SUFISM AND INDIAN SPIRITUAL TRADITIONS

An Educational Perspective

SUFISM AND INDIAN SPIRITUAL TRADITIONS

An Educational Perspective

Edited by

Mohammad Shaheer Siddiqui

NEW DELHI PUBLISHERS
New Delhi

Mohammad Shaheer Siddiqui, Sufism and Indian Spiritual Traditions: *An Educational Perspective*, New Delhi Publishers, New Delhi

First Edition 2015

Title Page by Mrs. Gulshan Khan

ISBN: 978-81-85503-05-9 (e-book)
ISBN: 978-81-85503-06-6 (print)

New Delhi Publishers
90, Sainik Vihar, Mohan Garden, New Delhi – 110 059
Tel: 011-25372232, 9971676330
ndpublishers@rediffmail.com/gmail.com
Website: www.ndpublisher.in

Dedicated to

Gurudev Rabindranath Tagore

And

Maulana Jalaluddin Rumi

...Who sustained

The Education of Heart

Contents

PART—II
SPIRITUAL TRADITIONS IN INDIA

PART—III
RABINRANATH TAGORE AND SPIRITUALISM

PART—IV
MUSIC, POETRY AND SPIRITUAL TRADITIONS

PART — V
EDUCATIONAL PERSPECTIVES

PART — VI
EPITOMES OF INDIAN CULTURE

Acknowledgement

This book is the outcome of the inspirational efforts, scholarly contributions and loving support of many people. First of all I would like to express my heartiest gratitude and humble regards to Prof. Sabujkoli Sen, Hon'ble Director, Studies, Educational Innovations and Rural Reconstruction (SEIRR) & Principal, Vinaya Bhavana for the endless encouragement and motherly motivation to do productive and fruitful work through the ways of academic activities. I am also thankful to Prof. K.C. Sahoo, the Head, Department of Education, for his moral and academic support and recurring reinforcement to do fruitful. I am also thankful to Subhankar Ghosh, my loving scholar, whose untiring efforts to check the proof and making modifications in the manuscript as required are invaluable. May God bless him with His special care and love.

I wish to express my deepest gratitude to the scholars, educationists, academicians and all the experts in the field who have contributed their valuable papers to make this volume possible for the service of academic world.

I am deeply thankful to **New Delhi Publishers** who extended their valuable cooperation to publish the book in time.

Last, but not the least, I am thankful to my loving wife Gulshan Khan and adorable daughters Mahek and Shireen for extending their untiring cooperation and loving support to complete the work.

Santiniketan

Thursday, 23rd April, 2015

(Mohammad Shaheer Siddiqui)

Acknowledgement

Preface

'If a man is truthful to his religion then he can understand the truth in the heart of a man of other religion. He will not be cruel to him.'

—**Maulana Jalaluddin Rumi** *(Masnawi-e-Manavi)*

It is generally felt that our schools and universities provide most of the education of mind and body and less of the education of heart and soul to the disciples. They are often ignored or undereducated. The result is agony, frustration and violence because heart and soul are lost and mind gets training in trades not in traits. Quality is concerned with the outcome of Educational process not by counting the first divisions, rank holders, pass outs etc. Quality of education can be best measured by observing decreasing trends of crimes, corruption, superstition, prejudices and hatred on the one hand and increasing breezes of love, fraternity, patriotism, inter-religious harmony, unity, peace and efforts to maintain the dignity, pride and happiness of the Nation, on the other. In Sufi teacher-training no one is given the responsibility to teach the pupil until he achieves his own refinement of heart. The Qur'an says, '*Qad af 'laha man zakkaha*' which means, "Whosoever cleanses his self (*nafs*), gets success." Peace is a condition which emerges and flourishes in a clean and purified heart. Trapped heart and self (*nafs*) creates hurdle and it pierces the process of purification. Real Education is concerned with peaceful and purified heart. Sufism is the manifestation of love, peace, knowledge and universal fraternity. Sufism is entirely a system of action, application and implementation.

Spiritual health is the part of overall holistic pattern of Educational Aims and Achievements in Indian Spiritual traditions. The following Vedic prayer is the best example of this invocation.

"O God, bestow upon us the best of treasures;
An efficient mind, and spiritual luster,
The increase of wealth, the health of bodies,
The sweetness of speech and the fairness of days."

—**Rig Veda (2.21.6)**

'Education for Peace' by NCERT (2006) quotes the complaint of a student "*With ever greater anger, the student shouted, 'You helped me extend my hands with incredible machines, my eyes with telescope and microscopes, my ears with telephones, radios and sonar, my brain with computers, but you did not help me extend my heart, love and concern for the human family.*" Education of heart and soul is much required today. Whatever we claim as quality of education in the name of infrastructure, number of teachers, pile of certificates, and circulation of books, is in fact the quantitative aspect. All these elements are concerned with heart. If Education of heart becomes the part of curriculum, it may be possible. If a seed is sown in a well cultivated land the calamity of nature can hardly harm it. The tender plant grows according to predisposed conditions of its cultivation.

Our major problems of education are related to hearts and souls of the teachers and pupils. Today we are in need of such torchbearers that can lead us to maintain the peace of heart, and soul and harmony and integration throughout the globe. Today we have broken hearts, disserted souls, polluted conscience, burdened brains, and tumult thoughts. We have no faith, no trust, no hope and no pleasure of genuine nature. We are leading a hollow life in the glinting and artificial environment of bare materialism. There is all around violence, degradation, agitation, terrorism and fear of death. All these things gave rise two world wars and hundreds of civil wars.

A single feature of ancient Indian civilization is that it has been moulded and shaped in the course of its history more by religious than by political, or economic, influences. The fundamental principles of social, political, and economic life were welded into a comprehensive theory which is called Religion in Hindu thought. The total configuration of ideals, practices, and conduct is called *Dharma* (Religion, Virtue or Duty) in this ancient tradition. *Srimadbhagvadgita* describes the essence of religion in the performance of duties and obligations in life. While describing the path of righteousness *(Dharma)* it is said that one who works in the path of righteousness his very intention lends him virtue's greatness. Lord Krishna tells Arjuna "*Whenever there is a decline of righteousness and rise of unrighteousness, O Bharata, (Arjuna) then I send forth (create, incarnate) Myself. For the protection of the good, for the destruction of the wicked, for the establishment of righteousness, and I come into being from age to age.*" Under the influence of such great religious ideas, the concept of this country ripens as a cultural or a spiritual possession, and broadly speaking, India came to be known with her cultural and intellectual wealth. While declaring the purpose of establishing Visva-Bharati, Santiniketan, Rabindranath Tagore wrote, "*Visva-Bharati represents India where she has her wealth of mind and it acknowledges India's obligation to offer to others the hospitality of her best culture and India's right to accept from others their best.*"

When Islam came to India it offered a religious system revitalizing all the activities of life with a blend of divine discipline and spiritual spark. Islam not only influenced the day to day activities as eating food, drinking water, meeting with people, sleeping posture but also the arenas of arts, music and literature were inspired by Islamic traditions. As far as pure religion is concerned, there is fundamental harmony in the inner spiritual experience of Hindus and Muslims. The heart of India which supplies life-blood to Muslims as well as Hindus has been so nurtured on the breadth of mind and vision of mystical traditions, that religious antagonism leading to war, a common phenomenon in Europe in the middle ages, was rare in Indian History. In the last thousand years when two religions, so entirely different as Hinduism and Islam, were brought together on the soil of India, her saints and Sufis created an atmosphere of not mere toleration but of harmony, so that while Hindu and Muslim princes were struggling for power, the common people of both religions could live amicably together.

The spirit of Indian culture rests in universal love, fraternity, expression of truth, beauty and purity of thoughts and deeds. For the first time in the history of mankind the Upanishads were translated by a Sufi Scholar, Dara Shikoh, the Mughal Prince. He composed *Majm-ul-Behrine* (the mingling of two oceans) reflecting the confluence of two great cultures in India viz. Islamic and Vedic. He realized and conveyed to the world that the two great cultures are like the two sacred streams of Divine love that mingled into the ocean of spirituality. Dara Shikoh got the Upanishads translated into Persian with the help of many Hindu and Muslim scholars who knew both Persian and Sanskrit. He himself wrote the book on this subject titled as *Sirr-e-Akbar* (the great mystery) which is the translation of 52 selected Upanishads. This translation brought the great knowledge of Upanishads to European countries in 18th century for the first time. To him Islam and Hinduism had great spiritual wealth which might be explored and exposed for the sake of universal love and fraternity. Thus he tried to bridge the cultural gap between Hindus and Muslims. If Akbar was the precursor of political and social unity among the two civilizations, Dara Shikoh played the prominent role in establishing spiritual unity through scholarly compositions. Dara Shikoh made arrangements for the translations of two great Sanskrit books in to Persian i.e. *Bhagavad-Gita* and *Yoga Vashishtha*.

Religion makes a person disciplined and sensible towards performing duties and responsibilities. This dedication for responsibilities in Islam (as *Huqooq e-Allah* and *Huqooq-al-Ibad*) is the pathway to spiritualism. Sufism is the very name of good conduct and beauty of thoughts. Thus spiritualism is a liberated and advanced stage of religion.

In fact Sufism and other Indian spiritual traditions are concerned with the purification of heart and inculcation of traits in human personality. All these tracts go towards the education of heart.

The present book is an effort to understand the Indian spiritual traditions with respect to their educational perspectives. The book offers papers by Academicians, Scholars and Experts in the fields.

Santiniketan **(Mohammad Shaheer Siddiqui)**

Thursday, 23rd April, 2015

List of Contributors

1. **Amit Kumar Verma,** Assistant Professor, Sangeet Bhavana, Visva-Bharati, Santiniketan, W. Bengal, email: kr.amitverma@gmail.com
2. **Arpana Singh,** UGC-Junior Research Fellow, Department of Education, University of Calcutta, West Bengal. email: arpanasinghh@gmail.com
3. **Atiqur Rahman,** Assistant Professor (Persian), Department of Arabic, Persian, Urdu & Islamic Studies, Visva-Bharati, Santiniketan. email: atiqura044@gmail.com
4. **Aurang Zeb Azmi,** Assistant Professor, Department of Arabic, Jamia Millia Islamia, New Delhi. email: azebazmi@gmail.com
5. **Biswajit Chatterjee,** Research Scholar, Department of Education, Visva-Bharati, Santiniketan, West Bengal. email: biswajit225@rediffmail.com
6. **Chandan Adhikary,** Assistant Professor, Government College of Education, Burdwan, West Bengal. email: cadhikry123@gmail.com
7. **Debika Guha,** Head, Dept. of B.Ed., Senior Faculty Department of Education, Loreto College, Kolkata, West Bengal. email: devika.guha@yahoo.com
8. **Feroz Haidry,** Department of Urdu, Vasantrao Naik Govt. Institute of Arts & Social Sciences, Nagpur. email: ferozhaidry3@yahoo.com
9. **Harikrishnan Bhaskaran**, Assistant Professor, Department of Journalism, Central University of Himachal Pradesh. email: harikrishnanbhaskaran @gmail.com
10. **Jayanta Mete,** Professor, Department of Education, University of Kalyani, Nadia, West Bengal. email: jayanta_135@yahoo.co.in
11. **Meraj Ahmad Meraj,** Assistant Professor & Head, Department of Arabic, Aliah University, Kolkata. email: merajjnu@gmail.com
12. **Manzoor Ahmad Najar,** Doctoral Scholar, Dept. of Modern Indian Languages, Aligarh Muslim University, Aligarh, email: mansurkhan13@gmail.com
13. **Minati Saha,** Assistant Professor, Institute of Education for Women, Kolkata, West Bengal. email: minati.saha@yahoo.com
14. **Mohammad Hammad Reaz,** Arabic Department, Aligarh Muslim University. email: hammadalig@gmail.com
15. **Mohammad Israr Khan,** Assistant Professor, Department of A & R Economics, M.J.P. Rohilkhand University, U.P. email: drmisrarkhan@gmail.com
16. **Mohammad Shafi Ahmed,** Raniganj Urdu High School, West Bengal email: mdshafiahmed87@gmail.com

17. **Mohammad Sirajul Islam,** Professor, Department of Philosophy and Religion, Visva-Bharati, Santiniketan, West Bengal. email: siraj_tuli@yahoo.co.in
18. **Moumita Gayen,** Research Scholar, Department of Arabic, Persian, Urdu & Islamic Studies, Visva-Bharati, Santiniketan. email: moumitagayen06 @gmail.com
19. **Mrs. Nasrin,** Professor, Department of Education, Aligarh Muslim University, Aligarh. email: nasrinamu@gmail.com
20. **Namrata Mishra,** Head, Department of Music, R.C.A. Girls P. G. College, Mathura, U.P. email: namrata.swaranjali@gmail.com
21. **Navneet Sharma,** Assistant Professor, Department of Teacher Education, Central University of Himachal Pradesh. email: harikrishnanbhaskaran @gmail.com
22. **Nazmul Hussain Laskar,** Assistant Professor, Department of Political Science, Dr. G. M. Roy College, West Bengal. email: mr.nazmulhussain@rediffmail.com
23. **Neeti Trivedi,** Research Scholar, Faculty of Education, Banasthali University Banasthali. email: trivedineeti16@gmail.com
24. **Piyali Dutta Chowdhury**, Department of Bengali, Vidyasagar College for Women, Kolkata, West Bengal. email: duttachowdhurypiyali@gmail.com
25. **Pramod Kumar Sharma,** Research Scholar, University of Hyderabad, email: pramodchu2009@gmail.com
26. **Prarthita Biswas,** Research Scholar, Department of Education, University of Kalyani, Nadia, West Bengal. email: prarthitab@gmail.com
27. **Priyadarsini Mitra,** Assistant Professor, School of Buddhist Studies & Civilization, Gautam Buddha University. email: priyamitra20@rediffmail.com
28. **Reshma Khatun,** Research Scholar, Department of Education, Visva-Bharati, Santiniketan, West Bengal. email: reshmakhatun87@rediffmail.com
29. **Ritu Singh,** Research Scholar, Department of Music and Performing Arts, B.H.U. Varanasi, ritujeets@gmail.com
30. **Rituparna Ghosh,** Ph.D. Fellow, Department of Pali, University of Calcutta, Kolkata. email: rituorseason@gmail.com
31. **Ruchi Gupta,** Associate Professor (Music), Sahoo Ram Swaroop Mahila Mahavidyalaya, Bareilly, U.P. email: kapilgupta23@yahoo.com
32. **Sanchita Dasgupta,** Assistant Teacher, Khairtala Nurpur High School, Khairtala, Malda, West Bengal. email: bird.doyel@gmail.com
33. **Sangeeta Pandit,** Senior Assistant Professor, Department of Vocal Music, Banaras Hindu University. email: dsangeetapandit@gmail.com
34. **Saumyajit Acharya,** Writer, email: saumyajit.me@gmail.com
35. **Shaikh Musak Rajjak,** Assistant Professor of History, Maulana Azad College, Aurangabad, Maharashtra. email: shaikhmusakrajjak@gmail.com

36. **Shamenaz Bano**, Associate Professor (English), Dept. of Applied Sciences & Humanities, Allahabad Institute of Engineering & Technology, Allahabad. Email: shamenaz@gmail.com

37. **Shivani Sonkar,** Research Scholar (JRF), Department of Music and Performing Arts, B.H.U. Varanasi, U.P. email: shivraaga@gmail.com

38. **Simanta Roy,** Research Scholar (J.R.F), Department of Arabic, Persian, Urdu & Islamic Studies, Visva-Bharati, Santiniketan, West Bengal. email: simantaroy365@gmail.com

39. **Sujoy Paul,** Research Scholar, Department of Education, Visva-Bharati, Santiniketan, West Bengal. email: sujoypaul58@gmail.com

40. **Susmita Bhattacharyya,** Assistant Professor, Department of Sociology, P. C Mahalanobis Mahavidyalaya, West Bengal. email: mithu_susmita@yahoo.com

41. **Trishna Banerjee,** Assistant Professor, Department of Education, Visva-Bharati, Santiniketan, West Bengal. email: trishnayan@gmail.com

42. **Vinay Chandra Pathak**, Research Scholar, Department of Education, Visva-Bharati, Santiniketan, West Bengal. email: vinaytruthprevail@gmail.com

43. **Vishal Jain,** Assistant Professor, Department of Music and Performing Arts, University of Allahabad, U.P., email: dhrupadvishaljain@gmail.com

44. **Yogesh Praveen,** Renowned Historian, Writer and Expert on Indian Culture, Lucknow, U.P., email: yogeshpraveen@gmail.com

PART—I:
SUFISM: VARIOUS DIMENSIONS

1

Sufi Culture and Social Values: An Integrated Approach in Indian Perspective

Mohammad Sirajul Islam

Abstract

Culture is a symbiotic structure without boundaries. The term culture refers to a state of intellectual accomplishments of man. The social and political forces that influence the growth of a human being and society as well are to be considered as culture. Indian culture is very rich and diverse in nature and unique in its way. It has assimilated with various cultures, thoughts, religions and etiquettes in its orbit from the time immemorial. Indian way of thinking, manners and communicating with one another are one of the important components of our culture. Its easy accessibility with all is unique features that lacks in the other parts of the globe. Even though Indian people are very accustomed to accept modern means of living and improved their life style, however, their values and beliefs are remaining unchanged. A person can change his clothing, way of eating, thinking and living standard but the rich values of the society always remain same because these are deeply entangled and rooted with the hearts, minds and souls of the peoples. These unchanging values are the inevitable parts of our culture. Sufism is basically a religious movement but in the course of time it became an inevitable component of world culture due to its diversified aspects and egalitarian outlook. At the outset we will discuss something on culture and then we will proceed to discuss about Sufi culture and its social values successively.

Keywords: *Sufis, Culture, Peace, Brotherhood, Love.*

Indian culture is basically composite in nature. Composite culture does not mean the merger of religious, ethnic and linguistic identities. Composite culture means the recognition of those identities to flourish for the cultivation of mind and intellect. Indian notion of value is deeply embedded in its culture that is related to religion and social atmospheres too.

Sufism is a spiritual movement to establish Islamic values and culture in the society without any discrimination of caste, creed and religion. Sufi spirituality is generally different from the other spirituality of the world because it does not recognize stoicism. Like Islam Sufis also believe that this mundane world is a battle ground of good and evil and as a human being it is the utmost duty to engage our own self for the well being of all. The egalitarian outlook of Indian Sufis helped to establish primordial values of the society that ultimately enriched Indian culture to disseminate integrated outlook in wider way. Sufism as a socio-cultural milieu integrated various cultures and values and says for preserving the cultural traditions of various groups, respecting elders; discharging brotherhood and friendship towards all, free mingling to accommodate tolerance, well-being of all sentient and non-sentient beings, joy and sharing with love and adjustment in mundane and supra-mundane life. According to Sufism, culture and values are not confined in a particular groups/community rather it is equally efficacious for all without any discrimination. In the age of globalization this eclectical attitude of the Sufis are very important to maintain communal harmony and social solidarity as well.

It is indubitable that we are enormously advance in science however at the same time moral values are degraded day by day. In this social turmoil and degradation the preservation and practice of socio-cultural values of the Sufis are the crying need in discharging humanitarian outlook and social stability for all so that our posterior generation may live with perfect peace, harmony and tranquillity.

This paper is an attempt to focus the social values embedded with Indian Sufi culture and their integrated implications as well.

What is Culture?

Culture is an important component of the particular nation. A country is to be considered as rich and developed if it is culturally rich and developed. Culture is to be conceived in diversified forms, such as colloquial meaning of culture that basically refers to the realm of intellectual production at a large and the sociological meaning of culture where intellectual, material and institutional realms are characterized.[1] Therefore, a very careful philosophical analysis of the notion of culture is a pre-requisite for any discourse of cultural analysis. The term culture possess broader outlook which encompasses all intellectual, material, spiritual and social accomplishments of human being, hence, a careful description of customs, folklore, religious rites, cooking, dress, etiquette, social and family ceremonies, industrial and technological progress, art, music so on are to be considered as an inevitable elements of culture.[2] It is a most valuable, potent and dynamic variable of the society. [3]

Generally, the term *culture* is a generic term that encompasses all kind accomplishments of the society/nation/world and through it the progress or development of them can be measured. Culture seems to be the heart of the society/nation where individual capabilities, talents and social potentialities are cultivated and exhorted in a systematic manner. The term *cultura animi* penetrated in the Western thinking since the beginning of our scientific era.[4] Edward B. Taylor says culture is a complex whole, which includes knowledge, belief, arts, morality, laws, customs any other capabilities and habits acquired by man as a member of society.[5] Al L. Kroeber opines culture is that which human species has and other social species lack.[6] As its lowest level an intuitive awareness of individual identities that needs personal commitment to their pursuit and actualization. At the highest level the consciousness of value implied in it in addition to their mutual cohesion. It is obvious that human accomplishments are varying from one culture to another culture; however, they helped enormously to dye human civilization that unhesitatingly accepts change and mutation in social milieu. In viewing the multifaceted dimensions of culture, it seems to me that culture is basically a conceptual and imaginative artifact of the individual and society that determine the evolution of human living and their ways of expressions. In fact, cultural relativism, pluralism and universalism are also appeared in this modern society where it is almost clear to us that each and every culture is an autonomous whole and a hierarchical structure of values that are deeply rooted in it that beyond criticism. Culture as a cream of the particular society that may claim universalism to address to all human beings.[7] Philosophers have greater role to penetrate in the abysses of the fact. In philosopher's viewpoint Culture is not an individual property, hence it is not a subjective entity rather it is a collective enterprise where all people of the globe have equal sharing to utilize its benefits. Some bodies in maintaining secular attitude are fascinated to devoid moral values from culture and based merely on intellectual calibre but moral values are essential to apprehend the real perspective of culture by which we can judge the invaluable accomplishments of the peoples.[8]

Sometimes the term civilization is also considered as the synonymous of culture but it is not true. There is no doubt that civilization is an inevitable part of culture and they have keen affinities to each other, however, both bear sharp distinctions. Civilization is basically entangled with industrial and technological artefacts and their progress but culture have much broader outlook that encompasses all types of progress/developments of the individual as well as the Nation. Therefore, to make difference between culture and civilization we will have to fulfil some conditions, like people may live in a certain geographical boundary, have a minimum requisite for Nationhood and that Nation must have an accepting political order for framing a State, where language, religion, art, ethnicity, racial history, sublime imagination etc. are to be considered as an inevitable conditions of culture.[9]

Indian Culture

Indian culture is an instance of unity, integrity and configuration where geographical and economic unity exists to such an extent, that naturally exhibit its cultural coalescence. In spite of its multifarious differences, there is the basic unity in thinking, feeling, living which waxes and wanes with the changing political constellation but never ceases. A.L. Basham maintains "no land on earth has such a long cultural continuity as India."[11] He also produced some ground for supporting his opinion that "India has carried their commerce and culture beyond their frontiers…. Her unique civilization has often been over rated."[12] It is vivid that in several occasions the disintegration forces in external and internal levels threatened to shatter its unity but India's spirit of oneness never been broken. At present in the changing pattern of thought India is still maintaining its harmonious and tolerable attitudes that undoubtedly an astonishing example towards the people of the globe. Sometimes Terrorism, regional dividing forces, separatism, religious violence, communal conflict, regional ethnicity & language etc. are stumbled down its integrated appeal but India handled over all these in very scientific and methodical ways. If we will look in the inner aspects of all these problems then it will obvious that all these are extraneous elements that unfortunately associated in its society and that quietly antagonistic to Indian mind.[13] In spite of all these India represents a fascinating coalescence of cultures, embodied in distinct unified civilizations. It can be considered as the greatest confluences of cultural strands, a laboratory of racial mixing, cross fertilization of religious, linguistic and cultural bonds. Its cultural diversities emerged as a most tenacious plural society that seldom found in the annals of mankind. In terms of cultural depth and integrity it becomes an intertwining thread of inter cultural synthesis, in which the values of man, plural thoughts, social ethics preserved as a composite culture in a systematic whole. Though Indian constitution is the safe guard of justice and equality of all sections of its people however, class between lower strata families, lower caste groups, minority and majority tussle are emerged as an unpalatable truth of India. But Indian Government (UPA) has taken strong measures to preserve its integrated outlook strictly. In maintaining equality and justice among all section of peoples Indian political leaders have given special attention to uplift its down trodden and backward peoples. In eliminating minority-majority gap the present government has formed various committees for their economic, political, educational and health progress which are the most praiseworthy initiatives and measures of our present Government. In economic aspect it has given special attention upon the basic needs of all peoples, like food, clothing, accommodation and fuel that help enormously to upgrade the life of its down trodden peoples that something different from previous Government.[14] Here the opinion of Amartya Sen is very worthwhile as he stated "Our identities cannot be defined independently of our traditions and past..... Our reading of the past and understanding of the present are independent.[15] The cultural attainment of India can be roughly viewed in the context of language, literature, religion, spirituality, arts, dance, drama, philosophy economics and politics. There is no doubt that India is a culturally rich country but poor in economy. From our past record it is clear that before the beginning of Christian era, the culture of India had begun to spread systematically across the country. Her religions and philosophies penetrated in the minds of the people of Thailand, Malaysia, Afghanistan, Persia, Cambodia, Vietnam, Srilanka, China, and Japan and also various other parts of the globe that made deep impact in the culture and civilization of several other countries of the world.[16]

If we discuss the philosophical outlook of India then it is quite evident that Indian philosophy is deeply entangled with her culture. Her Philosophy, Metaphysics and Religious thoughts have a symbiotic relationship with one another. Her ancient sages and sheers have provided information through *shruti* (Knowledge preserved and spread through oral system) and *smriti* (remembrance).[17] Thereafter, Buddhist and Jains philosophy also developed as a separate branch of Indian philosophical traditions. Their conception of non-violence (*ahimsa*) is undoubtedly a global in nature and still a firm philosophical foundation of contemporary philosophy and culture.[18] The emergence of six philosophical systems, like, Nyaya, Vaiseshik, Samkhya, Yoga, Mimamsa and Vedanta are conceived as a justified philosophical system which are strongly argumentative and logical.[19] Here different philosophical traditions and schools are differed considerably from one another in social, economic and political outlook but all they have shared some common philosophical pursuits and recognized as indigenous Indian culture.[20] Therefore, Indian philosophical acumen is basically rationalistic as well as humanistic too which is highly conscious for assimilation not for expulsion, integrity not disharmony, unity not separation. Philosophically, Indian culture means the rejection of mono-cultural regimentation or domination rather it reaffirms the value of pluralism and syncretistic thoughts, as a sound cultural effloresces. From the Vedic age certain glimpses are embodied with its idea, like, divine inspirations that helped a lot to discharge its tolerable and non-violent appeal towards all where it showed respect to all biotic and a biotic species as well as material objects.[21] Indian culture appreciates both homogeneous and heterogeneous creativities as a vast museum of technology. Here Hinduism, Christianity, Islam Zoroastrianism are not only different religions but are inevitable part of her culture.[22] Its intention is larger acceptability where tribal, rich, poor, elite, folk, religious, social, cultural traditions are equally important and valuable to enlarge its beauty. In its cultural fold Baghdad, Rome, Jerusalem, Afghan, Persian, Arabian,

European are intermixed from time immemorial without any antagonism that ultimately have made a single flower vase and discharging their significant fragrance without any reluctance. Here the term Hindustani culture reflected the attitude of National culture where Hindus, Muslims, Buddhists, Jains, tribal peoples all have equal sharing. [23] Hence, Jawaharlal Nehru in his *Discovery of India* provides suitable information concerning Indian cultural integration as" everywhere I found a cultural background which has exerted a powerful influence on their lives. This background was a mixture of popular philosophy, tradition, history, myth and legend and it was not possible to draw a line between any of these.[24] At present there are tremendous crisis in preservation or restoration of cultural identities in the entire world. As a result the promotion of cohesive mutual unity is globally stumbled down. Indian cultural philosophy is undoubtedly the most significant example to enrich global cultural synthesis as well as a worthy initiative in preservation of global humanism. Now it has changed its shape slightly and not only confined its outlook on spirituality and mere abstract thoughts but in this new millennium it's philosophy laid emphasis on social uplift as well the eradication of social problems. Its technological devices, industrial up gradation, space research development are going on process and as a Third World developing country its growing rate not only in philosophy but also in all aspects are gradually in high level. In seeing India's cultural coalescence and unity in diversity the formation of global unity sprouted in my mind, the reason is that if the composite culture and harmonious nature is possible in India despite her varieties then why the idea of global culture and one humanity will not possible? India has shown the way how unity may be established in plurality. This idea is deeply rooted in Indian culture because her sages and saints have viewed the entire world as one family and proclaimed (*Vasudhaiva Kutumvakam*).

Sufi Culture

Religion and culture are not antagonistic rather they are intimately connected to each other and at the same time both they are playing a pivotal role in cultural transformation. All religions emphasize principles like peace, truth, justice, non-violence, equality, love etc. which are the inevitable part of culture and its transformation. Religion is a commitment to practice cultural ideals in man's life. A person who lacks cultural pursuit conceived uncivilized. Islam as a universal religion is highly conscious concerning cultural homogeneity and rapprochement in avoiding all fundamentalisms. Its basic commitments and values are peace, love, truth, justice, equality and brotherhood which are considered as the most essential principles of cultural transformation. Sufism emerged in the Islamic society as a movement to revitalize Islamic religious values. These principles of Sufism help a man for his/her inner uplift and urge him/her for cultural coalescence. In Sufism a man will have to prove his credibility by practicing these principles, if anybody fails to practice these, cannot be considered as Muslim.

Sufism is a mystico-philosophical trend in Islam. A Sufi is always aspires to attain knowledge of the Reality through the unsurpassed love and friendship with Him. It believes that the main intention of the human being is to attain Divine wisdom (*marifah*) that elevates him to acquire Truth (*Haq*). Sufis claim these are highly metaphysical in nature and value embedded. Like Socrates they propagate the view that knowledge of self-means to know thy self and that is their most valuable saying. In the course of time Sufism extended its wings and mixed up with other faiths, philosophy and literatures that ultimately changed the shape of Sufism. In the western region, many people accepted Islam those who were belonged to Christianity, Zoroastrianism, Buddhists etc and they inhabited in the various towns of Persia, Syria, Egypt and Mesopotamia. At that period these regions were the main centers of Neo-Platonism. The influence of Greek and Christian thoughts and philosophies are discernible in the culture and values of the reputed Sufis. It is worthy to mention that the Greek wisdom flowed towards the Muslim East through Harran and Syria. The Syrian took special initiative to accept Greek speculations, i.e. Neo-Platonism and transmitted to the Muslim society. Both Plato and Aristotle are popular in Muslim community even today. Now we perceive through the Arab chronicles where they recognized the superiority of thoughts on Indian medicines, philosophy, mathematics and astronomy. Sufis are not satisfied only for these thoughts they are similarly interested to gather know ledges on metaphysical subjects and that are the main concern of them. Ba Yazid al Bistami, a celebrated Sufi learnt metaphysics and spirituality from his teacher Abu Ali Sindi, who was Indian origin. The pantheistic concept is originally Vedantic concept and the Sufi concept of Fana is highly resembled to Buddhist Nirvana. Sufis are very much conscious to attain the know ledges on metaphysical elements and values like God, soul, Concept of love, tolerance, brotherhood, mystery of the life and the Universe etc. They say the ideas of God's grace; goodness, beauty, truth etc. are metaphysical characters and the sole basis of our moral apprehension. The concept of love is beautifully epitomized as "Love is not to be learned from me, it is one of God's gifts and comes of His grace."[25]

Therefore, Sufis are falling in dichotomy in defending their faith in one hand on the other, they are reconciling it with Islam and that is a very difficult task for them.

There are many social values that are intimately embedded with Sufi thought and culture, some are maintained below:

Sufi Concept of Love

It is generally considered that Sufism is mainly based on the philosophy of love and Sufis have mainly utilized it as the main source of their realization of Truth/

Reality (*haq*). They have considered their relation with God just like the relation of the lover and beloved. In their eyes, a Sufi is a lover (*'ashiq*) and God is the beloved (*ma'shuq*). Sufis wants to unite himself with God to denote his concept of love as metaphysical element that cannot be articulated in the particular language. The feeling of love is purely mystical and metaphysical that is a matter of apprehension and realization only. The idea of love presumably borrowed by the Sufis from the holy quran, where the terms *mahabbah, hubb, wudd, muwaddah* are present that are depicts the various types and gradations of love. The *hubb* and *mahabbah* are inter-related and represent as a super category of love or overflowing love (*ashaddo huballillah*).[26] Prophet Muhammad also clearly expressed about the concept of love several times. In a Hadith he says— "My servant draws nigh unto Me by works of devotion. And I love him, I am the ear by which he hears, and eye by which he sees and the tongue by which he speaks (Bukhari).[27] The greatest Sufi and thinker of Islam al Ghazali in his *Ihya ulum uddin* maintains that love is a natural desire, which produces pleasure but when that desire assumes an intense form, it is called passionful love or *Ishq*. Sufis say whenever love going beyond extreme in affection and becomes intense it is called *Ishq*. Sufis regard Love is the essence of their metaphysics. A true Sufi is a lover of God as well as the lover of the whole universe. Whenever a Sufi is deeply fused in the love of God he sees all as his own without any discrimination of caste and creed, even in the highest ecstatic moment whenever a Sufi is fully intoxicated sees nothing except God and all the distinction between mine and thine is disappeared here. In this stage he proclaims anal haq (I am the Reality) as mansur al Hallaj uttered. Here a Sufi proclaims- "*ishq ashiq hai ishq hai mashuq khud ke upar khud fida hai ishq*"[28] i.e. Love is the lover and love is the beloved and love is fondly in love with itself. Again reputed Sufi al Jami says—*"ishq awwal, ishq akhir, ishq zahir was batun, ishq hi se tu banaeh har dar wa diwar hai ishq"*[29] i.e. love is the beginning, love is the end. Love is the manifest and love is hidden. Love is that sustains the world.

Sufi Concept of Equality and Brotherhood

Sufis are the lover of God and all creatures. They love all and sundry without any discrimination of caste creed and religion. According to their tradition anybody can take their discipleship without changing their own faith and all initiated members of the Sufi silsilah are considering as *pir bhai* (brother of spirituality). There is no caste classification, all the rigidities and barriers like high and low, superior and inferior are broken down in their society. They believe all human being are the descendant of one Adam and piety is the best criteria to measure some one's quality and goodness. Even Sufis pay regards to all creatures as they thought they are the inevitable part of environmental balance. Their universal brotherhood is based on the notion of *khidmat-e-khalq* (the service of humanity) as they apprehend it as their one of the best principles. So they uttered—

"tariqate bajuz khidmat-e-khalq nist
batasbih ws sajadeh wa dilaq nist"[30]

i.e. the path of Sufi is nothing but the service of humanity.

It is neither in a rosary, nor on the prayer carpet, nor in the garment of the Sufi.

Sufi Concept of Tolerance

Though the main aim of the Sufis is to unite their finite soul with the Infinite, nevertheless, they do not cut themselves off from the society. In India, Sufis achieved extra ordinary popularity due to their humane and tolerate attitude. Their eternal message is—

"awwal sakhawati chun sekhawat-e-darya
doam sefqati chun sefqat-e-uftab
sewan tawazui chun tewazu-e-zameen"[31]

i.e. a generosity, like that of the ocean, secondly, mildness like that of the sun and thirdly, modesty like that of the earth.

In extending tolerant outlook they open their khanqah for all human being and the guests those who arrived in their khanqah, lived, slept and ate all together without any ethnic distinction. The holy book and scriptures were open to all and accessible to all. The celebrated Sufi Nizam-al-din Awlia's humanism and toleration were very lofty, so he said "devotion to God does not mean detachment from the mundane world. Highest form of devotion to god is removal of misery of the distressed and extending helping hands to the helpless and the feeding of the hungry."[32]

In the dark ages of human civilization (*aiyam-e-jaheliyat*) Islam showed the light of rich culture towards all aspects of human life in transforming all spheres of the society, but it is very unfortunate that most of the people do not understand the true spirit of this cultural transformation. In the due course Islamic culture penetrated in India in the garb of Sufism and assimilated with Indian culture and its divergent natures. It assimilated with Indian composite values and developed various aspects of cultural sides through its scientific transformations. There is an erroneous thought that Islam is typically rigid and cannot able to adapt with the changing patterns of the society, but it is not true. Since Sufis were very much egalitarian in their outlook therefore, In the course of time Islamic culture has adapted with various cultures of East and West and accommodated the attractive and reasonable portions of other cultures in its fold. This philosophical enquiry is an initiative to understand the true nature of Indian cultural homogeneity and rapprochement. In this contemporary world Sufi culture and its ethical values, if practiced properly, it will help to annihilate most trivial problems of the world.

Sufi Notion of Peace

The most vital problem of the day which draws serious attention of the sages, savants, philosophers, politicians and the religious leaders of the world for establishing peace. Modern science is failure to establish peace because he is unable to invent any instrument to control the human mind. Violence is occasionally takes place in the society due to the fulfilment of the animal urges of human being where religions are generally misused. Peace is not a monopoly of any particular religion or sect. Peace is a natural principle and impulse. The heavens and the earth have always existed in peace. The sun, the moon, the stars, and the wind all perform their duty in perfect harmony. There is also the perfect harmony between the different organs of the body of human beings. Only man, who lives on this earth, has lost that peace. He only talks about it. He gives speeches about establishing peace, but then he disrupts the unity and sets out to rule the world. Is this not a wonder? But peace loving man must realize the deeper meaning of religion. Moral degradation is increasing day by day. If God's rule of righteousness, peace, justice, goodwill and solidarity among mankind is faithfully and sincerely adhered to war and violence will be disappeared and permanent peace will prevail in the world. Sufis are the real ambassador of peace. They preached peace for all and in their Sufi terminology it is called *sulhi kul*. In establishing peace a Sufi never makes any discrimination rather he works for peace to all and sundry.

References

1. Kucuradi Ionna and Agazzi Evandro, (1993), Philosophy and Cultural Development, (International Federation of Philosophical Societies, Philosophical Society of Turkey, Ankara), p. 2.
2. *Ibid.,* p. 9.
3. *Ibid.,* pp. 10-13.
4. *Ibid.,* 11.
5. Taylor Edward B., (1871), Primitive Culture: Researches into the Development of Mythology, Philosophy, Religion, Language, Art and Custom, (Murry, London), 3rd edition, Vol. 2, p. 1.
6. Anthropology: Race, language, Culture, Psychology, Pre-history, (1948), Oxford & IBH Publishing company, Calcutta, by arrangement with Harcourt, Brace & world, Inc, New York, p. 253.

7. Al Faruuqi Ismail, "Islam as Culture and Civilization", book- Islam and Contemporary Society. Longman, London, pp. 140-141.
8. Kucuradi Ionna and Agazzi Evandro, op. cit, p. 14.
9. Husain S. Abid, (1978), The National Culture of India, National Book Trust, New Delhi, India, pp. 3-5.
10. *Ibid.,* p. 6.
11. Basham, A.L., (1975), A Cultural history of India, Clarendon Press, Oxford, p. 2.
12. Basham, A.L., (1954), The Wonder that was India, Sidgwick and Jackson, London, p. 1.
13. Husain S. Abid, op.cit, p. 7.
14. *Ibid.,* p. 16.
15. Sen Amartya, (1996), On Interpreting India, The Asiatic society, Calcutta, p. 38.
16. Singh, B.P., India's culture, — The State, the Art and Beyond, Oxford University Press, Delhi, (1998), p. 37.
17. Jha, D.N., (1977), Ancient India—An Introductory Outlook, Delhi, pp. 10- 25.
18. *Ibid.,* p. 36.
19. Singh, B.P., op. cit, pp. 31-33.
20. Basham, A.L., (1964), Studies in Indian History and Culture, Sambodhi Pub. Pvt. Ltd., Calcutta, p. 58.
21. Husain, S. Abid, op. cit, p. 130.
22. W. Stern Robert, (1993), Changing India, Cambridge University Press, New Delhi, pp. 22-24.
23. Husain, S. Abid, op. cit, pp. 95-96.
24. Nehru Jwaharlal, (1981), Discovery of India, (OUP, Delhi), pp. 67-68.
25. Sharda, S.R, Sufi Thought, (Munshiram Monoharlal Publishers and Pvt. Ltd., 1974), p. 17.
26. Quran, 2:165.
27. Valiuddin Mir, 1968, Love of God, (Motilal Banarrasidass, Delhi), p. 82.
28. *Ibid.,* p. 133.
29. *Ibid.,* p. 133.
30. Islam Md. Sirajul, (1995), "National Integration in the Light of Sufism", Book-National Integration Problems in Perspective, Edt. By P. Jash, (Indira Gandhi centre for National Integration, Visva Bharati), p. 77.
31. *Ibid.,* p. 77.
32. Nizami, K.A., (1961), Some Aspects of Religion and Politics of India, Aligarh, p. 239.

2

Development of Sufism in India And Its Contribution

Atiqur Rahman

Abstract

Sufi philosophy includes the schools of thought unique to Sufism, a mystical branch within Islam. Sufism and its philosophical traditions may be associated with both Sunni Islam and Shia Islam. It has been suggested that Sufi thought emerged from the Middle East in the eighth century, but adherents are now found around the world. Perhaps the most notable one was the great theologian and philosopher Al Gazalli who lived in Iran around 1100 AD. His famous treatises, called the "Reconstruction of Religious Sciences," the "Alchemy of Happiness," and other works; set off to convince the Islamic world that Sufism and its teachings originated from the Qur'an and were compatible with mainstream Islamic thought and theology. It was Al-Gazali who bridged the gap between traditional and mystical Islam. It was around 1000 AD that the early Sufi literature, in the form of manuals, treatises, discourses, and poetry, became the source of Sufi thinking and meditations. Others were founded in different parts of the Islamic world by Sufi-masters such as Jalaluddin Rumi and Abdur Rahman Jami in Iran, and Muinuddin Chishti and Nizamuddin Aulia in India.

Keywords: *Sufi Orders, Impact of Sufism, Sufis in British India, Cultural and Religious Impacts of Hinduism, Responses to Modernity.*

Introduction

Sufism (Arabic:*tacawwuf*, Persian· *sufigari*, *tasavvuf*) is generally understood to be the inner, mystical dimension of Islam. A practitioner of this tradition is generally known as a *Súfi,* though some adherents of the tradition reserve this term only for those practitioners who have attained the goals of the Sufi tradition. Another name used for a Sufi seeker is dervish.

The term, *'Sufi',* is applied to Islamic spiritualists who attempt to achieve a development of exercise, contemplation, renunciation and self-denial. Sufism *(tasawwuf),* became a universal aspect of Islam social life whose influence spread to all Islamic world by 12th century A.D. Political expansion, sectarian controversies, theological and philosophical developments, all synchronized with the evolution of Sufism.

In the 11th and 12th century, there was a vigorous Sufi tradition in Khurasan (modern Iraq and Afghanistan). It was characterized by 'Orders' *(tariqa* or *silsilah)* of quiet recent historical development. These patterns of holy life and Sufi organization were transmitted from Khurasan to Delhi Sultanate. Through the order, Sufism became more widely known and practiced throughout different levels of society.

The massive geographic presence of Islam in India can be explained by the tireless activity of Sufi preachers. Sufism had left a prevailing impact on religious, cultural, and social life in South Asia. The introduction of the mystical form of Islam was done by Sufi saints. Sufi scholars travelling from all over continental Asia were instrumental in the social, economic, and philosophic development of India. Besides preaching in major cities and centres of intellectual though, Sufis reached out to poor and marginalized rural communities and preached in local dialects such as Urdu, Sindhi, Panjabi versus, Persian, Turkish, and Arabic. Sufism emerged as a "moral and comprehensive socio-religious force" that even influenced other religious traditions such as Hinduism. Their traditions of devotional practices and modest living attracted all people. Their teachings of humanity, love for God and Prophet continue to be surrounded by mystical tales and folk songs today. Sufis were firm in abstaining from religious and communal conflict and strived to be peaceful elements of civil society. Furthermore, it is the attitude of accommodation, adaptation, piety, and charisma that continues to help Sufism remain as a pillar of mystical Islam in India.

Chronologically, the history of Sufism in India is concerned with the establishment of Delhi Sultanate to the beginning of Mughal Empire. It is classified and discussed eight important Sufi *silsilahs (orders)* which has been analyzed here.

(a) The Chishtiyya

The Chisti order of Sufis is essentially an Indian one. Other branches emanating from the town of Chisti in modern Afghanistan did not survive for long in the Perso-Islamic world. Among the Sufi migrants to Chisti was Shaikh Abu Ishaq Shamsi from Syria. The Shaikh traced his origin from Ali and Prophet Muhammad, and then Hasan Basri.

The Chisti order remained important from the 13th to the 18th century. Starting from Rajasthan, its centers spread to Delhi and to Punjab, Uttar Pradesh, Bihar, Bengal, Gujarat and the Deccan. A large number of well-known Sheikhs belonged to this order. Among the early luminaries were Khwaja Muinu'ddin Chisti of Ajmer, Shaikh Bakhtiyar Kaki of Delhi, Shaikh Fariduddin of Paktattan, Shaikh Nizamuddin Auliya of Delhi and Shaikh Nasir'uddin Mahmud, 'the lamp of Delhi' (Chirag-i-Dilli). Khwaja Muinu'ddin laid the foundation of Chisti order in India and worked out its principles at Ajmer, the seat of Chauhan power. No authentic details are available about the way he worked in the population but it is known that common people flocked to him in large numbers. It would appear that the Khwaja lived in Ajmer fort and his simple, ascetic life was an inspiration to the people. His living reminds the social ethics of Islam, as interpreted by Sufi, which attached no importance to material power and wealth, stressing only piety, simplicity and devotion to God. Most Chisti saints lived in poverty and some of them did not even receive cash gifts and lived in their own labour. The Chistiya saints lived in extreme asceticism, severe austerities with piety and fasting. For instance, Baba Farid performed Chilla-i-Mak'us, which means fasting and praying for forty days and nights, with a rope tied around his feet and remain suspended in a well, upside down. The greatest Sufi saint of the 14th century in India and the most celebrated was Shaikh Nizamuddin Auliya. He was also an example for the Chistiyya Sufis. He ate sparingly in order to live like the poor people. He laid great emphasis on renunciation but does not emphasis on not wearing loin cloth in state of asceticism. For him, one should continue to wear clothing and also eat and also distribute to the poor. He also taught constantly about forbearance and peaceful relations between people.

The Chistiyya Sufis also observed what is taught by Shaikh Nizamuddin Mahmud as the mortification, fasting and prayers. The essence of the Sufi disciple was control of the breath and this should be practice during meditation. Every breath was related to mystic state. During the time of Akbar, Shaikh Jalal turned Thanesar into a major Chisti center. Shaikh Salim Chisti and his Khalifas became important in Fatehpur Sikri and the Agra region. Several new centers emerged in the Punjab during the 16th and 17th centuries. By the end of 17th century, Delhi became an important center with the presence of Shah Kalimullah.

(b) The Suhrawardiyya

The Indian soil was enriched by the migration from Iran and Transoxiana of a number of disciples of Shaikh Shihabuddin Suhrawradi. The real founder of the Suhrawardiyya in India, however, was Shaikd Bhahauddin Zakariyya (Multan), Shaikh

Jalaluddin Tabrizi (Lakhnaudi), Qazi Hamidudin (Nagaur) and Saiyid Nuruddin Mubarak (Delhi). They popularized Sufism in Uch and their influence spread to Punjab, Kashmir and Gujarat.

The Suhrawardi strongly discouraged Sufi seeking guidance from a number of different Pirs, urging them to lay their heads on one, rather than a number of thresholds. They laid great stress on performing *namaz* and admitted that all their achievements were result of it. Unlike the Chistis, the Suhrawardiyya did not observe incessant fasting and ate normally and they were quite rich as well. Occasionally, they seriously controlled their lower self in all conversations and actions. They greeted each other with *As-Salam Alaikum* (peace be with you) and expected disciples to finish their obligatory religious duties first and to greet him afterwards. The Chistis encouraged people to indulge in trade and commerce, agriculture and crafts for their livelihood, but these should not to interfere with spiritual exercises. However, the Suhrawardis were rich and concerned only with rich. For Chistis, association with rulers and noblemen was disastrous for spiritualists but for Suhrawardis, it wasn't. The Suhrawardi order did not retain its importance after 15th century.

(c) The Firdausiyya

This silsila traced its spiritual descent from Shaikh Saifuddin Bakharzi Kurba. The Firdausiyya order, a collateral line of Suhrawarddiya, was founded in Delhi by Khwaja Badruddin Samaraqandi but it became popular in Bihar due to Shaikh Sharafuddin Samarqand (1236-1381). A large number of his disciples established a network of *khanqahs* from Bihar to Sonargaon in Bengal. Like the Chisti saints, his teaching method was based on anecdotal formats.

(d) The Kubhrawiyya

The last quarter of 14th century saw the establishment of Kubrawiyya order in Kashmir. Saiyid Hamadani was imbued with the searing missionary zeal. This enthusiasm took the form of temple demolition and the enforced conversions of many Kashmiris. The best known work of Saiyid Hamadani's was on Islamic socio-political ethics which rulers and the governing classes were expected to follow. He believed the alleged "covenant of Umar", to be a legitimate basis for the relationship between the Sultans and the Zimmis (protected people).

(e) The Qalandars

The history of Sufism has been made infinitely more colourful by the role of Qalandars. Khwaja Abdullah Ansari wrote a treatise entitled the *Qalandar Nama* which contains his conversions with a Qalandar. According to the*Qalandar Nama,* Qalandars should possess these qualities – humility, lowliness, selflessness, asceticism, and renunciation. According to Al-Maqrizi, the Qalandariyyas first appeared in Damascus (1213-14). One of the early founders was a Spanish Arab from Egypt called Yusuf. They have shaven hair and have a habit of never being without razor. Ibn Batuta mentioned that this habit was taken over from Shaikh Jamaluddin of Sawa. Unlike other Silsilahs, they were not institutionalized. They were wandering Sufis and spread all over medieval India.

(f) The Shattariyya

This was founded in India by Shaikh Abdullah. Shattari centre were established by disciples in Bengal, Malwa, Gujarat, and the Deccan before the end of the 16th century. The most famous of Shattari Shaikhs was Shaikh Abdul Muyyad Muhammad. He wrote a number of Sufi works marked by a liberal and catholic spirit. His descendants and his disciples enjoyed great prestige in different parts of India like Gujarat, Malwa, the Deccan, Rajasthan, Bengal, Uttar Pradesh and Punjab.

(g) The Qadiriyyas

The Qadiriyyas order was one of the oldest of all mystical orders (1166 A.D.). In India, however, it gained a footing only at the end of 14th and during the 15th century. This order was introduced into India by Mir Nurulla. They were influential in Punjab, Delhi, Agra, etc. A few Qadiri *khanqahs* were established at Ahmedabad in Gujarat and at Mandu in Malwa. During the 17th century, Shaikh Mir Muhammad, popularly known as Mian Mir, rose into prominence in Punjab. Among his important disciples in Lahore, Sirhind and Sunam was Mulla Shah who was greatly admired by Dara Shikoh who himself is counted among the Qadiris. Some Qadiri *khanqahs* were established in U.P., Bihar and Bengal before the end of 17th century.

(h) The Naqshbandiyya:

This order flourished in India during the Mughal period. The Indian Naqshbandiyyas traced their spiritual descent from Khawaja Nasiruddin Ubaidullah Ahrar. The conquest of India by Babur in 1526 gave considerable impetus to development of the Naqshbandiyya order. Both the new Emperor and a large number of his central Asian soldiers were the spiritual followers of the disciples of Khwaja Ubaidullah. Many Naqshbandiyya Sufis also migrated from Central Asia to India, of whom Babur held a deep respect for Khwaja Abdush-Shahid and Khwaja Kalan. In the early years of Akbar's reign, the Naqshbandiyya influence returned to the Mughal court and many of them migrated from their homeland in Transoxiana to Agra who obtained high posts in civil and military administration. They retained their loyalty to the Emperor and even supported the broad based policies which Akbar introduced after 1579. The Naqshbandiyya Sufis produced people such as Khwaja Muhammad Baqi and Shaikh Ahmed Sirhindi (claimed to be Mujaddid-i Alif-i Sani). Sufism also moved down to Deccan especially during the time of Muhammad bin Tughlaq. **Gisu**

Daraz, a disciple of Shaikh Nasiruddin Mahmud made Deccan (in Gulbarga), his centre of activities. As it may be expected, all the Sufi orders were not equally important and same. However, principles of Sufism are same for almost all the orders. The central part of Sufism were the purification of heart, love of God and finally emerging with the Almighty God *(fana)*.

Impact of Sufism

The massive geographic presence of Islam in India can be explained by the tireless activity of Sufi preachers. Sufism had left a prevailing impact on religious, cultural, and social life in South Asia. The introduction of the mystical form of Islam was done by Sufi saints Sufi scholars traveling from all over continental Asia were instrumental in the social, economic, and philosophic development of India. Besides preaching in major cities and centres of intellectual thought, Sufis reached out to poor and marginalized rural communities and preached in local dialects such as Urdu, Sindhi, Panjabi versus Persian, Turkish, and Arabic. Sufism emerged as a "moral and comprehensive socio-religious force" that even influenced other religious traditions such as Hinduism. Their traditions of devotional practices and modest living attracted all people. Their teachings of humanity, love for God and Prophet continue to be surrounded by mystical tales and folk songs today. Sufis were firm in abstaining from religious and communal conflict and strived to be peaceful elements of civil society. Furthermore, it is the attitude of accommodation, adaptation, piety, and charisma that continues to help Sufism remain as a pillar of mystical Islam in India.

Sufism as we have seen is a very complex phenomenon. In India, it took root in both the rural and the urban areas. In some cases, the deep impact of Sufism and its popularity among the masses transformed rural region, such as Uch, Nagaur and Sylhet, into a flourishing urban centers. By the time of Muhammad Bin Tughlaq, *khanqahs* began to exercise a deep social, political, economic and cultural influence in India. The reliance of Sufis on God, particularly in the material sense, attracted both people from economically deprived classes and members of the oppressed elite into orders. *Khanqahs* gave to most people a feeling of hope and a vision of a bright future, both in this world and the one to come.

Various leaders of Sufi orders, tariqa, chartered the first organized activities to introduce localities to Islam through Sufism. Saint figures and mythical stories provided solace and inspiration to Hindu caste communities often in rural villages of India. The Sufism teachings of divine spirituality, cosmic harmony, love, and humanity resonated with the common people and still does so today. The following content will take a thematic approach to discuss a myriad of influences that helped spread

Sufism and a mystical understanding of Islam, making India a contemporary epicenter for Sufi culture today.

Sufi During British Rule

Sufi movement became dormant with the decline of Muslim power in India. With the failure of armed resistance against the British and Sikh-Hindu combined, the followers of hard line Sufism were forced to adjust with the ground reality of non-Muslim occupation of Indian subcontinent but did not reconcile with it. The failure of Sepoy mutiny and consolidation of British power in Indian subcontinent was a further jolt on the radical Islamists but all the Islamic revivalist movements like Deoband, Aligarh and Pakistan drew their inspirations from the anti-Hindu syndrome of Sufi saints like Sirhind and Shah Wali Ullah. Khilafat movement and subsequent Pakistan movement were the outcome of the jihadi interpretation of Walli Ullah brand of neo-Sufi jehad against the political domination of non-believers. The resistance of Muslims against the British and subsequently against the Indian National Congress was due to deep and hard line influence of Shah Wali Ullah over them.

Before the failure of 1857 Sepoy mutiny Sir Sayed Ahmad Khan was a follower of the neo-Sufi cult of Shah Waliullah. Elizabeth Syrriyeh (Sufis and Anti-Sufis, 1999) maintained that Syed Ahmad Khan gradually distanced himself fro Shah Wali ullah. But firmly rooted in the Indian Islamic mysticism he was deeply pained with the plight of Muslims after the collapse of Sepoy mutiny of 1857. He therefore, took up the challenge of modern education and transformed the revolutionary mystic ideology of Shah Wali Ullah for revitalization of Islamic glory through western education. Had he distanced himself from Wali Ullah, he would not have initiated the two-nation theory on the line of this Sufi Islamist to promote the movement of Muslim separatism through his Aligarh movement.

Sir Sayed's philosophy was a synthesis of progressive and orthodox Islam. On one hand he favored modern education on European pattern and on the other he supported Islamic orthodoxy for superior religious identity of Muslims. He reinterpreted the cultural heritage of Islam within the mystic ideological frame of Wali Ulla, His Aligarh movement was a tactical but a hidden alliance of the Muslims with British under latter's sovereignty to revive the supremacy of Muslims. He advocated for free discussion on Islam but due to his communal obsession he did not strive hard to prove his point for the socio-religious integration of Indian society.

According to Allama Iqbal, "he (Wali Ullah) was the first Muslim to feel the urge for rethinking the whole system of Islam without in any way breaking away from its past" (The Sufi Orders in Islam by J. Spencer Trimingham, Oxford, 1971, Page 198). Iqbal was a known follower of Islamic mysticism of Qadiriyya order.

He, synthesized the mystic ideology of Wali Ullah and the modern view on Islam of Sir Sayed Ahmad Khan and made his Islamic mystic approach completely subservient to political domination of the Muslims. Applying modern philosophy in his intellectual exploration of Sufism he gradually turned to an anti-Sufi philosopher. He said, "The present day Muslims prefer to roam about aimlessly in the dusty valleys of Hellenic-Persian mysticism, which teaches us to shut our eyes to the hard reality around, and to fix our gaze on what it describes as 'Illuminations' a blue, red and yellow reality springing up from the cells of an overworked brain" (Sufis and anti-Sufis by Elizabeth Syrrieh, 1999). "Sufi shaikhs constituting a spiritual aristocracy, Iqbal appealed to Muslim youth to cast off the Sufi noose from their neck" (*Ibid.* Page133). For Iqbal Sufism was a formulation of Islamic Persianism. It was contrary to the purity of Arabic faith in its original version. His rejection of Sufism was influenced by Wahhabi movement of Saudi Arabia, which was more concerned with Islamic power following the decline of Muslim power in eighteenth century.

Cultural and Religious Impact of Hinduism

Sufism gave birth to a very wide range of mystic symbolism and became an indispensable part of Persia poetry. Poetry was not only an expression of mystic love of a thirsty soul seeking an intuitive understanding of God, but an avenue for emotions and feelings which would otherwise have never been expressed due to fury of orthodox social inhibitions and political repression. Sufi poetry written in Hindi added a new dimension to Indian mysticism and a new lyrical and colourful way by which to achieve an estate state. The subtle refinement of Hindi music, combined with Persian conventions and artistry gave fresh meaning and depth to Indian Sufi thought. Hindi Sufi poets and the Bhaktas rebelled against all forms of religious formalism, orthodoxy, falsehood, hypocrisy and stupidity and tried to create a new world in which spiritual blessing was the all-consuming goal. The Sufis were influenced by the Hindu Bhaktas in controlling breath, composing songs, not eating meat etc. They even gave importance to the Hindu gods. Lala Yogeshwari influenced the Sufi movement as well. All these gave rise to a cultural and religious meaning to Sufism coming closer to Hindu religion.

In the nineteenth and twentieth centuries the different bûfî traditions were involved in many different ways in helping to shape Muslim responses to the West and also in defining Islamic forms of modernity. At the same time, although in changing contexts, many of the main themes of the older experiences of the orders continue. Among the many aspects of the history of bûfî orders in the modern era, it is important to examine a number more closely: the Sûfî orders continued to serve as an important basis for popular devotional life; they were important forces in responding to imperial rule; they helped to provide organizational and intellectual inspiration for Muslim responses to modern challenges to the faith; and they continued to be an important force in the mission of Muslims to non-Muslims.

Responses to Modernity

Súfî orders also were important in helping to shape the responses to the challenges to Muslim faith in the modern era. In the nineteenth century this was more in terms of providing organizational bases for opposition to European expansion and in the direct continuation of the traditions of activist reformist movements such as the Naqshbandìyah. In the twentieth century, *tarîqah*s responded to specific societal needs in a variety of ways. In some countries orders provided the direct organizational basis for modern-style political parties. In Sudan, for example, the Khatmîyah provided the foundation for the National Unionist Party, then the People's Democratic Party; late in the twentieth century the head of the order was also the president of the Democratic Unionist Party. In Senegal, the Murîdîyah provided an organization for the development of cash crops and played an important role in modernizing the agricultural sector of the Senegalese economy. In the days of Soviet communist rule in Central Asia, the popular local *tarîqah*s and the established traditional ones like the Naqshbandîyah provided the framework within which Islamic communal identity could be maintained in the face of the official efforts to suppress religion. In the holy war in Afghanistan after the Soviet occupation in 1979, leaders of established orders likc the Qîdirîyah and Naqshbandîyah Mujaddidîyah were among the most important organizers of *mujâhidîn* groups. These examples affirm the fact that in many different areas, the organizational traditions of the bûfî orders provided important bases for responding to specific challenges.

In the twentieth century, however, the role of the orders was sometimes different. The established *tarîqah*s might seem ineffective in meeting particular challenges of modernity, but the basic structures or the general approach might still provide models for new Islamic revivalist and reformist movements.

Conclusion

Sufism has an illustrious history in ***India*** evolving for over 1,000 years. The presence of Sufism has been a leading entity increasing the reaches of Islam throughout South Asia. Following the entrance of Islam in the early 700s, Sufi mystic traditions became more visible during the 10th and 11th centuries of the Delhi Sultanate. A conglomeration of four chronologically separate dynasties, the early Delhi Sultanate consisted of rulers from Turkic and Afghan lands. This Persian influence flooded South Asia with Islam, Sufi thought, synergetic values, literature, education, and The concept of Tawhid (Unity in God), which is the real formulation of Sufism suggests that Islamic mysticism has no difference with the formulations of other non-Islamic faiths about the oneness of God. On this basis Sufism became popular in India during the period of Muslim rule. But when the Sufis supported the Muslims in their political conflict with the Hindus and played important role in conversion of indigenous people to Islam, it gave birth to politicization of religion, which generated communal tension between the two major religious communities. The movement for purifying Islam from extraneous influences, which was launched by the Sufis like Saikh Ahmad Sirhindi and Shah Wali Ullah was against the spiritual doctrine of 'Tawhid' (Unity in God). Creating a far-reaching impact on the psyche of Indian Muslims it continues to keep the Muslim mass away from the modern global changes.

Sufism in India has commonly been viewed as a secular attempt for eternal quest of the soul for its direct experience of the ultimate Super power. For centuries the Hindus accepted Sufi shrines as symbol of communal harmony. A large number of them have been offering prayers in Sufi shrines without any reservation but this liberal gesture has not been reciprocated Muslims.

Contrary to the common perception that Sufism tried to unify the Hindu-Muslim spirituality for a communal harmony, the political Islamists of Sufi background used the doctrine of Tawhid to accelerate the process of Muslim separatism in Indian subcontinent. Their movements were the by-products of Sufi tradition of Islam. They were basically the mystics for the political domination of Islamic activists.

The basic creed of mystic movements is unity of God irrespective of religious connotation. Unity of God denotes social unity and universal brotherhood. But these political mystics not only divided the society on the basis of religion but their doctrine created a permanent Hindu-Muslim conflict in the region. The spirit of mysticism is to resolve any dilemma confronting the society. But Sufi movement failed to resolve confronting Hindu-Muslim dilemma in Indian society. In practice they launched a movement for systematic dehumanization of Islam and negated the concept of Islamic spiritualism of Tawhid (Unity of God).

References

Aziz Ahmad, *Studies in Islamic Culture in the Indian Environment*, Oxford University Press, 1964, p. 189.

Arberry, A.J. *Sufism: an Account of the Mystics of Islam.* London: Allen and Unwin, 1950.

Aquil, Raziuddin (2007). *Sufism, Culture, and Politics: Afghans and Islam in Medieval North India*. New Delhi: Oxford University Press.

Abidi, S.A.H. (1992). *Sufism in India*. New Delhi: Wishwa Prakashan.

Anjum, Tanvir (2011). *Chishti Sufis in the Sultanate of Delhi 1190-1400: From Restrained Indifference to Calculated Defiance*. Pakistan: Oxford University Press.

Askari, Syed Hasan, Tazkira-i Murshidi—Rare Malfuz of the 15th-Century Sufi Saint of Gulbarga. Proceedings of the Indian Historical Records Commission (1952).

Akhbarul Akhyar' By Abdal Haqq Muhaddith Dehlwi (d.1052H-1642 CE). A short biography of the prominent sufis of India have been mentioned in this book including that of Hazrat Akhi Siraj Aainae Hind).

Binge, John Kingsley. *The Bektashi Order of Dervishes.* London: Luzac and Co., 1994.

Burckhardt, Titus. *An Introduction to Sufi Doctrine.* Trans. D.M. Matheson. Wellingborough, Northamptonshire: Thorsons Publishers Ltd., 1976.

Jafri, Saiyid Zaheer Husain (2006). *The Islamic Path: Sufism, Politics, and society in India.* New Delhi: Konrad Adenauer Foundation.

Jagadish Narayan Sarkar, *Islam in Bengal,* (Calcutta, 1972).

Rizvi, Saiyied Athar Abbas, *History of Sufism in India*, Vol. 2, 1992, p. 180.

Robert Heilbrunn Institute for International Interreligious Understanding, American Jewish Committee. p. 204.

Schimmel, Annemarie. *Mystical Dimensions of Islam.* Chapel Hill: University of North Carolina Press, 1975.

Sajida Sultana (2012). *Perspectives on Mughal India: Rulers, Historians, Ulama, and Sufis.* Karachi: Oxford University Press.

Schimmel, Anniemarie (1975). "Sufism in Indo-Pakistan". *Mystical Dimensions of Islam.* Chapel Hill: University of North Carolina. p. 344.

S.A.A. Rizvi, *A History of Sufism in India, Vol.* I, (Delhi, 1978), p.143.

Schimmel, Anniemarie (1975). "Sufism in Indo-Pakistan". *Mystical Dimensions of Islam.* Chapel Hill: University of North Carolina, p. 344.

Trimingham, Spencer J. *The Sufi Orders in Islam.* Oxford: Clarendon Press, 1971.

Walsh, Judith E. (2006). *A Brief History of India.* Old Westbury: State University of New York, p. 58.

ZH Sharib (2006). *The Sufi saints of the Indian subcontinent.* Munshirm Manoharlal.

Ziya-ul-Hasan Faruqi. (1996). *Fawa'id Al-Fu'ad—Spiritual and Literary Discourses of Shaikh Nizammuddin Awliya.* South Asia Book. Originally compiled by Amir Hasan 'Alâ' Sijzî Dehlawî ; English translation with introduction and historical annotation by.

3

Sufism: A Way Towards Retaining Peace, Solidarity and Harmony

Sanchita Dasgupta and Chandan Adhikary

Abstract

23rd December, 2014 near about 80 people belonging to 'Adibasi' or 'Santhal' community in Assam were brutally shot to death. 16th December, 2014 the world lost its speech in grief as hundreds of innocent flowers were pathetically shot dead in Pakistan. These incidents register to the fact that despite a havoc progress in different sphere of our lives, we are not happy at all. A gigantic 'Black Hole' is gradually approaching us and we are helplessly giving in. How can we rescue ourselves from this trap? Where is that very light that will ensure the victory of humanity, love, tolerance and absolute peace? If we look at the Indian spiritual tradition we will find that India is the epitome of different religious transfusion. The Bhakti Movement led by Sri Chaitanya, Kabir, Nanak was a kind of reform movement that attempted to bring a fresh air in the Indian society. On the other hand, Sufi Movement chiefly during the 10th and 11th centuries emerged as the liberating force that inspired free thinking, fellow-feeling and unorthodox ideas. The Movement had a significant role in establishing harmony among Hindus and Muslims & even among different sects of Hindus. Sufism indulged in love and peace; it embraced all irrespective of their social, religious and political status. It was solely a humanitarian call to the common mass who were extremely troubled and confused by social and religious distinction or segregation. Sufism is in fact a journey towards inner soul, a search of the self, and the enlightened soul ultimately succeeds in understanding the divine. This journey to find the God or the 'Beloved' is synonymous with the journey of the 'Bauls' to find their 'moner manush'. What is most striking about Sufis is that they have given birth to new kinds of folk genre, Murshidi and Marifati song in the field of folk culture in India. Their simple and modest life, devotion to God by constant self-denial attracted the hearts of the ordinary people. Now, when the humanity is pitifully groping in this land of 'nothingness', that very hand and heart with voice of love can definitely take the whole humanity to the realm of peace once again. The ideas & values of Sufi mystics if re-discovered, re-kindled and re-assessed with a new zeal, it can serve the humanity as a panacea, yet to be treasured.

Keywords: *Bhakti Movement; Sufi Movement; Enlightenment; Illumination of soul*

Introduction

"Dike dike naginira felichhe bishakto niswas,
Shantir lalit bani sonaibe bartho porihas"

"Pardon me, O Lord! We forgot to celebrate your birthday, this December. We forgot to sing carols, instead, with wet eyes were busy in singing elegies". This was, indeed, our sincere apology to our beloved Jesus on the cursed December of 2014. We are ashamed of belonging to that civilization which stands 'motionless and still' witnessing the brutal killing of innocent children and some poor, marginalized people. From Pentagon to Palestine, from Kabul to Kashmir the only story is of utter destruction. With wounds, bleeding profusely, we entered into a new year. 'The poisonous breath of serpents', as our poet, Tagore once realized, has entirely entangled this so-called 'advanced' civilization. 16th December 2014, the day broke with the wail of hundreds of helpless parents. Can we in any way justify the brutality executed in Assam on 23rd December? We are passing through a sterile and vacant period when the words of love, peace & harmony are being desperately proved to be futile. It's in fact an erosive ailment that is devouring modern civilization at a rapid pace. But is the world destined to end in such a way? As Eliot out of extreme frustration uttered in 'The Hollow Men':

"This is the way the world ends
This is the way the world ends
This is the way the world ends
Not with a bang but with a whimper."

In our attempt to discover the best possible treatment we have to look behind and throw some light on the spiritual tradition and rich mystic heritage that we have been nurturing from times immemorial. The Bhakti and Sufi Movement in India acted as a liberating force that suddenly brought a fresh air in an era of utter political and social turbulences. Sufism originating from the heart of Islam with its message of love, tolerance, humility, equality, fraternity, peace and harmony paved the way towards salvation. This paper is a spontaneous effort on our part that attempts to investigate and explore the relevance and implication of Sufism in context of sustaining universal peace and harmony.

Origin of Sufism

There are differences of opinion regarding the actual origin of the word 'Sufi'. Lexically the word is said to have been derived from the Arabic word, *'safa'* meaning 'purity'. Some hold the view that it has originated from *'suf'* meaning 'wool' in Arabic. It refers to the ascetics who used to wear woolen cloak. Another opinion is that the word has been derived from *'Ahl-as-Suffah'*, i.e., the people of the bench. These people belonging to weaker sections of society were the dedicated followers of the prophet. Again, Abu Rayhan al-Biruni, a medieval scholar said that the word has originated from Greek word *'sofia'* which means 'wisdom'.

Introduction and Development of Sufism in India

Sufism emerged in the 8th century Iran when the struggle for political power reached its peak. Amidst this political and social turmoil, Sufism began to flourish gradually in its own course. During the 11th & 12th century AD Sufism reached in India and consequently it extended its periphery at a rapid pace during the Mughal Dynasty. There are eight different Sufi orders (*tariqa* or *silsila*) in India:

> Among these orders *Chistiyya* Sufis were very popular among common mass. This order gained popularity during the 13th & 14th century with Khwaja Moinuddin Chisti of Ajmer, Shaikh Bhaktiyar Kaki of Delhi. Shaikh Bhaharuddin Zakariya, Saiyid Nuruddin Mubarak, Shaikh Jalauddin Tabrizi were the founders of *Suharawardiyya* order. Sufis belonging to this order were more prone to Islamic rigidity of practicing religious rites. The *Kubhrawiyya* was much orthodox and engaged them in demolishing temples, and forced people to accept Islam. On the other hand, the *Qalandars* used to emphasize on exercising humility, modesty, asceticism, renunciation & self-denial. These Sufis were wanderers and they spread all over the medieval India. *'Qalandar Nama'* written by Khwaja Abdullah Ansari is a remarkable printed document that exhibits the lives and philosophy of these saints. One of the oldest of all mystical orders in India are the *Qadriyyas*. Mir Nurullah was its chief proponent. During the Mughal period *Naqshabandiyya* order extended its periphery. In 1526, the conquest of India by Babar served as a catalyst in the extension of *Naqshabandiyya* order. Many *Naqshabandiyya* Sufis like especially Khwaja Abdush-Shadid, Khwaja Kalan were very close to Babar. What is striking is that unlike others, Sufis belonging to this order used to aspire for royal presents and flattering and was too much concerned with the Mughal Court.

Multi-dimensional Impact of Sufism on Indian Life

Social Life

It was indeed a bold task on the part of the Sufi saints to open their mouth for establishing equality on a land extremely distorted and fragmented by year-old beliefs justifying castism and hierarchical racial structure. Teaching of Sufism and Sufi principles being based on universal brotherhood and amity played a pivotal role in establishing a bridge among people belonging to different communities and religious beliefs. The aim of a Sufi saint is two-fold: (i) Self-illumination by the way of complete surrender to Allah, the Almighty; (ii) Love for mankind. What is notable is that the Sufi saints despite practicing Islam assimilated themselves with the very core of Indian life and culture. Among *Chistiyya* Sufis Baba Farid, Khwaja Moinuddin Chisti of Ajmer, Nijamuddin Awliya of Delhi were highly esteemed by the Indians. The great Mughal emperor Akbar himself was highly impressed by the Sufi brothers Abul Fzal and Faizi, and invited them to his court.

Religious Life

Sufism may be called less a religion more a way of life, rather an enlightened way of living. The journey of the Sufi saints is that of a quest simultaneously for realizing the Divinity and in so doing for knowing the inner self, by a rigorous and constant process of self-denial. These saints indulged in free-mixing among people regardless of their racial, social religious and cultural differences. They preferred to live in contact with poor and down-trodden people instead of aristocratic sections of society. Many Hindus belonging to lower sects felt attracted by the words of equality imbibed in Islam and accepted it in an attempt to live a life of dignity. Impartial regards to and even adoption of different local rituals and customs on the part of these Sufi saints brought them much closer to the Hindus in India.

Economics & Politics

The *Chistiyya* saints encouraged to indulge themselves in trade and commerce, agriculture and crafts. Most of the Sufi Saints dedicated their lives for the service of human being; in time of natural calamity or any other crisis they used to serve and console the common mass. The Sufis played a significant role in influencing the king to be kind and considerate to his subjects and reminded them of the ethical aspects of Islam. They even influenced the king to be impartial and responsive to their non-Muslim subjects. The whole Mughal Dynasty owed much to the Sufi saints; they in fact believed in the spiritual power of the Sufis. Khwaja Moinuddin Chisti was called 'Sultan-ul-Hind'.

Literature & Music

Sufi mysticism has immense influence on the classical as well as folk culture and music in India. Sufi *'Khanqahs'* (hospice) and '*Dargahs*'(shrine) were the most notable instances of spiritual confluence where both Muslims and Hindus used to gather. As far as classical arena is concerned, the Sufis introduced and developed the genre of '*ghazal*' and *'nazm'*. In the field of devotional song they introduced the genre of *'qawwqli'* which was based on Indian classical *ragas* and was invented by Amir Khosru, the most talented and promising disciple of Nizamuddin Awliya. In fact the contribution of Amir Khosru to Indian classical music specifically '*kheyal*' genre is beyond measure. He was rightly entitled 'The Parrot of India'. The most significant contribution of Sufism on Indian folk culture is the emergence of a new folk genre, i.e., '*Murshidi*' and *'Marifati'* song that got assimilated and dissolved in the Indian heart.

Education

The Sufi saints, unknown to them, remained as a strong source of formal, non-formal and informal education in the medieval India as well as in the Central Asia. Moral education propagated by Islam got a free breeze in the hands of the saints. If education in its broader sense refers to an all-round development of an individual, then these Sufis undoubtedly exercised the pivotal role in spreading moral and ethical education among people, highly confused and staggered by the existing socio-political anarchy and discord.

Sufism in The Light of Liberal Humanism

Humanism with its different connotations was indeed a revolution that shattered the year-old rigid and orthodox feudal orientation. With Socrates in the West and Boccaccio in the East Humanism began its journey and established its dominance during the succeeding periods of human civilization. Acceptance of the needs, desires and welfare of human beings propounded by philosophers like Descartes, Spinoza, Leibniz, was seen to be manifested in the chief concerns of the Sufi ideology. Human beings regardless of age, sex, social and religious identity found a dignified way of living in the theory and practice of Sufism. Therefore, human beings dared for the first time to speak out and many Sufi saints encouraged the common mass to raise their voice against any kind of exploitation exercised upon them by the ruler or royal authority.

Sufism exhibits the property of scientific attitude, another characteristic feature of Liberal Humanism, in its denial of any kind of superstition. Though having Islamic mysticism as its background Sufism reached beyond the limitations of any religion and represented a comprehensive way of life. This comprehensiveness today is said to be the guiding force to be adopted in the field of education and culture as modern social-scientists and educationists have emphasized.

We all know that folk literature and music is the mirror of rural life. In the language of Maxim Gorky, "The true history of the toiling people cannot be learnt without knowledge of the folklore." If we analyze different sections of Sufi music and literature we will find that many of them are the accounts of the struggles, sufferings and deprivation of the common mass. Let us see how Durbin Shah has depicted the helplessness of a poor farmer who in his struggle for existence scarcely gets time for prayer:

> It's really overwhelming to think that these religious leaders in their practice of simple, meek and humble living contributed a lot to the triumph of Liberal Humanism on earth, *"Namaj amar hoilo na adaay,*
>
> *Namaj ami Porte parlam Na, darun khannachher day.*
> *Fojorer namajer kale, chhilam ami ghumer ghore,*
> *Johor galo aaite- jaaite, aachhor galo kamer day."*

though remained unattended & unsung for a long period of time.

Sufism: A Concord Within

Sufism in its theory & practice is itself an incarnation of integrity and harmony. In fact, the essence of harmony is inherent in the doctrine of Sufi way of living. The doctrine of *'wahdat-al-wujud'* (the unity of being) propounded by Ibn Arabi advocates the existence of only the Absolute, i.e., God. It is solely out of His wish that the whole Creation came into being. What is truth is the existence of God, nothing exists except Him. God is omnipresent, & everything is a unified form of the One, i.e., God. Without Him everything is meaningless. Here we can find a close resemblance between the basic philosophy of *Wahdat-al-Wujud* with that of 'Upanishasd' where the universe is conceived as the manifestation of the Supreme power or *'Brahmo'*. The opening 'mantra' of *'Ees Upanishad'* reflects the concept of His omnipresence:

> *"Eesha basyamidang sarbang jot kincho jagatyang jagat,*
> *Teno takteno vunjitha ma gridho kasyaswid dhanam."*

(Think that everything in this moving world is shrouded with God, He is there in every object; so it's unethical to be greedy)

"*sarbang khlawaidong Brhomo*" (everything is Brhomo; as everything emerges from Him & dissolves in Him) as depicted by the '*Chhandogyo Upanishad*', has much similarity with Sufi belief of the Unity of Existence.

Enlightenment or the illumination of self is one of the highest aims of the Sufi saints. 'Know Thyself' (*Atmanang Bidhdhi*) is also the sole concern of the Indian philosophy. Sufi saints attempt to acquire 'wisdom' or '*ilam*' (Arabic) or 'consciousness' to understand the universe as well as the whole creation. Self-realization is a long standing perception of Indian saints too. Sri Aurobindo wrote in 'Life Divine':

> "Our surface existence is only a surface and it is there that there is full reign of the ignorance; to know we have to go within ourselves and see with an inner knowledge. All that is formulated on the surface is a small and diminished representation of our secret greater existence."

Mysticism, a simple word conveying a profound implication within it had played a very significant role in the formation and sustenance of different religious and theological tradition throughout the world. Sufism like Indian philosophy too is deeply soaked in the essence of mysticism. Self-purification can only be attained through mysticism, as it is capable, according to the Sufis, of breaking the wall standing between God and His followers. Eminent Sufi poet Hafez wrote in his 'A Tethered Falcon':

"Beloved, I am waiting for you to free me
Into Your Mind
And Infinite Being
I am pleading in an absolute helplessness
To hear, finally,
Your words of Grace
Fly! Fly into Me"

Rabindranath Tagore quite in similar tone surrendered himself saying:

"Amare dei tomar hate
Nuton kore nuton prate. S
Dine dinei fulje fote, temni korei fute othe
Jibon tomar anginate
Nuton kore nuton prate."

The fact that Sufi mysticism is nothing but an essential and indispensable flow of the mystic realization as a whole regardless of socio-cultural and religious distinctions, is registered as we find the instances of the same perception in Tagore and even in British poet William Wordsworth. The mystic orientation is notable in Wordsworth's '*Tintern Abbey*':

".........And have I felt
A presence that disturbs me with joy
Of elevated thoughts; a sense sublime
Of something far more deeply interfused,
Whose dwelling is the light of setting suns?
And the round ocean, and the living air,
And the blue sky, and in the mind of man;
A motion and a spirit, that impels
All thinking things, all objects of all thought,
And rolls through all things."

What we are experiencing is that Sufi mysticism is shining as a single entity embracing different shades of oriental & occidental philosophical traditions.

The success of Sufism reached its peak in Bengal as the Sufi saints & the *'Bauls'* of Bengal became the two opposite sides of a single coin. The rural folk culture of Bengal & Sufi mysticism got assimilated on the soil of Bengal and rest is a very fertile history of Bengali as well as Indian folk tradition. The common quest of the Sufis and that of the *Bauls* to find their 'Beloved' and '*Moner Manush'* respectively was the chemistry that worked between them and they came very close to each other. This '*Moner Manush'* or 'Beloved' is none but the inner soul, who is sacred & pure, who is light and joy. The Sufis and *Bauls* have long been aspiring for union with the Beloved. Sufis and the *Bauls* are in fact two the separate strings of a single *'Dotara'* which if well attuned produce a harmonic tune. "Drink on the Wind of the Beloved" is an ecstatic creation of Hafez that exhibits how the poet is ardently awaiting the moment of the very union:

"Don't sit there thinking; go out and immerse yourself in God's sea.
Having only one hair wet with water will not put knowledge in that head.
For those who see only God, there vision
Is pure, and not a doubt remains.
Even if our world is turned upside down and blown over by the wind,
If you are doubtless, you won't lose a thing.
O Hafiz, if it is union with the Beloved that you seek,
Be the dust at the Wise One's door, and speak!"

We can find similar aspiration in the *Bauls* of Bengal like Lalan Fakir, Hasan Raja, Shah Abdul Karim, Duddu Shah to get dissolved in the Divine existence. Let's see what Karim Shah,one of them is saying :

"Eso byather sathi ogo tumi amar snai
Tomar moto byathar byathi brohmande keho nai"

The influence that Sufi and *Baul* mysticism has exerted upon the society in terms of ensuring communal harmony is beyond exaggeration. l. Especially *Bauls & Fakirs* of Bengal for centuries have been struggling hard for establishing the doctrine of common identity, common recognition and common religion for all human beings. What moves us is the fact that most of these people were illiterate, but they were not uneducated; they derived education from their lives through their blessings of mysticism. Lalan Fakir, one of the most popular Sufis in Bengal, an illiterate rural guy, makes us spellbound when we find him repenting at the hypocrisy of social order:

"Jaat galo jaat galo bole eki aajob karkhana.
Sotyo pothe keu noy raaji,sob dekhi tana-nana".

On the other hand, Hafez has open-heartedly declared what he has learnt in divine contact:

"I Have Learned
So mush from God
That I can no longer
Call Myself
A Christian, a Hindu, a Muslim
A Buddhist, a Jew."

The Sufism of Iran and the *Vedantic* philosophy of India–one emanating from the core of Islam and the other from the heart of Hinduism commenced a journey together of course ignoring the existing religious and social orthodoxy & thus proclaimed the beginning of a new era in the history of Indian theological movement. The goal of both was to establish the dominance & victory of Humanism in a cordial air of love, tolerance, equality and fraternity. Hazrat Inayat Khan, a distinguished Sufi scholar himself said, "The Sufi sees the truth in every religion."

Sufism and Peace Education

Following the devastation caused by two succeeding wars (World War-I and II) voices were raised especially by International Institute for Intellectual Cooperation (IIIC), a preceding entity of United Nations Educational, Scientific and Cultural Organization (UNESCO), on the need of fostering international understanding and cooperation. In 1946, with the formation of UNESCO international peace & harmony became an essential part of its agenda. In this context, if we look back we will be surprised to find that the Sufism is the history of cultivating & instilling education of peace and value in a society utterly fragmented by prevalent socio-cultural milieu. The way towards tranquility that the Sufis have long been suggesting is relevant today & even of course in its rather heightened implication. Modern Sufi scholar Hazrat Inayat Khan declared: "The peace for which every soul strives, and which is the true nature of God and the utmost goal of man, is but the outcome of harmony."

Hazrat Inayat Khan, the founder of 'Universal Sufism', expressed his views on how can peace and harmony be achieved saying, "harmony is brought about by attuning oneself to all beings, to all things, to all situations; and one who cannot tune himself tries to tune others." Here, we find that a modern Sufi or may be called a dedicated follower of Sufism, has exquisitely summarized one of the modern connotations of Education.

Extension of Sufi Idealism: Modern Scenario

Among the hardcore followers of Sufi idealism Hazrat Inayat Khan (1882-1927) very sincerely took up the task of introducing & extending Sufi principles all over the world specifically in the West. He founded an institution named, 'The Sufi Order in the West' in London in the year of 1914; though 'International Sufi Movement', the revised version of 'The Sufi Order in London', started in 1923. He was a dedicated teacher of 'Universal Sufism'; and it was due to his sincere and continuous endeavor that the essence of Sufism reached Netherland, France, Germany, England, U.S.A, Canada, Australia and Russia. 'The Sufi Way' founded by Inayat Khan, now directed & supervised by Pir Elias Amidon, has become a distinguished institution today in expanding Sufi messages all over the world.

It's really a very positive and inspiring phenomenon that a nine-month training and seminar entitled; 'Open Path Training' is going to be organized in London & Germany by 'The Sufi Way'. This training will be an integrated approach relating to both classical and modern Sufi practices, philosophy pertaining to *Vedantic, Upanishodic*, Buddhist theology and meditation practices & even post-modern psychological trends. Another notable effort on their part is that they have arranged a year-long teleconference program by the name, 'Living Sufism' which has already started on October 2014 and will be continued till October 2015.

'Institute for Sufi Studies: Educational and Research Center' regularly organizes lectures, workshops, conferences for all who are interested in Sufism. This institute is the educational department of International Association of Sufism (IAS) that offers even on-line classes through internet.

Sufism: A Panacea to All Ailments

Let us look at a glance at the chief orientation of Sufi way of living:

- Simple living
- Total surrender to God
- Self-denial
- Self-illumination
- Contact with common people
- Secular outlook
- Philanthropic attitude

The ultimate aim of the Sufi saints is the derivation of spirituality at the cost of perishing the self; yet these are the persons who preached philanthropy in an era distorted by political & social unrests & upheavals. A Sufi saint used to shun and rule out anything that could divide human beings from one another. Despite being possessed entirely in the thought of the Divinity they had a profound social concern. They were actually a kind of social reformer who with words of love, tolerance, non-violence, fraternity and equality attempted to rescue the humanity from their extreme downfall. Spirituality and Philanthropy are the two important pillars of Sufism. Love and only love is the solution to any kind of unrest within and without. According to Sufi saints only love can enlighten and educate the inner being, awaken it from the state of inertia. Sufi poet Idries Shah said:

> *"The union of the mind and the intuition which brings about illumination, and the development which the Sufis seek, is based upon love."*

People flocked around these saints as their presence and their words were indeed a '*marham*' on their wounds, a solace to their burdened hearts. Jalal-uddin-Rumi, the great Sufi mystic as well as philanthropist has asserted:

> *"Love is the beginning and the end.*
> *Love is the eternal, infinite and everlasting.*
> *Love is the energizing elixir of the universe.*
> *Love is the cause and effect of all harmonies."*

Therefore, today the salvation lies in our hands as we have to choose our own way. The message of tranquility and peace delivered by Sufi way of living should reach the common mass. Though organizations like Universal Sufism, International Association of Sufism (IAS) are trying their best for the purpose of infusing Sufi ideology into the minds of the people, yet all of their efforts have remained concentrated on a definite section of society. Both print and electronic media specifically television should be more fruitfully used to transmit the principles of Sufism to all living throughout the Globe. The introduction of Peace Education with Sufism as its indispensable part should be our highest concern today.

References

1. R.N. Tagore: *Poem No.18, Prantik.*
2. T.S. Eliot*: The Hollow Man from The Waste Land,1922.*
3. A. Wahab: Banglar baul sufi sadhana o sangit, page no.194, 2011.
4. A.M. Nuri: Sufibad, 2008.
5. Upanishad, Haraf Prakasani, 2009.
6. Sri Aurobindo: The Life Divine,1982.
7. Tagore: Gitabitan, page no.151.
8. W. Wordsworth: Tintern Abbey.
9. Uzayyr, S.B. (2012). *Sufism: A Brief History*. Notion Press.
10. Dehlvi, S. (2009). *Sufism: The Heart of Islam*. Harpercollins.
11. Wahab. A (1999). *Banglar Baul Sufi Sadhana O Sangit*. Ratnaboli, Kolkata.
12. Nuri. A.M. *Sufibad.*
13. *Upanishad*. Haraf Prakasani, Kolkata.
14. Sri Aurobindo (2001). *The Life Divine*. Sri Aurobindo Ashram.
15. Dwivedi, A.N. (2002). *T. S. Eliot: A Critical Study*.

4

Relevance of Sufism in the Contemporary World as a Propagator of Peace and Harmony

Vinay Chandra pathak

Sufism in India has commonly been viewed as a secular attempt for eternal quest of the soul for its direct experience of the ultimate Super power. For centuries the Hindus accepted Sufi shrines as symbol of communal harmony. The Sufis were the peaceful emissaries of Islam who dedicated their lives in spreading the Islam and to the service of humanity. They laid Emphasis on the principle of nobility to achieve their goals. The massive geographic presence of Islam in India can be explained by the tireless activity of Sufi preachers. Sufism had left a prevailing impact on religious, cultural, and social life in South Asia. Sufism emerged as a "moral and comprehensive socio-religious force" that even influenced other religious traditions such as Hinduism. Their traditions of devotional practices and modest living attracted all people. Their teachings of humanity, love for God and Prophet continue to be surrounded by mystical tales and folk songs today. The introduction of the mystical form of Islam was done by Sufi saints; Sufi scholars traveling from all over continental Asia were instrumental in the social, economic, and philosophic development of India. Besides preaching in major cities and centers of intellectual thought, Sufis reached out to poor and marginalized rural communities and preached in local dialects such as Urdu, Sindhi, and Panjabi versus Persian, Turkish, and Arabic. Sufis were firm in abstaining from religious and communal conflict and try to be peaceful elements of civil society.

So in this circumstances Sufism provides guidance to mankind. Sufism teaches that the whole of existence, from atoms to galaxies to human beings, all submitted to their informed center and are guided by their innate knowledge. There is quite similarity between Hindu monism and Sufi monism. Monism is most clearly identified in Advaita Vedanta. In Advaita Vedanta, Brahman is the eternal, unchanging, infinite, immanent, and transcendent reality which is the Divine Ground of all matter, energy, time, space, being, and everything beyond in this Universe. The nature of Brahman is described as transpersonal, personal and impersonal by different philosophical school. Many followers of Sufism advocated monism. Most notably the 13th-century Persian poet Jalal ad-Din Muhammad Balkhi-Rumi (1207–73) in his didactic poem Masnavi espoused monism. Rumi says in the Masnavi, In the shop for Unity (wahdat); anything that you see their except the One is an idol.

The Sufi community is a global community, and the global community is a beloved community. From a Sufi perspective, this global community is possible because all of humankind (*insan*) is ultimately one people – a single community that transcends creed, caste, class, country, and color. Every human community has received streams of divine truth and revelation. Each civilization has a unique contribution to make to the human prospect, and every culture is intrinsically valuable. Moreover, each culture can benefit from contact and exchange with other cultures: the whole world needs the whole world.

The most relevance contribution of Sufism to present world is constructive approach for the peace and harmony. Sufism has a vital and essential role to play in these efforts, in which it can harmonize relations between Islam and other great religious cultures and direct attention to issues that are of perennial importance in the moral and spiritual development of humanity. Sufism tried to bridge the gulf between orthodoxy and devotion and played a important role in propagation of peace and harmony. Because of its capacity to inspire human solidarity and deeply ecumenical spirituality, Sufism can greatly expedite the emergence of a global peace culture. Like other religious and spiritual traditions Sufism must be respond to the problems of contemporary context of human life.

Increasingly in this century the mediating presence of Sufism enables man to pursue a harmonious path with the communities and society. Sufism is a school for the actualization of divine ethics. It involves an enlightened inner being, not intellectual proof; revelation and witnessing, not logic. By divine ethics, we are referring to ethics that transcend mere social convention, a way of being that is the actualization of the attributes of God. Sufism calls for attitudes of humility and deep respect. Every individual and every nation or culture is capable of manifesting divine qualities. Sufism in India has commonly been viewed as a secular attempt for eternal quest of the soul for its direct experience of the ultimate super power. For centuries the

Hindus accepted Sufi shrines as symbol of communal harmony. Sufi saints have played a major role in promoting religious harmony and Hindu-Muslim unity in medieval India. But, the present generation is largely unaware of their contributions; Sufi saints dedicated their entire lives to the promotion of secular values, religious toleration and Hindu-Muslim unity. The values propagated by them were still relevant and could be used to fight evils such as communalism & terrorism. Sufism believed in the concept of *wahdat-ul-wajud* (unity of being). According to the Sufis, the highest form of devotion to god was the service of mankind. The Sufism encouraged equality and brotherhood.

Because of its capacity to inspire human solidarity and deeply ecumenical spirituality, Sufism can greatly expedite the emergence of a global peace culture. Though most religious and ethical systems promote reciprocity and goodwill, their institutions and outlooks are too frequently identified with just those aspects of the past that contribute to current division and conflict.Sufism competent enough of bring together on the agenda of humanity and it has different technique to achieve this object. All the mystic thoughts developed in different religions in vis-à-vis different places and times but with similar feelings. No one deny the there are differences between the great religions on the fundamental viewpoint. The unity on existence of one and only God is the way which can lead us to achieve the universal outlook for solving the problems. So it is the need of time that we must work together for peace and prosperity under the shadow of Sufism The most significant part of mysticism/ Sufism is the motivation for the universal unity of human beings without any discrimination. It shows that how Sufis have love and care for the mankind. Sufism modifies the human behavior with broad thinking of universality. This expected spiritual understanding goes to beyond to humans for examining global idea of unity and harmony. Sufism promises for progress in human behavior in practical forms to universal level.

Sufi mysticism has long exercised a fascination upon the Western world, and especially its orien list scholars. Figures like Rumi have become well known in the United States, where Sufism is perceived as a peaceful and apolitical form of Islam. The Islamic Institute in Mannheim, Germany, which works towards the integration of Europe and Muslims, sees Sufism as particularly suited for interreligious dialogue and intercultural harmonization in democratic and pluralist societies; it has described Sufism as a symbol of tolerance and humanism—no dogmatic, flexible and non-violent.

Sufism is the science of the supreme knowledge of God, its doctrines and methods are derived from the Holy Quran. Sufism freely makes paradigms and tallies with Greek and even Hindu sources, and it is not at all strange that the most recent of the great revealed religions should take account of the intellectual developments which preceded it when these are compatible and useful in bridging the gap between human reason and sure knowledge of the Divine Sufism inculcates the notion that all religions are the religion of God. If each one of us would come to the realization that my God is the God of man we would find it impossible to greed for a world of overpowering our fellow being and infliction them with agonies. Definitely Sufism is the best way to heal and cure our physical and spiritual injuries in these turbulent times. We are brought up to believe that from about the sixteenth century onwards the east began to stagnate, whereas the West developed and progressed, Sufism is the only bridge between the East and the West spreading its wings beyond the boundaries of this mortal world.

So we conclude that Sufism provides guidance to mankind in all ages and shall continue to do so in future. The teaching of peace and harmony in Sufism (*tasawwuf*) ought to be just as important today as it has ever been throughout its long history. Being a way of purifying the soul – a necessity for each new generation – its role should never diminish with changing times and circumstances.

References

Alavi, M.A. (2011). *Relevance of Sufism in the contemporary world as an antidote to violence & terrorism,* 15-21.

Angha, N. (2002). *Sufism: A Bridge Between Religions*, MTO Shahmaghsoudi Publication.

Nasir, R. (2013). *Role and importance of Sufism in modern world. International journal of advancements in research & technology,* Vol. 2, issue1, January-2013.

5

Dakhani Poetry of Manpuri Yoganand Swami and Sufism

Shaikh Musak Rajjak

Abstract

'Yaro Allah dekhaa Jahaa Tahaa. Sijdaa Namaaz Karo Kahaa Kahaan. Guru Ko Murid Bhayo. Palme Agyaan Gayo.' This is the one pad from the collection of Dakhani poems of Swami Yoganand Manpuri Prasad (d. 1730) in Seventeenth - Eighteenth century Deccan. Manpuri Swami explained the ideas of Sufism in his Dakhani poem. 'All where Allah is seeing by me, I should pray but where and where? All places full of the existence of Allah. The Guru meet to me, I am free from 'unknowingness' and now enlightened the truth'. Swami Yoganand Manpuri was the famous Gosawi Saint at Daulatabad in Deccan. He was the contemporary of Emperor Aurangzeb of Mughal Empire. Manpuri Swami wrote the number of Dakhani poems on Bhakti and Sufism. He was influenced by Yogi Practices, Gosawi cult of Shri Datta Sampradaya, Nath, Varkari, Shri Vitthal and Sufism. Daulatabad Fort town is the dominant historical sites of the Marathwada division of Maharashtra. Daulatabad Fort was the capital of Muhammad Tughlaq in Deccan region. Daulatabad town is famous for other saints like, Swami Janardan, Saint Eknath, Saint Chaand Qadiri and the number of Sufis. The Fort located in the center of and around the Hindu, Buddhist, Jain and Sufi sites. Verul or Ellora Caves are famous for Hindu, Jain and Buddhist Cave temple sites. Khuldabad or Roza is famous for several Chishti Dargahs of Tughlaq – Bahamani period. Swami Yoganand Manpuri Math is located in Sayyadpur of Daulatabad town. The interactions between Sufi Saint Shahnur Qadiri (d. 1692) of Aurangabad and the

Swami are famous today in folk oral sources. Shahnur visited number of times to Manpuri Math at Daulatabad. The archaeological remains, Samadhi, two painted photo of Manpri Swami and Shahnur give the information about the spiritual history of Deccan. The Dakhani poetry of Manpuri Swami explained the religious co-existence and Sufi influences on him. In the term of methodology, the paper has been made by both primary and standard secondary data by historical research method.

Keywords: Sufism, Dakhani, Deccan, Spiritual co-existence, Hindu Bhakti cults etc.

Manpur Yoganand Swami was the contemporary of Emperor Aurangzeb during the seventeenth and eighteenth centuries. Manpuri was the Bhakti poet and Guru within the Yogi Gosawi cult of Shree Datta Sampradaya. The Hindu spirituality were spread over the poetries of Manpuri. He explained and remarked the thinking of Shri Vitthal cult, Shri Datta Cult, Nath, Gosawi and the Sufism in his Dakhani poetries. His writing had the Hindavi Dakhani flavor and medieval Marathi touch. The manuscripts are available at Manpuri Math of Daulatabad today.

Polity & Cultural Synthesis In Deccan

The Deccan region in which Manpuri Swami lived is deeply marked by the footprints of multiple kingdoms and cultures with different spiritual thinking. The first Marathi speaking dynasty, the Yadava kingdom was based at the fort town of Daulatabad (old name *Devagiri*). Saint Jnaneshwar had composed his rendering of the *Gita* into Marathi *Jnaneshwari* at the end of the thirteenth century. He referred the last Yadava king Ramdeva in his colophon. In 1294, Daulatabad fort captured by Alauddin Khilji and the Deccan region come under the Muslim Sultanate. In 1327, Muhammad bin Tughluq decided to make Daulatabad, the southern capital of the Delhi Sultanate (Sherwani, 1985:13). Later, the Deccan ruled by Bahamani empire from Daulatabad, Bidar and Gulbarga sub capitals. Till the seventeenth century, a prominent center of Sufism was established at *Roza* or Khuldabad near Daulatabad town (Carl Ernst, 2004). The Bahamani and later the Nizam Shahi sultanate had open attitudes towards religion and languages. In the beginning of seventeenth century, the Deccan conquered by Akbar and the Mughals. Emperor Aurangzeb ruled over the Deccan till his death at 1707. His Mughal head-quarters were at Daulatabad, Aurangabad and Ahmadnagar.

During the Bahamani Empire, the religious and cultural synthesis had been happened. The Sufis spread over the Deccan from Khuldabad, Daulatabad, Bidar, Gulbarga, Kandhar and Bijapur region. During the Nizam Shahi of Ahmadnagar, the topic of Muslim authors and poets were of Marathi poetry on devotional *bhakti* thinking of both religions (Dhere 1967, Pathan U.M., 2001).

Devotional Dakhani Poetry of Manpuri Swami

Manpuri was very much influenced by *tasawwuf* or Sufism. He repeated the Sufic philosophy in his Dakhani poetries, he was influenced by Sufism both spiritual and socially, so that he treated all people as equal regardless of caste and class (Nile Green, 2005). The Math of Manpuri Swami located at the Road of Daulatabad in District Aurangabad, Maharashtra. State. He noted the fort capital of Daulatabad as '*Takhat Dawlatabad'*, in his poetry (Telang, 1953). Manpuri Yoganand Swami was the Brahmin of *Kanyakubj* Brahmin branch. He had born in Multani Gosawi cult of Northern Himalayas. He migrated to Deccan from the travel over Kashmir, Punjab, Kashi, Mathura, Burhanpur and Aurangabad. He visited Paithan, Pandharpur and Daulatabad in Deccan number of time in his life (*Sant Charitra*, 1960). He was also the regular visiter of Sant Janardan Swami Samadhi, Shri Vitthal Mandir Pandharpur, Nipat Niranjan Swami Math Begumpura and the sites of devotional importance in Maharashtra region. The Marathi inscription at the Samadhi or tomb of Manpuri Swami as (*epitaph*) —

> *Pahaa Devgiri Samul Awudhi saadhu jani sewili, tethe Manpiri pavitra nagari, samaadhi sampaadili. Solaasewili baawanaatil baraa saadhaar samwastari, jyeshti shuddha. Hi panchami ravi dini he bolilo uttari.* (Inscription of Black stone at Math, Daulatabad, Dist Aurangabad, Maharashtra State)

It means that, at Sunday, *Jyeshth Shudha* 5, *Saka* 1652 (1730 AD), the Swami had buried himself alive into the '*Samadhi'*, as the devotional practice of *Gosawi Datta* cult. Manpuri Swami explained the bhakti philosophy into his Marathi poetry. He noted the contributions of Saint Jnaneshwar, Eknath and Gosawi cult into his poetries. He called Saint Ramdas as '*Dnany Mothe'*, means the big scholar. The Dakhani poetry of Swami Manpuri is contained the number of facets of Sufism with examples. The fort town of Daulatabad had the long tradition of religious and theological synthesis. The former killedar of Daulataad fort, Swami Janardan was the follower of Datta cult. He was the pupil of Muslim Qadiri Sufi Pir, named Chand Bodhale Qadiri too. The shrine of Shaikh Chand Bodhale Qadiri located the opposite side of Daulatabad fort. The Samadhi of Janardan Swami is at the topside of the Daulatabad fort. Swami Manpiru visited number of times to the Samadhi of Janardan Swami. Saint Eknath of Paithan was the disciple of Swami Janardan. Another disciple or Murid of Shaikh Chand Bodhale Qadiri was Shaikh Muhammad of Shrigonda, Ahmednagar. Shaikh Muhammad wrote the '*Hindu Muslim ducheshma'*, on the symbolic similarities and monotheism in between the Hindu and Muslim philosophies (Deshpande, 1973; Dusan Deak, 2005; Musak, 2008). It was the cultural coexistence at Daulatabad Deccan region. Also, Swami Manpuri had the friendship with Sufi Shaikh Shah Noor of Aurangabad during Mughal period. There are number of evidences on the spiritual interactions between Hindu and Muslims, saints, poets and Sufis (Datar, 1936). Manpuri Swami had the spiritual relation with number of Sufis at Khuldabad, Daulatabad and Aurangabad Deccan. The two Mughal style paintings had painted on the wall of Manpuri Math in eighteenth century. It can be seen today also. The first one is the painted photo of Shri Swami Manpuri Yoganand and second one is the painted photo of Hazrat Shah Noor Qadiri. The ston sculptured platform (chairs, *chabutara*) located inside the Math. It was used by both saints for spiritual yogic practices and rest. Here are some Dakhani poems written by Manpuri as following:

Al-al lillah. Jit tit Allah Allah,
Jaha dekhate tahaa aapahi dikhe,
Daras path dikhaa ghar ghatlla ghalla.
Paak najar so dekho yaaro,
Nahi na barran hi bhallah bhallah.
Manpuri swami har ghat maahi,
Tan ko milo galla galla.
Yaro Allah bharpur dekhaa jahaa tahaa
Sijdaa namaaj karo kahaa kahaa.
Guru ko murid bhaayo,
Pal mo agyaan gayo.
Paripura jan liyo yahaa yahaa.
Alif kahe aadi ant ko mul,
Jaa kaaran suchan aag,
Ek alif bit aur kucchu nahi,
Sab jag Alif Alif hi maahi.
Praaniyaa tu kaun hai re,
Yah jaan.
Hindu Musalmaan.
Kaunso der konsi pujaa,
Kounsi aatmaa gyaaan.
Naad bind ki aadi vichaare,
So na chatur sujaan.
Manpuri prabhu rup naam ninaa sab ghat
Sadaa hai samaan.
Mohi miyaan dekhi didaar,
Koti bhanu surati wato,

Manmohaa matwaar,

Manpuri prabhu har dam nahi bhule, Zikir karo yaar yaar. (Telang, 1953)

[Oh Allah Allah. Everywhere Allah Allah. Where I see there is Allah. The chapter recited everywhere and every home. See with pure vision everywhere. Manpuri Swami joining together additions with the followers shoulder to shoulder greetings, on friends. Allah has been seen everywhere, here and there. Where should I perform prayer and *sijda*. The disciple followed the Guru. Suddenly the disciple enlightened with true knowledge and free from *agyaan*. The all knowledge absorbed from him. The *Alif*, first word of Arabic script, is the beginning knowledge. The original beginning of the life, will be good upto the end of life. The *Alif* Allah is truth. The all world has the *Alif Alif*. The word Allah is starts with *Alif*. The human being is 'what?', and 'Why?'. *Hindu* and *Musalaman*? What deity and Which God? Which soul and which knowledge? The all name and things, without it, all where He. All are equal before Him. Manpuri will not forget Him. Recite His name again and again *zikr*.]

Paintings on the Wall of Math, at Daulatabad

Manpuri's Sufi friend Shah Noor Qadiri was originally from Baghdad. He migrated to Deccan in Mughal period. His *Khanqah* and Shrine or *Dargah* located today at *Shahnoorwadi* area of Aurangabad town.

Shah Noor belongs to Qadiri Sufi order. The revenue minister of Emperor Aurangzeb, Diyanat Khan was the murid of Shah Noor. *Maasi al Umara* of Shah Nawaz Khan explained the political and cultural history of Aurangabad Deccan. Shah Nawaz noted the entire life and philosophy of Sufi saint Shah Noor of Aurangabad. Bahauddin Hasan wrote a Persian book on life of Shah Noor named, *Noor al Anwar*. Shah Noor died at 1699 in Aurangabad. The shrine of Shah Noor is visited by number of devotees from Deccan region including Hindu Muslim milieu (Hasan, 1994; Baig, 1931). Shah Noor visited number of times to Manpuri Math at Daulatabad in his life. He performed the Mugaqaba and Yogic practices inside the Math. The painting and the chair stone shows the spiritual history of Math.

Conclusion

The Dakhani poetries of Swami Manpuri Yoganand has the essence of Sufism and religious coexistence. He wrote the recitation, *Zikar* practice of Sufism in his poetries. His expansion of philosophy is covered the all Hindu Muslim bhakti in Deccan. In some poetries without surprise Manpuri Swami focuses on the Islamic theology. The oral source, *Bhajan* and the paintings at the wall recalculated the history of meeting, re-meeting, Yogic practices and visits of virtuous personalities at Daulatabad Math. During Mughal India, number of Hindu Muslim *sampradayas* had spiritual relations. Entire medieval times of Indian subcontinent has the long list of spiritual coexistence background with such personalities like, Baba Farid, Nizamuddin Auliya, Amir Khusro, Nanak, Kabir, Kara Shukov etc. Another example of these lines, are the poetry and Math of Swami Manpuri Yoganand at Daulatabad. The Marathi *Bhajan* and Dakhani poetries have the very significance role in spiritual and social history of Deccan. It educated us the spiritual history for communal harmony within the new society for national integration in India.

References

Baig, A.M. (1994). Tazkhira-e-Riyaz Husaini, Maseer, Aurangabad : Mahaveer Pier Press, p. 24.

Bhalchandra Telang (1953). "Aurangabad ki Hindu Santvani, Aurangabad" Marathwada Vidyapith Prakashan.

Carl, W. Ernst, (2004). Eternal Garden: Mysticism, History and Politics at a South Asian Sufi Centre, IInd Edition. New Delhi: Oxford University Press.

Datar Vyankitesh Madhao, (1936). Shri Dnyaneshwari and Sufi Panth, Shri Dnaneshwari Part II, Ahmednagar: Fedi. M.B. Deshmukh Pub. :199-294.

Deshpande, A.N. (1973). History of Marathi Literature Volume II, Pune: Venus Pvt. Ltd.

Dusan Deak, Maharashtra Saints and the Sufi Tradition: Eknath, Chand Bodhale and the Datta Sampradaya, Deccan Studies, Hyderabad, III, No. 2, 2005:27-28.

Haroon Khan Sherwani (1985). The Bahamanis of the Deccan, Delhi: Munshiram Manoharlal Publishers, p. 13.

Hasan Bahuddin Johar Khan (1931). Noor al Anwar, Persian Text, Aurangabad: Shah Noor Dargah Collection Library.

Nile Green, (2005). Who's the King of the Castle? Brahmins, Sufis and the Naratives Landscape of Daulatabad, Contemporary South Asia, 14, No. 1: 21-37.

Pathan, U.M. (2011). Muslim Marathi Sufi Saint Kavi, Mumbai: Maharashtra Rajy Sahitya va Samskriti Mandal.

Ramchandra Chintaman Dhere, (1967). Musalman Marathi Santkavi, IIIrd Edition. Pune: Padmagandha Prakashan.

Sant Ammatray Charitra Series, (1960). Aurangabad: Eknath Samshodhan Mandir Library: 86.

Shaikh Musak Rajjak, Bhakti Panth and Sufi Parampara, in Samshodhak Quarterly, Rajwadi Institude, Dhule, Sep. 2008:3, 40-49.

6

Sufi Influence in Bengal: Exploring the Cultural Conglomeration

Reshma Khatun

Abstract

The earliest record of Sufism in Bengal goes back to 11th century AD in connection with the continuation of Sufism in northern India. Shah Sultan Rumi was the first Sufi to come to Bengal, when he came to Mymensingh in 1053 AD. The noble intention of preaching Islam was the main factor which drove them to leave their hearth and home for Bengal. They came to Bengal, often alone, and preached Islam in the secluded areas throughout their lives under unfavourable circumstances. The earliest Sufi attempts at religious conversion began in the very hostile environment maintained by the orthodox sena rulers. Sufi masters taught monotheism (the oneness of Allah), the teachings of Holy Quran and the Hadith to their followers. Before the advent of the Sufis, most of the local population was either Hindu or Buddhist. Sufis were able to convert many of them to Islam by preaching about the magnanimity of the religion and the essence of love, brotherhood and equality. The indomitable zeal and uncommon piety of the Sufis, and the wide belief that they could perform miracles were the prime causes of the success of the Sufi mission in Bengal. This paper attempts to show the influence of the enlightened Sufis who devoted their major efforts to developing the spiritual dimensions of the Bengali minds.

Keywords: *Sufi, Devotion, Spiritual, Magnanimity, Islam.*

Introduction

The word Sufi is derived from the Arabic word 'safa' meaning purity. Sufism worked for purification of the human soul (*nafs*) by cleansing the spiritual heart (*qalb*) to give it a mirror-like transparency for the reflection of Almighty's love (*Ishq*). As one of the mystic corollaries of Islam, Sufism helped illuminate the spirit (*ruh*) by emptying it of egoist drives and filling it with Allah's attributes (*Zekr*), and also to complete the journey of life with absolute purification. From 1200-1500 AD Sufism attained its 'Golden Age' in Bengal, being influenced by the diverse Sufi orders of *Qadiriya, Chistia, Naksbandia, Mujaddedia, Suhrawardiya* etc. During this period the Sufis of northern India, especially Hazrat Khawja Muinuddin Chisti and Khawja Bahauddin, sent their deputies to Bengal as torch-bearers of the Islamic faith. In Akbar's reign many religious teachers, including Mujaddid Alf Sani, were sent to this province, where they continued preaching their faith Islam among non-believers. Bengal's earliest sustained contact with Islamic civilization occurred in the context of the geopolitical convulsions that had driven large numbers of Turkish-speaking groups from Central Asia into the Iranian plateau and India. Whether as military slaves, as adventurers, or as refugees fleeing before the Mongol advance, Turks gravitated not only to the older centers of the Islamic world—Baghdad, Cairo, Samarkand—but also to its fringes, including Bengal. Immigrant groups were often led by a man called *alp* or*alp-eren*, identified as "the heroic figure of old Turkic saga, the warrior-adventurer whose exploits alone justified his way of life." Migrating Turks also grouped themselves into Islamic mystical fraternities typically organized around Sufi leaders who combined the characteristics of the "heroic figure of old Turkic saga," the *alp*, and the pre-Islamic Turkish shaman—that is, a charismatic holy man believed to possess magical powers and to have intimate contact with the unseen world. It happened, moreover, that the strict authority structure that had evolved for transmitting Islamic mystical knowledge from master (*murshid*) to disciple (*murîd*) proved remarkably well suited for binding retainers to charismatic leaders. This, too, lent force to the Turkish drive to the Bengal frontier.

One of the major factors of Islam impacting the subcontinent as well as creating predominantly Muslim influence in Bangladesh was the spiritual and humane influence of Sufism during the medieval period. Sufi masters taught monotheism (the oneness of Allah), the teachings of Holy Quran and the Hadith to their followers. Before the advent of the Sufis, most of the local population was either Hindu or Buddhist. Sufis were able to convert many of them to Islam by preaching about the magnanimity of the religion and the essence of love, brotherhood and equality. The indomitable zeal and uncommon piety of the Sufis, and the wide belief that they could perform miracles were the prime causes of the success of the Sufi mission in Bengal. Their zeal was so great that it could not be curbed or checked by the atrocities of the ruling monarchs.

In his book *Religion in India: A Historical Introduction*, Fred W. Clothey (2006) maintained that Sufis followed ten basic principles to popularise Islam in India. They were: (i) repenting for misdeeds and emptying of self-orientation; (ii) living simple lives; (iii) focusing on the sovereignty and accessibility of God; (iv) taking vow to possess nothing other than what is needed as daily necessities; (v) practicing self-discipline; (vi) being grateful for the mercies of God; (vii) fearing God; (viii) acquiring and filling by Divine nature; (ix) being content with one's spiritual stature and (x) submitting to the divine will.

Bengali Sufis and Hindu Thought

From the beginning of the Indo-Turkish encounter with Bengal, one section of Muslims sought to integrate into their religious lives elements of the esoteric practices of local yogis, together with the cosmologies that underpinned those practices. Contemporary Muslims perceived northern Bengal generally, and especially Kamrup, lying between the Brahmaputra River and the hills of Bhutan, as a fabulous and mysterious place inhabited by expert practitioners of the occult, of yoga, and of magic. During his visit to Sylhet, Ibn Battuta noted that "the inhabitants of these mountains. Are noted for their devotion to and practice of magic and witchcraft." Around 1595 the great Mughal administrative manual *â'în-i Akbarî* described the inhabitants of Kamrup as "addicted to the practice of magic [*jâdûgarî*]." Some twenty-five years later a Mughal officer serving in northern Bengal described the .... And in 1662–63 another Mughal chronicler, referring to the entire Assam region, of which Kamrup is the western part, remarked that "the people of India have come to look upon the Assamese as sorcerers, and use the word 'Assam' in such formulas as dispel witchcraft." Since Sufis were especially concerned with apprehending transcendent reality unmediated by priests or other worldly institutions, it is not surprising that they, among Muslims, were most attracted to the yogi traditions of Kamrup. Within the very first decade of the Turkish conquest, there began to circulate in the delta Persian and Arabic translations of a Sanskrit manual on tantric yoga entitled *Amròtakunòdòa* ("The Pool of Nectar"). According to the translated versions, the Sanskrit text had been composed by a Brahman yogi of Kamrup who had converted to Islam and presented the work to the chief *qâzòî*, or judge, of Lakhnauti, Rukn-al-Din Samarqandi (d. 1218). The latter, in turn, is said to have made the first translations of the work into Arabic and Persian. While this last point is uncertain, there is no doubt that for the following five hundred years the *Amròtakunòdòa*, through its repeated translations into Arabic and Persian, circulated widely among Sufis of Bengal, and even throughout India. The North Indian Sufi Shaikh 'Abd al-Quddus Gangohi (d. 1537) is known to have absorbed the yogic ideas of the *Amròtakunòdòa* and to have taught them to his own disciples. In the mid seventeenth century, the Kashmiri author Muhsin Fani recorded that he had seen a Persian translation of the *Amròtakunòdòa*, and in the same century the Anatolian Sufi scholar Muhammad al-Misri (d. 1694) cited the *Amròtakunòdòa* as an important book for the study of yogic practices, noting that in India such practices had become partly integrated with Sufism. In both its Persian and Arabic translations, the *Amròtakunòdòa* survives as a manual of tantric yoga, with the first of its ten chapters affirming the characteristically tantric correspondence between parts of the human body and parts of the macrocosm, "where all that is large in the world discovers itself in the small." In the mid sixteenth century, there appeared in Gujarat a Persian recension of the *Amròtakunòdòa* under the title*Bahòr al-hòayâtò*, attributed to the great Shattari shaikh Muhammad Ghauth of Gwalior (d. 1563). A prologue to this version, written by a disciple of the shaikh, records how these yogic ideas were thought to have entered the Bengali Sufi tradition:

This wonderful and strange book is named Amròtakunòdòa in the Indian language [i.e., Sanskrit]. This means "Water of Life," and the reason for the appearance of this book among the Muslims is as follows. When Sultan 'Ala al-Din [i.e., 'Ali Mardan] conquered Bengal and Islam became manifest there, news of these events reached the ears of a certain gentleman of the esteemed learned class in Kamrup. His name was Kama, and he was a master of the science of yoga.

In order to debate with the Muslim *'ulamâ* [scholars] he arrived in the city of Lakhnauti, and on a Friday he entered the Congregational Mosque. A number of Muslims showed him to a group of *'ulamâ*, and they in turn pointed him to the assembly of Qazi Rukn al-Din Samarqandi. So he went to this group and asked: "Whom do you worship?" They replied, "We worship the Faultless God." To his question "Who is your leader?" they replied, "Muhammad, the Messenger of Allah." He said, "What has your leader said about the Spirit [*rûhò*]?" They replied, "God the All-nourishing has commanded (that there be) the Spirit." He said, "In truth, I too have found this same thing in books that are subtle and committed to memory."

Then that man converted to Islam and busied himself in acquiring religious knowledge, and he soon thereafter became a scholar (*muftî*). After that he wrote and presented this book to Qazi Rukn al-Din Tamami [Samarqandi]. The latter translated it from the Indian language into Arabic in a book of thirty chapters, and somebody else translated it into Persian in a book of ten chapters.…And when Hazrat Ghauth al-Din himself went to Kamrup he necessarily spent several years in studying this science.…The name of this book is *Bahòr al*-hòayâtò.

Sufis of the Capital

The principal carriers of the Islamic literary and intellectual tradition in the Bengal sultanate were groups of distinguished and influential Sufis who resided in the successive capital cities of Lakhnauti (from 1204), Pandua (from ca. 1342), and Gaur (from ca. 1432). Most of these men belonged to organized Sufi brotherhoods—especially the Suhrawardi, the Firdausi, and the Chishti orders—and what we know of them can be ascertained mainly from their extant letters and biographical accounts. The urban Sufis about whom we have the most information are clustered in the early sultanate period, from the founding of the independent Ilyas Shahi dynasty at Pandua in 1342 to the end of the Raja Ganesh revolution in 1415.

The political roles played by Sufis in Bengal's capital were shaped by ideas of Sufi authority that had already evolved in the contemporary Persian-speaking world. We have already referred to the central place that Sufi traditions assigned to powerful saints, a sentiment captured in 'Ali Hujwiri's statement that God had "made the Saints the governors of the universe." Being in theory closer to God than warring princes could ever hope to be, Muslim saints staked a moral claim as God's representatives on earth. In this view, princely rulers possessed no natural right to earthly power, but had only been entrusted with a temporary lease on such power through the grace of some Muslim saint. This perspective perhaps explains why in Indo-Muslim history we so often find Sufis predicting who would attain political office, and for how long they would hold it. For behind the explicit act of "prediction" lay the implicit act of appointment—that is, of a Sufi's entrusting his *wilâyat*, or earthly domain, to a prince. For example, the fourteenth-century historian Shams-i Siraj 'Afif recorded that before his rise to royal stature, the future Sultan Ghiyath al-Din Tughluq, founder of the Tughluq dynasty of Delhi (1321–1398), had been one of many local notables attracted to the spiritual power of the grandson of the famous Chishti Sufi Shaikh Farid al-Din Ganj-i Shakar (d. 1265). The governor made frequent visits to the holy man's lodge in the Punjab, and on one occasion brought along his son and nephew, the future sultans Muhammad bin Tughluq and Firuz Tughluq. All three were given turbans by the saint and told that each was destined to rule India. The length of each turban, moreover, exactly corresponded to the number of years each would reign. In this anecdote one may discern the seeds of the complex pattern of mutual patronage between shaikhs of the Chishti order and one of the mightiest empires in India's history.

Leading Chishti Sufi Saints of Bengal

In Bengal as in North India, the connection between political fortune and spiritual blessing is most evident in the early history of the Chishti order, the order to which the most ascendant shaikhs of early-fourteenth-century Delhi belonged. "Anybody who was anyone," as Simon Digby puts it, visited the lodge of Delhi's most eminent shaikh of the time, Nizam al-Din Auliya (d. 1325). Indeed, the two principal Persian poets of the early fourteenth century, Amir Khusrau and Amir Hasan, together with the sultanate's leading contemporary historian, Zia al-Din Barani, were all spiritual disciples of this shaikh. Since Delhi at this time happened to be the capital of a vital and expanding empire, it is not surprising that the literary, cultural, and institutional traditions of that city—together with the shaikhs and institutions of its dominant Sufi order—expanded along with Khalaji and Tughluq arms to the far corners of India, including Bengal. But there was a deeper reason why Indo-Muslim courts patronized Chishti shaikhs. By the fourteenth century, when other Sufi orders in India still looked to Central Asia or the Middle East as their spiritual home, the Chishtis, with their major shrines located within the Indian subcontinent, had become thoroughly indigenized. Seeking to establish their legitimacy both as Muslims and as Indians, Indo-Muslim rulers therefore turned to prominent shaikhs of this order for blessings and support. For the same reason, leading Chishti shaikhs dispersed from Shaikh Nizam al-Din's lodge to all parts of the empire and often enjoyed the patronage of provincial rulers. Conversely, many young Indian-born Muslims journeyed from all over India to live in or near that shaikh's lodge, later to return to their native lands, where they would establish daughter Chishti lodges and enjoy the patronage of local rulers. Leading Chishti Sufis of Bengal are as follows—

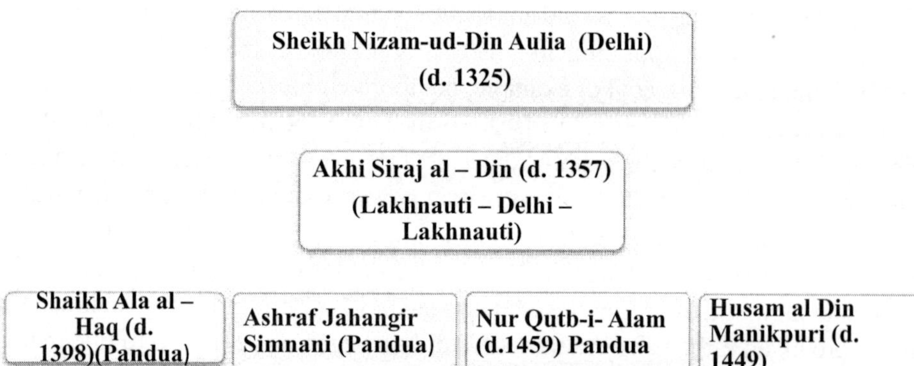

Fig. 1: Leading Chishti Sufis in Bengal

The first Bengal-born Muslim known to have studied with Shaikh Nizam al-Din was Akhi Siraj al-Din (d. 1357), who journeyed to Delhi as a young man. Having distinguished himself at the Sufi lodge of the renowned shaikh, Siraj al-Din received a certificate of succession and so thoroughly associated himself with the North Indian Chishti tradition that he was given the epithet "âyina-yi Hindûstân," or "Mirror of Hindustan." Returning to Bengal some time before 1325, when his master died, he inducted others into the Chishti discipline, his foremost pupil being another Bengal-born Muslim, Shaikh 'Ala al-Haq (d. 1398). But unlike his own teacher, who had no known dealings with royalty, Shaikh 'Ala al-Haq was destined to play a special role in the political history of Muslim Bengal.

In fact, the earliest-known monument built by the founder of Bengal's longest-lived dynasty, the Ilyas Shahi line of kings (1342–1486), was dedicated to this shaikh. On a mosque built in 1342 in what is now part of Calcutta, Shams al-Din Ilyas Shah praised the Sufi as "the benevolent and revered saint (Shaikh) whose acts of virtue are attractive and sublime, inspired by Allah, may He illuminate his heart with the light of divine perception and faith, and he is the guide to the religion of the Glorious, 'Alaul-Haqqmay…his piety last long."

The importance of this inscription derives from its political context. Shams al-Din Ilyas Shah, an ambitious and politically astute newcomer to the delta, was just then launching a bid for independence from Delhi, evidently using southwestern Bengal as his power base. The imperial governor of nearby Satgaon having recently died, Shams al-Din, aware that Delhi was convulsed by the various crises provoked by the eccentric Sultan Muhammad bin Tughluq, seized the moment to attain province wide power. As his earliest-known coin was minted at Pandua inA.D. 1342–43 (A.H.743), Shams al-Din's ascendancy exactly synchronizes with the dedication of this mosque and his patronage of Shaikh 'Ala al-Haq. Moreover, the patronage of the two men was mutual, since Shaikh 'Ala al-Haq, attaching himself to this rising political star, adopted Shams al-Din as a recipient of his teachings and blessings. This early connection cemented an alliance between government and prominent Chishti shaikhs that would last for the duration of Muslim rule in Bengal.

Not all alliances between Sufis and sultans were initiated by would-be rulers seeking to broaden their political bases. Some Sufis were drawn to the court out of a fervent desire to advance the cause of Islam as they understood it, and to augment the welfare of Muslims in the realm. We see this in the correspondence between Muzaffar Shams Balkhi (d. 1400) and Sultan Ghiyath al-Din A'zam Shah (r. 1389–1410). An immigrant from Central Asia, Muzaffar had left his native Balkh for Delhi, where he taught at the college of Firuz Shah Tughluq. But the man's restless spirit led him to Bihar city, where, after meeting and becoming the disciple of the great Firdausi shaikh Sharaf al-Din Maneri (d. 1381), he experienced a major change in life-orientation. Abandoning his pride in scholarship, Muzaffar subjected himself to various austerities and distributed all his worldly possessions in charity. He also made several pilgrimages to Mecca, where he once stayed for four years, teaching lessons in *hòadîth* scholarship.His extant letters reveal him not as an ecstatic, quiescent, or contemplative sort, but as committed to imposing his understanding of the Prophet's religious vision on the here-and-now world, a man inclined to scrutinize human society by scriptural standards and, finding it wanting, to transform it so as to meet those standards. In the sultan of Bengal, the Sufi found an outlet for these impulses.

Conclusion

Bengal's Sufis and sultans, then, were fatefully connected by ties of mutual attraction and repulsion. Generally, when they were first establishing themselves politically, and especially when launching new dynasties, rulers actively sought the legitimacy powerful saints might lend them. Sultan Ghiyath al-Din 'Iwaz's earliest chronicler situated the launching of Bengal's first independent dynasty (1213) in the context of the grace, or *baraka*, of two simple dervishes in Afghanistan. And in 1342, when Sultan Shams al-Din Ilyas Shah launched the longest-lived dynasty in Muslim Bengal, he did so with the blessings of a renowned scion of the prestigious Chishti line. Struck by the awesome spiritual powers people attributed to charismatic shaikhs, or believing that their own lease on power was somehow extended by such forceful men, new Muslim kings sought their favor, built lodges or mausolea for them, or made public pilgrimages to their tombs. Conversely, some Sufis sought royal patronage out of their own reformist impulses to bring "the world" (*dunyâ*) into proper alignment with their understanding of the dictates of normative "religion" (*dîn*).

On the other hand, once dynasties were securely entrenched in power, some kings no longer considered it necessary to call upon the charismatic authority of holy men to legitimate their rule. In fact, the wealth and influence of charismatic shaikhs were sometimes seen as potential threats to royal authority. Sikandar Ilyas Shah only begrudgingly patronized a saint on whose mausoleum he heaped more praise on himself than on the saint. And he actually banished the most eminent shaikh of the day from his capital when he felt his authority rivaled. Only after the death of Nur Qutb-i 'Alam in the mid fifteenth century, when Sufism's intellectually vibrant tradition was replaced by a politically innocuous tomb-cult, did the state once again wholeheartedly ally itself with the Chishti tradition.

Reference

Abdul Karim (1960). "*Corpus of the Muslim Coins of Bengal"* Asiatic Society of Pakistan, Publication No. 6, Dacca.

Enamul Haq, (2013). "*Sufi Influence in Bengal*".

M.I. Borah, (1935). "*An Ac- count of the Immigration of Persian Poets into Bengal*" *Dacca University Studies* 1.

R. Ahmed, (1981). "*The Bengal Muslims, 1871-1906: A Quest for Identity"*, Delhi.

Richard Maxwell Eaton (1996). "*The Rise of Islam and the Bengal frontier 1204-1760*".

S.K. Abdul Latif, (1974). "*The Muslim Mystic Movements in Bengal from the 14th to the Middle of the 16th Century, A.D.,"* Ph.D. dissertation, Aligarh Muslim University.

7

Development of Sufism in India and Its Contribution to promote Peace and Harmony

Meraj Ahmad Meraj

Abstract

India is the land of spirituality. The notion of peaceful co-existence is not alien to India. India, being greatly addicted to this philosophy was well suited for Sufism. Sufis came to India from the Middle East during 11th and 12th centuries A.D. It was by the overpowering spell and charm of their magnetic personalities, spiritual powers and exemplary conduct. India, with her multi-racial, multi-religious and multi-lingual society has always welcomed men imbued with high moral and spiritual ideas by the overflow of their consciousness of God. Sufism in India was not confined to influencing a specific place or a shrine or a mosque and its units. Its impact was felt on the culture of the people, on the entire interlocking aspects such as environmental, geographical, social, economic, artistic and devotional. The Sufis had an especial impact on the Indian subcontinent and helped to shape many devotional Bhakti faiths such as Sikh Philosophy and Islamic thought. Sufism in India has commonly been viewed as a secular attempt for eternal quest of the soul for its direct experience of the ultimate Supreme power. Peace and harmony constitute the soul of Sufism. It offers streams of philosophical, ritualistic, literary and artistic forms. Beyond their love for humanity and tolerance, Sufi imprints in music, poetry and literature are monumental. The aim of this paper is to highlight the contribution of Islamic Sufism to promote religious harmony, its message of universal brotherhood as well as its impacts on India societies and culture.

Keywords: *Sufism, Spirituality, Humanity, Love, Peace, Harmony*

Introduction

Sufism is the spiritual essence of Islam. It attempts to clean the heart, to purify the soul and to beautify the self through attaining and enacting praiseworthy traits like charity, compassion, humility, honesty and justice. Sufism provides an insider's understanding of Islam in all its aspects. Sufism is much misunderstood by both Muslims and non-Muslims alike. Muslims think that Sufis are innovators in the religion and therefore unacceptable whereas non-Muslims think that Sufism offers a peaceful alternative to violent face of Islam, but as a matter of fact, Sufism is the spiritual undercurrent that flows through Islam. It is a journey that emphasizes more on the **inner struggle** and **dimensions** of a human being. It is a journey of self-discovery, and self-discovery ultimately leads to a state of oneness, peace and love. The *dhikr* meditation is one of the fundamental courses to purifying the heart and to understand the *tawhid* oneness of God is the ultimate goal of Sufism. The ideal perfection is called *Baqa* or *Fina fi Allah* by Sufis what is termed as "Najat" in Islam, "Nirvana" in Buddhism, "Salvation" in Christianity and "Mukhti" in Hinduism. Sufism is commonly called the mystical branch of Islam. Sufism always emphasized people to live with tolerance, harmony, love, brotherhood and peace on the earth adding that humanity is more precious than any of the religions. But, the present generation is largely unaware of their contributions. The Sufi saints dedicated their entire lives to the promotion of secular values, religious toleration and Hindu-Muslim unity. The values propagated by them are still relevant and could be used to fight evils such as communalism and extremism.

Origin and Development of Sufism

The origin of Sufism is traced back to the practice during the time of Prophet Mohammad. However, it took a formal shape much later with the first known Sufi, Hasan of Basra. Thereafter, from time to time, new elements and modification were introduced into the teachings and practices of Sufism. Sufism went through three different stages- Taifa stage, Khanqah stage and Tariqa stages.[1] It also gave birth to fraternities in Sufi orders *silsilahs.* Sufism is derived from the Arabic word "Suf" which means "wool", refer to the garments worn by early Sufis. Some says it is derived from "Suffa" or "bench" referring to a group of poor Muslims living at the time with Prophet Mohammad (P.B.U.H), known as the people of bench. The word Sufi is derived from *Safa* meaning pure, purified of ignorance, superstition, dogmatism, egotism, and fanaticism, as well as free from barriers of caste, creed, race and nation. The Sufis believe in God as the Absolute, the only Being and that all creation is the manifestation of His nature. There have been Sufis at all periods of human history. Though, they have lived in different parts of the world, speaking different languages and born into different faiths and beliefs. The Islamic Sufism began as a spiritual revolt against the rampant materialism of the Ummayad and Abbasid Caliphates within the first couple of centuries of the emergence of Islam. Ibn. Khaldun, an Arabic Historian, contends that Sufism emerged in 2nd century Hijra.[2] The first person having used the nomenclature was Abu Hashim Sufi. Famous early figures of the moment include Bayazid Bustami, Rabiya Basari and Hasan Basari who led simple, ascetic lives and aspired to achieve union with God through mediation and other spiritual disciplines.[3] The Sufi movements which took place in Persia in the later periods and Sufism came to be regarded as a Persian philosophy. Al-Ghazali, Junaid al- Baghdadi, Fariduddin 'Attar are some of the very important figures who played the leading role in advancing Sufism in the world at large. Shams Tabréz, Sa'di, Khagani, Firdausi, Omar Khayyám and other great Sufi poets have very substantially established the reputation of Sufism by their inspired poetical works on divine wisdom. Sa'adi's works (*Gulistan* and *Bostan*) illuminate the intellect, the Divan of Hafiz expands the heart with divine love, Jalaluddin Rumi's poems, the *Masnavi e Ma'navi* inspire the souls.

Development of Sufism in India

India, being greatly addicted to the philosophy of spirituality was well suited for Sufism. Sufis came to India from the Middle East during 11th and 12th centuries A.D. It was by the overpowering spell and charm of their magnetic personalities, spiritual powers and exemplary conduct that they won the hearts of millions of people thus laid the foundation of Islam and unity in diversity in this country.[4] India, with her multi-racial, multi-religious and multi-lingual society has always welcomed men imbued with high moral and spiritual ideas by the overflow of their consciousness of God. The concept of*Tawhid* oneness of God is the real formulation of Sufism. It suggests that Islamic mysticism has no difference with the formulations of other non-Islamic faiths about the oneness of God. Sufism became popular in India during the period of Muslim rule. The essential spirituality of life was hardly found in any Muslim ruler or Prince except Dara Shikoh (1615-1659) who was perhaps the only sincere Muslim prince, who made formidable efforts to find out a common ground between Hindu and Muslim religious thoughts.[5] He wrote "Majma al-Bahrain' '*The meeting of the two oceans*" referred to in the title of the book denote Islamic Sufism, on the one hand, and the vedantic thoughts as contained in the Upanishadic texts of the Hindu tradition on the other.

Sufism was introduced in India immediately after its origin. It entered the country with a stronger foothold at the khanqah stage and after the development of Sufi silsilahs. The arrival of Moin al-Din Chishti just before the Sultanate period[6] marked the beginning of the revolutionary change in the religious ethos of the country. In the next three hundred years, during the Sultanate period, Sufism reached every nook and comer of the country and the khanqahs spread over nearly all political nerve centers. The first among the Sufis who come to India appears to be Abu Hifs Rabi bin Sahib al-Asadi al-Basari, a traditionalist and ascetic, who came to Sind, where he died in 776-77 A.D. Among the Sufis of the earliest times who visited India, tradition mentions the name of Mansur al-Hallaj, who made a voyage to India by sea in the l0th century.[7] The first Sufi to visit Lahore that history mentions was Ismail Lahori (1005 A.D.-1054 A.D.). Bathad Vali who was born of a princely family in Turkey, but later became a saint and devoted his life towards the spreading of Islam, came to Madurai and Trichinapalli in 1039 A.D. His tomb stands in Trichinapalli.[8] His disciples, Sayyid Ibrahim Shaheed and Baba Fakhr al-Oin also preached in India. Among the earliest Sufis of India, Baba Ratan's name is prominent who is said to have visited Mecca twice and fmds mention is *'As'aha fi' Ma'rifatis-Sahaba'* of Ibn Hajar Asqalani and *Tajrid* of Ad-Dhahabi. In the former, he is ranked as a companion of the Prophet whom he had met and accepted Islam. He is said to have lived for seven hundred years and is buried in 'Tabar Hind' in modern Bhatinda, Punjab.[9]

Development of Various Sufi Orders in India

By the early thirteenth century, Delhi emerged as the brimming hub of the Sufi movement that had sprung in Central Asia and swept across much of north India. Soon it became the popular religion of the masses as opposed to the orthodox, often puritanical Islam represented by the theologians. Of the various Sufi orders, Muslims of India prominently follow Chistiya, Naqshbandiya, Qadiriya and Suhrawardiya. However, the impact of Chisti order is more visible even in small villages of Indian subcontinent. Kwaja Moinuddin Chisti introduced this order in India. He was born in Afghanistan in 1142 A.D, came to India with the army of Shihabuddin Ghuri in 1192 A.D and selected Ajmer as his permanent abode since 1195 A.D. His shrine became a place of pilgrimage mainly with the support of Muslim rulers. Akbar used to have annual pilgrimage there.[10] Suhrawardi order of Sufism was founded by Shihabuddin Suhrawardi of Baghdad and introduced in India by his disciple Bahauddin Zakariya of Multan. Suharwardi order of Sufism became popular in Bengal.[11] Qadiri order was founded by Abdul Qadir Jilani in Baghdad. Its influence is extensively among the Muslims of south India. Naqshbandi order of Sufism was founded by Bahauddin Naqshbandi (1318-1389) in Turkistan. Insistence on rigid adherence to Shariat and nurturing love for Prophet was the essence of this order.[12] However, various Sufi orders became significant because they lived and wrote in a multi-religious context addressing and attracting people of different faiths Muslims, Hindus and others alike. Some of them developed an understanding of Islam and other faiths that went beyond narrowly constructed communal boundaries.

The Impact of Sufism on Indian Societies

Sufism played a pivotal role in reshaping the Indian society. Sufism in India was not confined to influencing a specific place or a shrine or a mosque and its units. Its impact was felt on the culture of the people, on the entire interlocking aspects such as environmental, geographical, social, economic, artistic and devotional. Sufism's ethos was egalitarian, charitable and friendly. It blended with local cultures and cemented Islam's place from North Africa to the Indian subcontinent. The Sufis had an especial impact on the Indian subcontinent and helped to shape many devotional Bhakti faiths such as Sikh Philosophy and Islamic thought. They were surprisingly contributors in bringing many people willingly into the fold of Islam.[13] The most significant impact the Sufi institution left in the region was creating a society based on communal harmony in a highly diverse region culturally, ethnically and socially. Although mysticism in all religious traditions strives for coexistence with others, the mystic traditions of Hinduism, Islam, Sikhism and Buddhism historically are intertwined with grassroots movements connecting people beyond religious, ethnic and cultural boundaries.

Sufism offers streams of philosophical, ritualistic, literary and artistic forms. Beyond their love for humanity and tolerance, Sufi imprints in music, poetry and literature are monumental. They are the most tolerant and music loving people. The literature and philosophy of the Sufism stress on the purification of the heart. Miracle stories (*karamat*) are important part of Sufi literature.

Amir Khusrow, a known mystic poet and disciple of the great Sufi of his time, Nizamuddin Auliya, was also a pioneer of the Indian music who invented several musical instruments and ragas. The Punjabi poetry of Bulhay Shah and Baba Farid, and the Sindhi poetry of Shah Abdul Latif Bhitai, all are assets of Sufi legacies in the subcontinent. It is because of this heritage that the Sufi music is still a popular genre in the subcontinent today.[14]

The Contribution of Sufism to the humanity

Sufism is the mystical dimension of Islam. Throughout the world of Sufism, love has become the eternal theme. Interfaith dialogues (Sulh-e-kul) and service to humanity (Khidmat-e-khalq) are important aspects of Sufism. There are many Sufi khanqahs (hospices) and dargahs that serve only vegetarian food respecting Hindu sensivities. Many dargahs provide important mental and physical health services to everyone without any discrimination. According to sprit of Sufism, religion has no meaning unless it is warmed by emotions of love. So, if it rightly interpreted, Sufism is the heart of Islam. Sufis have in many cases realized and shown the greatest perfection in humanity. The most important attributes that have contributed to their wide acceptance are their love for the humanity, purifying of mind and perfections in their conducts. Spirituality does not need to follow of any particular religion. Customs and rituals are only the outer forms of religion. Spirituality is however, seeking the Truth and self-realization that are the matter of heart and soul which are equal and same in every individual.

Sufism in India and its Contribution to Promote Peace and Harmony

The essence of Sufism is that the only way to Love the Almighty, is to love all His creation because love goes beyond all religious beliefs, and is larger and more profound than any religion. Peaceful coexistence is one of the most important human ideals. Peace and harmony constitute the soul of Islam. Sufism has laid the foundation of peace and has thus leveled the path to peaceful coexistence. Sufism, the mystical dimension of Islam had contributed significantly to India's rich cultural and religious legacy. Sufi saints have played a major role in promoting religious harmony and Hindu-Muslim unity in medieval India. The Sufi saints dedicated their entire lives to the promotion of secular values, religious toleration and Hindu-Muslim unity. Sufism always persuaded people to live with tolerance, harmony, love, brotherhood and peace on the earth adding that humanity is more precious than any of the religions.

Sufis for centuries have been the bridging gap between Hinduism and Islam. Sufi religious establishments in India were the major means of spreading Islam and adapting it to indigenous cultural tradition. Sufis played a significant role in bringing together major Indian religious communities by creating conditions for a composite culture.[15] The mysticism, in all religious traditions strives for coexistence with the people of other faith but Islamic Sufism served as a connection between religious, ethnic and cultural identities. It involved common people with its message of tolerance and love for God and humans. Sufis in the sub-continent are known for providing a common venue for people of all religions and ethnicities. Sufi shrines are still highly popular among the believers of Hindu, Muslim, Sikh, Christian and other faiths. Sufism has made significant contributions to Islamic civilization in music and philosophy, dance and literature.

Sufism, the mystical dimension of Islam had contributed significantly to India's rich cultural and religious legacy. When Sufism came into contact with the people of other religions, some of the influence of the latter upon the former's social and cultural conditions was inevitable. The idea of *Wahda-tul-Wojood* and several techniques of mediation brought the Sufism very close to certain non-Muslim religious tradition which already existed in Indian subcontinent. For example, the *Advaita:* a Hindu stream believed that the *Aatma* (human soul) and *Parmatma* (God) were one and the same, a theory similar to *Wahda-tul Wojood*. Similarly, the Sufis found much to learn from Hindu disciplines such as Yoga which influenced and strengthen their mediation techniques. In the same way, local Indian traditions were also powerfully affected by the principles of Islam as represented by Sufi Saints. The teachings of Kabir and Guru Nanak show the clear imprint of Sufi Islam.[16]

All mystic traditions tried to comprehend divinity, universe and life from personal subjective and individual perspectives. Sufism can provide a conceptual framework for grassroots movements working for equity, gender equality and communal harmony. It would not be wrong to ascertain the potential of Sufism in providing a common platform to world religions for reducing unnecessary religious animosities and tensions. Sufism historically played in promoting tolerance, peace and harmony. Despite its religious orientation, the most significant impact of the Sufi institution left in the region was creating a society based on communal harmony in a highly diverse region culturally, ethnically and socially. For centuries the Sufi creed and Sufi music has been a great symbol of spiritualism and promoters of peace and harmony between Hindus and Muslims. The concept of Sufism and spirituality has been unquestioningly accepted as the hallmark of Hindu-Muslim unity. It has played a major role in promoting religious harmony and Hindu-Muslim unity in medieval India. Sufism always emphasized people to live with tolerance, harmony, love, brotherhood and peace on the earth adding that humanity is more precious than any of the religions.

Conclusion

Sufism means purity, purification of self, contentment, help of others, betterment of the humankind and love for all. Sufism is not an innovation, but the continuity of a thoughtful process that links Muslims to their religious predecessors all the way to Prophet Muhammad. The essential principles of Sufism have remained free from the dimensions of time or place, gender or race, cultures or ceremonies and all human qualities. Sufism of various orders in the name of their founder saints has become a universal aspect of Islam. Sufism in India has commonly been viewed as a secular attempt for eternal quest of the soul for its direct experience of the ultimate Supreme power. Sufism has some potential in providing a common platform to world religions for reducing unnecessary religious animosities and tensions. It can also provide a conceptual framework for grassroots movements working for equity, gender equality and communal harmony. The teachings of Sufis can help in eliminating the communal tensions in India and building up the nation's moral discipline and religious character. Indian and other parts of the world are facing serious problems of extremism and intolerance whereas peace and harmony is the need of the day. Love and respect for the entire humanity and unconditional devotion to the Almighty are the basic tenets of Sufism. Sufism is a science having objective of turning of hearts towards motivation for global peace and harmony. Sufism teaches that all aspects of life - from nature to other people - are signs of God, and yet the grandeur of God is beyond human comprehension. The teachings Sufism may help in bringing peace and security at National and International level. In the light of above discussion the role of Sufism became clear towards ideal society and all social and religious problems could not be solved with the intolerance but society can solve problems by following teachings of Islam and Sufism.

Endnotes

1. J.S. Trimingham, The Sufi Orders in Islam, London, 1971, p.103
2. Ibn Khaldun, Muqaddam, tr. in Persian by M. Parveen Gunabadi, Vol.II, Teheran, 1347, p. 987.
3. In the name of Allah: Understanding Islam and Indian History by Raziuddin Aquil, p. 25.
4. Encyclopedia of Sufism: Edited by Masood Ali Khan, S. Ram, p. 14.
5. Islamic Mysticism in India by Nagendra Kumar Singh, p. 179.
6. Amir K.hwurd, Siyar al-Auliya, Lahore, reprint 1978, p. 27.
7. Tara Chand, Influence of Islam on Indian Culture, Allahabad, 1936, p. 46.
8. *Ibid.*, p. 46.
9. Asrar al-Tasawwuf, Lahore, 1925, pp. l0-11.
10. Indian Islam by Murray T. Titus, 1979, p. 117.
11. Contemporary Relevance of Sufism, 1993, published by Indian Council for Cultural relations.
12. In the name of Allah: Understanding Islam and Indian History by Raziuddin Aquil, p. 12.
13. Islamic Mysticism in India by Nagendra Kumar Singh, p. 183.
14. In the name of Allah: Understanding Islam and Indian History: by Raziuddin Aquil, p. 45.
15. 80 questions to understand India: History, Mythology and Religion: by Murad Ali Baig, p. 55.
16. History of Sufism in India by Syed Athar Abbas Rizvi, Vol. 2, 1992, p. 180.

8

The Quest For *Ma 'Rifat* (Gnosis) In Kashmiri Sufi Poetry

Manzoor Ahmad Najar

Abstract

This paper begins with an overview of the process within which the concept Ma'rifat emerged as an expression of the specific kind of knowledge proper to the Sufi discipline. In Kash_ful Mahjoob, Muhammad Fadl al-Balkhi says: "knowledge is of three kinds—from God, with God, and of God." Knowledge of God is the science of Gnosis (ilm-I ma'rifat), whereby He is known to all His prophets and saints. It cannot be acquired by ordinary means, but is the result of Divine guidance and information. The significance of the concept is examined in relation to Kashmiri Sufi poetry, where the finest expressions of Ma'rifat can be found. The existence of Human Being in Sufism is seen as a macrocosm and of the Universe as microcosm. When a Sufi attains the stage of Al-Arif (Gnostic) he fathoms the Ultimate Truth and from his head flows a shower of Ultimate knowledge, which becomes an Elixir to his life, and he realizes the unrealized. In this paper it is argued that the definitive and ultimate content of Ma'rifat can be seen more clearly in relation to the principle of tawhîd. For while the tawhîd of the theologian means affirming that there is but one God as opposed to many gods, for the Aarif bi -Llah, the 'knower through God', it entails the spiritual realization that there is but one Reality. The article focuses on the quest of a Sufi to gain Ma 'rifat as revealed aptly in Kashmiri Sufi poetry.

Keywords: *Ma'rifat (Gnosis), Aarif, Sufi, Tawhid, Realization, Ultimate Truth, Shahada.*

Overview of Sufism and the process of *Ma 'rifat* (Gnosis)

Sufism is the most universal manifestation of the inner dimension of Islam; it is the way by which man transcends his own individual self and reaches God. (Nasr 32) It provides within the forms of the Islamic revelation the means for an intense spiritual life directed towards the transformation of man's being and the attainment of the spiritual virtues; ultimately it leads to the vision of God. Islam is primarily a "way of knowledge," (Schuon-13) which means that its spiritual method, its way of bridging the illusory gap between man and God—"illusory," but none the less as real as man's own ego—is centered upon man's intelligence. Man is conceived of as a "theomorphic" being, a being created in the image of God, and therefore as possessing the three basic qualities of intelligence, free-will, and speech. Intelligence is central to the human state and gains a saving quality through its content, which in Islam is the *Shahâda* or "profession of faith": *Lâ ilâha illâ 'Llâh*, "There is no god but God"; through the *Shahâda* man comes to know the Absolute and the nature of reality, and thus also the way to salvation. The element of will, however, must also be taken into account, because it exists and only through it can man choose to conform to the Will of the Absolute. Speech, or communication with God, becomes the means—through prayer in general or in Sufism through quintessential prayer or invocation (*dhikr*)—of actualizing man's awareness of the Absolute and of leading intelligence and will back to their essence. (*ibid.* 13-18)

Through the spiritual methods of Sufism the *Shahâda* is integrally realized within the being of the knower. The "knowledge" of Reality which results from this realization, however, must not be confused with knowledge as it is usually understood in everyday language, for this realized knowledge is "To know what is, and to know it in such a fashion as to be oneself, truly and effectively, what one knows."(René Guénon 10) If the human ego, with which fallen man usually identifies himself, were a closed system, such knowledge would be beyond man's reach. However, in the view of Sufism, like other traditional metaphysical doctrines, the ego is only a transient mode of man's true and transcendent self. Therefore the attainment of metaphysical knowledge in its true sense, or "spiritual realization," is the removal of the veils which separate man from God and from the full reality of his own true nature. It is the means of actualizing the full potentialities of the human state.

Metaphysical knowledge in the sense just described can perhaps be designated best by the term "gnosis" (*Ma'rifat*), which in its original sense and as related to Sufism means "Wisdom made up of knowledge and sanctity." (Palmer 8) The *Ma'rifat* of the Sufis is the 'gnosis' of Hellenistic theosophy, i.e. direct knowledge of God based on revelation or apocalyptic vision. It is not the result of any mental process, but depends entirely on the will and favor of God, who bestows it as a gift from Himself upon those whom He has created with the capacity for receiving it. It is a light of divine grace that flashes into the heart and overwhelms every human faculty in its dazzling beams. "He who knows God is dumb." (Nicholson 30)

The online Encyclopedia Britannica defines *Ma 'rifat as:*

> Ma'rifa, (Arabic: "inside learning") in Islam, the enchanted information of God or the "higher substances" that is a definitive objective of devotees of Sufism. Sufi magic came to ma¿rifa by taking after an otherworldly way that later Sufi masterminds sorted into an arrangement of "stations" that were trailed by an alternate arrangement of steps, the "states," through which the Sufi would come to union with God. The procurement of ma'rifa was not the consequence of learnedness however was a kind of gnosis in which the otherworldly got brightening through the beauty of God. The finest statements of ma¿rifa can be found in the verse of the Sufis Jalâl al-Dîn al-Rûmî (1207–73) and Ibn al-'arabì (1165–1240). In spite of the fact that the quest for ma'rifa is most usually connected with the Sufis.

Many Sufis speak of gnosis as being synonymous with love, but "love" in their vocabulary excludes the sentimental colorings usually associated with this term in current usage. The term love is employed by them because it indicates more clearly than any other word that in gnosis the whole of one's being "knows" the object and not just the mind; and because love is the most direct reflection in this world, or the truest "symbol" in the traditional sense, of the joy and beatitude of the spiritual world. Moreover, in Sufism, as in other traditions, the instrument of spiritual knowledge or gnosis is the heart, the center of man's being; gnosis is "existential" rather than purely mental. (Schuon 50)

Sufism deals first and foremost with the inward aspects of that which is expressed outwardly or exoterically in the Sharî¿a, the Islamic religious law. Hence it is commonly called "Islamic esotericism."(Burckhardt chap. 1) In the view of the Sufis, exoteric Islam is concerned with laws and injunctions which direct human action and life in accordance with the divine Will, whereas Sufism concerns direct knowledge of God and realization—or literally, the "making real" and actual—of spiritual realities which exist both within the external form of the Revelation and in the being of the spiritual traveller (sâlik). The Sharî¿a is directly related to Sufism inasmuch as it concerns itself with translating these same realities into laws which are adapted to the individual and social orders.

Purifying the Soul

Sufis agree on the necessity of devoting oneself to the purification of the soul (*tazkiyat an-nafs*), which is the only way that can bring about the emergence of a noble character (*khuluq*) and the proper inward and outward attitude (*adab*) in a human being. In doing this their intention is to follow the model of the Prophet:

"Surely thou art endowed with a tremendous character (*khuluq*)," says the Koran addressing the Prophet (68:4). The noble virtues (*akhlâq*, pl. of *khuluq*) that Sufis endeavor to acquire are therefore the same as those of Islam, but Sufis give them particular weight by bringing them to life within themselves; thus these virtues are transmuted into initiatic stations. This type of Sufism, it goes without saying, has been accepted by the general body of *'ulamâ'*. In this perspective, it represents one of the three parts of the religion, along with the dogma (*aqîda*) and the Law (*Sharî'a*). He who travels the Path would not try therefore to experiment with supernatural phenomena but would try instead to ascertain the truth of the Law and to perfect his submissiveness to God.

Other Sufis, going further, considered purification to be just a means and not an end in itself, since its goal is to arrive at the knowledge of God in order to better adore Him. "They have not appreciated God equal to His true measure" (Koran 6:91). According to Al-Qushayrî, this verse means "They did not know God in His true measure." The doctrinal seeds of "knowledge," of gnosis (Ma'rifa), are present in the first masters, and it may be that it is necessary to see in this the beginning of a Neo-Platonism influence which would later provide Sufism with conceptual tools. According to Ma'rûf al-Karkhî (d. 815), who was regarded as the founder of the Sufi school of Baghdad, Sufism consists in "seizing upon Divine Realities (*haqâ'iq*) and forsaking all that comes from creatures (*khalâ'iq*)." During this same period, al-Bistâmî affirms that the "knower," the gnostic, "flies towards God, while the ascetic only walks," and Ruwaym says that "the hypocrisy of Gnostics is better than the sincerity of aspirants [who aspire only to purification]."(Michon and Gaetani 84) Knowledge is a mirror, adds Ruwaym, in which the gnostic sees God revealing Himself. Dhû'n-Nûn insists on this direct grasping of God: "How did you (come to) know your Lord?" someone asked him. "I knew my Lord through Himself."(*ibid.* 84)

Inspiration and unveiling are indispensable for he who wants to clear a path towards this God who appears as "the Light of the heavens and the earth" (Koran 24:35). It is for this reason that all Sufis sought to make room in themselves for the "radiation" (*tajallî*) of this light. Unblocking human nature from its opacity, just as the sun drives away darkness, (Cf. Koran, 92:2.) this theophany reveals God to the heart of man. As-Sarrâj observes that the simple believer sees by the light of God, while the gnostic sees by God Himself. (Luma 41) Later, Ibn ¿Arabî would explain how multiplicity is spread from its start in Unicity through a succession of uninterrupted theophanies that take innumerable forms. The Sufi thus sees God in all being, in every manifested thing. Unlike the ascetic, he does not reject the world, because to him it is illuminated by the divine Presence. "Beings were not created so that you would see them, but so that you would see their Master in them," said Ibn "Amâ' Allâh. (Michon and Gaetani 85) Again and again the Koran encourages man to decipher the "signs" (*âyât*), to contemplate God by contemplating His Manifestation. "We shall show them our signs in the universe and in themselves until they see that it is the Truth [God]" (Koran 41:53).

Uniting Oneself With God, or "Extinguishing Oneself" in Him?

The ultimate goal of the mystical life cannot be to know God but to be united with Him. However, in Islam one cannot speak of a *via unitiva* in the same sense as in Christian theology. From the point of view of the central dogma of *taw%îd*, which focuses only on "the divine Unicity," the very concept of "union" with God is eminently paradoxical. (Michon and Gaetani 86)

The central concern of the bûfis, as of every Muslim, is *taw%îd*, the witness that "There is no deity but God." This truth has to be realized in the existence of each individual. A prominent Kashmiri Sufi, Sheikh ul Alam Says:

La : Ila:ha Ill_Allah sahiy korum/ vahi korum panun pa:n
waju:d travith mu:ju:d sorum/ ada boh vo:tus la:maka:n

(There is no deity but God, did I verify and confirm; myself "I" quite burnt away. Ignoring the manifest, I mediated on the Everlasting. So was the Space less realized to me)

Indeed, union presumes the coming together of two entities, of two substances. Now, the profession of faith (*shahâda*) of Islam affirms: "There is no god but God." For the Sufi, this negative assertion actually means: "Only God is," since that which is created, the contingent, vanishes in the face of the Absolute. Therefore the Sufi doesn't live in a state of union, strictly speaking, since in Islam there is no continuity of substance between God and creation. His goal is "extinction in God" (fanâ'). Removed from the various solicitations of the world, the initiate then knows the intoxication of immersion in the divine Presence. Being completely unaware of himself as subject-consciousness, he becomes a mirror in which God contemplates Himself. This state paradoxically opens up the horizons of Knowledge, for man can only have access to divine realities when his ego no longer interposes itself in his contemplation, that is to say when divine Being shows through in him. (*ibid* 86)

In order to react against the slippery slope made use of by the "intoxicated" mystics, other Sufis, called "temperate," emphasized that in the ecstatic state of *fanâ'* man always had to keep a glimmer of lucidity, especially as this state, being paroxysmal but still transient, was only the prelude to a more complete experience, that of *baqâ'*: having burnt away his individual attributes, the initiate "subsists" henceforth in and by God so that it is the divine Attributes that now act in him. According to a *'adîth qudsî* frequently cited by Sufis, God becomes "the ear with which he hears, the sight through which he sees, the hand with which he grasps, and the foot with which he walks." Maulana Rumi Says:

> "Make everything in you and ear each atom of your being, and you will hear at every moment what the Source is whispering to you... You are, we all are, the beloved of the beloved, and in every moment of your life, the Beloved is whispering to you exactly what you need to hear and know."

In the first phase, the one of *fanâ'*, a person doesn't see anything outside of God; in the second, the one of *baqâ'*, he sees Him in everything. After the intoxication of immersion in God comes the soberness that allows the initiate to be with God and with the world at the same time. Letting God do with him as He will, he achieves his ontological servitude while at the same time putting himself at the service of men.

This double experience of *fanâ'/baqâ'* is so essential in Sufism that Junayd thought that it is this experience alone which defines it. "Tacawwuf," he said, "is summed up thus: the Real [or, the 'Truth,' i.e. God] makes you die to yourself, and causes you to come alive again through Him." (A-Qushayri 280) This theme is the transposition onto a mystical plane of the Koranic verse: "All that is on earth is passing away. There remaineth (yabqâ) but the Countenance of thy Lord of Majesty and Munificence" (Koran 55:26-27). The initiatic death, as implied by the experience of *fanâ'/baqâ'*, is a response to the Prophet's injunction: "Die before dying!" Specifically, it is inscribed in the example of Muhammad, he who "has been sent" among men to guide them. Extending the dogma of the divine Unicity and the spiritual "tasting" of *fanâ'*, some Sufis explained that God is One in the sense that He alone possesses Being: in manifesting creatures, He endowed them with an existence emanating from His Being, but this has only an ontological content that is relative, or even non-existent. Many exoteric scholars have fought against this metaphysical formulation, which is known as the "oneness of Being" (*wahdat al-wujûd*) because it has seemed to them to deny divine transcendence. The meaning of *wabdat al-wujud*, if not the actual expression, can be found in sources ranging from certain Qur'anic verses, such as "Whithersoever ye turn there is the Face of God" (2:1 15), to certain sayings of the Prophet, such as "I am Ahmad without the m" (meaning Ahead or the One, referring to the inner oneness of the Prophet with the Source of all being). It is also the theme of many poems, some of which are among the greatest masterpieces of Sufi poetry. (Nasr 55)

Prophet Muhammad (SAW) is also described as light from light, and from his light all the prophets are created, constituting the different aspects of this light. In its fullness such light radiated from the historical Muhammad and is partaken of by his posterity and by the saints; for Muhammad has the aspect of sanctity in addition to that of prophecy. An apocryphal tradition makes even God attest: "I am Ahmad (= Muhammad) without 'm' (i.e., Ahad, 'One'). (Encyclopaedia Britannica) In the words of a Kashmiri Sufi poet Rahman Dar, the same thought can be observed as he says:

Nur nish nur paedeh draav
Ahadas ahmad kornai naav
Muhammad laaegith bazar draav
Bahar aav jani jananai

(Spiritual light originated from Spiritual light. In the same way Ahad (the unidentical One) was named Ahmad. In the guise of Muhammad (SAW), He sends Ahad into this world and the world was bloomed with His coming.) (He sent his Beloved Muhammad SAW to manifest Himself and to bloom this universe).

As for its full exposition, it must be sought in works of Sufi metaphysics. The poems of Sheikh Noor-ud Din wali do reveal that he did receive God's grace and in ample measure. The veil of illusion was lifted, as Sufis claim, from the face of the Truth. Light of God shone upon him destroying darkness of doubt and ignorance. His intense penance, unalloyed faith, strict control of his sense organs, and absolute riddance from the powerful forces of obscuration, such as greed, lust, egotism and desire for worldly goods had, at last, borne fruit. He attained the realization of the Divine Being. The affirmation of this 'state' is made in the following verses:

Da:l go:m mi:lith Aliphas ta Hayas/ Ami hayan kornam bayas na:sh
Sheshikal troprim Ahadakis payas/ Meema_rous Ahmad logum ra;sh
Sheyi_wanna phyu:rus mo:yas mo:yas/ Ada par mokalyom ta kodum va:sh

('*Da:l'* got suffixed to '*Aliph'* and '*Hai*'. And '*hai*' destroyed my fear!. Six (apertures) of sense did I close to gain clue to the One. Minus '*Meem*', Ahmad (became Ahad)- the source of my joy. I roamed about the six forests, every nook and corner; lo! And behold! My wings came unfolded and I stretched myself.)

Tsha:nja:m bhava_nan beyyi shen dishen/ neib ta nisha:n lobmas na konei
Pristsha:m mala_ba:ban ta tapa_reshan/ tim lagi bu:zi revanei
Dab yelli dyutamas fikran ta andeishan/ ada sui dyu:nthum boh na kunei

(I looked for Him in the Bhawans and six directions. Neither any mark nor clue did I come upon. I enquired of the Mullahas and the Hermiits. Hearing me they only bemoaned (their ignorance) as I subdued my logic and doubts. Lo! I found Him all-pervading and myself naught.)

Su me nishe boh tas nishe/ Me tas nishe qarar aav
Na:haqqa tso:ndum me pardishei/ pananei dishei qarar a:v

(close by me stood He, and I by Him. Relaxed felt I by His vey side. Wrongly had I looked for Him in alien lands. (When) I found solace within myself)

In any case, to understand even the theoretical meaning of the oneness of Being on any level requires a certain intellectual intuition as well as intellectual preparation, in addition to Divine grace, while only the saint who has reached the end of the Sufi path and become drowned in the Ocean of Divinity can know its meaning fully and in the ultimate sense.

The knowledge of which Sufism speaks is not mental knowledge but a light that illuminates the beholder of this knowledge and in fact all around it and finally returns the human being to its Source, the Supernal Sun. On the highest level, the subject as well as the object of this knowledge is God. The gnostic in Sufism is called al- 'Arif bi'Llah, one who knows by God and not one who knows God, for ultimately it is only the Divine Spark within us that can know the Divine. Our duty is to remove the veils within that prevent such a unitive knowledge from taking place.

The Prophet has said, "Knowledge is Light," and one can add that the Quran speaks of God being the Light of the heavens and the earth. Now, existence itself is a ray of light that issues from the Divine Sun. Knowledge is therefore also being. The more one knows in a principia} manner, and not only discursively, the more one is. On the highest level the knower, knowledge, and the known are one. To know the Truth with one's whole being is ultimately to "become the Truth," to realize that the root of our "I" is the Divine Self I self, who alone can ultimately utter "I." It was not the individual ego of Al-Hallaj who uttered *Ana'l-Haqq*. That would be blasphemy, and that is how those ignorant around him who did not understand interpreted it. In reality, one who does not utter *Ana'l-Haqq* is still living as a polytheist and idol worshipper, positing his or her own ego as a reality separate from God as *Al-Haqq* and idolizing that ever-changing and evanescent ego as well as the world as a divinity. In any case, the quest for the Truth lies at the heart of Sufism, and the goal of the adept is to be able to ascend the levels of certitude until one's separate existence is consumed by the Truth and one is given access to the Garden of Truth. (ibid. 32)

The description and theoretical exposition of the Truth is contained in Sufi doctrine while the realization of the Truth is possible only through spiritual practice. Sufi doctrine, which is also called theoretical gnosis is itself the fruit of spiritual realization and not simply philosophical speculation. It is presented to those in quest of the Truth as a map of the structure of reality and the road that is to be followed to transcend the cosmic labyrinth. One might say that the Sufi masters first climbed the cosmic mountain and then flew into the sky of the Divine Presence and after that, upon descending, drew a map for other climbers who wished to reach the summit and fly to the Beyond. Sufi doctrine is like the lore of certainty and its realization the truth of certainty. From the operative point of view, the doctrine is presented and then its truths realized, but in reality it is the realization of the truths of the path that have made it possible in the first place for master expositors of Sufi doctrine to formulate their teachings and guide men and women on their journey to the One. (ibid. 33)

Classical Sufi texts are replete with the description of the virtues. I shall mention later some of the early Sufis, who wrote on this subject and whose writings culminate in Al-Ghazzali's *Ihyia'ulUm al-din* (Revivification of the Sciences of Religion), the most important work of spiritual ethics in the history of Islam. (Greenwood 19) Since the steps to God or the stations can be enumerated in different ways and seen from different perspectives, the number of stations and their ordering is not the same everywhere. Some speak of three main stations, some of seven, some of forty, and some of even higher numbers. In what follows I shall mention some of the main stations, whose understanding opens the door for the comprehension of this subject in general. Before turning to the schools of Baghdad and Khurasan, it is important to mention a ninth-century figure that did not belong to either school, Thawban ibn Ibrahim, known as Dhu'l-Nun al-Misri (d. circa 86r). An Egyptian Sufi who travelled to Baghdad and was also known as an alchemist and philosopher, he not only spoke of the love of God and called Him the Beloved but was also the first Sufi to develop the theory of gnosis, or Ma 'rifa. He also developed the theory of annihilation (*al-fana'*) and subsistence (al-*baqa'*), discussed above, on the basis of Qur'anic teachings. (Rizvi 18)

The Sufi then dwells in a various spiritual stations (*maqâmaat*). Kashmiri Sufis have described some these *maqaamaats* for instance Shams Fakir talks of seven *maqaamats* in his poetry:

Sath samandar chhim peth mmeani taaley
Ath daryaavs kati tari naav
Ani gatti Shamso tsoung kous zaaley
Meha gos baaley choun deedar

(there are seven oceans upon my head, how to cross a boat across the river. Oh Shams who shall dare to ignite a lamp in the night, I wish to see my beloved.)

The Sufi who sets out to seek God calls himself a 'traveller' (salik); he advances by slow 'stages' (*maqamat*) along a 'path' (*tariqat*) to the goal of union with Reality (fana fi'l-Haqq). Should he venture to make a map of this interior ascent, it will not correspond exactly with any of those made by previous explorers. Such maps or scales of perfection were elaborated by Sufi teachers at an early period, and the unlucky Moslem habit of systematizing has produced an enormous after crop. The 'path' expounded by the author of the Kitab al-Luma', perhaps the oldest comprehensive treatise on Sufism that we now possess, consists of the following seven 'stages', each of which (except the first member of the series) is the result of the 'stages' immediately preceding it—(l) Repentance, (2) abstinence, (3) renunciation, (4) poverty, (5) patience, (6) trust in God, (7) satisfaction. The 'stages' constitute the ascetic and ethical discipline of the Sufi, and must be carefully distinguished from the so called 'states' (*ahwal*, plural of *hal*), which form a similar psychological chain. The writer whom I have just quoted enumerates ten 'states'—Meditation, nearness to God, love, fear, hope, longing, intimacy, tranquility, contemplation, and certainty. While the 'stages' can be acquired and mastered by one's own efforts, the 'states' are spiritual feelings and dispositions over which a man has no control:

> "They descend from God into his heart, without his being able to repel them when they come or to retain them when they go." (Nicholson 29)

The Sufi's 'path' is not finished until he has traversed all the 'stages,' making himself perfect in every one of them before advancing to the next, and has also experienced whatever 'states' it pleases God to bestow upon him. Then, and only then, is he permanently raised to the higher planes of consciousness which Sufis call 'the Gnosis' (*Ma'rifat*) and 'the Truth' (*haqiqat*), where the 'seeker' (*talib*) becomes the 'knower' or 'gnostic' (*Arif*), and realizes that knowledge, knower, and known are One. (ibid.12)

Mystical poetry in Kashmiri (spoken by the natives of the valley) has a richness and variety of its own, traceable to the mingling of several cultural streams. Its growth began in the fourteenth century with the famous woman poet and saint, Lal Ded. It was in her time that Sufism first came to Kashmir through Muslim saints and mystics. Consistent with her Saivite background, Lal Ded, in her vakhs, neither characterizes the world as illusory nor recommends external renunciation. She looks upon the objective universe as the Swarupa Itself (the Real Form) that parallels the Sufi view of the physical world as *Wahadat-ul-wajud*.

To the discerning reader, Shamas Faqir's description of the Sufi path must appear suggestively similar to the spiritual 'adventure' given in other varieties of religious mysticism (including Hindu and Christian mysticism). In several poems, he makes use of the via-negative and via-affirmative approaches in his accounts of the Divine. Each of these approaches to Reality involves a characteristic language use, which the poet accomplishes so well; sometimes we find the two approaches deftly interwoven in the same poem. In quite a few poems, we come across direct allusions to the Persian mystic, Mansur-ul-Hallaj, and the doctrine of An-ul-Haq (I am Truth) that he boldly preached.

Several lyrics of Shamas Faqir center round the theme of the mystic's quest for the primal cause of this universe. As an illustration, the lyric titled 'Agur Kami Manz Drav' repeatedly poses the question, 'what is the fountainhead of the stream?', which serves as its refrain. Here is my translation of some significant lines of the poem (attempted to convey the essential meaning):

Day and night does Pavan flow
Through the four Bhavans non-stop;
Whence did it come
And whither did it go?
It was even (all of one hue),
Whence did the stream come forth?

....

O Shamas, to attain gnosis,
Throw open your heart's door;
Sun-like, roam the sky through
(To fathom the Secret);
What is the fountain-head?

We can see that the poem poses vital and thought- provoking questions regarding the First Cause. It instructs the seeker to pursue the spiritual journey inwardly to realize the Self. This would naturally call for annihilation of the little self. The answer to the imponderable question regarding the source of the Cosmos is provided through the intertwined images of the 'drop' and the 'river'. In the concluding lines, that lay stress on cleansing the heart as a means to inward transformation, the tone of the poem changes as the poet addresses his own self. Without sounding the didactic, the changed tone stimulates self- introspection in the reader/listener.

The Persian Sufi poets have often used the word *rinda* in their lyrics. It refers to the true lover, a liberated soul (not tied to this or that school). With its rich associations, it has been absorbed into Kashmiri mystical poetry and has by now got into common usage among the Kashmiris. (Cyprian 28) It occurs frequently in Shamas Faqir's verse too. One poem titled 'Rinda Sara Ho Sapdi Kunu Ye' is specifically addressed to the rinda. This is how the poet instructs the aspiring gnostic:

O rinda, in order to realize the One,
Learn to die while still alive. (trans. A.N. Dhar)

Emphasis is laid in the poem on self-conquest as being the stepping stone to advancement in spirituality. An *Arif's*, devotion has to consist in 'cleansing of the doors of perception', which involves a disciplining of the mind and the senses. He has to be discriminative and mentally alert throughout. Shamas Faqir is explicit about this quality required of the true aspirant:

Seemingly blind, look keenly for
What you seek, O rinda!
Sifting the pure grain
From the impure,
Winnowing the grains a hundred times
Will reveal the Precious One to you. *(trans. A.N. Dhar)*

The poet draws our attention to the strenuousness and pains involved in the spiritual effort, in these lines:

Break the stones at the dead of night,
To take away the Gem guarded
by the cobra;
Feed the burning lamp
with your blood,
Eat up your own flesh;
Thus will you, O rinda, realize the One.
Special stress is laid in the closing lines on belief and divine grace:
Believe before you verify,
That's Shamas Faqir's gospel;
When you get the 'Word'
As a God-sent gift,
O rinda, you'll realize the One. *(trans. A.N. Dhar)*

In one particular poem titled 'Walo Mashoka Deedar Hav', the poet employs 'dark imagery' throughout, from the beginning to the end, and mentions 'black light' specifically in these lines:

The Elixir of life is hidden in the dark,
The light divine is dark, too;
Light itself is grounded in darkness,
Pray, meet me Beloved! *(trans. A.N. Dhar)*

This poem reminds us of the images of 'darkness' that are so recurrent in St. John of the Cross, especially in his poem titled 'Dark Night of the Soul', there is a close parallel between the Christian concept of 'divine dark' and what Shamas Faqir conveys through his images. Similarly, the names of Hindu divinities such as Krishna, Shyama, Kalaratri, Megashyama, suggest 'the night of the great release into the oneness of Self', which is dark only to the senses, not to the spirit.

The 'human form divine', in its feminine aspect, is celebrated conspicuously in the poetry of Persian Sufis. Parallel motifs and images are seen to occur in both Hindu and Christian mysticism. The form functions as a wisdom figure, which is, in fact, a recurrent image in literature. It is also identifiable as the 'theophanic figure through whom the manifestation of God takes place'. (Jankinath 38)

After Sheikh Nur-ud-Din Rishi of Charari Sheriff, it is he (before others followed them) who paid glowing tributes to Lal Ded in a poem wholly devoted to her, titled 'Zan Mila Nav Bhagvanas Sooty'. The poem shows how high he held her in his esteem, how familiar he was with her story and how thoroughly acquainted he must have been with her vakhs. Lall Ded says that one who thinks himself not different from the other; one who accepts sorrow as good as pleasure; one who frees himself from duality; he and he alone tells the beads of Lord of the Lords-Almighty and this is the basic thinking of Shaivism. She held a key to many mystic truths. (Parimoo 6)The following stanza illustrates her deep mystic thought:

So my lamp of knowledge afar,
Fanned by slow breath from the throat of me.
They, my bright soul to my self-revealed.
Winnowed I abroad my inner light.
And with darkness around me sealed,
Did I garner truth and hold Him tight. *(Trans. Sir Richard Temple)*

Lal Ded thinks dissolution of 'self' (Aham) essential for Realization. According to her, Sadhaka has to reach that mental attitude where there is no difference between 'Him' and 'self'. She says one who considers his own self and others alike ends the distinction between 'I' and 'you', who treats days and nights alike, who is above sorrows and pleasures, can only realize God in his own self. According to her, differentiation between the human soul and Divine-self was Zero.

A Sufi on his way to illumination undergoes many changing spiritual states such as *qabd* and *bast.* He feels at certain times "constraint and happy spiritual expansion, fear and hope, and longing and intimacy, which are granted by God and last for longer or shorter periods of time, changing in intensity according to the station in which the mystic is abiding at the moment." (Encyclopedia Britannica) The Sufi reaches to a point of his spiritual development in *Ma'rifat* ("gnosis") or in *ma'abbah* ("love"), the central subject of Sufism since the 9th century, which implies a union of lover and beloved. In Sufism the final goal is *fanâ'* ("annihilation"), primarily an ethical concept of annihilating one's own qualities and Sufis stress on complete extinction of personality/existence. (Arberry 17) In the words of a Shams Fakir:

Hasti dur kar near ats andrai
Wuchh_han jani jaanaan
(Extinct your existence and go inside your own. You will see the Beloved)

According to the prophetic saying "Take over the qualities of God," but slowly developing into a complete extinction of the personality. Some Sufis teach that beyond this negative unity where the self is completely effaced, the *baqâ'*, ("duration, life in God") is found: the ecstatic experience, called intoxication, is followed by the "second sobriety"—i.e., the return of the completely transformed mystic into this world where he acts as a living witness of God or continues the "journey in God." The Sufi has reached *%aqîqah* ("reality"), after finishing the *marîqah* ("path"), which is built upon the *sharî¿ah* ("law"). Later, the disciple is led through *fanâ'fi ashshaykh* ("annihilation in the master") to *fanâ' fiar-Rasûl* ("annihilation in the Prophet") before reaching, if at all, *fanâ' fi-Allâh* ("annihilation in God"). In conclusion, I reiterate that Kashmiri Sufi poetry is outstanding in its grasp and assimilation of many mystical concepts like *Ma 'rifat*.

The Sufi poetry of Kashmir is an expression of inner states of mind and manifestation of several metaphysical experiences. Because of strong spiritual and mystic traditions, Sufi poets of Kashmir have found the atmosphere quite conducive to their quest. The way these Sufi poets have preserved and enriched the mystic and spiritual traditions of Kashmir is quite appreciative. They do not reject the Sharia, which is fundamental to Islamic Sufism, but come up with a new and creative interpretation of it in the light of their own intense spiritual experiences. In their verses they describe the spiritual attainments of the saint concerned, pay their tribute, and makes a fervent prayer to God to bless them the same way. Accentuation is laid in the Kashmiri Sufi poetry on triumph toward oneself as being the venturing stone to headway in otherworldly existence. An Aarif's commitment needs to comprise in 'purging of the entryways of observation', which includes a training of the brain and the faculties. He must be rationally cautious all through. Kashmiri Sufi poetry is explicit about this quality required of the true aspirant.

References

Saiyid, A.A. Rizvi, *A History of Suf sm in India* New Delhi: Munshiram Manoharlal Pub., Pvt. Ltd., 1978), Vol. I, p. 18.

A.J. Arberry, *Sufism* (London: George Allen & Unwin, Ltd., 1950; rpt. 1956), pp. 17, 27.

As-Sarrâj, *Kitâb al-Lumâ¿*, ed. R.A. Nicholson, London: E.J. Gibb Memorial Series XXII, 1963, p. 32.

B.N. Parimoo, *The Ascent of Self* (Delhi: Motilal Banarsidass, 2nd rev. edn., 1987), p. 6.

Cyprian Prince, O.P., *The Persian Sufis* (London: George Allen & Unwin Ltd., 1964), p. 28.

E.B. Greenwood, 'Poetry and Paradise: A Study in Thematics', Essays in Criticism, 17 (1967), p. 19.

Encyclopaedia Britannica, http://www.britannica.com/EBchecked/topic/1549151/marifa, accessed on 20.01.2015, at 17.04 pm.

Frithjof Schuon, "*The Quintessential Esoterism of Islam": Sufism: Veil and Quintessence, World Wisdom, forthcoming in 2007.* Translated from French by Mark Perry. Understanding Islam, pp. 13.

Frithjof Schuon, "*G.E.H. Palmer, in the foreword to Schuon, Gnosis: Divine Wisdom* (London, 1959), p. 8.

Jankinath Kaul *'Kamal', tr & annotator, Indrakshi Stotram* (Srinagar, Kashmir: Sri Ramakrishna Ashram, 1995), p. 38.

Motilal Saqi, ed., *Kashmir Sufi Shairi* (Srinagar: J&K Academy of Art, Culture & Languages, 1985), Vol. 1, pp. 311-439.

Reynold A. Nicholson, *The Mystics of Islam*, Rutledge, Kegan Paul, London, 1914.

Seyyed Hussein Nasr, *Ideals and Realities of Islam* (London, 1966), chapter 5, p. 32

Seyyed Hossein Nasr, "*The Spiritual Needs of Western Man and the Message of Sufism":Islam and the Plight of Modern Man*, ABC International Group, Inc., 2001, pp. 71-100.

Seyyed Hossein Nasr, *"The Garden Of Truth": The Vision and Promise if Sufism, Islam's Mystical Tradition.* E book. 2007, Harper Collins, and Harper One™ are trademarks of Harper Collins Publishers. Web site: http:/ /www.harpercollins.com

Titus Burckhardt, "*Sufi Doctrine and Method"* (the chapter in the present volume includes the chapters "At-Tacawwuf," "Sufism and Mysticism," and "Rites" from): An Introduction to Sufi Doctrine, Thorsons Publishers Limited, 1976, pp. 15-27, 99-105. Translated from French by D. M. Matheson.

René Guénon, "*$aqîqa and Sharî¿a in Islam"* (the chapter in the present volume includes the chapters "Islamic Esoterism" and "The Shell and the Kernel [Al-Qishr wa al-Lubb]" from): Insights into Islamic Esoterism and Taoism, Sophia Perennis, 2004, pp. 1-13. Translated from French by Henry D. Fohr.

PART—II
SPIRITUAL TRADITIONS IN INDIA

1

The Spiritual Quotient –The Ultimate Intelligence: In The Light of Srimadbhagvadgita

Saumyajit Acharya

Abstract

The educationists gave their focus light on Intelligence Quotient (I.Q.) which was considered as a success mantra in all sections of life. The concept changed when Howard Gardner focused on the narrow I.Q. view in his book "Frames of Mind" and extended the unitary concept of intelligence to multiple dimensions. The concept of Emotional Quotient (E.Q.) emerged. But in the world of xenophobia E.Q. fails to maintain the equilibrium of modern society. Now thinkers and psychologists have identified Spiritual Quotient (S.Q.) which plays a crucial role in balancing such turbulent times. They recognize Spiritual Quotient is the ultimate intelligence. Although the modern psychology emphasizes the concept of S.Q., from the very beginning ancient Indian thinkers identified Spiritual Intelligence as ultimate intelligence. This paper tries to explore the role of Srimadbhagavadgita (the ancient Indian Holy Book) to cope with the frustrations of the society.

Keywords: Spiritual Quotient, Sustaining the education of heart, Srimadbhagvadgita.

Introduction

For many decades, the world has put great stock in the intelligence quotient (IQ). To predict success in life, psychologists came up with ways of testing IQ—

one's rational intelligence. IQ testing was first coined by Alfred Binet and his colleague Theodore Simon. IQ is a number representing a person's reasoning ability (measured using problem-solving tests) as compared to the statistical norm or average for their age, taken as 100. One could expect the higher the number of IQ means higher intelligence and therefore the higher the success. But sheer intellect is only part of the true measure of our intelligence. Although researchers proved the importance of IQ in professional accomplishments, they also discuss the fact that only 25% of the success in devoted to it. Moreover, Howard Gardner focused on the narrow I.Q. view in his book "*Frames of Mind*" and extended the unitary concept of intelligence to multiple dimensions.

Emotional intelligence is another important aspect. In the 1990s, psychologist Daniel Goleman popularized the concept in his book *Emotional Intelligence: Why It Can Matter More Than IQ*. He used findings from neuroscience and psychology to show the importance of an emotional quotient (EQ) to success in life. Daniel Goleman defines emotional intelligence "*as a set of skills, including control of one's impulses, self-motivation, empathy and social competence in interpersonal relationships*" (www.danielgoleman.info).

Actually EQ is the ability to perceive emotion, integrate emotion to facilitate thought, understand emotions and regulate emotion to promote personal and corporate growth. But in the world of xenophobia E.Q. fails to maintain the equilibrium of modern society. Now thinkers and psychologists have identified Spiritual Quotient (S.Q.) which plays a crucial role in balancing such turbulent times.

Yet most people have never heard the term Spiritual Quotient (SQ). Some may think they know the meaning, but they may be confusing the term with spiritual knowledge. This is the intelligence involved in questions about the meaning of life and ultimate values.

Spiritual Quotient

Dana Zohar and Ian Marshal, in their book, named, "*Spiritual Intelligence-the Ultimate Intelligence*" focused on Spiritual Quotient (S.Q.) and they emphasized S.Q. as the ultimate intelligence of soul. In her joint book Dana Zohar said "*SQ is what we use to develop our longing and capacity foe meaning, vision and value. It facilitates a dialogue between reason and emotion, between mind and body. SQ allows us to integrate the intrapersonal and interpersonal, to transcend the gap between self and other*"(Zohar and Marshall 2001: 22-35).

In another definition of SQ from the scientific point of view is that, "...*the intelligence with which we address and solve problems of meaning and value, the intelligence with which we can place our actions and our lives in wider, richer, meaning-giving context, the intelligence with which we can assess thatone course of action or one life-path is more meaningful than another"* (Zohar and Marshall, 2004:26)

Spiritual Quotient is the ability of an individual to see his personal vision and the ensuing endeavour to achieve the same through the prism of the larger good to the society, bringing good health and happiness to him and the world at large.

Spiritual Intelligence is entirely innate. Spiritual Intelligence (S.I.) makes a man self-aware and self-guided. Spiritual Quotient focuses on self-esteem and makes an individual emotionally mature. Spiritual Quotient gives high intelligence to individual. It is the intelligence with which we ask fundamental questions and with which we reframe our answers.

SQ allows individual to dream and to strive in this complicated world. SQ relates our relationship with all the living being, defines a moral-ethical path. SQ nourishes loving attitude (Buzan 2001: 25-40) SQ takes part in the journey of within, to find our inner-self.

The Ultimate Intelligence

Instead of measuring SQ with 'test' researchers prefer to use the observation technique. After monitoring the qualities, we have to find out some ways to improve SQ. The following qualities should be possessed by an individual to develop SQ:

- a high degree of self-awareness
- Identifying our deepest value
- sense of meaning of life
- thrust of intuitive wisdom
- the quality of being inspired by vision
- love and compassion
- a capacity to face and transcend pain
- the capacity to be flexible
- a capacity to face and use suffering
- capacity for forgiveness
- capacity to manage emotions and behavior
- capacity to think and work against convention

While I.Q. helps us to think, E.Q. helps us to relate, S.Q. transmit energy to transform our surrounding system into a whole new order of being. According to IQ happiness is wealth, fame and present pleasure. According to EQ happiness is related with emotional matters. According to SQ "*happiness is continual road to enthusiastic luminous- be it in happiness or in sorrow*" (Bozdag, 2002:38). We can understand these by the following picture:

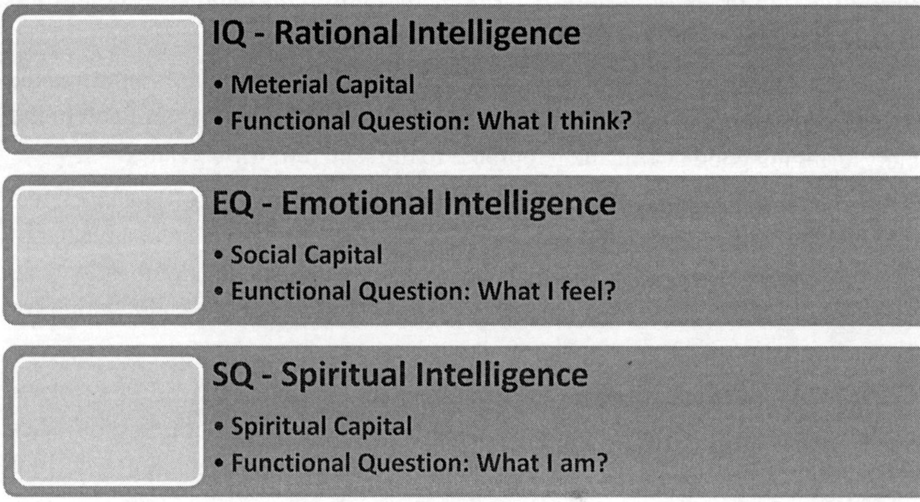

Picture 1: IQ, EQ and SQ

The search of self is the ultimate goal of SQ. That is also the search of Education. Truly Socrates said "*Education is the process of knowing thyself*". How can I discover myself? This is also a pertinent question of SQ.

Actually, SQ conveys an inner guidance whether a change and transformation is needed or not. People are born with it. It can never be taken from individual. Yet many have not named it and do not make a conscious choice when they use it (Edwards 1999: 2-4).

But is this so-called spiritual quotient really new? Don't the ancient Indian writings of the Srimadbhagvadgita indicate that man needs this added dimension to be able to attain his full human potential?

Srimadbhagvadgita-The mine of Spiritual Intelligence

The major schools of Indian philosophy accept and elaborate the conception of internal experience, self and totality. They emphasize on insight learning. In the epistemology of Indian philosophy, most of the schools said that self is the main source of gaining knowledge. It gives us self-consciousness and self-knowledge.

The Bhagavadgita is the divine word of Sri Krishna, the great teacher of humanity. The scripture is a mine of endless teaching. The *Bhagavad Gita* is the sealing achievement of Hindu synthesis. When Arjuna, who had sought refuge in the Lord, asked about the certain means of driving away his grief, Krishna described the truth about the Self. In the practice of the *Yoga* of Knowledge, the primary emphasis is laid on hearing as well as reflection and constant meditation on the truth about the Self. For example, in the forth chapter of the Bhagavad Gita Krishna said to Arjuna-

> "*What is action and what is inaction? Even men of intelligence are puzzled over this question. Therefore, I shall expound to you the truth about action, knowing which you will be freed from the evil effect*" (IV-16)

The word 'Kavayah' in this Sanskrit verse stands for men of intelligence, well-versed in the scriptures. The verse says that even they are at a loss of understand what is action and what is inaction. When even men of great learning and wisdom are at a loss of understand the truth of this matter, there is no wonder that ordinary men should get confused and puzzled over it. The truth about action, which Krishna, the great teacher, promised to expound, has been explained from verses 18 to 32 of this chapter. He who comes to know this truth in reality can never perform an action or practice renunciation of action, which may lead to bondage. That is why knowing this truth, one gets freed the pandemonium of the society.

In this chapter of the Bhagavad Gita Krishna said to Arjuna—

> "*He, who sees inaction in action and action in inaction, is wise among men; he is yogi, who has performed all actions*" (IV-18)

As ordinarily understood, the word 'Karma' in Sanskrit verse is action which denotes all activities of mind, intellect, senses and body. The point to be considered, therefore, is what is meant by seeing inaction in action which is prescribed by the scriptures? All duties enjoyed by the scriptures, such as performance of sacrifices, practicing charity and austerity as well as all vocational duties pertaining to one's order in society and those which are essential for keeping the body and soul together, when they are performed without attachment, the feeling possession and egoism, do not bear fruit in the form of pleasure and pain in this world, both good and evil they bring about liberation from the bondage of worldly existence. These are as same as SQ qualities. According to Srimadbhagvadgita, therefore, even through performing actions man does not contaminated by others. It is this sense that he is called '*wise among men*'. To achieve this stage *yoga* is important activity. Yoga is the crucial variable of both real knowledge and peaceful life. Through the practice of *yoga* and meditation Krishna represents himself as extreme knowledge. *Taittiriya Upanishad* defines yoga as the mastery of body and senses. According to Srimadbhagvadgita, the Holy Book, the purpose of *yoga* is experience of *Brahman* or*Âtman* pervading all things. Sri Krishna told to Arjuna,

> "*Tasmad asaktah satatam*
> *karyam karma samacara*
> *asakto hy acaran karma*
> *param apnoti purushah.*"
>
> —Bhagavad Gita (III-19)

"Therefore, without being attached to the fruits of activities, one should act as a matter of duty, for by working without attachment one attains the Supreme".

In the fifth chapter of the Srimadbhagvadgita Krishna said to Arjuna—

"*He who happy within himself, enjoys within himself and delight of the soul and even so illumined by the inner light (light of the soul), such a Yagi identified with Brahma attains Brahma, who is all Peace.*" (V-24)

God is the parameter of the whole universe. God, who is all peace, the embodiment of Truth, Knowledge and Bliss, Attribute less, Formless and Absolute. The following verse describes the characteristics of those who have thus realized God, the supreme reality.

The Srimadbhagvadgita combines many different elements from*Samkhya* and *Vedanta* philosophy. The book may be treated as a great synthesis of the ideas of the impersonal spiritual monism with personalistic monotheism, of the *yoga* of action with the *yoga* of transcendence of action, and these again with*yogas* of devotion and knowledge. The Srimadbhagvadgita is part of the Prasthanatrayi, which also includes the Upanishads and Brahma sutras. These are the key texts for the *Vedanta*.

According to *Vedanta*, the ideal of the *Yagi* is eternal peace and love through omniscience and omnipotence.All hatred and anger and jealousy have been burnt out of this *Yogi*. Nothing can make him react; he is infinite love all the time and he is omnipotent in his power of love. "*They have conquered relative existence in this life that is firm-fixed in sameness. God is pure and same to all. Therefore such are said to be living in God*" (Bhagavad Gita, V. 19). Swami Vivekananda explained, "*So when the Vedantist has realized his own nature, the whole world has vanished for him...The prison of misery has become changed into Sat, Chit,Ananda-Existence Absolute, Knowledge Absolute, Bliss Absolute- and the attainment of this is the goal of Advaita Philosophy*(Swami Vivekananda,1995).

A person is often the most miserable when consumed solely with self-interest and when he shuns contact with others. When we understand that we have the responsibility of stewardship of the earth, there should follow a sense of duty to our Creator and Benefactor. Like Spiritual Intelligence, Srimadbhagvadgita promotes mankind to learn the way of life that produces peace and joy for all. Sri Krishna leads Arjuna through his meditation to overcome the pandemonium of the society. Through that process one becomes isolated from external chaos and can be a happiest man.

Conclusion

It wasn't long before western authors were recognizing a new dimension to human intelligence—a spiritual quotient (SQ). This is the intelligence involved in questions about the meaning of life and ultimate values. But this so-called spiritual quotient is not really new. Although the modern psychology emphasizes the concept of S.Q., from the very beginning ancient Indian thinkers, like in Srimadbhagvadgita identified Spiritual Intelligence as ultimate intelligence. From the beginning to the end in the text of *Srimadbhagvadgita*—to develop Spiritual Intelligence-Sri Krisna has given the sermons of carrying out one's duty inspired by one's own inborn nature. This is a unique text of metaphysics (the science of reality) and ethics (the art of union). We human beings can only reach our full potential when SQ, IQ and EQ all work in harmony. If we want to implement them for the benefit of educators we may refocus these properly. The untested process and ideas may be tested in our present education system. If Education will be heart-oriented, focuses on soul development, it may be possible to regain our legacy of Spiritual Traditions. Sustaining of Education of heart can be the solution to cope with the turbulent society. Heart expanding Education also can rebuild the harmony of Hindus and Muslims.

References

Buzan, Tony (2001), The Power of Spiritual Intelligence, USA: Harper Collins.

Bozdað, Dr. Muhammed (2006), The Spiritual Intelligence. Handbook, USA: Emmanual Meals.

Bozdað, Dr. Muhammed (2006), SQ: Spiritual Quotient Çankaya/Ankara-TR ISBN 975-6503-13-0

Gardner, Howard (1993), Frames of Mind: The Theory of Multipal Intelligence, NY: Basic Books.

Goyandka, Jayadayal (2000), Srimadbhagavadgita Tattvavivecani, India: Gita Press.

Powell, David (2003), Spirit Intelligence,. Thorogood Publishing ISBN 1920688196.

Spiritual http://amansharma5.wordpress.com/2014/03/18/spiritual-quotient-and-leadership-2/

The Complete Works of Swami Vivekananda (1995), Calcutta: Advaita Ashrama, Vol. 1, p. 357.

The Bhagavadgita with an Introductory Essay, Sanskrit Text, English Translation and Notes. London: George Allen & Unwin Ltd., 1948.

Zohar, Dana, (2000), SQ: Connecting with Our Spiritual Intelligence London: Bloomsbury ISBN 1-58234-044-7.

Zohar, Dana, Marshal Ian.(2001), SQ: Connecting with Our Spiritual Intelligence, USA: Berrctt-Koehler.

Zohar, Dana, Marshal Ian. (2004), Ruhsal SQ (cev: B. Erdemli, K. Budak), Istanbul: Meta Tayin Lari.

www.danielgoleman.info

2

Gurubad in the Kala Samhati Satras of Assam: A Study

Nazmul Hussain Laskar

Abstract

Gurubad or extreme veneration to the guru is one of the most important characteristics of the Kala Samhati Satras. The disciples of these Satras considered the guru as the supreme representation of God and venerated him accordingly. However, gurubad is not peculiar to the Kala Samhati Satras, in other samhati also (Brahma, Purusha and Nika) veneration to the guru exists, although not in extreme form. Gurubad owes its origin to the Bhagawat Gita, where Lord Krishna emphasised upon the importance of a guru in clearing the confusions from the mind of devotee regarding God and philosophy of human life. In Assam, it was Srimanta Sankardeva and his disciple Madhavdeva and lateron Gopaldeva and Anirudhadeva popularised the idea of gurubad. They not only emphasised on the importance of guru in the life of a devotee but also practiced it in their own life. To them, gurusewa or serving one's guru is the best religion and it is the best way for salvation. In this paper an attempt is made to find out the traces of gurubad in the Kala Samhati Satras of Assam with special reference to the neo-vaishnavite movement launched by Sankardava in the late 15th and early 16th century in Assam.

Keywords: *Guru, Satra, Sankardeva and Kala Samhati Satra*

Introduction

Gurubad or extreme veneration to the guru is one of the most important characteristics of the Kala Samhati Satras[1]. The disciples of these satras considered the guru as the supreme representation of God and venerated him accordingly. However, gurubad is not peculiar to the Kala Samhati Satras, in other samhati also (Brahma, Purusha and Nika) veneration to the guru exists, although not in extreme form.

Gurubad owes its origin to the Bhagawat Gita, where Lord Krishna emphasised upon the importance of a guru in clearing the confusions from the mind of devotee regarding God and philosophy of human life. After learning the secret of human life from Lord Krishna, Arjuna, the third Pandava, took initiation from him and declared him as his guru. The words he had disclosed on that occasion are reproduced by Sankaradeva in his Bhakti Pradip as follows:

Mura maha sanka dura kara deva hari
Tumise parama guru haiba aji dhari,
Sariraaka samarpilu pawata tomar
Guchoka Mura maha ajyana andhar[2].

(Remove all fear from my mind; you are my guru from this day. I have surrendered my body to your feet. Let all my ignorance get removed through your kindness).

In the Rajasuya Yagna of Yudhisthira, the eldest son of Pandavas, there gathered a large number of rishis or saints. Different rishis pointed out different ways to attain salvation. When some of them expressed faith in gyana or knowledge as the real path to attain mukti, some other gave importance on Karma or work and still others held that the only way to attain salvation is Bhakti or devotion. Arjuna then requested Lord Krishna to clear his mind by pointing out the real path. Lord Krishna then related the story of a Chandaloni or a low caste woman, who was a true devotee of Lord Krishna and how she got salvation by surrendering herself with undivided devotion to him which implied the indispensability of a guru for a devotee. In the Gita, Arjuna represents the perplexed materialistic person who surrenders to a guru. He did not go to anyone else. So the real guru is Krishna who is guru not only to Arjuna but also to everyone[3].

Gurubad and Srimanta Sankardeva

Sankardeva did not take initiation from any guru although he had high respect for Sridhara Swami of Puri and also Kabir. But he could realise the importance of a guru in the life of a devotee. In the Bhakti Ratnakar, he says that without a guru a devotee cannot conquer or control his mind. Only a guru can liberate him from all troubles and show him the right path in all matters[4]. He even discusses certain qualities which a guru must possess. Thus he must be a man of character and must have the ability to control his mind. At the same time, he must have mastery over the religious texts so that he can remove all doubts from the mind of a devotee regarding any question of salvation. Besides, he must be man of justice and free from pride and all kinds of temptations.

Sastraka janaya matra nuhike bhakat
Tara upadeshe budha nopaje lokat
Jadiba bhakat huwe sastra najanay
Nepare Khandite tebe sisyar samsaya
Eteke uttam guru ashraya kariba
Krishnata bhakati kari sansara tariba[5]

Srimanta Sankardeva could give the best explanation of the Hindu religious scriptures and could remove all doubts; therefore he alone deserved to be regarded as 'Guru'. His unalloyed disciple Madhavdeva has stated in his 'Namo ghosa' as follows:

Sankare samsaya chedi sastara tattvaka bhedi
Pracarila Krishnara Bhakati
Tanaka eri ki karan anaka bolaya guru
Kino loka moha mudhamati *(Namaghosa, 54)*

(Having cut asunder the doubts and penetrating to the essential principle of the scriptures has Sankara preached devotion to Krishna. I do not understand how people leave him aside and call others guru. Oh! How foolish and deluded people are).

Gurubad: Reflection in the life of Madhavdeva and his followers

It was Madhavdeva, who not only emphasised on the importance of Guru in the life of a devotee but also practiced it in his life. He added the element of guru to the three elements *Deva*, *Nama* and *Bhakata* already introduced by Sankaradeva. It formed the fundamentals of Assam Vaisnavism. He hailed Sankardeva as unique personality and repository of all good qualities to whom prostrated a million times out of intense devotion.

Jaya guru sankara sarvagunakara
Jakeri nahike upama

Tohari charane renu satakoti
Bareka karuho pronam[6].

He said that Sankara was like a kalpataru or wish yielding tree to his devotees and there was no one superior to him as guru. (Srimanta Sankara hari bhakatara, Jana Jena kalpataru tahanta binayee nai nai amara param guru)[7].

In the Guru Bhatima Madhavdeva says that without a guru nothing could be accomplished as only the guru can show the devotees the real path of salvation (Vine guru charane bhakati rakati mukuti kabahu nahoi)[8].

At the time of taking initiation from Madhavdeva, Gopaldeva put him two questions, first as to why sravana and kirtana were considered the best of the nine ways to attain salvation and how one can follow this; secondly, how one can serve his guru? It is related in the biography of Gopaldeva that Madhavdeva answered these questions referring to Sankardeva who said that *gurusewa* or serving one's guru is the best religion. A true devotee must always obey his guru and perform sravana and kirtana taking the name of his guru in his heart. Gopaldeva was so much satisfied with the discussion he had with Madhavdeva that he considered serving guru's wife and children also as equivalent to serving one's guru. In his biography it is described as follows:

Jata dharma ache sabato karia
Guru sewa sesthatar
Guru putra guru bhajyaka sevite
Guruse sewa hai.[9]

Gopaldeva considered that by intense devotion to both Sankardeva and Madhavdeva one can get mukti or salvation. Thus he says,

Namu Sankardeo Madhava Sahete duiyu
Mura esta guru duyujan
Madhavara sikyadhari bhakti vabe bhaju hari
Bandu hena Bhaktara charan[10].
Sankara Madhava Abheda Iswara
Guru nuhe duita pare,
Duhanu namara Kirtana karia
Kitya kitya huwe nare[11].

Once Pursuttom Thakur abused Gopaldeva in the presence of the later's disciple Ramachandra. Ramachandra unable to tolerate the aspersions cast on his guru violently struck his head against a solid slab of stone and as result sustained injury in his head which caused profuse bleeding[12]. Gopaldeva was so much devoted to his guru Madhavdeva that he was ever ready to perform any kind of job for him. He was a good architect but gave up three houses he built at Barpeta Satra's campus one after another at the suggestion of his guru for the use of bhakatas[13]. He digged a well with Sriram Ata and others and removed the problem of water of Kalindi, the wife of Sankardeva as ordered by his guru Madhavdeva.

The tradition of *gurusewa* had highly influenced Gopaldeva'a daughter Padmapriya, the first woman poet of Assam, who composed a number of devotional songs. She added the name of Gopaldeva to Sankardeva and Madhavdeva and considered all three as representation of God. She said guru is God and God is guru (Guru Brahma Guru Bishnu Gurudeva Maheshwara)[14].

Srimanta Sankara Srimanta Madhava
Srimanta Gopaldeva
Tinio Iswara eku vinna nai
Pawe pari karu sev.[15]

The same feelings are expressed by Bar Jadumanideva, the founder of Bansbari Satra in 1584[16], who was a disciple of Gopaldeva. In the same way, Anirudhadeva, the founder of Mayamara Satra and one of the most trusted disciples of Gopaldeva places Gopaldeva on line with Sankardeva and Madhavdeva and considered all three as his guru. In his Bhakti Mongol Ghosa he writes as follows: *"Gopalese esta guru suhrida parama deva Gopalata pare nahe ana. Tahenta charane pasi nirmala bhakati rati diyuka tana charanate thana*." In the 5th Skandha of Bhagawata (n. 582), he explains that unless one listens to the exposition of the religious texts from the mouth of a guru, he would not be able to cultivate Bhakti and make distinction between right and wrong. In the Bhakti Mongol Ghosa (v.127) he states that the guru is the image of God and it is only he who can remove all confusions regarding Bhakti from the mind of devotee and explain to him all matters relating to God[17].

Most of the hymns composed by Aniruddadeva echo his veneration for the guru. According to him, one who learns the greatness of the chanting the name of the God by the grace of his Guru is unequalled in the three worlds *(guru charanara anugraha laiya jijane jane namake, kahe Aniruddha tini lokata, same kona sijananta)* (Bhakti Mongol Ghosa, VV. 341-353)[18]. Guru can help the devotee to make himself free from the bondage of worldly pleasure and make him conscious of the value of human life and show him the right path of salvation. He believes guru cannot die because guru is an image of God. The disciples of Aniruddhadeva used to cut the doors of their houses through gable ends only, because if they did it on the side walls which were very low, they would be required to lower their heads, which go against their customs of not bowing their heads to anyone except their guru. A custom still prevails among the disciples of Kalasamhati Satra's according to which every disciple who visit his guru's house brings with him a gift to the guru (*gurur grihaloi jaba, huda hate najaba*). So, unstinted was their devotion to their guru that two Mayamara disciples lost their lives in undergoing a test taken by the Ahom king Pratap Singha (1603-41) in which four of them were asked to gallop their horses against swords placed horizontally to their necks. To vindicate the insults heaped upon their guru by the Ahom Government, the Mayamarayas rose into the rebellion in 1769. Their war cry was "*Mari yaon mari yaon guru en suji yaon*", I will kill or get myself killed and thus repay my debt to my guru. Such a rebellion had never happened before. The Mayamarayas believe that an ideal *guru* is an image of God. He cannot die. He simply changes his human form. Therefore when a guru dies, the disciple say, *"terar icha hal or terai nat lila Samarile"* meaning he wants to depart or close the drama of his life.

The reasons for which gurubad received an extreme form in Mayamara Satra may be due to the reason that bulk of the disciples of these satras were backward communities, mostly tribals. When Aniruddhadeva forbade the worship of any kind of *bigraha* or idol, they must have been looking for something visible to worship as deity. In the absence of this, the devotees considered the guru himself as the living embodiment of God and worshipped him accordingly. Any insult done to the guru, they considered as done to their own persons and they became determined to avenge it. Indeed Gurubad played a vital role in the Assamese society during the medieval period.

References

Baruah Harinarayan Dutta : Bhakti Pradip (ed) Guwahati, 2000, p. 6.

Baruah S.L: Life and Teachings of Sri Sri Aniruddhadeva (ed), Dibrugarh University, 2004, p. 180.

Bhattacharya S: Asamar Satra Parichay (ed), Jorhat, 2004, p. 280.

Dewan M : Buranji Vivek Ratna (ed.), Saikia N, Department of Assamese, Dibrugarh University, 2003, p. 77.

Dutta S: The Mataks and their Kingdom: Castes and Tribes of Assam, Allahabad, 1985, p. 59.

Mahanta M.C and N. Bordoloi : Mahapurush Sri Sri Gopaldeva Carit, (eds.), Jorhat, 1978, p. 29

Mahanta N : Sri Sri Gopaldevar Geet Ghosa aru Padmapriya Air Geet Ghosa, (ed), Nazira, 1998, p. 69.

Mahanta N: Sri Sri Gopaldevar Geet Ghosa aru Padmapriya Air Geet Ghosa, (ed), Nazira, 1998, p. 64.

Ibid., p. 66.

Mahapurush Madavdevar Bakyamrit : Srimanta Sankardeva Sangha, (ed.) Nogaon, 1994, p. 201.

Mahapurush Madavdevar Bakyamrit : Srimanta Sankardeva Sangha, (ed.) Nogaon, 1994, p. 202.

Neog M : Kirtan Ghosa aru Namghosa, (ed.) Guwahati, 1962, p. 182.

Pathak G: Mahapurush Sri Sri Gopaldeva Carit, Borpeta Satrar Itihas, Borpeta, 2003, p. 144.

Prabhupada Swami: The Journey of Self-Discovery, The Bakti Vedanta Book Trust, New Delhi, 1993, p. 36.

Sarma S.N: The Neo Vaisnavite Movement and the Satra Institution of Assam, Guwahati, 1999, pp. 122-123.

Thakur Ramcharan : Ratnakara Bhakti (Trans), Jorhat, 1949, p. 6.

Ibid., p. 6.

3

Indian Buddhist Tradition and Literature in Tibet

Rituparna Ghosh

Abstract

Tibet, known to most of us as the Hidden Land, the Mystic Land, the Forbidden Land, or the Land of Lâmas is still the most isolated and impenetrable country in the world. Located in the heart of Asia, the country, Tibet is a unique nation. As many of great countries on the planet, Tibetan people not only have great cultural traditions, profound philosophy and sophisticated language and literature but also have very rich and wonderful religion, the Buddhist religion, which is deeply rooted in Indian Mahâyâna Buddhist tradition.

Twelve centuries after the Buddha's Mahâparinirvâna, Buddhism crossed the Himalayan ranges and reached Tibet, the Land of Snow, in the 7th century A.D. In the following centuries Buddhism penetrated into all aspects of Tibetan life and culture and Tibetan people found in the teaching of Gautama the Buddha a source of deep peace, happiness and fulfilment.

Keywords: *Avalokiteúvara, Bu-ston, Úâkyamuni, Nâlandâ, Buddhism, Bon*

Just as Indian history begins to be recorded in writing from the days of the great Buddhist emperor, Asoka, Tibetan history, too, begins to be written down from the reign of Tibet's most gifted ruler, *Sron-btsan-sgam-po* (born in 617 A.D.),[1] who is historically the starting point of the Indo-Tibetan contact.

It is quite remarkable that Buddhism have come from India to Tibet, but between India and Tibet, there is a tremendous barricade, the Himalayas. The two countries are therefore practically cut of from each other. They are also different climate and environment, different inhabitants and ways of life different economy and so on. But, strange after these vast differences between them, the Tibetans choose to accept the Indian Buddhism. According to Sangharakshita, "it was not that one day someone went from India to Tibet and preached Buddhism and then few years later the Tibetans were all Buddhists. The Tibetans, specially the Tibetan nobles put up considerable resistance and the establishment of Buddhism as the religion of Tibet was a long and sometimes difficult process".[2]

When Indian Buddhism reached Tibet, it encountered the ancient native religion called *Bon* and also completely different culture and way of life. The follower of this ancient religion of Tibet is called a *Bon-po*. S.C. Das says "The ancient religion *Bon* was fetishism, demon-worship and propitiation by means of incantations, which was followed by Tibetans before the introduction of Buddhism"[3]. *Bon* was a type of Shamanism in which the spirits of the sun, moon, mountains and trees were worshipped. For several centuries Buddhism and *Bon* were in conflict with one to another in Tibet. Buddhism emerged as victor but *Bon* has remained a living tradition until the present day. As a result of its encounter with Buddhism, *Bon* underwent deep and lasting changes. Buddhism also had a profound effect on the political situation in Tibet. Part of the reason for its dramatic and almost total success within the country was because of the reverence and devotion of some of Tibet's greatest kings toward the teaching and principles of Buddhism. In giving an account of the development of Buddhism in Tibet, we must consider the activities of these, because their support and patronage was crucial to the spread of Buddhism in Tibet.

The very common myth in Tibet about the advent of the population and first king of Tibet-came originally from India. Surprisingly, the Tibetan historians try to substantiate even these claims by scriptural evidences, by which are meant the evidences of *Mahâyâna* texts.[4] Tibetans have traditionally considered their ancestors to be of Indian origin. A popular myth of early Tibet also contends that its first king came from India. According to *Bu-ston*, an ancient king named *Rûpati* was also military commander of the *Kaurava* army. *Rûpati* led his soldiers in a war against the *Pândavas*. After suffering defeat, the king fled to the northeast and established Tibet, and their descendants were the Tibetans. S.C. Das says that "after migrating to Tibet, Tibetan people welcomed *Rûpati* as their king and then by his gentle behaviour he won their affection and ruled over them for many years"[5]. One account notes that King *Shar-ba's* son was born with unusual marks, webbed fingers and eyelids closing from below, and so was cast into the Ganges in a box. Rescued by peasants, the child grew up and ran off in grief to the Himalayas, where he became the ruler of Tibet. The Tibetans carried him on their shoulders with high esteem; he, therefore, was called *Nathi-tsanpo* or *gNa'-khri btsan-po,* 'the neck-chaired Mighty One'. It was he who became the first king of Tibet. According to legend, he built Tibet's first house and began introducing Indian civilization. He and lineage of kings that descended from him extended their control over the whole Tibet. This lineage came to be known as the *Chogyal* dynasty. Some sources tell such a story about the fifth son of *Bimbisâra'*s youngest son, while other theories say the Tibetan king was the fifth son of *Prasenajit* or the son of *Œuddhodana*, father of *Úâkyamuni* Buddha; some favour the lineage of *Úatânîka (dMag-brgyad-pa*), father of King *Shar-ba* of Vatsa[6]. According to *Bu-ston* and *Sum-pa*, another origin myth asserts that Tibetan people descended from a male monkey, who was, an incarnate of the *Avalokiteœvara*. Following Rockhill, Waddell says that the name given to this monkey ancestor is *Hilumandju*, "evidently intended for *Hanumânji,* the Hindu monkey-god".[7]

S.C. Das says that "during the reigns of twenty six generations of kings, counted from *Nathi-tsanpo* the first of Tibetan kings to *Namri-sron-tsan* Buddhism was unknown in Tibet". He also says that "in the 27th generation of the royal succession that the *Bon* religion rose to the zenith of its power and when the sun of Buddhism was sinning in its meridian lustre all over *Jambudvîpa,* snow-girdled Tibet remained buried in the impenetrable darkness of *Bon* mysticism".[8]

In 441 A.D.[9] the 28th king of the *Chogyal* Dynasty, *Lha-Tho-thori-Òan-tsan,* who was the well-known as an incarnation on *Samanta Bhadra*, [10] received some Buddhist scriptures and religious objects from heaven. He did not understand the meaning of the scriptures but perceived that they and the sacred objects were things of great value and treated them with great reverence. As the king, sitting in council with his ministers, was debating on the value and merit of the divine gift, there was heard a voice from heaven, saying that in the fifth generation the meaning of the contents should be revealed. This was the first appearance of Buddhist scriptures in Tibet.

To the 32 ruler, *Namri SroE-tsan*, a son was born in A.D.600/ 617[11]. He was named *Tri SroE-tsan,* better known in later days as *SroE-tsan Gampo*, who seems to have been a remarkable man. Tibet enters her classical age from the period of this noble king, who may be described as first sovereign ruler of Tibet. He was really one of the greatest kings of Tibet under whose leadership the Tibetans moved from barbarism to civilization.[12] According to traditional histories, the definitive establishment of Buddhism in Tibet occurred during the reign of *SroE-tsan Gampo,* later he was portrayed as the first three *Chai gyel (chos rgyal*), or 'Religious Kings'. He is considered to have been an incarnation of *MahâkâruGi-Avalokiteœvara*, who took rebirth as a king in order to further the dissemination of Dharma.

The 33rd emperor of Tibet had unified all regions of Tibet as one great nation and he had conquered many neighbouring countries. "Thirteen years of age", says *Bu-ston*, "he ascended the throne and brought under his power all the petty chieftains of the borderland who offered him presents and sent their message of submission"[13]. But this success was not sufficient for *SroE-tsan Gampo*. Sangharakshita says that, "at the time Tibet was surrounded by a number of highly civilized states. All these states were Buddhist in those days. *SroE-tsan Gampo* saw that although Tibet was politically united and in military terms a force to be reckoned with, where civilization and culture were concerned she very much lagged behind all her neighbours, king had observed that the culture of the surrounding countries was very closely linked with Buddhism, and this led him to decide that Buddhism should be introduced in Tibet."[14]

The story of Tibet moves in the 7th century from colourful legend into the realm of history. The change is the result of two new arrivals — Indian Buddhist tradition and literature. While yet very young *SroE-tsan Gampo* evinced great intelligence and sagacity in dealing with his dependent princes and improving friendship with independent potentates. By his exertions the prosperity of the country of *Himavat* increased. Till then there existed no written language in Tibet, and did not have a cultural tradition. The king keenly felt its want especially when it was found that his Court had no means to reply to the messages of foreign potentates. His people were ignorant of the arts and sciences of the Indians and Chinese. He had learnt many of the border languages, which helped him in conducting conversation with the Indian and Chinese ambassadors. He acquired a fair knowledge of the Sanskrit, Palpa (Newari) and Chinese[15]. These rare qualifications and especially his inclination towards Buddhism, made people believe him to be an incarnation of some divinity. He devoted his attention to the propagation of Buddhism in Tibet. He clearly saw that a written language was most essential to the establishment of religion, and more particularly to the institution of laws for the good of the people, and that as long as this all-important want remained unsupplied, no success in either could be ensured.

According to Tibetan historian *SroE-tsan Gampo* was also inspired to the work for Buddhism by his two wives, — a Nepalese princess and a Chinese princess. The talented young prince, *SroE-tsan Gampo* suffering from a sense of isolation and inferiority, must have felt keenly the urge to find all possible ways of removing the backwardness of his people, because when he came to the throne he determinedly increased his military prestige to such an extent, that King *ACœuvarman* of Nepal in the South, and later the powerful Chinese emperor, *T'aitsung*, in the North, thought it wise to seek an alliance with him and respect his ardent wishes by giving their own royal princesses to him in marriage. These two queens, *Bhrûkuti* of Nepal and *Wen-Ch'eng* of China, bringing with them to Lhasa the images of *Akcobhya, Maitreya* and *Úâkyamuni* as gifts from their respective homes, greatly helped him achieve his ambition to bring his people to the forefront of civilization by introducing Buddhism into Tibet.[16]

According to Tibetan historians, both these princesses were devout Buddhists and it was because of their influence that *SroE-tsan Gampo* became a convert to Buddhism. During the course of his reign he built first Buddhist temples in Tibet. *Bu-ston* refers to the image of eleven-faced *Avalokiteœvara* brought from South India for the spread of Buddhism in Tibet. It has been said that writing language, of course literature was not existent in Tibet till the reign of king *SroE-tsan Gampo*. Through his endeavours the art of writing and literature were introduced in Tibet. *SroE-tsan Gampo's* zeal for introducing literacy into Tibet, according to Tibetan historians, led him to send a team of chosen Tibetans headed by Thonmi *Sambhom*a to India, from were literacy was brought to Tibet. After returning to Tibet he propitiated *Mañjuúrî*, the god of learning and framed the system of written language into Tibet and composed the great grammatical work called '*Sum Chu dag-yig*'. So that he came to be recognized for all time as the father of Tibetan literature.[17]. After the introduction of writings language in Tibet a huge number of Indian texts were translated into Tibetan. These texts in translation have been looked upon by Tibetans as their sacred heirloom and kept in the monasteries all over their country as holy articles of daily worship. The Tibetan translated Indian literature, chiefly Buddhist, have been preserved in two great collections known as the *Kanjur* and *Tanjur*, somewhat similar to the *Œruti* and the *Sm[ti* of the ancient Indian literature[18]. The king invited scholars from India, Nepal and china. Besides these literary activities *SroE-tsan Gampo* encouraged the Indian Buddhist art and architecture in Tibet.

The great king *Sron-tsan*, was the first to have introduced legal codes into Tibet prescribed by Buddhism. S.C. Das gives a list of his 16 ethico-legal codes. The king ordered the intelligent class of people to be taught the art of reading and writing, and many Sanskrit Buddhist books to be translated into Tibetan, and thus he laid the foundation of Buddhism in Tibet. According to tradition, the very first text to be translated was the *Mani kabum*. *Mani* here refers to the *om mani padme hûm* mantra and *kabum* means 100,000 words, the text being a sort of encyclopaedia about the mantra.[19] Then started one of the bright histories of the Tibetan translated literature. *Sron-tsan Gampo's* work did not come to an end when he died. More and more texts were translated from Indian languags into tibatan. Alaka Chattopadhyaya tell us that "literacy began in Tibet with the beginning there of the spread of Buddhism and as inseparably related to it. The pioneers of Tibetan education had their own education in India, presumably at some Buddhist *vihâra*. The Tibetan script was modelled on Indian script, the Tibetan grammar on Indian grammar. Throughout the subsequent history of Tibet education remained primarily Buddhist. Knowledge of Buddhism was the highest mark of Tibetan learning and at least up to the 14th century the translation of an Indian text under an Indian *pandita* was the peak of academic ambition for a Tibetan scholar"[20].

Thus the great king practically created Tibetan culture at least in its rudimentary from. In fact, *Sron-tsan Gampo's* interest in Buddhism appears to have been more cultural than religious. Historically, the Indo-Tibetan cultural contact starts since the reign of the first historical king *Sron-tsan Gampo*. He laid the foundations of the Tibetan nation, of its culture and literature and of Tibetan Buddhism itself- surely a very considerable achievement for one man. The Tibetan people show their gratitude to their Dharma king and his two said queens even to this day by regarding them as a manifestation of the great *bodhisattva Avalokiteœvara* and *tara*, who had come for the introduction of Buddhist tradition in Tibet.

Naturally, Indian Buddhism entered directly and played an important part in Tibet. Indeed, *Nâlandâ* University was a seat of great learning in ancient India. Most of the Buddhist scholars learnt and taught from *Nâlandâ* and contributed their own scholastic works, which were preserved in *Nâlandâ* Unversity library. Unfortunately, almost everything was destroyed. As a result, we have lost almost all priceless Buddhist texts, which were written in Sanskrit.

The Tibetan became prolific translators of Indian Buddhist texts from the seventh century CE and continued this process as long as it was possible for them to obtain texts from India – through Tibetans who visited India or from Indian teachers –up to about the early fourteenth century CE. It is for this reason that the Tibetan translations of Indian texts are so important for a complete understanding of the development of Indian Buddhist philosophy during this period of lost Indian history.

References

Bapat, p.v. (1959). *25oo years of Buddhism*, Delhi. Publication Division, p. 65.

Sangharakshita. (2010). *Tibetan Buddhism an Introduction*. New Delhi. New age books, p. 18.

Chattopadhyaya, Alaka. (1967.) *Atisa and Tibet.* Delhi. Motilal Banarsidass Publishers Pvt. Ltd., p. 164.

Ibid., p.151.

Ibid., p.1562.

Yeshe De Project. (1986). *Ancient Tibet*. Berkeley,USA. Dharma Publishing, p. 142.

Chattopadhyaya, Alaka. (1967.) *Atisa and Tibet.* Delhi. Motilal Banarsidass Publishers Pvt. Ltd., p. 152.

Ibid., p. 164.

Das, Sarat, Chandra. (1894). *Tibetan studies.* Calcutta. K.P. Bagchi and Company, p. 30.

Sharma S.K. and Sharma Usha. (1997). *Religious Heritage of Tibet*. New Delhi. Anmol publications Pvt.Ltd., p. 55.

Das, Sarat, Chandra. (1894). *Tibetan studies.* Calcutta. K.P. Bagchi and Company, p. 32.

Chattopadhyaya, Alaka. (1967). *Atisa and Tibet.* Delhi. Motilal Banarsidass Publishers Pvt. Ltd., p. 180.

Ibid., p. 182.

Sangharakshita. (2010). *Tibetan Buddhism an Introduction*. New Delhi. New age books, p. 19.

Das, Sarat, Chandra. (1894). *Tibetan studies.* Calcutta. K.P. Bagchi and Company, p. 33.

Bapat, P.V. (1959). *2500 years of Buddhism*, Delhi Publication Division, p. 65.

Ibid., p. 66.

Pathak Suniti kumar, (1974). *The Indian nitisastras in Tibet.* Delhi. Motilal Banarsidass, p. xii.

Sangharakshita, (2010). *Tibetan Buddhism an Introduction*. New Delhi. New Age Books, p. 20.

Chattopadhyaya, Alaka. (1967). *Atisa and Tibet.* Delhi. Motilal Banarsidass Publishers Pvt. Ltd., p. 145.

Bapat, P.V., (1959). *2500 years of Buddhism*, Delhi. Publication Division.

Banerjee, Anukul Chandra. (1973). *Buddhism in India and Abroad*. Calcutta. The World Press Private Ltd.

Bell, Charles. (1990). *Tibet past and present*. New Delhi. Munshiram Manoharlal Publishers Pvt.Ltd.

Bu-ston. (1931-1932). *History of Buddhism*. 2 Vols, Tr. From Tibetan by D.E. Oberamiller, Heidllberg.

Chattopadhyaya, Alaka. (1967). *Atisa and Tibet.* Delhi. Motilal Banarsidass Publishers Pvt. Ltd.

Das, Sarat, Chandra (1893). *Indian pandits in the Land of Snow*. Calcutta. Baptist mission press.

Das, Sarat, Chandra. (1894). *Tibetan studies.* Calcutta. K.P. Bagchi and Company.

Dutt, Nalinaksha. (1973). *Mahâyâna Buddhism*. Culcutta. Firma K.L. Mukhopadhyay.

Ligeti Louis, (1984). *Tibetan and Buddhist studies*. New Delhi. Munshiram Manoharlal Publishers Pvt. Ltd.

Power John, (1995). *Introduction to Tibetan Buddhism*. Newyork. Snow Lion Publication.

Pathak Suniti kumar. (1974). *The Indian nitisastras in Tibet*. Delhi. Motilal Banarsidass.

Roerich, G.N. (1988). *(The) Blue Annals*. Delhi, Motilal Banarsidass.

Sangharakshita. (2010). *Tibetan Buddhism an Introduction*. New Delhi. New Age Books.

Sanyal P.K. (2004). *Golden age of Tibet*. Varanasi.Sanjay book centre.

Sharma S.K. and Sharma Usha. (1997). *Religious Heritage of Tibet*. New Delhi. Anmol publications Pvt.Ltd.

Sinha Nirmal C. (1975). *An introduction to the history and religion of Tibet.* Calcutta. Amibica Charan Bose.

Waddell, L.A. (1895). *Buddhism of Tibet or Lamaism*. London, Asian Publishers.

Yeshe De Project. (1986). *Ancient Tibet*. Berkeley, USA. Dharma Publishing.

4

The Confluence of Souls: The Bhakti Philosophy of the Hindus and the Sufis

Trishna Banerjee

Abstract

The life of a human being attains its fulfilment when the body is united with the soul. It is man's insatiate demand for material prosperity and success that leads to mutual hatred and antagonism. On the other hand, when the same man could realize the bonding of his soul with his fellow being, it marks the end of all disharmony, and consequently brings mutual love, peace and toleration. From its antiquity, India had witnessed the birth and growth of different religious traditions on its soil. Interestingly, all these religions, though diverse in their character and forms, were one in their ideals and philosophies. They unanimously preached the union of human hearts and soul irrespective of class, caste, religion and community. The great sages and saints of our country preached that only a man's self-less love towards his fellow being could make him realize the spiritual pleasure, as divinity resides in every human soul. Thus, the different cultures and religious sects which came to India and mingled with its tradition and custom had enriched the Hindu culture, and provided the depth in its philosophy. Though political leaders in India were engaged in bloody wars for personal aggrandizement, the general mass could somehow find solace in the preachings of these saints and sages—both Hindus and Muslims. The doctrine of love, peace and unity, which had been advocated by these sages, had kept the faith alive in the internal union of hearts, in spite of the political strife and upheaval.

Keywords: *Bhakti Movement, Sufis, Songs, Communal Harmony, Hermitages, Khanqah*

The Bhakti Movement in medieval India came into being as a result of the socio-political conflict of the Hindus and the Muslims. This movement had consequently played a crucial role in building harmony between these two religious sects. Along with the Hindu saints and reformers, the other religious preachers who dedicated their lives in spreading the message of unity and peace, and in the well-being of the humanity were the Muslim Sufis. Talking about the combined effort of the Hindu *Sants* and the Muslim Sufis in reforming the medieval Indian society, Shahabuddin Iraqi commented:

> *The Bhakti Movement was led by the people of socially backward classes whose inner urge coincided with the liberal ideas of the Sufis. It was for this reason that both groups worked not for their personal ends but for the spiritual culture of all humanity. They played a vital role in bringing people closer to one other. There were many Sufi Shaikhs and Bhakti gurus who were equally popular among the Hindus and the Muslims, and there was an effective literary and cultural interaction between the two communities. (p. 245)*

From the beginning of the Muslim rule in India, the Sufis came to live in the country and started to make a great impact on its socio-cultural life. The name 'Sufi' originated from the Arabic word, 'safa', which means purity. The Sufis were the true mystics. Abandoning all external rituals and worldly pleasures, they preached the purity of the inner human soul and led a life of renunciation. These sages first established their habitation in the Sindh and Punjab regions. The two Sufi sects, which gained prominence in the Mogul period in India were the "Chishti" and the "Surabardi" (Silsila) sects. Beside these two sects, the "Kadiri" and "Nakashbandi" Sufis too settled in India and advocated their philosophy of mysticism. The Chishtis were prominent in Delhi, Uttar Pradesh, Rajasthan, Punjab, Bihar, Orissa and South India; whereas, the Surabardi Sufis mostly settled in Sindh, Multan and in certain regions of Punjab. The most notable Sufi-saints of medieval India included Khwaja Mainuddin Chishti, Khwaja Fariduddin Masud Ganjeshkar, Shah-Jalal Tabareji, Shekh Jalaluddin Tarbiji, Jalaluddin Rumi, Bahauddin Jakariya, Shekh Nizamuddin Auliya, Shah Abdul Latif and others.

Since their arrival in India from the tenth century onwards, there developed a harmonious relation between the Hindu saints and the Muslim Sufis. Both these communities mutually shared with each other's culture, religion, custom and tradition. This consequently helped in bridging the gulf between the Hindus and the Muslims, which had already been widened by the bitter political feuds and antagonisms. Regarding the religious and philosophical interactions that took place between the Hindu sages and the Sufis, Shahabuddin Iraqi stated:

> *The Early exposition of spiritual thought found in the Upanishads formed an ideological bridge between Vaishnavism and Sufism. The Sufis of several orders were*

> *so impressed by Indian thought and practices that some adopted these ideas ... Similarly, some Kayasthas, Khatris, Kashmiri Pandits, and Sindhi Amils adopted Muslim culture, cultivated Persian language and literature, and participated in the administration of Islamic states. (p. 241)*

The Chishti Sufis used to pay regular visits to the Hindu saints and shared many spiritual and religious thoughts with them. In fact, they had a great respect to the Hindu rituals and customs. Khwaja Mainuddin Chishti was the founder of the Chishti sect of Sufism. He was born in 1142 at Sistan in Afghanistan. He came to North India in 1193 and lived for a while in Delhi. From Lahore he came to Ajmer, which he chose as his place of worship. In 1236 he died in Ajmer and was also buried there. Later on, this holy place came to be known as "Ajmer Sharif."

Shekh Jalaluddin Tarbiji was one of the most notable Sufi saints. He used to spend most of his time in singing Bhakti songs with his disciples. The poor and the destitute were given food in his hermitage. His dissemination of the Bhakti philosophy in North Bengal made a great impact on the contemporary socio-cultural life. Along with the Muslims, the Hindus too paid a great respect to this Sufi saint. It was due to his influence that the worshipping of Satyapir was initiated in the Hindu culture. The Persian Sufi poet Jalaluddin Rumi was born on 1207. He composed a lot of poems and songs in the Persian language and thus drew the people towards the Bhakti cult. Rumi believed that in the Kingdom of God, all the people are one and there is no place of class or caste prejudices.

Bahauddin Jakariya was the founder of the Surabardi sect. He was born on 1227 in Multan. Like Jalaluddin Tarbiji, he too served the poor and the helpless. He was also a great musician and composed a number of *ragas*, like 'Multani Dhanasri' and others. Shekh Nizamuddin Auliya was born at Badayun, near Delhi. He was initiated to the Sufi theology by the sage, named Fariduddin Shakarganj. He preached the philosophy of Bhakti through the *bhajan* songs. Amir Khasru, who was the court poet of Mahammad Bin Tughlag in Delhi, studied under Nizamuddin's tutelage. In Nizamuddin's Dargah, many Hindu and Muslim devotees visit regularly till this day.

One of the major vehicles of the Bhakti Movement in India was Bhakti-*sangit* or the *Bhajans*. The great medieval sages preached their ideals, philosophies and thoughts of social reformation through the medium of *sangit*. According to them, music has a greater value than the *shastras* or the theological knowledge. Nizamuddin Auliya always urged his disciples to offer their prayer to God through music. He used to organize several religious and musical assemblies. Amir Khasru too participated in Nizamuddin's assemblies, which were the congregations of saints and sages of different religions and communities. One of the famous musical compositions of Nizamuddin is—

Parbata-bansa mangaba mere babul nike marba chhabare!
Sona Dinha, rupa dinha, babul dil dariyab re!

Amir Khasru composed a song which he dedicated to his guru, Nizamuddin:

Hazrat Nizamuddin Chishti
Jarjari Baksh Peer
Moyee Moyee Dhyabe Tayee Tayee
Phala Pabe
More Manki Murad Bhara Dijayi
Amir.

Shah Abdul Latif (1689-1752) was another renowned Sufi saint, who spent most of the years of his life in Laha Haveli, Kotri and Bhitshah of Hyderabad. Abdul Latif was a great composer and practitioner of Bhakti Music. People from different religions and communities used to visit him to hear his preachings. For both the Hindus and the Muslims, he built a shrine in Ahmadabad, named Bhitsharif. Till today, this shrine is regarded as the holy place for different religious communities and it appears as an embodiment of the Hindu-Muslim communal harmony. People from Sindh, Beluchistan, Rajputana, Punjab, Kashmir and from several other regions come to visit this shrine regularly to offer their prayer to God. Shah Latif was a true devotee of peace and love and his philosophy of Bhakti played an instrumental role in spreading the message of unity and communal harmony between the Hindus and the Muslims. Motilal Jotwani commented:

> *The religion of the saint-poet (i.e. of Shah Latif) even as of his other contemporary poets all over India was essentially of a man in direct relationship with God and not of a particular religious group looking towards the scriptural instructions and injunctions. As is abundantly evident from his poetry, he did not hold the traditional view of forming a part of any particular religious community. (p.116)*

To Shah Latif, it is the path of love which can lead man to realize the inner spirituality within every human soul. His conceptualization of the attainment of love was different and interesting, as he sang—

Kamuna so ashika kabej jehama tuhanji saraha thiye
Rin malamat ka mathe mor deha to tana diya.

It means— If you want to attain love, do not aspire to earn praises. Rather, try to face adversities of life and earn hatred from people. This could only lead you to the true path of love.

Along with the Sufi mystics, there were other notable Muslim saints who played crucial roles in spreading the Bhakti Movement in India. Among them Kabir (1440-1518) was the most influential figure. However, Kabir could not be called as a Hindu or a Muslim, rather he is regarded as a devoted worshipper of God, a saint-poet beyond all religions, creed or caste. Kabir was born in the household of a weaver in Varanasi. Later he became the disciple of Ramananda Swami. Throughout his life, Kabir had sung the songs of love and harmony. He became the epitome of Hindu-Muslim cultural integration and nurtured an ideal of communal harmony. Monotheism was the basis of his philosophy of Bhakti. Talking of Kabir's religious ideals, R.P. Tiwari wrote:

> *For him (i.e. Kabir) there was no distinction between man and man. He knew that the God of all religions is the same. He has said that if we explore our hearts we will find that there are both Rama and Rahim and we owe our existence to Ali and Rama and therefore we should show similar tenderness to all that lives. His outspokenness and bitter criticism of the deadening weight of rituals and complications of thought with which Brahmanism and Islam were overlaid was in reality prompted by his love for his fellow creatures. (p. 94)*

Kabir had a strong aversion to all forms of institutional religion. He orally composed his songs which were transcribed by his disciples. Many of Kabir's *dohas* are sung like *bhajans*. Kabir's preachings are now regarded with respect in diverse literary realms, including Hindi literature. Like other renowned poets, Rabindranath Tagore was highly influenced by Kabir's philosophy of monotheism. Tagore translated the Saint's hundred poems and named the collection— *One Hundred Poems of Kabir*. One of these famous translations is:

Original Song—

Mo ko kanha dhundo bande,
Main to tere pass me.
Na main debala, na main masjid,
Na kabe kailasa me.
Na tou koun kriya kamma me,
Nahi jog bairag me.
Khoji hoy to turate milihou,
Pal bharki talas me.
Kahain Kabir suno bhai sadho,
Sab sanso ki sans me.

Rabindranath Tagore's translation—

O Servant, where dost thou seek me?
Lo! I am beside thee.
I am neither in temple nor in mosque; I am neither in Kabba,
nor in Kailash.
Neither I am in rites and ceremonies, nor in Yoga and renunciation.
If thou art a true seeker, thou shalt at once see me;
thou shalt meet Me in a moment of time.
Kabir says, 'O Sadhu! God is the breath of all breath. (p.499)

Along with the Muslim saints and Sufis, the Hindu sages and *mahatmas* equally contributed in the dissemination of the Bhakti cult in medieval India. Guru Nanak was one of the most notable preachers of the Bhakti philosophy, and he was also the founder of Sikhism. Nanak was born in a place called Talmandi near Lahore in 1469 A.D. His compositions celebrate the glory of God and speak of religious harmony. The sermons and preachings of the five Gurus starting from Sri Guru Nanak to Guru Arjun Dev are compiled in *Sri Guru Granth Sahib*. This was the first and foremost holy book of Sikhism. These five Gurus are— Guru Nanak, Guru Angad, Guru Amardas, Guru Ramdas and Guru Arjun Dev. The Sikhs refer to the preachings of these Gurus as "Sabd" (teachings). Along with the sayings of the five Gurus, the *Granth Sahib* also embodies the preachings of several other saints, namely— Jaydev, Kabir, Namdev, Rabidas Trilochan, Ramananda, Paramananda and others. The sermons of these sages were compiled in order to be sung as songs, which are still in vogue.

Dadu (1544-1603) was another notable religious preacher of the Bhakti cult of medieval India. He was the disciple of Kabir's son, Kamal. He regarded both Hinduism and Islam with equal respect. His conceptualization of the "Brahma", reflected in his compositions, suggests that he regarded Brahma as his Guru. In fact, he conceived Brahma as the deity of all religious creed. In 1572, he organized "Brahma-sampraday" to spread the message of equality and religious harmony. Dadu composed almost four hundred *bhajans*. A deliberate mixing of Hindi and Rajasthani dialect is a unique feature of his compositions. He composed almost five thousand "Abhangs".

The chief purpose of the Bhakti Movement coordinated by the saints of medieval India was to disseminate truth. They did not believe in any particular religious creed, nor did they believe in the ritualistic conventions; rather they aimed to reform the society foregrounding the ideals of truth. They preached open perspectives and thoughts. They had no sense of Hindu-Muslim disintegration. They used to sing the notes of their own compositions liberating their minds from the artificial values of the society. Theirs was the song of universalism that reflected the ultimate truth. By birth, some of them were Hindus and some were Muslims. Yet, they did never resort to the ideals of differentiation.

It can be said that the role of such sages in human life is inspirational. Thus, if our present society can accommodate their ideals, the unity among diversity will be preserved forever, mind will be free from the narrow social constraints, and there will be the glorious emergence of national integration and communal harmony.

References

Iraqi, Shahabuddin. *Bhakti Movement in Medieval India: Social and Political Perspectives*. 1991. 106-16. Print.

1991. 87-95. Print.

Jotwani, Motilal. "Shah Abdul Latif." *Devotional Poets and Mystics*. Vol. II. New Delhi.

New Delhi: Manohar Books, 2009. Print. Publications Division, Ministry of Information and Broadcasting, Government of India.

Rabindranath Tagore. Ed. Sisir Kumar Das. Vol. I. New Delhi: Sahitya Akademi, 1994.

Tagore, Rabindranath. "*One Hundred Poems of Kabir*." The English Writings of *Tagore*.

Tiwari, R.P. "*Kabir.*" *Devotional Poets and Mystics*. Vol. I. New Delhi.

5

Spirituality in Buddhism: Relevance To Modern Aspect Through Education

Priyadarsini Mitra

Introduction

There are twelve recognized classical religions in our world. Buddhism is one of them. Buddhism is the indigenous religion in India.Buddhism is a pragmatic and humanistic religion among the twelve classical religions. In Buddhism Spiritualism is a process of transformation. This transformation is the transformation of mind. Buddhist spirituality is concerned with the end of suffering through spiritual path, the enlightened understanding of reality. According to Buddha, life is full of suffering but we can remove the suffering from our life after following the spiritual eight fold path and cultivation of wisdom and compassion which are spiritual practice. In Buddhism mind is the spiritual reality. If we guide our mind by our wholesome action and right knowledge then we will be happy and we will make others happy. For following the spiritual path we should also understand the Buddha's philosophical principle, three marks of existence. Education has a great role to make Buddhist spiritualism understandableand its practical importance in our present society.

Spiritualism in Buddhism

The term spirituality has a long and diverse character. Spirituality is derived from the Latin word '*spiritus*', spirit, the essential part of the person (Piles, 1990), which 'controls themind and the mind controls the body' (Neuman, 1995:48). Goddard (1995) proposed "spirituality as integrative energy", served to highlight its importance while at the same time seeking to transform its nature. Spirituality is a process of personal transformation, either in accordance with traditional religious ideals, or, increasingly, oriented on subjective experience and psychological growth independently of any specific religious context. In a more general sense, it may refer to almost any kind of meaningful wholesome activity or blissful experience. There is no single, widely-agreed definition for the concept. Every major religion follows the spiritualism. Buddhism is unique among the world's major world religions. Buddhism is the one world religion that has no God. It is an atheistic religion. In Buddhism Spirituality is a process of personal transformation. Buddhism describes a nonmaterial, spiritual reality which is pragmatic and humanistic because it is about us, our minds, and our suffering. Buddhist spiritual goal is the end of suffering through the enlightened understanding of reality.

Wali Ali Meyer of the Sufi Ruhaniat describes that process of "making ready" in these terms:"As Hazrat Inayat Khan says in no uncertain terms in *The Inner Life,* a person needs to be whole to take the journey. The point of this is to get your basic self in tune with your higher self. We are talking here about wounded psyches, fractured consciousness and dysfunction. Without addressing these issues, a person can become quite advanced in many ways and yet at a certain point find it necessary to self-destruct because she/he has not made a true accommodation in her/himself to sustain realization. Many of us started on the path even sneering at the psychological aspect of things, but had to go back to do such things as address our inner child, align the three selves, do a 12 step program, or some form of individual or group therapy."[1]

This same idea, the idea that we must prepare ourselves to be capable of manifesting the Divine Presence, is the very foundation of all religions including Buddhism. That is, in order to truly make significant spiritual progress we must be "clear", we must be empty of the little self. Many people are fighting for freedom, but all too often our battles are fought outside, when the greatest battle is the personal conquest which must happen within.

Buddhism is a teaching of transforming. It transforms our understanding of ourselves and our world. It gives rise to a broader and more inclusive perspective. It changes attitudes and intellectual horizons. Particularly it transforms our human relations and how we deal with people. Buddhism is not something to be merely believed like a set of doctrine and beliefs. It is not simply a ritual or a set of rules to follow. It is a spiritual force that works in our lives.

Enlightenment in principle means transformation, bodhi or awakening. We waken to the truth. We wake up from ignorance, delusions, greed, hatreds and prejudices. For avoiding all this negative approaches wisdom and compassion should be cultivated in person's mind. Buddha was the first person in the world who proclaimed that one is indeed one's own master. He told that one's mind is the forerunner of one's action. So if a person's mind wants then a person can acquire the spiritual life by following the Buddha's eightfold paths.

> *"Mind is the forerunner of all (evil) conditions.*
> *Mind is their chief, and they are mind-made.*
> *If, with an impure mind, one speaks or acts,*
> *Then suffering follows one*
> *Even as the cart wheel follows the hoof of the ox.*
> *Mind is the forerunner of all (good) conditions.*
> *Mind is their chief, and they are mind-made.*
> *If, with a pure mind, one speaks or acts,*
> *Then happiness follows one*
> *Like a never-departing shadow."*[2]

These words, which are the opening lines of the Dhammapada, werc spoken by Gotama Buddha 2500 years ago. The central theme of these verses is the human mind. We are the master of our own mind. So if we can guide our mind after following the Buddha's spiritual path then we will achieve Buddhist spiritual goal.

Four Noble Truths for being a Spiritual Seeker

The teachings on the four noble truths are among the very first of many teachings that Buddha preached in Sarnathafter attaining *enlightenment* in Bodhgaya. These teachings are known to contain the essence of the Buddhist spiritual path. The Four Noble Truths is the four fundamental principles of nature (Dhamma) that emerged from the Buddha's honest and penetrating assessment of the human condition and that serve to define the entire scope of Buddhist practice. These Truths are not fixed dogmatic principles, but living experiences to be explored individually in the heart of the sincere spiritualseeker:

1. *The Noble Truth of dukkha (suffering):*

life is fundamentally fraught withunsatisfactoriness and disappointment of every description; Suffering is a fact of life. There are four unavoidable physical sufferings; birth, old age, sickness and death. There are also three forms of mental suffering; separation from the people we love; contact with people we dislike and frustration of desires. Happiness is real and comes in many ways, but happiness does not last forever and does not stop suffering. Buddhists believe that the way to end suffering is to first accept the fact that suffering is actually a fact of life.Buddha's discovery of the solution of suffering began with the recognition that life is suffering. This is the first of the Four Noble Truths.

When the Buddha said that there is suffering in life, He also spoke about happiness. According to Buddha happiness is real but impermanent because it does not last forever and when happiness fades it leads to suffering. Buddhists learn that many people try to escape from the suffering in life by distracting themselves with temporary pleasures. There are many examples of people who try to block out sadness, pain, loss and grief by indulging in pleasures they think will bring happiness but actually end up disguising their real feelings, and making them feel even worse when the temporary happiness runs out. "Suffering is a big word in Buddhist thought. It is a key term and it should be thoroughly understood.

The Pali word is dukkha, and it does not just mean the agony of the body. It means that deep subtle sense of unsatisfactoriness which is a part of every mind moment and which results directly from the mental treadmill. The essence of life is suffering, said the Buddha. At first glance this seems exceedingly morbid and pessimistic. It even seems untrue. After all, there are plenty of times when we are happy. Aren't there? No, there are not. It just seems that way. Take any moment when you feel really fulfilled and examine it closely. Down under the joy, you will find that subtle, all- pervasive undercurrent of tension, that no matter how great this moment is, it is going to end. No matter how much you just gained because you are either going to lose some of it or spend the rest of your days guarding what you have got or scheming how to get more. And in the end, you are going to die. In the end, you lose everything. It is all transitory."[3]

In this way, the Buddha taught his followers not to be distracted by momentary pleasures, but to look at the bigger picture of their life experiences where happiness and pleasures are temporary and therefore that people should learn more about what Buddha taught as the true way to end suffering.

2. The Noble Truth of the cause of dukkha:

The cause of the dissatisfaction is tanha (craving) in all its forms; the reason that we experience suffering comes ultimately from our mind. By watching people Buddha found out that the causes of suffering are craving,desire and ignorance. The power of these things to cause all suffering is what Buddhists call The Second Noble Truth.

The Dhammapada states:

"From craving springs grief, from craving springs fear,
For him who is wholly free from craving, there is no grief, much less fear."[4] *(V. 216)*

This craving is a powerful mental force latent in all, and is the chief cause of most of the sufferings of life. It is this craving, grossor subtle, that leads to repeated births in Samsâra and makes one cling to all forms of life. Craving can be explained as the strong desires that people have for pleasing their senses and for experiencing life itself. Buddhists believe that anything that stimulates our senses or our feelings can lead to craving. None of the pleasures we crave for ever give us lasting happiness or satisfaction. This is why people can crave to repeat these experiences again and again, and become unhappy and dissatisfied until they can satisfy their craving.Craving is like a great tree with many branches. There are branches of greed, bad thoughts and of anger. Buddha taught that the tree of craving has its roots in ignorance. It grows out of ignorance, and its seeds fall and flourish whenever they find ignorance. According to Buddha ignorance is not just being uneducated or not knowing many things. Buddhists see ignorance as the inability to see the truth about things, to see things as they really are. This inability happens because of the limits of their right understanding.The way to end suffering in life is to understand what causes it. Craving and ignorance are the two main causes of suffering. Craving and misunderstanding can be solved by developing the mind, thinking carefully and meditating. Solving these main causes of suffering will lead a person to true happiness.

3. *The Noble Truth of the cessation of dukkha*: an end to all that unsatisfactoriness can be found through the relinquishment and abandonment of craving.After the Buddha realized the Truth about suffering and its causes, he spent six years committed to discovering a realization about the end of suffering and his achievement of Nirvana, was his ultimate achievements. Buddha discovered: there is an end to suffering; it can happen to anybody, anywhere, here and now; and the key to ending all suffering is to remove of three poisons of life(all desire or attachment or raga, ill will oraversion or dveshaand ignorance or avidya). After suffering, the Buddha taught, there is supreme happiness. Every step of the removing of the causes of unhappiness brings more joy. The second fruit of the end of suffering is what Buddhists call supreme Enlightenment. Enlightenment can be called liberation which is a total, absolute and permanent end of all suffering. It is the ultimate and final goal of Buddhist spiritualism.

The Buddha has described Nirvana in different ways. He has called it supreme happiness, peace, immortality. He also described Nirvana as uncreated, unformed, as beyond the earth, as beyond water, fire, air, beyond the sun and moon, unfathomable, immeasurable. It is also described as freedom from conflict and selfishness, the eradication of craving, hatred and delusion. Buddhists believe that we can eradicate all the causes of suffering in this life after following eight fold paths which is a spiritual path and achieve enlightenment(nirvana) which is our spiritual goal. After reaching at our spiritual goal we can live in bliss and we can help others to live in peacefully in this world. So Nirvana is a spiritual journey inour present life.

The reasoning behind this Third Noble Truth is the fact that suffering and the causes of suffering are dependent on the state of our own mind, so if we can change our own mind, we can also eliminate suffering. When we are ill, we go to a doctor. He knows what is wrong and prescribes medicines and gives us advice, which we need to take and follow up to get well again. Likewise, when a spiritual teacher prescribes us a practice and the development of wisdom to end our suffering, we still need to follow the instructions; otherwise there will be no effect. That leads us to the last Noble Truth of the Path of the 'medicine'.

4. *The Noble Truth of the path leading to the cessation of dukkha:*

There is a method of achieving the end of all unsatisfactoriness, namely the Noble Eightfold Path. "The noble truth of marga, the right track,is this:it is the noble eight limb way,namely right view, right thought, right speech, right action, right livelihood, right effort, right mindfulness,and rightsamadhi"[5]. The Noble Eightfold Path offers a comprehensive practical guide to the development of those wholesome qualities and skills in the human heart that must be cultivated in order to bring the practitioner to the final goal, the supreme freedom and happiness of Nibbana. These eight elements can be divided into three ways of practice; Moral Conduct(sila), Mental discipline(Samadhi) and Wisdom (prajna).

The goal of the Noble Eightfold Path is to bring a true understanding of the Four Noble Truths and deliver their ultimate Teaching-the end of suffering. To each of these Noble Truths the Buddha assigned a specific task which the practitioner of spiritual life is to carry out: the first Noble Truth is to be comprehended; the second is to be abandoned; the third is to be realized; the fourth is to be developed. If we can control our body and mind in a way that we help others instead of doing them harm, and generating wisdom in our own mind, we can end our suffering and problems. The Buddha explained that we can use the *Four Yardsticks* to assess if we are practicing the correct way: one should feel happiness, compassion, love and joyous effort when practicing.

The Noble Eightfold Path as Spiritual Path

The teaching of noble eight fold path is spiritual path which describes the spiritual life; a life that flows in a direction of purposeful action.The teaching is also a description of a process. One element flows from another. If we have the right vision,we think right way. If we think the right way,we speak the right way. If we speak the right way,we act the right way. If we act right way,we employ ourselves ethically; if we employ ourselves ethically, we put in full effort. Ifwe put in full effort,we become mindful and if we are mindful we experience Samadhi. Samadhi, the state of clear,meditative mind, in turn brings us vision. The eight steps therefore make a complete cycle, and the Buddha called this Dhamma Wheel.

The spiritual path can be seen as a description of the spiritual life and also as a method of spiritual training. On the other hand, the eight fold path can represent a description of the life of faith or spiritual confidence.If one trusts the spiritual teachings and is oneself trustworthy; one naturally lives this path and finds oneself carried along by it. The path is intrinsically satisfying and we find ourselves gaining faith in it. In this way, faith becomes self-reinforcing. It is thus possible to get on to a good path that continues to grow under its own momentum.On the other hand, we can train ourselves in all the elements of the Eightfold path, knowing that each will provide the conditions for the arising of all the others. Just as the Buddha and his followers led a disciplined life, following particular codes of behavior and observing and eliminating those mental processes which hindered their work, so too training can be an important aspect for all of us in becoming more fully alive. The elements in the eightfold path are each concerned with positive application. The prefix right in each element carries an implication of wholeheartedness.

In practice, the Buddha taught the Noble Eightfold Path to his followers according to a "gradual" system of training, beginning with the development of *sila*, or virtue (right speech, right action, and right livelihood, which are summarized in practical form by the five precepts), followed by the development of *samadhi,* or concentration and mental cultivation (right effort, right mindfulness, and right concentration), culminating in the development of *panna*, or wisdom (right view and right resolve). Progress along the path does not follow a simple linear trajectory. Rather, development of each aspect of the Noble Eightfold Path encourages the refinement and strengthening of the others, leading the practitioner ever forward in an upward spiritual maturity that culminates in Awakening.Seen from another point of view, the long journey on the path to Awakening begins in earnest with the first tentative stirrings of right view, the first flickering of wisdom by which one recognizes both the validity of the first Noble Truth and the inevitability of the law of karma, the universal law of cause and effect. Once one begins to see that harmful actions inevitably bring about harmful results, and wholesome actions ultimately bring about wholesome results, the desire naturally grows to live a skilful, morally upright life, to take seriously the practice of *sila* (moral behavior). The confidence built from this preliminary understanding inclines the follower to put one's trust more deeply in the teachings.

Compassionate and Wisdom an Inevitable Aspect for Spiritualism

For achieving enlightenment perfect wisdom and great compassion both has a great role. The real of heart of spirituality is the quest of wisdom and compassion.They are the result of complete freedom from craving and from ignorance and the tremendous transformations from ordinary life that Buddha's teachings exemplified. Through perfect wisdom He understands the real nature of all things. Through great compassion He is able to help countless beings overcome their suffering.In the Buddhist view, wisdom and compassion are intrinsically linked together. One cannot be truly compassionate without wisdom. Wisdomreveals the deep interrelatedness and impermanency of all things in this world. When we genuinely recognize this, compassion is our natural response. Wisdom can feel compassion and compassion can realize wisdom. Living compassionately means to think and act for betterment of me and others. To recognize that the whole of existence does not revolve around these little entities we call ourselves is the beginning of wisdom. Thus wisdom and compassion arise together. As we become more compassionate, we gain wisdom; as we become wiser, our compassionate natures are more fully revealed.

Wisdom and compassion are also innate.

So Compassionate and Wisdom both are essential condition for achieving spiritualism.

Three Marks of Existence to follow the spiritual path

"All conditioned things are impermanent...
All conditioned things involve suffering...
All things are not self.
When one sees this with wisdom, then one
turns away from suffering.
This is the path of purification."[6]

Change or impermanence is inherent in all phenomenal existence.According to Theravada, impermanence (*anicca*) is the first of the "Three Empirical Marks of Existence" (*ti-lakkhana*) and is usually considered as the basis for the other two marks: *duhkha* and not-self (*anatta*). Observation andreflection make it evident that existence is continually in a state of change and a state of becoming from moment-to-moment.

The Buddhist teaching of *anicca*, the impermanence of conditioned phenomena implies that all conditioned things and phenomenal processes, material as well as mental, are transient and unstable. Impermanence serves asa doorway to the other two characteristics of existence, namely duhkha and not-self. Thus, to understand impermanence is to understand both *duhkha* and not-self. In effect, to "see things as they really become" means to see them in the light of the three marks of existence as impermanent, unsatisfactory, and selfless. As the Buddha has noted: The five aggregates, monks, are *anicca*, impermanent; whatever is impermanent, that is *dukkha*, unsatisfactory; whatever is dukkha, which is without attaa, self. What is without self, that is not mine, that I am not, that is not myself. Thus should it be seen by perfect wisdom (*sammappannaaya*) as itreally is? Who sees by perfect wisdom, as it really is, his mind, not grasping, is detached from taints; he is liberated"[7].

The impermanent nature of existence leads to an important conclusion:what is impermanent,that is also unsatisfactory or *duhkha*.As a necessary corollary of *duhkha*, we come to the third basic characteristicof all phenomena, namely *anatta*. If self is characterized by impermanenceand unsatisfactoriness, it follows that it cannot be identified as abiding orpermanent: what is *anicca* and *dukkha* is also *anatta*. The standard formulationin the Nikayasuses the characteristics ofimpermanence to reveal the characteristics of suffering and both together toreveal the characteristics of non-selfand the subtle nature of the characteristics of *anatta* as follows: The Suttas take this indirect route to the characteristic of nonself because the selfless nature of things is so subtle that often it cannot be seen exceptwhen pointed to by the other two characteristics. When we recognize thatthe things we identify as ourselves are impermanent and bound up with suffering,we realize that they lack the essential marks of authentic selfhood andwe therefore stop identifying with them. The different expositions of threecharacteristics all thus eventually converge on the eradication of clinging. They do so by showing with regard to each aggregate, "This is not mine,this I am not, and this is not myself." This makes the insight into non-self theculmination and consummation of the contemplation of the three characteristics.

A*natta* (egolessness) is the principle philosophical teaching ofBuddhism; and without having realized the reality of egolessnessno real progress is possible on the path to deliverance.So all these thingswill become clear to one when one will able to understand the egolessness and conditionednature of all phenomena of existence. On the understanding of these tworealities depends the understanding of the entire teachingof the Buddha.

All things are impermanent; therefore attachment to all material possessions is painful. Man should remain detached from them as far as possible. There is no permanent soul; therefore, man should be selfless and should condemn selfishness because there is no separation between you and me.So the Buddha's philosophy, three Empirical Marks of Existence is essential teaching to achieve this spiritual goal(the end of suffering).

Connectivity with Education

Education is the key to open the door towards personal growth because education is the process of training and developing of the knowledge, skill, mind and character of human being. "Education is simply the soul of a society as it passes from one generation to another".[8]So education has a great role to build a good peaceful society through making a perfect human being.According to Tagore Education enables the mind to find out the ultimate truth, which gives us the wealth of inner light and love and gives significance to life. And according to Vivekananda Education does the manifestation of divine perfection already exist in man. Buddhism is itself an educational system. The goal of Buddhist education is to attain wisdom. The Buddha taught us that the main object of our mind to practice and cultivate wisdom and compassion. He further taught us that everyone has the potential to realize this state of ultimate wisdom, as it is an intrinsic part of our nature, not something one obtains external.After learning Buddha's teaching when we will practice compassion and wisdom to achieve the enlightenment which is spiritual practice then we will be able to remove our suffering that is the spiritual goal of Buddhism.After achieving that goal we will be able to remove the suffering from us and fromthe society. We will make us happy and will make others happy and we will be able to make a peaceful society which is the spiritualism in Buddhism.

It is very much understandable that the concept of education of Tagore and Vivekananda is very much related to Buddha's concept of education.Buddhism is an educational system aimed at regaining our own intrinsic nature. It also teaches absolute equality which stemmed from Buddha's recognition that all sentient beings possess this innate wisdomand nature. Therefore, there is no inherent difference among beings. Everyone is different now because we have lost our true nature and have become confused. The degree of wisdom exhibited by individuals depends on the degree of delusion and has nothing to do with the true nature of the individual.The Buddha's teaching helps us to realize that innate, perfect, ultimate wisdom. We can solve all our problems by our wisdom and turn suffering into happiness. So the cause of suffering is delusion and the source of happiness is our own wisdom. So if we preach this Buddha's educational system through education then it will be more accepted and followed by more people.

All those learners able to enhance the happiness of themselves and others people of society also. This education must be spiritually based andecologically sound and must offer a holistic view of life. This education can help to move individuals from selfishness to compassion, from a lack of meaning inlife to fulfillment, and from negativity to positive thinking. Then we can hope for a better society and innovative ideas for new beginnings for personal growth, social equity and ecological balance.So education has a great role to preach the Buddha's dhamma for spiritual goal which is the end of suffering. So a proper educational system is capable to promote humaneness and moral wisdom. Ideally and properly, education should cultivate our basic humanness in order to make humankind righteous and peaceful. Since the word manussa (human being) in its original sense means 'one of noble heart'. The right educational system should endow students with noble hearts and make them complete human beings. Once people become human beings, peace can be restored to the entire world.

Conclusion

Buddhist spirituality is imminently pragmatic and humanistic.For that Buddhist Spiritualism is more needful for our modern society than ever before.Buddhist spirituality provides an antidote to the stresses of modern living. Buddhism is not an otherworldly spirituality. It recommends that one should live following one's present moment without looking towards future. Buddhist spirituality is not about absenting oneself from this reality but rather fully, completely, and courageously facing it. It provides discipline for the mind and the body, for treating others and oneself. It does not merely say, "Love others"; it shows us how to love others. It does not merely say, "Be wise and compassion"; it shows us how we may become wise and compassion. Because it is practical rather than theoretical, it may be compatible with other religious perspectives as it is humanistic. Another important part of Buddhist Spirituality is leadingus to inner freedom. This inner freedom is a happiness that is not dependent on externals exploiting nature or our fellow beings. We become more and more capable of finding contentment within our own minds and through our own wisdom. The ability to be content without exploiting nature or our fellow humans can also be called the ability to be content independent of natural or social conditions. With a more independent kind of happiness, social and physical freedom will be preserved and strengthened. Human beings will then have the best possible relationship with both the natural environment and the human society.

Footnotes

1. Sufi Ruhaniat Mureed's Manual by Wali Ali Meyer, 2005, p. 77.
2. Dhammapada, I pairs,1-2 verses.
3. Mindfulness in Plain English by Henepola Gunaratana.
4. The Dhammapada, Verse 216.
5. Samyutta Nikaya 61.11. 8.
6. Dhammapada, Verse 277-279.
7. Samyutta Nikaya, 22.45.
8. G.K. Chesterton, English author & mystery novelist (1874 - 1936).

References

The Central Philosophy of Buddhism: A Study of Madhyamika System by T.R.V Murti, New Delhi: Munshiram Manoharlal Publication, 1998.

The Selfless Mind by Peter Harvey, Curzon Press, 1995.

Buddhist Thought in India by Cone, Edward, University of Michigan Press: 1962.

What the Buddha Taught by Walpola Rahula, New York: Grove Press, 1959.

Mindfulness in Plain English by Henepola Gunaratana Boston: Wisdom Books, 1991.

The Mind and the Way: Buddhist Reflections on LifebyAjahn Sumedho Boston: Wisdom Publications, 1995.

An Illustrated Outline of Buddhism: The Essentials of Buddhist Spiritualityby William Stoddart World Wisdom, Inc, Bloomington, 2013.

In the Path of the Masters: Understanding the Spirituality of Buddha, Confucius, Jesus, and Muhammad by Denise Lardner Carmody, M.E. Sharpe, 01-Jan-1996.

Reformation of Present Society by Practicing the Buddha's Ethics by Dr. Priyadarsini Mitra Article in the Book, Language and truth in Buddhism, Edited by – Prof. Ragunath Ghosh and Joytish Basak, Published by Northern Book Center, New Delhi-2010.

6

Ancient Indian Treasure of Knowledge and the Arab Muslims

Aurang Zeb Azmi

Introduction

The Arabs had strong relations with the Indians since ancient period. They first travelled to them in search of Indian products; swords, medicines, horses and herbs. They were so impressed with the beauty of the Indian women even they used a simile of them to theirs'. Here are some Arabic verses, from Pre-Islamic period, which prove to be strong evidence for these long historical relations.

The Pre-Islamic poet larfah s/o al-'Abd says:

وظلم ذوي القربى أشدّ مضاضة　　　على المرء من وقع الحسام المهنّد

Tr.: The oppression done by the nears and dears is more painful for a man than a wound met with by the Indian sword.

Here the word 'المهنّد' has been used for the sword imported from India.

Another poet 'Antarah s/o Shaddâd says:

ولقد ذكرتك والرمـــــــــاح نواهل　　　مني وبيض الهند تقطر من دمي

Tr.: I remembered you while the spears were pierced into my body and the Indian swords were dropping with my blood.

Here the word 'بيض الهند' is used for Indian swords.

Imru-Ul-Qais, the famous Pre-Islamic poet, says:

إذا قامتا تضـــــوّع المسك منهما   نسيم الصبا جاءت بريّا القرنفل

فهل ينكر هذا الفضل إلا الرجل الأخطل

Tr.: When she stands musk bursts profusely from her body as if the Breeze has come with the sweet smell of the Clove.

Here the word 'القرنفل' has been taken from India.

A poet says concluding Indian's distinction:

لقد أنكر أصحابي وما ذلك بالأمثـــــــــل   إذاما مدح الهند وسهم الهند في المقتـــــل

لعمري إنها أرض إذا القطـــــــــر بها ينزل   يصير الدر والياقـــــوت والدر لمن يعطل

فمنها المسك والكافـــــور والعنبر والمندل   وأصناف من الطيب ليستعمـــــــل من يتفل

وأنواع الأفاويه وجـــــــوز الطيب والسنبل   ومنها العاج والساج ومنها الفيـــــل والدغفل

ومنها الكرك والببغـــــاء والطاؤوس والحوزل   ومنها شجـــــــــر الرائج والساسم والفلفل

سيوف ما لها مثل قد استغنت عن الصيقـــل   وأرماح إذاما هزّت اهتزّ بها الجحفـــــــــل

In this poem, the poet has mentioned all Indian products including pearls, camphor, campherena, spikenard, snakes, coconut, odoriferous wood, ivory, teak, elephant, wolf, parrot, peacock, short, sîsam, pepper, sword, and spears.

Not only this the Arabs translated the books of Indians into poetic form. 'Abd al-Hamîd al-Lâhiqui who belongs to the Abbasside period translated the famous Indian story book 'Kalîlah wa Dimnah' into poetic form. He says:

هذا كتاب أدب ومهنـــــــة   وهو الذي يدعى كليلة ودمنة

فيه دلالات وفيه رشـــــــد   وهو كتاب وضعته الهنـــــــد

فوصفـــــوا آداب كل عالم   حكاية على ألسن البهـــــائم

فالحكمـــــاء يعرفون فضله   والسخفاء يشتهون البهـــــائم

Not only this even their poets prayed their God for development of India and its long life. Abul 'Abbâs al-Zabbi says:

سقى الله بلد الهنـــــد مغناهما   سمــــاء من المزن غير السماح

ولا زال وكراهمــــــا عامرين   بنسل مبــــــاح وخير متاح

Aspects of Impact of Indian Treasure of Knowledge upon the Arabs

The Arabs got impressed with the Indians in two fields; language & literature and the sciences. Here we wish to discuss each field separately:

Language & Literature

In the field language & literature the Arabs got impressed with the Indians in four ways; words & terminologics, proverbs & wise sayings, rhetorics and short & long stories. Here we wish to shed some lights on each way:

1. *Words & Terminologies:* There are numerous Sanskrit words which got place in the Arabic language and literature after being Arabiacised. I am giving a list of some words with pointing out their origin and meanings:

Barûs (بروص) : It is originally 'Bharûch' which is a famous city of Gujrât. The famous author al-Balâdhri says in his book 'Futûh al-Buldân':

"The king sent also him to Barûs while he sent his brother al-Mughîrah bin Abi al-'Âs to the heart of a-Dîbal where he faced the enemy and got victory"[1].

Al-Mas'ûdi says:

"There is al-Dîbal city through which Indian cost is united with Barûc which is famous in making spears"[2].

The Arabs used it in their poetry. One Arab poet says:

ألفت قوساً ذا انتقاء   جاء بها جالب برصاء

Another Arab poet says:

من شفق خضر بروصات   صفر اللجاء والخلوقيات

Al-Nîlaj (النيلج) & al-Nainîlaj (النينيلج): This is Arabiacised form of Nîl which is an Indian word used for blue powder to colour the clothes after wash. The famous Arab poet Ibn al-'Arâbi says:

سوداء لم تخطط به نينيلجا

Al-Mauz (الموز) : It is a famous Indian fruit; banana. Its Indian origin is 'Mûsha'. Al-Maqdisi says about Sindh:

"It a hot area where found date, coconut and mauz (banana)"[3].

Al-Fotah (الفوطة): Its origin is 'pot' which means trouser or turban. The famous traveler Sulaimân al-Tâjir says:

"The Indians, both men and women, wear two *fotas* and decorate it with the bangles of gold and diamond"[4].

Al-Nârjîl (النارجيل): Its Arabiacised form of Nâriyal (coconut). The famous writer of the dictionary 'Lisânul 'Arab' says:

"al-Nârjil is Indian coconut"[5].

The famous traveler Sulaimân al-Tâjir says:

"These islands which are ruled by the woman are full of coconut tree"[6].

Al-Qust (القسط): It is originally 'Kust' (costus). In the famous dictionary 'Lisânul 'Arab':

"al-Qust is a wood which is imported from India and used for perfume and medicine"[7].

Al-'Ud (العود): Its origin is 'Aud'. Ibn-e-Manzûr says:

"al-'Ud is a wood found nearby sea and used for perfume"[8].

The Prophet Muhammad says:

"Be stick with the Indian 'Ud"[9].

Al-Filfil (الفلفل): It's originally 'Pipli'. It reached to the Arabs through the Persian language which is sister language of Sanskrit. The famous poet Imru-Ul-Qais says:

ترى بعر الصيران في عرصاتها　　　وقيعـــانها كأنه حبّ فلفل

He again says:

كأنّ مكاكي الجـــــــــواء غدية　　　صبحن سلافاً من رحيق المفلفل

Al-Qaranfal (القرنفل): Its origin is 'Karan fal' or 'Kiran fûl'. Ibn-e-Manzûr says:

"al-Qaranfal or al-Qaranful is Indian plant. It is not of the Arabia"[10].

The famous poet Imru-Ul-Qais says:

كأن القرنفـــل والزنجبيل　　　باتا بفيها وارياً منشورا

Al-Rakh (الرخ): It is originally 'Rath'. Al-Yaqûbi says:

"al-Rakh is of the horses"[11].

Al-Fîl (الفيل): Its origin is 'Pilû' but it came to Arabic through Persian which is sister language of Sanskrit. The Qur'an says:

"ألم تر كيف فعل ربك بأصحاب الفيل، ألم يجعل كيدهم في تضليل"[12].

2. *Proverbs & Wise Sayings:* The second thing in which India influenced Arabia was the proverbs and wise sayings. We know very well that the Arabs were fond of proverbs and wise sayings. When they met with the Indian wise men[13] they tried their best to take benefits from them. Consequently, Kalîlah wa Dimnah was translated into Arabic. In this book we find numerous proverbs and wise sayings.

For we have narrow space here we quote here only some Indian proverbs and wise sayings which the Arabs borrowed from the Indians mentioning them in their books that they took it from the Indians. The author 'Uyûn al-Akhbâr' Ibn-e-Qutaiba quoted the following proverbs and wise sayings from the Indians:

Justice of the king is more useful for its people than the full help of time.	• عدل السلطان أنفع للرعية من خصب الزمان
The worst wealth is that which is not spent.	• شر المال ما لا ينفق منه
The worst friend is that who forsakes.	• شرّ الإخوال الخاذل
The worst king is that from whom the people are afraid.	• شرّ السلطان من خافه البريء
The worst country is which is not fertile and peaceful.	• شرّ البلاد ما ليس فيه خصب ولا أمن
The king who is less faithful and is careless of his friends is like a prostitute.	• إنما مثل السلطان في قلة وفائه للأصحاب وسخاء نفسه عمن فقد منهم مثل البغي والمكتسب كلما ذهب واحد جاء آخر
The wise king increases with the advice of wise ministers like a sea which increases with the rivers falling into it, and take with wisdom and advice which cannot be taken with power and army.	• الملك الحازم يزداد برأي الوزراء الحزمة كما يزداد البحر بمورده من الأنهار وينال بالحزم والرأي ما لا ينال بالقوة والجنود

The person who seeks leave from the friends at the time of advice, from the doctors at the tile of treatment, and from the Juries at the time of any doubt, he will commit mistake, will increase in disease, and will face consequence.

- ومن التمس من الإخوان الرخص عند المشورة ومن الأطباء عند المرض ومن الفقهاء عند الشبهة أخطأ الرأي وازداد مرضاً وحمل الوزر

Three things make an increase in familiarity and confidence; Increase in travel, mutual trust and recognition of own people.

- ثلاثة أشياء تزيد في الأنس والثقة الزيادة في الرحل والمواكلة ومعرفة الأهل والحشم

Four people are in loss; who whispers to the deaf, who scatters seeds in the mud, who lights candle in the bright day, and who does favour with the unfaithful.

- أربعة ليست لأعمالهم ثمرة مسار الأصمّ والباذر في السبخة والمسرج في الشمس وواضع المعروف عند من لا شكر له

Six things are not permanent; shadow of the cloud, friendship of the mischief, love of the women, abundance of wealth, wrong king and untrue praise.

- ستة أشياء لا ثبات لها؛ ظل الغمام وخلة الأشرار وعشق النساء والمال الكثير والسلطان الجائر والثناء الكاذب[1]

Similarly Ibn-e-Duraid the author of 'al-'Iqd al-Farid' has pointed out the richness of the Indians in this field and mentioned numerous proverbs and wise sayings of the Indians[15].

3. *Rhetorics:* It is also astonishing that the Indians help the Arabs to develop the Rhetorics. It was narrated by al-Jâhiz that he asked one of the Hindu Pandit about Rhetorics there in India. His name was sâleh. He replied that he is not expert of this field except that he has one treatise of this field which he summarized to al-Jâhiz who in turn took benefit from it in developing the Rhetorics[16].

2. *Short & Long Stories:* In this field the Arabs also took benefits from the Indians. They not only translated Indian short stories but also rendered the Indian books of long stories. Here we mention a few of them:

- *Forty Years:* It is narrated by Muhammad bin 'Abdûs al-Jahshiyâri that some clothes and ornaments were gifted to one of the Indian kings. Then he called his two wives and asked them to select. When one lady came the minister made his eye at the clothes. The lady took the ornaments so that the king should not know that the minister has made his eye at the clothes and on the other hand the minister used to put one of his eyes half-closed for the whole life of forty years. The king at the time of his death called upon his son and advised him to do good with the minister because he paid the price of one fault for forty years".[17]

Similarly Ibn-e-Qutaibah has narrated one of the Indian stories of a priest who thought of making abundance of wealth with a little bit of butter[18].

- *Alf Laila wa Lailah:* This book is basically known among the readers of *'Thousand Nights and One Night'* and in Urdu we know with the name of *'Alif Laila'* whose correct pronunciation is *'Alf Lailah'*. Here 'alf' means thousand and 'laila' is night. It is said that several short stories of this collection of stories have been taken from the Indian sources.
- *Al-Sindbad:* It is in two parts; small and big. It has been translated from Sanskrit. Ibn-e-Nadîm says:

  "Kitabus Sindbâd is in two parts; Small and Big. It is made on the pattern of Kalîlah wa Dimnah. Keeping the majore parts of it into mind it looks that it is the handiworks of the Indians"[19].

  Al-Masûdi sayd:

  "He has seen Sindbâd whose book is 'Kitab al-Wozara al-Saba wa al-Muallim was Imratul Malik'. This book is known as 'Kitâb al-Sindbâd'. The author was employed in the medical factory"[20].
- *Bozasf wa Balohar:* Its Sanskrit name is Budhi Satu Pradhitra. It deals with the story of Budh who left his kingdom for search of spirituality. In his way to search for spirituality he met with a priest who put up some questions to him. This story has been rendered first into Pahlavi then into Arabic during the Abbasside period. It was also rendered into poetic form by Abbân bin 'Abdul Hamîd[21].
- *Hudud-o-Mantiqil Hind:* Its topic, as looks from the title, is the conversation of the birds. It contains stories of good morals in the language of birds[22].
- *Shânâq al-Hindi:* Shânâq is Chanakya in Sanskrit. The book contains five chapters on morals and manners. In this books war and its ways have been mentioned in the way of story[23].
- *Kalîlah wa Dimnah:* The most famous Sanskrit book of stories is Kalîlah wa Dimnah who Sanskrit name is Panchtantra. It was written by Baidba for the king Dibshalîm. It was first translated into Pahlavi then into Arabic and from Arabic into all languages. The person who translated it into Arabic was 'Abdullah bin al-Muqaffa. The book is available in the market and taught in the Arabic *madrasas*. It is full of wise saying and moral lessons in the language of animals and birds.

Sciences

The Arabs took much benefit in the fields of different sciences like medical sciences, mathematics, astrology, astronomy, chemistry etc. Here we wish to shed some lights on each science in which the Arabs were benefitted by the Indians:

1. **Medical Sciences:** In this field the Arabs took much benefit even they developed it and made their own medical science named as 'Arabian Medicine'. The books translated in this regard are as follows:

(*a*) *Sushuriti Sanhita:* This book was written by the famous Indian physician 'Sushurat' who learnt medicine from Dewdas in Varanasi. The book contains diseases, its symptoms and its treatment. It is in ten chapters. Ibn-e-Nadîm says:

"Kitâb-o-Susrad is in ten chapters. Yahya bin Khâlid ordered to render it into Arabic"[24].

Al-Râzi has took benefits from this book in his famous book of Unâni medicine[25].

(*b*) *Chark Sanhita:* It is the book written by famous Indian physician Chark who was in the courtyard of the king Kanishk. Al-Bairûni says about him:

"The Indians have a book in medicine which they give weightage. It is known with the name of its author, Chark. His family tree of knowledge reaches upto Perjapati the father of Indian medicine"[26].

'Abdullâh bin 'Alî translated this book into Arabic.

(*c*) *Kitâb al-Sumûm:* The author of this book is Chânakya whose Arabiacised form is 'Shânâq'. Chânakya was the Minister of Chandragupt Mauriya. Ibn Abi Usaibi'a says about him:

"Among the famous Indian physicians is Shânâq. He has many experiments in the medical science"[27].

Abbâs bin Sa'îd al-Jauhari translated it from its Persian version which was done by Kanka the famous Indian translator.

(*d*) *Kitâb fi Ilâjât al-Nisâ':* It was written by one of the Indian lady physicians. Al-Râzi has taken benefits from this book.

(*e*) *Kitâb fi Ajnâs al-Hayyât:* It was written by Roy.

Similarly *'Kitab al-Namuzar fi al-Amâr'*, *'Kitâb fi al-Tawahhum'*, *'Kitâb Nidan'* and *'Kitâb Tauqishnal'* were translated into Arabic.

2. ***Mathematics:*** In this field India not only did favour upon the Arabs but through the Arabs it did faour upon the whole world. Before the Indians the humanity was unaware of full numbers. It is the Indians who taught it to them and from them the Arabs took and made it famous in the whole world. Till the date they named it as 'al-Arqâm al-Hindiyyah' (Indian Numbers). Its story has been narrated by al-Bairûni in details. See his book 'Tahqîq-o-Ma Lil Hind', Page no. 82-84. Arabs not only took it from them but also they wrote original books on the topic. Among some Arabs who wrote books on the topic are Abu Nacr Mohammad bin 'Abdullâh al-Kaluzani, Abu Yûsuf Yaqûb bin Is.hâq al-Kindi, Ahmad bin 'Umer al-Karabisi, Sinân bin al-Fat.h, Abul Qâsim Ali bin Ahmad al-Mujtaba and Muhammad bin Ahmad bin Yûsuf al-Khawârzmi.

To this science Algebra is related. Though it was invented by the Arabs themselves they based it upon the Indian numbers. The famous book on this topic is *'Kitâb al-Jabr wa al-Muqâbala'* by al-Khawârzmi.

3. ***Astronomy & Astrology:*** These two sciences are related to the Indians. The Arabs did not anything about this science before their contact with the Indians. They had only 'al-Tanjîm' (Natural Astronomy). The Indians were expert of this science as al-Bairûni said[28].

   The famous book on this topic translated by the Arabs was 'Barham Sidhdhânt' which was written by 'Barham Gupt'. He wrote this book at the age of 30 and presented it to the king Dayagharmukha. It was translated in the period of Abu Jafar al-Mansûr as al-Qifti said[29].

   Al-Bairûni has mentioned it in details and pointed out its contents[30].

   The second Indian book translated into Arabic from Sanskrit is Arjubhuz. It was written by Arya Bhat. He was born in 471AD and hailed from Patna. He started writing books at the age of 23. This is his last book which contains 12 chapters.

   There is another book translated on the topic is Khanda Khadyaka. It is known in Arabic as 'al-Arkand'. It was also written by Braham Gupt. It was translated into Arabic by Yâqûb bin Târiq. The translation has been revised by al-Bairûni. There is another Sanskrit book 'Panchasidhdhanta' written by Virahamira. It was also rendered into Arabic among his other books on the topic.

4. ***Horoscope***: Its Sanskrit name is Jâtuk. On this topic several books were translated such as *'Asrârul Mawâlîd'* of Kanka al-Hindi[31], *'Kitâbul Mawâlîd'* of Ghaudar al-Hindi[32], *'Kitâbul Mawâlid al-Kabîr'* of Sanghal al-Hindi[33] and *'Kitâbul Mawâlîd'* of Brahmur who wrote two books on the topic[34].

   Not only this, but the Arabs have developed this science writing books on the topic. Among some famous Arabs writers on the topic are Muhammad bin 'Umer al-labri, Abu Sahl Fazl bin Naubakht, Sahl bin Bashîr, al-$asan bin Ibrâhîm al-Asajj and al-$asan bin al-Khatîb.

5. ***Chemistry:*** Though Arabs developed this science they took benefits in this regard from the non-Arabs including the Indians whom Ibn-e-Nadîm considers among its inventors[35].

   Among the Indian books translated on the topic is *'Kitâb-o-Khâtif AL-Hindi'*. It was written by Khätif al-Hindi whose two books were translated on the topic[36].

   Arabs did not translate much on the topic and started writing original books from which the Europeans took benefits.

Footnotes

1. Futûh al-Buldân, Pg: 188
2. Târîkh al-Masûdi, 1/139

3. Al-Masâdir al-Hindiyyah li al-Ulûm al-Islâmiyyah, pg: 26
4. Silsilah al-Tawârîkh, pg: 59
5. Lisânul Arab: al-Nârjil
6. Silsilah al-Tawârikh, pg: 6
7. Lisânul Arab: al-Qust
8. Ibid, pg: al-Ud
9. Al-Masâdir al-Hindiyyah li al-Ulum al-Islamiyyah, pg: 27
10. Lisânul Arab, pg: al-Qaranfal
11. Târikh al-Yaqûbi, 1/109
12. The Qur'an: Chapter 'al-Fil': 1-2
13. Al-Qâzi Said al-Undulusi says pointing out the richness of the Indians in this field: "India is the mine of wisdom and spring of justice. Its people have high opinions, good proverbs, and unique researches'. Tabqâtul Umam, Pg: 16
14. Uyûnul Akhbâr, 1/3, 5, 25, 27 and 112, and 3/24, 161 and 169
15. Al-Iqd al-Farîd, 1/70, 123, 215 and 314 and 2/135 and 168
16. Al-Bayân wa al-Tabyîn, Pg: 40
17. Kitâb al-Wuzara wa al-Kuttâb, Pg: 8
18. Uyûnul Akhbâr, 1/263
19. Fihrist Ibn-e-Nadîm, Pg: 424
20. Târîkh al-Masûdi, Pg: 1/162
21. Al-Masâdir al-Hindiyyah li al-Ulûm al-Islamiyyah, Pg: 112
22. Al-Fihrist, Pg: 424
23. *Ibid.,* Pg: 437
24. Al-Fihrist, Pg: 435
25. Uyûn al-Anba fi Tabaqât al-Atibba, 2/33
26. Kitâb-o-Tahqîq ma lilhind, Pg: 76
27. Uyûn al-Anba fi Tabaqât-i-al-Atibba, 2/33
28. Tahqîq-o-Ma lil Hind, Pg: 73
29. Tarîkhul Hukama, pg: 270
30. Tahqîq-o-Ma lil Hind, Pg: 74
31. Al-Fihrist, Pg: 392
32. Uyûnul Anba fi Tabaqât al-Atibba, 2/32
33. Al-Fihrist, Pg: 392
34. Taqîq-o-ma lil Hind, Pg: 175
35. Al-Fihrist, Pg: 521
36. Ibid, Pg: 517

Bibliography

1. Abu 'Uthmân al-Jâhiz: al-Bâyan wa al-Tabyîn, Dâr-o-bâdir, Beirût, 1997
2. Al-Yâqûbi: Târîkh al-Yâqûbi, Dâr-o-bâdir, Beirût, 1990
3. Ibn Abi Usaibiah: 'Uyûn al-Anba fi Tabaqât al-Atibba, Beirût, 1965
4. Ibn al-Nadîm: al-Fihrist, Dâr al-Marifah, Beirût, 1978
5. Mahmûd Hasan Qaisar Amrohawi: al-Macâdir al-Hindiyyah li al- 'Ulum al-Islamiyyah, Dârul Fikr, Syria, 2010
6. Mu%ammad 'Abdur Razzâq Kanpûri: al-Barâmikah, Navalkishore Press, Lahore
7. Sa'îd al-Undulusi: labaqât al-Umam, al-Matba al-Katholikiyyah, Beirût, 1912
8. Shibli No'mâni: al-Mamûn, Afzalul Matabe, Delhi, 1889
9. Wasîm A%mad Azmi: Baitul $ikmat ki Tibbi Khidmât, 1988
10. Zakriya al-Qazweni: Âthârul Bilâd wa Akhbârul 'Ibâd, Dâr-o-bâdir, Beirût, 1380H

PART—III
RABINRANATH TAGORE AND SPIRITUALISM

1

Tagore's Idea of "*Manassundari*"

Piyali Dutta Chowdhury

Abstract

Tagore has visualised his "MANASSUNDARI" in various distinct forms among the people of this world as well as among nature. He has visualized his "MANASSUNDARI" sometimes as a lover and sometimes in the realization of death. Sometimes he is saying, "Debotare jaha dite pari, di tai/priyojane-priyojone jaha dite pai/tai di debotare; ar pabo katha!/debotare priyo kori priyere debota" and at other times he is writing death is his lover and he will become one with death. However diverse Tagore's idea of spiritualism may be in his writings, but in his heart this spiritualism is one complete thought. He has called this very thought or idea as "MANASSUNDARI" or "JIBANDEBOTA". Tagore's spiritualism is not bound to any particular religion, place, caste or class. This realization or feeling is eternal and for everyone. In Tagore's contemporary world, many spiritualists have referred to God either as male or as female. However, Tagore has never referred to his God as male or female. His idea of spiritualism is neither of walking on a path of any particular religion nor of worshipping any particular God. In Tagore's spiritualism, the God he believes resides in himself does not have any form- He is formless and infinite. This thought of spiritualism is found all over his literary work. It is not possible to give a full account of his idea of spiritualism as found in his literary works in so few words. So I have chosen a particular period called "SONAR TORI".

Keywords: Spiritualism, Sonartori, Jeebatma, Vishanvas, Manassundari, Jibandebota

Introduction

Tagore's "MANASSUNDARI" is not a theory but a beautiful realization of his ideas of spiritualism. His spiritualism is also not a rigid idea- it is rather a philosophical thought. It is very clear from his writings that he believed in the existence of God. At the same time, he did not believe in any particular form of God. The God which we get in the writings of Tagore is not bound to any particular religion, caste or country. Tagore's idea of God is also not bound to any form or idol. In Tagore's spiritualism, the God he believes resides in himself and does not have any form- He is formless and infinite. He has also not bounded his God in any masculine or feminine form. In addition, Tagore tells us of the meetings between the finite and infinite, the Soul *(atma)* and Supreme Soul *(paramatma)*, and incomplete and complete. It is essentially his own individual feeling. In Tagore's idea of spiritualism, on one side we get words like finite, Soul *(atma)* and incomplete and on the other side we get words like infinite, Supreme Soul *(paramatma)* and complete. So it is thought that these words are synonymous in Tagore's writings, i.e. **finite=Soul *(atma)*= incomplete and infinite=Supreme Soul *(paramatma)*=complete.** Similarly, he is thinking of life as being synonymous to incomplete and death synonymous to complete. When this idea of his spiritualism had matured further he has made the lives of each and every creature on this planet one with the lives of all other creatures of the entire universe. In this way, Tagore's idea of spiritualism gave way to his idea of universal brotherhood. Probably, this realization of spiritualism has led Tagore to overcome the narrow boundaries of nation, caste-creed-race and religion and reach the stage where all people are one and his very own. He has written, "*Bishwa sathe joge jethae biharo/seikhane jog tomar sathe amaro/naeko bone,noe bijone,/noeko amar apon mone,/sabar jethae apon tumi,he priyo,/sethae apon amaro*" [GITANJALI/ POEM NO. 94].

Tagore's SONARTORI

This idea of spiritualism is not a new thought. He got the essence of it from the literature of ancient and medieval India like the *Upanishads, Vedas, Vaishnav Padavali,* etc. Tagore started reading these books from an early age under the guidance of his father, Maharshi Devendranath Tagore, and it had left a deep mark in his heart. As a result, the essence of his spiritual that we in his writings from the very beginning was inspired by this philosophy. In addition to this inspiration, the growth of Rabindra philosophy was also due to Tagore's contact with nature that came about during the Shilaidaha period. During this period, he had to spend time alone in a boat with the nature as his only companion. Thus, he got the opportunity to take in and realize the beauty and significance of the nature. It was during this time that he realized the infinity of God through the infinity of the nature. Tagore has written, "*Ekhane manush kom abong prithibitai beshi-charidike emon sab jinish dekha jae ja aaj tairi kore kal meramod kore porshudin bikri kore phelbar noe,ja manusher janmamrityu kriyakalaper moddhe chirodin atol bhabe dariye ache-protidin saman bhabe jatayat korche ebong chirokal abisranto bhabe probahito hochhhe.*"[Chhinno patrabali, [Chhinno patrabali, letter number 34]. In this Shilaidaha period, Tagore wrote "SONAR TORI" where we can get a glimpse of Tagore's "MANASSUNDARI".

In the poem "SONAR TORI" from the book "SONAR TORI" Tagore wrote about a human soul (atma) who is waiting for someone he does not know but wants to give up his everything to that person. The poet has shown this person who is waiting as being alone and very lonely with only his own belongings. At this point of time, the person sees someone whom he partially recognizes sailing away in a boat. Eagerly, he asked the person on the boat to come near him because he wanted to give up all his belongings and all that he acquired in his life and load it on the boat. He also promises that after putting everything on the boat, he would not demand any right on his belongings. Tagore, about the request of this person, has said, "*Bar ek phirao tori kulete eshe/jeo jetha jete chao jare khushi tare dao/jare khushi tare dao/sudhu tumi nie jao/khonik heshe/amaar sonar dhan kulete ese*". Finally, all his belongings get a place in the boat; although he himself does not get a place. His loneliness then changes to tremendous mental pain and he says, "*Thai nai thai nai-choto se tori/amari sonar dhane giyeche bhori/...sunno nadir tire rahinu pori/jaha chilo nie gelo sonar tori*".

In the context of explaining this poem, Tagore has said,

> "*...manush somosto jibon dhore fasal chaas korche. Tar jiboner khet tuku diper mto, charidikei abbyakter dara se beshtito,oi ektukhani e tar kache byakto hoe ache. Sei jonne GEETA bolechen -*
>
> *abyakta deeni vutani byakto moddhani bharat*
>
> *abyakta nidhana nebbo tatro ka poridebona*
>
> *jakhon kal ghonie asche, jakhon charidiker jal ghonie uthche,jakhon abar abbyakter moddhe atr oi char tuku taliye jabar samay holo atkhon tar somosto jiboner karmer ja kichu nityu phal ta se oi sansarer taranite bojhai kore dite pare. Sansar somoto e nebe, ekti konao phele debe na. ...*" *['TORI BOJHAI'/ SANTINIKETAN]*.

Our interpretation is that Tagore's realization is that every soul(*atma)* is alone and it waits consciously or sub-consciously to become one with Supreme soul(*paramatma)*. But why did he mention the word 'alone'? It is because realization of God is a personal feeling. So, this realization cannot be achieved along with others. Thus, each and every devotee pays homage to God all alone. In the

VAISHNAV PADABALI too, Sri Radhika performed "*avishar*" for Sri Krishna. Here, Sri Radhika symbolizes soul and Sri Krishna symbolizes the Supreme Soul and "*avishar*" symbolizes the walk across the path between the Soul and the Supreme Soul all alone. In the poem "SONAR TORI", this human soul is also waiting to give up everything he acquired in his life to the Supreme Soul like Sri Radhika. But in this poem there is a boat onto which this human soul wants to unload all his belongings. Possibly, Tagore, in this poem, has referred to the boatman as the Supreme Soul and symbolized the boat for eternal time. Every human soul wants his belongings not to get lost with time. He himself also wants to remain eternal. However, this desire of man is never fulfilled because eternal time preserves the creations of man but not his ego. Therefore, although the human soul may say, "*ekhon amare laho karuna kore*", his desire is not to be fulfilled. The meeting between two souls as well as the meeting between the Soul and the Supreme Soul is possible only without ego.

Spiritual Manifestations

Tagore believes that the Soul wants to meet the Supreme Soul; otherwise the soul would not be complete. Therefore, Tagore wants to know the supreme soul completely. At times, Tagore searches for this Supreme Soul in an idol and sometimes it is just an abstract idea. He wants to know the roots of his own as well as every other human soul. Tagore has said, "*Mone hoe, jeno mone pare/jakhon bilinbhabe chinu oi birat jathore/ajato bhubanbhruno-majhe,lokkhokotu barsha dhore/ oi taba obisram kalotan antare antare/ mudrito hoiya geche; sei jonmo purber swaran,/ garbhostho prithibi-pore sei nitya jibonspandan/taba matri hridoy er- ati khin abhasger moto/jage jeno somosto shirae...*". [SOMUDRER PRATI/ SONAR TORI]. The human soul wants to know its own identity in this way. The love for nature has made this realization of the poet stronger. The poet realizes his own identity is nothing different from the trees, water, animals and all other human beings. In this way he realized all other souls of creatures also a part of the universe and likewise, a part of the Supreme Soul, because the universe is a creation of the Supreme Soul. At the same time, the poet has also noticed a difference between the universe and the Supreme Soul. He has shown that in the universe there is birth and death, joy and sadness, but the God or the Supreme Soul is indifferent. The poet thinks that he and all other human soul actually loves this world of life where there are tears and laughter, birth and death. He has written, *"Ami ei prithibi ke baro bhalobasi. Er mukhe bhari ekti sudurbyapi bishad lege ache. Jeno er mone mone ache, 'Ami debotar meye, kintu debotar khamota amar nei. Ami bhalobashi kintu rokkha korte pari ne. arombho kori, sampurna korte pari ne. Janmo di mrityur hath theke bachate pari ne!' Ei jonne swarger opor ari kore ami amar doridro mayer ghor aro beshi bhalobashi-eto asohai, asamortho, asampurna, bhalobashar shahashro ashonkae sarboda chintakator bolei...."* [CHINNO PATRABALI/ LETTER NO. 13]. Tagore accepted that every soul is born out of the Supreme Soul and thus he wrote, *"Ami debotar meye"*.

Tagore, after all this, has said that he is frantically searching for the Supreme Soul in idols- *"Khyapa khuje khuje phire paras pathar"*. He wants to acquire the knowledge through which he can reach the Supreme Soul. In the quest of this knowledge he lost all consciousness. The entire world laughs at him and maybe, the Supreme Soul too laughs. But the poet does not even think of these- *"Jalarashi abiral koriteche kalokal/atol rahasya jeno chahe bolibare/kamya dhon ache kotha/jaane jeno sab katha/se bhasha je bojhe sei khuje nite pare/kichute bhrukkhep nahi, mahagatha gaan gahi/samudro aponi sune aponar swar/ keho jae keho ase, keno kade keho hashe/khyapa tire khuje phire paras pathar."* so, even after so much devotion, the poet is unable to find the Supreme Soul. Moreover, he realizes that in this quest he did find the *"paras pathar" (Supreme Soul)* but also lost it. So, the poet begins the quest for this knowledge with much more vigor and realizes that he has already lost half of his energy in search of the knowledge to know the Supreme Soul. He also realizes that searching outside one would never be able to understand the true form of the Supreme Soul. He then started searching for this knowledge in his conscience.

The poet realizes that the Supreme Soul he has been searching for so long is within himself. It is present in his own conscience. He says, *"Ami paraner sathe khelibo ajike/maranokhela/nishitho bela"* [JHULON/SONAR TORI].. He has imagined the supreme soul as "*paranbodhu*" and "*maronkhela*" as that devotion through which his soul will become one with the Supreme Soul. He has also referred to this *"maronkhela"* as *"jhulonkhela"*. He wrote, *"Amate pranete khelibo dujone/jhulonokhela/nishithobela"* [JHULON/SONAR TORI]. 'Jhulon' is a very common word in VAISHNAV PADAVALI which means a swing on which swung Sri Radha and Sri Krishna as one at kalpavrindavan. Tagore too in his imagination is sitting on a swing just beside the Supreme Soul and yet he is unable to completely understand the Supreme Soul. Somewhere there is a curtain between them. The poet realizes that there is an infinite distance between them. In order to overcome that distance, to completely know the Supreme Soul, his feelings need to grow more strong. Possibly, only then he will be able to lift up that curtain and know the Supreme Soul- *"Ae re jhonjha, paran bodhur/aboranrashi koria de dur/kori lunthan abogunthan-/basan khol..."*. At the time of meeting of Sri Radha and Sri Krishna, Sri Radha could not even tolerate the obstruction caused by a string between them. A Vaishnav poet has written, *"Duhu krore duhu kande bichhedo bhabia"*. Similarly, Tagore is not able to tolerate the obstruction caused by the curtain between the human soul and the Supreme Soul. He says, *"Pranete amate mukhomukhi aaj/ chini labo donhe cgari bhoy-laaj/ bokkhe bokkhe poroshibo donhe/bhabe bibol"* [JHULON/SONAR TORI]. Finally, the Soul and the Supreme Soul are becoming one in the poet's conscience. The *"khyapa"* who was searching for God or Supreme Soul(*paramatma)* outside as well as within himself has now become one with the Supreme Soul-*"Swapno tutia bahireche aaj/duto pagol"* [JHULON/ SONAR TORI].

The Concept of Death

Rabindranath Tagore, most of the times, has visualized the Supreme Soul in black or blue colors. In his conscience, death also has the black color and he has seen death as the completion of life and not the end of it. He has said, *"ogo mrityu, sei lagne nirjan sayan prante/ eso bar beshe/amar poran bodhu klanto hosto prosharia/bohu bhalobeshe/dharibe tomar bahu"* [PROTIKKHA/SONAR TORI]. According to Tagore, the meeting between the Soul and the Supreme Soul is possible only through death. Thus, in the philosophy of Tagore, death is synonymous to completion. Like eternal time, death is also inevitable. No one can control their motion. In Tagore's spiritualism, death is the other name for eternal time. In other writing, he says, *"Bedomontre ache mrityu o tar chhaya, amrito o tar chhaya-ubhoyke e tini nijer modhhe ek kore rekhechen. Jar moddhe samosto donder abashan hoe ache, tini e hochhen charam satya. Tini bishudhhatama jyoti, tini nirmaltama andhakar."* [PREM/SANTINIKETAN]. Now, the question arises, why has Tagore visualized the Supreme Soul along with death in blue and black colors? So, has he found the Supreme Soul in Sri Krishna, just like in the Gauriya Vaishnav philosophy? Although he has said that the love songs composed by the Vaishnav poets were inspired by the love between the common people-*"Eto premkatha-Radhikar chittadirna tibra byakulata/churi kori laiacho kar mukh, kar/ ankhi hote*!" [VAISHNAV KABITA/SONAR TORI].

The Concept of Love

But, he then realized that, since love originates in the heart, there is no difference between the love for a person and the love for God- *"Debotare jaha dite pari, di e tai/priyojane-priyojane jaha dite pai/ tai di debotare; aar pabo kotha!/ debotare priyo kori, priyere debota"* [VAISHNAV KABITA/SONAR TORI]. Tagore, in his writings, has visualized the Supreme Soul or Death in the color blue, the sea water, the color black and the darkness of night. Simultaneously, he has visualized the origin of life in the first rays of the sun in early morning, the eastern direction and in dawn and has said that one is the consequence of the other. In this context we can refer to Tagore's own interpretation-".*amar barabar e kathai mone hoe je,diner belata mortoloker, aar ratribelata suroloker.maus bhoy pay,manus kajkormo kare,manus tar payer kacher pothta spasta kore dekhte chay, eijonne etoboro ekta alo jwalte hoyeche. Devotar bhoy nei,devotar kaaj nishsabde gopone, devotar chalar sange stabdhater kono birodh nei,eijonnei asim andhakar devsabhar astoron. Devota ratrei amader batayane ese dekha den."*[JAPAN-YATRI] In the same essay, the poet also wrote-*"din aloker dwara abil,andhakari param nirmal. Andhakar ratri samudrer moto; ta anjaner moto kalo,kintu tabu niranjan. Aar din nadir moto; ta kalo nay, kintu pankil".* Tagore has considered the color black as the Supreme Soul or his 'MANASSUNDARI' and this is evident from his writings-*"...Jedik theke oi manoharan ondhokarer bansi bajche oi dikei manusher somostp aradhona, somosto kabya, somosto silpokala, somosto beeratya, somosto atyatyag much phirie ache; oi dike cheyei manush rajyasukh jalanjali diye bibagi hoe berie geche, maranke mathae kore nieche. Oi kaloke dekhe manush bhuleche. Oi kalor bansitei manushke uttor meru dakkhin meru te taane...."*[JAPAN-YATRI]

Tagore's spiritualism which he realized during the period of 'SONAR TORI' and 'CHHINNO PATAVALI' originates from his deep love for life. He has written, *"...e jeno ei brihat dharonir proti ekta narir taan-ek samaye jakhon ami ei prithibir song eek hoe chillum, jakhon amr opor sabuj ghaas uthto, sarater alo porto, surjo kirane amar sudur bistrito shyamal onger protyek romkup theke jouboner sugandhi uttap utthito hote thakto, ami kato dur durantor, kato desh deshantarer jal, sthal, parbot byapto kore ujjal akasher niche nisstabdho bhabe shue pore thaktum, takhan sarat surjaloke amar brihat sarbange je ekti anandaras ekti jiboni sakti ottonto obbyakto, ardhachetan ebong ottonto prokanda brihat bhabe sancharito hote thakto, tai jeno khanikta mone pare-amar ei je moner bhab e jeno eii protinioto onkurito mukulito pulokito surjo santha adim prithibir bhab. Jeno amar ei chetonar probaho prithibir prottyek ghaase ebong gacher shikare shikare shirae shirae dhire dhire probahito hochhe. Somosto sosshyokhetra romanchito hoe uthche ebongg narkel gacher prattyek pata jiboner abege tharthar kore kanpche...."*[CHHINNO PATRAVALI/LETTER NO. 70]. In the poem 'VASUNDHARA' and 'SAMUDRER PRATI' from 'SONAR TORI', the poet has had the same realization.

Spirit of MANASSUNDARY

The realization of infinity within the finite has introduced the poet's 'MANASSUNDARI' to him. 'MANASSUNDARI' is the combination of two words- 'MANAS' and 'SUNDARI'. In Bengali, the meaning of the word 'MANAS' is heart and 'SUNDARI' means a beautiful woman. The poet, in his conscience, has realized that the energy to move on with life is provided by this 'MANASSUNDARI'. He has realized that his 'MANSSUNDARI' easily travels between the finite and the infinite. She is present in water, on land and in the universe. She is always entering and leaving the poet's mind. In the words of the poet, *"swarga hote marta bhumi/ koricho bihar; sandhar kanak barne/rangicho anchal! Usher galito swarne/goricho mekhola; purno totinir jale/koricho bistar..."* etc. [MANASSUNDARI/SONAR TORI]. In the same poem, in another line, the poet has said, *"snigdho hasta hani/lalate bulae dao; na kohia bani,/santwana bhoria prane, kobire tomar/ ghum paraiya dia kakhon abar /chole jao nisshobdo charane"*. Therefore, he did get 'MANASSUNDARI' in his life but understood that it is not possible to get her in a permanent form. The poet realized that in the varieties of nature, its infinities and in the various situations of the mortal being there is present 'MANASSUNDARI' or the Supreme Soul. Since the poet realized this 'MANASSUNDARI' from his inner conscience, we could understand the complete meaning of the word 'MANAS'. 'SUNDARI' is a feminine word, but, we have already discussed that the Supreme soul is neither feminine nor masculine. The poet himself has explained this contradiction. He has said, *"Manasi rupini ogo basanabasini,/alokbasona ogo, nirobbhasini,/parojonme tumi ki go murtimoti hoe/janmibe manabgrihe nariroop loe/anindosundari?"*. [MANASSUNDARI/SONAR TORI]. Tagore was the worshipper of love. To him, beauty is that in which resides truth and goodness. The poet, in this poem, has imagined this beauty as a woman. However, he questions himself, *"Sei tumi murtite dibe ki dhara?"*. It means that the heart of the poet does not want to give the beauty of the nature, which is abstract and absolute, any particular form. But, in any form, that is, in an idol or as an abstract idea, Tagore's 'MANASSUNDARI' is the Supreme Soul. At the end of the poem, in Tagore's language itself, we get his acceptance-*"Eso supti, eso santi/ eso priye, mugdho mouno sakarun kanti,/ bokkhe more laha tani; soao jatane/ maranshusnigdho shubhro bismriti sayone"*.

Tagore found his 'MANASSUNDARI' in the infinite mysteries of the world. She is the inspiration for all of the poet's works. At one point of time, we feel that maybe the poet has given up his fate in the hands of this 'MANASSUNDARI'. He has asked, *"Aar kato dure niye jabe more/he sundari?/bolo, kon paar bhiribe tomar/sonar tori"*[NIRUDDESH JATRA/SONAR TORI]. In the first poem of the book 'SONAR TORI', the poet had mentioned about a boat which we took as a symbol for eternal time. In this poem, the poet again talks about that same boat. The only difference is that in the first poem the poet could not completely recognize the boatman whereas in the poem 'NIRUDDESH JATRA', the poet has referred to this boatman as 'MANASSUNDARI'. She is Tagore's 'JIBONDEVATA'. He wants to know from his 'JIBONDEVATA', in which direction his life will head after that point of time. The Supreme Soul or 'JIBONDEVATA' informs him, *"Nirabe dekhao onguli tuli/akul sindhu uthiche akuli/dure poschime dubiche tapan/gagano kone/ki ache hothae-chalechi kisher/anneshane"*. The poet then realizes that he has to gain knowledge of the literature of the west.

Tagore's realization of the Soul and the Supreme Soul has grown upon the ancient philosophy of India. According to the directions of 'MANASSUNDARI', the poet now wants to gain knowledge of the west. He clearly realizes this instruction of 'MANASSUNDARI'-*"Jakhon prothom dekechile tumi/ke jabe sathe/ chahinu barek tomar nayane/ nabin prate/ dekhale samukhe prosaria kar/ poschim pane asim sagar/ chanchol alo ashar moton/ kanpiche jale/ torite uthia sudhanu takhon/ache ki hothae nabin jibon/ ashar swapon phole ki hothae/ sonar phole?"*. In another place, the poet has written, *"Asimer sadhana ei sundarir jonne, seijonnei tar bansi birat andhakarer bhitar diye emon byakul hoe bajche; asimer sadhana ei sundarike nutan nutan malaye nutan kore sajachhe. Oi kalo ei rupasike ek muhurto buker theke namie rakhte paren na, kenona, e je tar parama sampad. Chotor jonne baror ei sadhana je ki asim, ta phuler paprite paprite pakhir pakhae pakhae megher ronge ronge manusher hridoyer aparup labannye muhurte muhurte dhora porche."* [JAPAN-YATRI].

Concluding Thoughts

It may be said in this context that the poem 'MANASSUNDARI' has been written within 15-18 December, 1892 [RABIJIBANI VOL 3, Prasanta Kumar Paul]. Regarding this poem, in the later years, in a letter, Tagore has written, *"Kabita amar bahu kaler preyosi. Bodhoe jakhon amar rothir moto boyosh chilo takhon theke amar songe bagdutta hoechilo..."* [CHHINNO PATRAVALI/LETTER NO. 94]. Two years before writing this poem, he went to Europe for the second time. His experience of each and every day of this journey can be found in the essay, 'EUROPE-YATRIR DIARY'. In this diary, we get Tagore's acute observation and interpretation of eastern western literature. After returning to India, according to the instructions of Maharshi Devendranath Tagore, he went to Siladaha to look after their land. This poem was written during his time in Silaidaha. But Tagore's idea of 'MANASSUNDARI' began from his previous book 'MANASI'. In a letter, Tagore has informed about his 'MANASSUNDARI', *"Bhalo kare bhebe dekhte gele manasir bhalobasha angsatukui kabyakatha- baro rokomer sundar rokomer khela matra- or asal satyi katha tuku hochhe ei je, manush ki chae ta kichu jane naa-...ami emon obosthae moner songe aposhe bojhapora kore kalpanar kalpobrikkher mayaphal parbar chesta korchi.... Manusher mone ishwarer moto asim akansha ache, kintu ishwarer moto asim khamata nei-keu ba bolche ache- bole bohirjagat e chesta kore berachhe- keu ba jane, nei- tai akansha- rajye bosei ardho -niraswas bhabe kalpanaputtoli gorie take pujo korche. Ekei bolo bhalobasha? ...ami bhalobashi anekke- kintu manasi te jake khara korechi se manoshei ache.- se artist er hathe rochito ishwarer prothom asampurna pratima."*[CHITHIPATRA 5/ to PROMATHA NATH CHOWDHURY/LETTER NO. 7].

Tagore has referred to this same thought in the essay 'JAPAN-YATRI'-*"Ei prakasher jagat, ei gourangi, tar bichitro ranger saaj pore avishar e choleche- oi kalor dike oi anirbochonio abbyaktor dike. Bandha niyomer moddhe bandha thakatei tar maran- se kulkei sarbosso kore chup kore bose thakte pare naa, se kul khuie berie poreche. Ei berie jaoa bipader jatra, pathe kanta, pathe saap, pothe jhar-bristi- somosto ke atikram kore, bipad ke upekkha kore se je choleche, se kebol oi abbyakto asim er taane. Abbyakter dike, aror dike prakasher ei kul khoano avishar-jatra,proloyer bhitor die, biplaber kantapathe pade pade rakter chinho eke"*. Tagore's spiritual thought has a unique characteristic. It is not the theory of any particular religion. Tagore was inspired by the philosophy of Soul and Supreme Soul from ancient literature, especially from the *Upanishads,* and the philosophy of Sri Radha and Sri Krishna from 'Gauriya Vaishnav Darshan'. But his own philosophy of *'atma'* and *'paramatma'* is much vaster because he combined the beauty and characteristics of the nature along with the philosophy of the Soul and Supreme soul. In Tagore's spiritualism, just as the Soul is eager to meet with the Supreme Soul, the incomplete desires to be complete, the day wants to lose itself into night and brightness wants to become complete in darkness. Tagore has written, *"Ei abbyakto keboli jodi na-matra, sunno-matra hoten ta hole prakasher kono arthoi thakto na, tahole bigyaner abhibyakti kebol ekta shobdomatra hoto. Byakto Jodi abbyakteri prakash na hoto tahole ja kichu ache ta nishchal hoe thakto, keboli aaro-kichur dike aponake nutan kore tulto na. ei aaro-kichur dikei somosto jagater anondo keno. Ei ajana aaro-kichur bansi shunei se kul tyag kore keno. Oi dike shunno noe bolei oi dikei she purnoke anubhav kore bolei. Shei jonnoi Upanoshad bolechen- bhumoibo shukhong, bhumattweabo bijiggyashitabyah. Shei jonnoi to srishtir ei leela dekhchi, alo egie choleche andhakarer akule, andhakar neme asche alor kule."*[JAPAN-YATRI]. So, Tagore's 'MANASSUNDARI' is not a theory. It is his completely individual realization which grew due to his vast knowledge about ancient and medieval philosophy and literature and an acute interpretation of our universe. He has said, *"...idear probaho anadi utso theke ucchosito hoe satasahasra moner moddhe diye anantakaler dike probahito hoe choleche, sei sutre amar songe somosto otit kaler ebong anagata kaler jog...sekhane amar anondo ebong bedona bishwabyapi."* [CHINNO PATRAVALI/ LETTER NO. 243].

References

Bharatiya Atijhya O Rabindranath/Nihar Ranjan Ray/ Satabarsho Purti Granthamala 2/ Sanskaran January 2004

Chinno Patravali/ Vishwabharati Sanskaran Ashar 1411

Chithipatra/ Vol. 5/ Vishwabharati / Sanskaran Boishak 1400

Rabijiboni/ Tritiyo Khanda/ Prothom Sanskaran/ Prasanta Kumar Paul

Rabindra Rachanavali/ Vishwabharati/ 125th Rabindra Jonmo Jayanti Upolokkhe Prokashito Sulabh Sanskaran/ Volume No. 2

Rabindra Rachanavali/ Vishwabharati/ 125th Rabindra Jonmo Jayanti Upolokkhe Prokashito Sulabh Sanskaran/ Volume No. 6

Rabindra Rachanavali/ Vishwabharati/ 125th Rabindra Jonmo Jayanti Upolokkhe Prokashito Sulabh Sanskaran/ Volume No. 7

Rabindra Rachanavali/ Vishwabharati/ 125th Rabindra Jonmo Jayanti Upolokkhe Prokashito Sulabh Sanskaran/ Volume No. 8

Rabindra Rachanavali/ Vishwabharati/ 125th Rabindra Jonmo Jayanti Upolokkhe Prokashito Sulabh Sanskaran/ Volume No. 10

Rabindra Rachanavali/ Vishwabharati/ 125th Rabindra Jonmo Jayanti Upolokkhe Prokashito Sulabh Sanskaran/ Volume No. 14

Rabindranath/ Sri Subodh Chandra Sengupta/ Sanskaran November 2000

Rabirashmi/ Charuchandra Bandyapadhya

Shardhasatabarshe Rabindranath/ Bangladesher Sraddhanjali/ Edited By Anisujjaman/ Vishwabharati/ Sanskaran Boishak 1419

2

Spiritualism in Rabindranath Tagore's Philosophy

Prarthita Biswas and Jayanta Mete

Abstract

Spiritualism, in philosophy, is a characteristic of any school of thought that affirms the existence of immaterial reality which is imperceptible to our senses. Defined in this way, spiritualism embraces a vast array of highly diversified philosophical views. Most patently, it applies to any philosophy that accepts the notion of an infinite, personal God, the immortality of the soul, or the immateriality of the intellect and will. It also includes belief in such ideas as finite cosmic forces or a universal mind, provided that they transcend the limits of gross materialistic interpretation. In Tagore's philosophy all concepts of God, self, the immortality of the soul etc. as interrelated. Tagore believes God, self and nature to be inseparable aspects of reality. They are essentially the same. Tagore sees that the goal of religion is attaining union with the Infinite. Philosophy is concerned with the knowledge of reality, and the realisation of reality is the concern of religion. Tagore assumed that "True knowledge is that which perceives the unity of all things in God." Tagore through his vast immortal literary works, educated us that, the whole world is a expression of God, and that there is no unbridgeable gulf between our world and God's, and that God is the one who can offer the greatest love and joy.

***Keywords**: spiritualism, Rabindranath Tagore, philosophy, soul, religion*

Introduction

Tagore's conception of religion springs from his conception of reality. He believes that the finite, imperfect self is real but the underlying infinite and the perfect self are much more real, hence the religion of human being is the realisation of this perfect self or the Infinite. Tagore also affirms that diversity is quite true but there is a unity which is truer which we discover behind diversity. It finds expression in various forms and ways. He knows and makes use of this world where it is endless and thus attains greatness, but he realises his own truth where it is perfect and thus finds his fulfilment. It is clear thus that to Tagore, religion is the breath of life. For him there is no defined religion of any particular church or creed, but it is one that illumines all religions. It bestows its divine light to show the real value of things, it is the source of human being's deepest longings and aspirations, and it makes death beautiful. His every thought is dominated by the consciousness of God, and this consciousness pervades his being, bringing his mind into a perpetual attitude of worship. Tagore gives us a pure religion, which is substantially the same in all ages and all climates, in which the purified spirit of human being can find its congenial home. Finally, the most beautiful thing about Tagore is his belief in unity in diversity.

Rabindranath Tagore was a universal personality. His genius was versatile, synthetic and original. He was influenced by the Christian conception of the fatherhood of God and might have been inspired in his early years by Shakespeare, Goethe, Wordsworth, Ruskin, Shelley, Keats and Browning. But the roots of his intellectual creativism and emotional make-up lie in the Upanishads, in the majestic poetry of Kalidas, in the lyrics of Vaisnavas, in the mystic poems of Kabir and the religious atmosphere of the Brahmo Samaj. Different philosophers have described the character of Tagore's philosophy differently. Hirendrenath Datta describes his philosophy as Concrete Monism. It is monism because reality is conceived as one, and it is concrete because the one reality is not an abstract principle negating completely the reality of the many, but is a concrete whole, comprehending the many within its bosom. Radhakrishnan says, "We do not know whether it is Rabindranath's own heart or the heart of India that is beating here". Tagore in his philosophy tries to revive the ancient ideals of life; and then, they have been re-stated in accordance with the needs of the present times. The traditional philosophical notions of India have been brought out by Tagore from the dark abyss of abstraction, where they were lying all the time, into the open to be viewed in the light of the present philosophical beliefs. Tagore was a writer of deep originality and creative attainments. He was a patriot. During the day of the agitation against the partition of Bengal his stirring words rang with strength and he was later on venerated as a national poet. He stood for social reform, Swadeshi and the solidarity of the country. He was not a politician but a political prophet who taught unity, harmony peace and co-operation. He has given to modern India a philosophy of world-and-life-affirmation.

Spiritualism, in philosophy, is a characteristic of any school of thought that affirms the existence of immaterial reality which is imperceptible to our senses. Defined in this way, spiritualism embraces a vast array of highly diversified philosophical views. Most patently, it applies to any philosophy that accepts the notion of an infinite, personal God, the immortality of the soul, or the immateriality of the intellect and will. It also includes belief in such ideas as finite cosmic forces or a universal mind, provided that they transcend the limits of gross materialistic interpretation.

In Tagore's philosophy we find all these concepts such as God, self, the immortality of the soul etc. as interrelated. Tagore believes God, self and nature to be inseparable aspects of reality. They are essentially the same. According to Tagore, consciously or unconsciously we have in our life this feeling of the truth which is ever larger than its appearance; for our life is facing the infinite, and it is in movement. Its aspiration is therefore infinitely more than its achievement, and as it goes on, it finds that no realization of truth ever leaves it stranded on the desert of finality, but carries it to a region beyond. This reference to the beyond is the essential element in religious longing. He not only speaks of God or Self or the infinite but also speaks of the ways to be one with the infinite.

Rabindranath Tagore and Spiritualism

Rabindranath is often regarded as some sort of a spiritual leader, a prophet. Some noted Westerners were openly contemptuous of Tagore's apparent mysticism, while, needless to say, many others embraced it. Tagore's almost-saintly appearance and the poems which, on the surface, express some mysticism, perhaps discouraged – and encouraged – those who believe a book should be judged only by its cover and they refused to delve deeper into the images Rabindranath painted with words. After his death, Rabindranath became our official Thakur (the Bengali surname for the Tagores, which also means "god", of all things) apart from the seasonal ones. According to Rabindranath Tagore, the notion of God as an impersonal entity does not appeal to him. Tagore feels that a Brahman, who stares at people with frozen eyes, regardless of their selfless devotion and silent suffering, does not appeal to our religious instinct. He feels that God has to be brought nearer to man. One can take interest in God only when He is humanized. Tagore asserts that the supreme has to be a person. He tries his best to show that this would, in no way, imply any limitation or imperfection on the part of God. He says, 'If this universe is not the manifestation of a person, then it is a stupendous deception and perpetual insult to him'. Hence, for Tagore, the world is not unreal or maya as is said in Vedanta. It is as real as reality because it is the manifestation of reality.The religion Tagore is talking about here has nothing to do with the religion the texts of which describe an omnipotent figure creating the universe out of nowhere according to His will and being vengeful on not being worshipped.

Tagore's Spiritualism and Idealism made him a cult figure among the educationists of the times. He wants to achieve the essential unity of the universe through God. For Tagore, 'the object of education is to give man the unity of truth'. Tagore believes in a spiritual world which is the innermost truth of this world. Tagore wants to make ' the purpose of education nothing short of the highest purpose of man, the fullest growth and freedom of soul' He strongly advocated that moral and spiritual education is more important than bookish knowledge for an integral development of human personality. Tagore fought against the dominance of materialistic outlook of life and he was an idealist to the core. But he believes that education should be related to the life-currents of the people for which it is meant. Tagore writes, "Joy flows through the universe, the sun and moon drink of it, A full measure. The light of the joy of goodness, Stays ever effulgent... Why are you all by yourself, confined to your own ego?"

Tagore's Contribution to education is highly relevant in the modern scenario and many of his innovations have now become part of general educational practices. The visionary in Rabindranath and the great educationist in him solved the problem of today a century earlier. The problems of modern education are attendance, use of other unfair means and indiscipline. It is more certificates oriented irrelevant of intelligence and correlation with Nature. Tagore solved these problems in a grand way. Freedom in the class solved the problem of attendance, absence of invigilator solved the copying or use of unfair means. Thus Tagore's educational system is a great achievement. It is regretted that we did not try to apply the formulas suggested by Tagore. That is why his Tagore's Santiniketan, Vishwa Bharti and Sriniketan may said to constitute Tagore's educational trinity through which he tried to developed his education theme.

The poet selected for its motto an ancient Sanskrit verse, "Yatra Vishwam bhavatieka nidam", *which means, where the whole world meets in a single nest.".* Tagore rightly observed:

"The world today is wild with the delirium of hatred,
The conflicts are cruel and unceasing in anguish,
crooked are its paths, tangled its bonds of greed.
All creatures are crying for a new birth of thine,
O thou of boundless life,
save them, raise thine eternal voice of hope,
let Love's lotus with its inexhaustible treasure of honey
open its petals in thy light."

Spiritualism in Rabindranath Tagore's Poetry

Rabindranath Tagore's spiritual outlook and humanism were derived from man, nature and Brahma or God. He held the view that the route to spiritual development was from 'body to society, from society to totality and from totality to the spiritual domain'. In this way, the melody of the soul was intertwined with the universal power. But what was required for this inter-mingling was connecting the world of nature with that of human beings. To Tagore, the whole human body appeared to be reverberating with the touch of light, air, affection, love, bliss, joy and electricity, as if embedded in a supernatural flute. Although he might have been influenced by the romantic movements of the time, the Brahma Samaj, the Bauls, Sufism or the Vedanta philosophy of Upanishads, those views were in some respects Tagore's very own. We can very well comprehend how his spirit was liberated by connecting with the universe, the nature and the environment which surrounded him, by looking at the following lines:

> *"Where He has given himself up through his infinite mirth and youthfulness, there is no dearth of affluence there, no limit to variety, and the riches are unending. There, the sky is lit in a thousand directions wearing the girdles of stars; there, beauty surfaces in so many new forms, the gushing of the spirit never stops."*

By connecting with our environment in this manner, our self-consciousness becomes sweeter, deeper and brighter. The man within us grows into a fuller entity. Our soul seems to mingle with His colours and flavour. Rabindranath had identified this phenomenon as devotion. He said, "The poet's task is to ignite this awareness in the consciousness of man, to transform indifference into a newer zeal. That poet is great in the eyes of humans who diffuses human hearts with the attributes of constancy, grandeur, freedom, omnipresence and depth."

This theme of liberation of the spirit is found in many of Rabindranath's poems. There is thus a new excitement for self-expansion in 'Kalpana' "Oh bird, my bird / blind, don't fold your wings now". The formula for revival of the self-encompassed the spirit of the universe. This inseparability of the self is made clearer in the poem 'Anobachchhinna Ami' "I saw under the infinite sky / I rock while seated on the swing of light". In the 'Geetanjali-Geetimalya-Geetali' phase, the soul of Rabindranath could become one with the cosmos. Overwhelmed by the unified voice of the waves and the forests, the ocean and the land, the sky and the earth, the poet wrote in his later years:

> *"I have tied you with my two joints,*
> *Your creations are with you and me,*
> *Your pain today is my pain.*

Today you know yourself
With my knowledge.
My surprised eyes are touched by a wand of gold,
It has revived the sense of beauty
In your own consciousness." ('Doita', Shyamoli)
Then in 'Prantik', Tagore says,
"I have bought my freedom from bonds
Crossing the far away sky of soul, the Milky Way,
In the pilgrimage of light, on the fine coast of extinction."
In the same vein, Tagore asserts in 'Nabojatak',
"The human child brings back again and again
The message of eternal hope
As if bringing along
The light of freedom in a new dawn."
The theme is even more pronounced when in the poem 'Shesh lekha' Tagore declares,
"Let the bonds of the world come to an end,
The vast universe has opened its arms,
The soul is fearless to know
The great unknown."

In these autobiographical poems, Rabindranath strove to look at his own self in different light and perspectives. In the process, he has equated the spiritual force with the eternal force of the universe. The Bauls and Kirtans of Bangla had a great influence on the poems and songs of Tagore. He stayed almost permanently in East Bengal for around a decade from the age of thirty. He belonged to an affluent high-class society in Kolkata, but was exposed to mainstream Bengali society while living in Shilaidaha-Shahjadpur-Patisar. He was especially captivated by the Baul songs he heard in Kushtia and made wide use of these Baul tunes in his patriotic, love and prayer songs. He was even termed as the greatest Baul of Bangla at that time.

Spiritualism had transcended all aspects of Rabindranath's life and he looked at man and nature as images of God. He wrote in a letter, "If I have realized God or got any hint about him, then it was from this world, its people, trees, animals, dust and soil from all these objects." We therefore find the poet comprehending God as dearest to man and his companion in times of sorrow, as in the volumes of 'Geetanjali'-'Geetimalya'-'Geetali'. In 'Balaka' (1916), he depicted God as the determinant of human destiny. Ultimately, this God finds His place in the heart of man and becomes one and the same in the eyes of the poet.

Relevance of Tagore's ideas in the Modern World

Gurudeva Rabindranath Tagore (1861-1941) was a man of vision and viewpoint. Tagore was the Renaissance man of modern India - the bridge from an Indian culture traditional education system. Tagore's educational ideals have been agreed by other educationists and many of his innovations have now become part of general educational practices, but his special role lay in the emphasis on harmony balance between materialism and spiritualism in total development of personality. Talking about the crisis of education, Tagore said that a boy should be permitted to read books of his own choice including to the prescribed textbooks he must read for his school work. Our education system is without delight. Small children are burdened with bundle of books .Tagore wrote: From childhood to adolescence and again from adolescence to manhood, we are coolies of the goddess of learning, carrying loads of words on our folded backs. Gurudeva was always concerned regarding socialization. His educational institution represented a way of thinking, feeling, and living, both in society and in education. Some of his students, indeed, became teachers, national leaders and Nobel prizewinners.

Education is worthwhile which enables a human being to have 'Mukti' or freedom from all vices. India had visualized a socialistic democratic pattern of society in its constitution. The modern philosophy of Education builds up with development of critical thinking and reasoning. The Twentieth century thinkers of India developed the philosophy of Humanism, equality, brotherhood, world economy, and world government. Among leading Educators of India, Tagore has done much to shape the future course of educational practice at home and abroad.

Rabindranath Tagore who was a leading spokesman for compassionate humanism, nationalism, internationalism and culture in India. Tagore's song 'jana gana mana adhinayaka' (1911) invoking the same goal of a larger humanity was chosen as our national anthem remains a symbol of modern India's legacy of universal humanity. He was one of the first in India to argue for a humane educational system that was in touch with the environment and aimed at overall development of the personality. Tagore is known as the benefactor of humanity and expressed his faith in God and advocated spiritual, humanistic and character development.

The core of Tagore's contribution was learning from nature, music and life. This is the reason why his education is easily acceptable by human mind. The visionary in Rabindranath and the great educationist in him solved the problem of today a century earlier. The problems of modern education are attendance, use of other unfair means and indiscipline. It is more certificates oriented irrelevant of intelligence and correlation with Nature. Tagore solved these problems in a grand way. Freedom in the class solved the problem of attendance, absence of invigilator solved the copying or use of unfair means. Thus Tagore's educational system is a great achievement. It is regretted that we did not try to apply the formulas suggested by Tagore. That is why his Tagore's Santiniketan, Vishwa Bharti and Sriniketan may said to constitute Tagore's educational trinity through which he tried to developed his education theme. The poet selected for its motto an ancient Sanskrit verse, "Yatra Vishwam Bhavatieka Nidam", which means, where the whole world meets in a single nest.

Conclusion

Rabindranath Tagore was not an ordinary person; he is a genuine manifestation of the Indian spirit in the nineteenth century. He epitomises peace and beauty in the world where the forces of racial rivalry and religious division are very strong. His vision of religion is universal in the sense that he identifies religion with love. For Tagore religion is the hunger for unity through joy and sorrow. This hunger for unity is the spiritual substance of his religion. This desire for unity is the desire to discover the rest of the world in oneself, just as a mother discovers herself in her child.

Tagore's religion is an aspect of human spirit. It does not come from God, it is rooted in human being, and, therefore, his religion is a poet's religion. Religion, for him, is a principle of unity that binds us together; it is our essential quality, inherent in us. Religion enables us to cultivate and express these qualities in us. Thus, to realise the principle of unity is spiritual and our effort to be true to it is our religion. Religion trains our attitude and behaviour towards the Infinite in its human form. Religion emerges from ultimate self-consciousness. It is to see the Infinite in the finite, to find God in all things. Religion does not consist in knowledge or philosophy, truth is the essence of realising one's personality, fulfilment. Religion enables us to experience the deeper unity of all that exists, it is God. All the same, religion is not the ultimate goal but it ushers us to our perfect liberation in the universal spirit across the furthest limits of humanity itself.

Tagore introduces us to a human God, who has human qualities. His God comes to our lives in our daily experiences— God comes to us every moment of our life, He comes in the sunny April through the forest path, He is present in the gloom of July night, He comes to us through our joys and sorrows. Tagore's God is not in the temple, but in the place where the tiller tills his field, He is present in the pathmaker breaks the stones. This is really the God of our day-to-day experience. It is the God of every person. This God lives among the poor and the lowliest. Tagore, here, calls us to find God in our own life and our life experiences. Tagore's experience of God is an invitation for us to experience the silent footsteps of God in our life.

Finally, the most beautiful thing about Tagore is his belief in unity in diversity. He was fortunate enough to be born in a country where cultural diversity is so rich and beautiful. Tagore explored this unity in diversity to the maximum. This type of religion cuts across the religious barrier, it is universal in human being. His religion challenges us to look upon human beings as ends in themselves and not as means. If we dwell upon his vision of religion, irrespective of our religious differences, we will be merged in a beautiful harmony that is our Indianness. As long as Tagore lives in our memory, he will continue to stir the conscience of the world.

References

Dutta, Hirendranath, "Rabindranath as a Vedantist", Visva Bharati Quaterly, May-Oct 1941.

Prasad, Devi, Rabindranath Tagore, Philosophy of education and Painting, p. 1.

Rabindranath Tagore, Education in the Ashram, in Shiksha, p. 311.

Rabindranath, Personality, Kessinger Publishing, U.K., pp. 25-26.

Radhakrishnan, "The Philosophy of Rabindranath" Macmillan 7 co, London, 1941 p. vii.

V.P. Varma, Modern Indian Political Thought, Lskshmi Narayan Agarwal, Agra, 1987, p. 76.

3

'*Sadhana*' by Tagore: A Spiritual Approach to Life

Mohammad Hammad Reaz

Abstract

This paper seeks to study the collection of Tagore's lectures in the book Sadhana, a breath-taking collection of spiritual discourses given by Rabindranath Tagore to the boys in his school. A repository of the timeless wisdom of the East, Sadhana is one of the most profound books on spirituality that we would ever find. Compiled and translated by Tagore from his Bengali lectures, the book consists of eight essays in which Tagore answers some of the most profound questions of life: why did God create this world? Why would a perfect being, instead of remaining eternally concentrated in Himself, go through the trouble of manifesting the universe? Why does evil exist? Do love and beauty have a purpose? Tagore masterfully brings the spiritual truths behind these profound questions to light with his lucid explanation of the Sanskrit verses of the Upanishads and the teachings of Jesus and Buddha Spiritualism, in Tagore's philosophy, is a characteristic of thought that affirms the existence of immaterial reality, which is imperceptible to our senses. Defined in this way, spiritualism, in general, embraces a vast array of highly diversified philosophical views. Most patently, it applies to any philosophy that accepts the notion of an infinite, personal God, the immortality of the soul, or the immateriality of the intellect and will. It also includes belief in such idea as finite cosmic forces or a universal mind, provided that they transcend the limits of gross materialistic interpretation. In Tagore's philosophy we find all

these concepts such as God, self, the immortality of the soul etc. as interrelated. Tagore believes God, self and nature to be inseparable aspect of reality.
***Keywords**: Tagore, Sadhana, Spiritual, Upanishad*

Rabindranath Tagore (1861-1941), the poet- saint of India with his creative soul endeavoured upon varied literary enterprises- poetry, drama, novel and short stories to mention a few, that are truly the manifestation of his realization of man's integral presence in the overall infinite and sublime purpose of the cosmic Godhead. *Sadhana*, a collection of Tagore's discourses delivered at various instances to his students at *Bolpur*, *Bengal*, contrary to his claim that these lectures do not carry any philosophical bent of mind, in fact represents the culmination of the poet's philosophy of life in a comprehensive manner[1]. The Indian poet and the artist is not a philosopher in the academic sense of the term-in the sense in which on reads and writes on philosophy as an academic discipline. Moreover, he is neither an analyst nor a system builder. Instead he has always considered himself to be a poet and neither a scholar nor a philosopher[2]. He acknowledges that his religion is a poet's religion. In the Times Literary Supplement, the following is written:

> *"Perhaps no living poet was more religious and no man of religion was more poetical than this great Indian[3].*

Deeply indebted to the *Upanishads* and the teachings of *Buddha*, Tagore speaks from his own personal experiences at once instinctual and individual, the values of the sprit, which enables man to achieve communion with the divine in his everyday life. He sees creation as the revelation of truth. His mystic mind gets absorbed in his personal God and becomes an instrument in the hands of God. In his spiritual vision, Tagore advocates a poet's religion, which is all embracing and all loving. His religion does not come from his knowledge of the world as a phenomenon that revolves and rotates. His religion is that of an artist trying to explain the relationship between the finite and the Infinite, and his spiritual vision has a beauty, power and sweetness of its own which is unique, unequalled and original. *Swami Adiswaranandaof* the *Ramakrishna-Vivekananda* Centre of New York, in his preface to Tagore: The Mystic Poet writes:

> *"The inner seeking spirituality of India infused all of Tagore's writings. He wrote in many genres of the deep religious milieu of Hinduism. The values and core beliefs of the Hindu scriptures permeated his work." Says Swami: "Rabindranath Tagore's philosophical and spiritual thoughts transcend all limits of language, culture, and nationality. In his writings, the poet takes us on a spiritual quest and gives us a glimpse of the infinite in the midst of the finite, unity at the heart of all diversity, and the Divine in all beings and things of the universe."[4]*

Sadhana comprises of eight titles- 'The Relation of the Individual to the Universe', 'Soul consciousness', 'The Problem of Evil', 'The Problem of Self', 'Realization in Love', 'Realization in Action', 'The Realization of Beauty' and ' The Realization of the Infinite', the poet has offered in this collection the way and means of attaining the ultimate purpose in human life –that is to become one with the Infinite.In his treatment to these means and ways, he deeply focus on a particular approach to human life in accordance to his spiritual vision strewn from Upanishad, this approach of Tagore to human life entertain with a steady balance between two form of human life; inner one and outer/material one.

In his book, *The Philosophy of Rabindranath Tagore*, *S. Radhakrishnan* states that:

> *"Rabindranath's philosophy of life is viewed.....as nothing but the ancient wisdom of India restated to meet the needs of modern times. His writings are a commentary on the Upanishads by an individual of this generation on whom the present age has had its influence. The soul of ancient India is mirrored in them".*[5]

However, *Dr S. Radhakrishnan* discusses Tagore's philosophy of life as is exemplified throughout the creative literary output of the poet ranging from his early writings, including *Sadhana* and so on. However, it would be valuable to study *Sadhana*, wherein the poet–philosopher has gathered the entire thesis of his philosophical knowledge and wisdom between the covers of a single text which seeds are strewn and spread separately in his other creation. As Dr *RamaswamiSastri* writes:

> *"All other works of his seems to be like beautiful individual notes while the Sadhana is like the sweet tune running through them all.*[6]

In the first lecture, 'The relation of the Individual to the Universe', Tagore distinguishes between the western ideas of the relationship between nature and man, with those of the Indian concepts. He sees that the forest is the birthplace of human civilization and through the constant intercourse with her varying aspects; it revealed to him that his aim was not to acquire but to realize, to enlarge his consciousness by growing with and growing into his surroundings. He felt that truth is all-comprehensive, that there is no such thing as absolute isolation in existence, and the only way of attaining truth is through the interpenetration of our being into all objects. To realise this great harmony between man's spirit and the spirit of the world was the endeavor of the forest-dwelling sages of ancient India. In the contrary, The West always believed in the mastering of nature because to them nature consisted of inanimate things and the beasts. This kind of thinking stemmed from the sense of superiority that manstood first in the scale of creation that he is born to rule over the universe. Intoday's world situation, this attitude of man has led to diverse problems between not only man and nature but also between man and man. The emphasis of the West on man as a superior being has resulted in the dislocation and destruction of our environment. Whereas in the Indian context, right from the ancient times, India believed that, the forest/nature was the sanctuary to the rishis, a place where the soul of man found reconcilement with the soul of the world. For India, also man is a supreme being but understood that "superiority is not in the power of possession but in the power of union". When confined within the walls of human self, man loses the inner perspective. As *Radhakrishnan* aptly points out:

> *"Rabindranath advocates life in nature and in the open as the best means of spiritual progress, for in nature the religious eye will see the infinite lying stretched in silent smiling repose. According to him the best way to derive inspiration is to lose oneself in the contemplation of nature."*[7]

Only perfect harmony between man and everything else in nature would enable man's soul to comprehend the mysteries of reality and realize the Infinite. Man must thus cross barriers to become more than man, experience the freedom of consciousness, to unite with All: "To be truly united in knowledge, love and service with all beings, and to realize one's self in the all- pervading God is the essence of goodness…Life is immense"[8]

In the next discourse titled 'Soul Consciousness', Tagore lays emphasis on man's search for a system in expediting his everyday affairs of the world:

> *"This search for system is really a search for unity, for synthesis; it is our attempt to harmonize the heterogeneous complexity of outward materials by an inner adjustment. In the search we gradually become aware that to find out the One is to possess the All; that there, indeed is our last and highest privilege".*[9]

To know one self is to understand the world around. Hence, when we understand something, it means then that we find in it something of our own. Tagore draws illustrations from the family, where the parents love their children. It is nothing but the fact that whomsoever we love, we find in him or her, our own soul. We tend to realize that the same supreme soul in us is as well as in our children. The *Upanishad* teaches that in attaining consciousness of one's soul, one attains cosmic consciousness or God-consciousness. First of all man must know how to segregate his soul from his self. The self is the body that causes him pain and suffering, greed and pride, fear and death. However true greatness lies in the realization of the fact that we are not just the physical self or body but our soul is part of the larger consciousness. Man travels from ignorance to light when his soul attains freedom from mundane activities of the physical world:

> *"When a man's life rescued from distractions finds unity in the soul, and then the*

> *consciousness of the infinite becomes at once direct and natural to it as the light is to the flame. All the conflicts and contradictions of life are reconciled; knowledge, love, and action harmonized; pleasure and pain become one in beauty, enjoyment and renunciation equal in goodness; ... it is only the soul, the one in man, which by its very nature can overcome all limits, and finds its affinity with the Supreme One."*[10]

'The Problem of Evil', deals with the fact that suffering and pain and evil in world are only impermanent though we imagine it to be standstill and therefore exaggerate its presence. Tagore too similarly questions the idea of death when he says: "Life as a whole never takes death seriously. It laughs, dances and plays, it builds, hoards, and loves in death's face... we lose sight of the wholeness of a life of which death is part... but the truth is, death is not the ultimate reality" (*Sadhana* 299). There is evil in the world in various forms that we encounter in our everyday life, which is but a manifestation of imperfection in this world. We are forced to learn the limiting weaknesses of human efforts to survive. Man understands that "evil cannot altogether arrest the course of life ... for evil has to pass on, it has to grow into good; it cannot stand to give battle to All" (*Sadhana* 300). Tagore firmly believes that existence cannot be an evil and calls upon the intellect of man "to realize the truth through untruths, and knowledge is nothing but the continually burning up of error to set free the light of truth" (300). The very goal of life is to move from imperfection to perfection, as the poet establishes that:

> *"This life process is going on- we know it, we have felt it; and we have a faith, which no individual instances to the contrary can shake, that the direction of humanity is from evil to good. For we feel that good is the positive element in man's nature and in every age and every clime what man values most is his ideal of goodness." (300)*

Tagore distinguishes between goodness and pleasure and says that while pleasure is limited to one's own self, "goodness is concerned with the happiness of all humanity and for all time" (302). Again, to live in perfect goodness means to realize one's life in the infinite. He draws from *Buddha*'s teachings now to reiterate the point that when the individual is merged in the universal then man is freed from the thralldom of pain. It is therefore important to realize the 'world man' in oneself who remains un- affected by death and suffering and one who understands that pain is but the other side of joy.

In the lecture on 'Problem of Self', Tagore discusses how the self is responsible for the sufferings and the sins that man commits; "It has led man to shame and crime and death; yet it is dearer to him than any paradise where the self lies, securely slumbering in perfect innocence in the womb of Mother Nature" (306). It is in a state of ignorance that we believe that self is an end in itself. It is only *Dharma* that can deliver man from his selfishness or self-centeredness. '*Dharma*' as Tagore interprets for us is the "the innermost nature, the essence, the implicit truth, of all things. *Dharma* is the ultimate purpose that is working in our self" (308). The true nature or essence of our being is the godliness inherent within us. This can be realized only when selfishness is extinguished from us. In recalling the words of *Buddha*, Tagore says:

> *"The emancipation of our physical nature is in attaining health, of our social being in attaining goodness, and of our self in attaining love. This last is what Buddha describes as extinction- the extinction of selfishness. This is the function of love, and it does not lead to darkness but to illumination. This is the attainment of bodhi, or the true awakening; it is the revealing in us of the infinite joy by the light of love."(312)*

In the journey from Self to Soul, the freedom of self-will has to be negated, for which purpose Tagore lays great emphasis on love. Just as God created the universe not out of necessity but out of joy and love, so should man strive to attain freedom from self through love. It is in action that we tend to manifest our nature. The poet gives the example of a mother, who "reveals herself in the service of her children, so our true freedom is not the freedom from action but freedom in action, which can only be attained in the work of love" (310). He brings out the distinction between *maya* and truth, in that *maya* is the self-separate from God, while love is truth or *satyam*. Man has to discard his selfish desires, which hang on to him as his second skin, seeming to be his very nature. But once he starts giving in love then he finds fulfillment in that as is his true nature. Therefore, when the self sees itself in isolation from the soul as the absolute it lives in futility. But it becomes *satyam* when it recognizes its essence in the universal and the infinite:

> *"It is the end of our self to seek that union. It must bend its head low in love and meekness and take its stand where great and small meet. It has to gain by its loss and rise in its surrender...We must know that it is only the revelation of the infinite which is endlessly new and eternally beautiful in us and gives the only meaning to our self."(315)*

In echoing the words of Tagore, *Radhakrishnan* also expresses a similar view when he says that in the annihilation of the self lies the fulfillment of love, which leads man from the self-centered life to a god-centered one.[11]

Tagore's talk on the 'Realization of Love' hinges upon the concept of the infinite love of *Brahma* that manifests itself through finite forms. It is said that though bound by the laws of the world, so as to lead a disciplined and moral life, the human soul sets on its passage from bondage in law to freedom in love. Tagore alludes to *Buddha*'s idea of *Brahma-vihara*, or the joy of living in *Brahma*. This idea entails the proposition that the one, who overcomes pride, hatred, deception, anger, cruelty, and antagonism towards fellow beings and fellow creatures, cultivates the quality of love for all creatures in the process of exercising universal goodwill, attains perfection of consciousness (Tagore 321). Imbibing this key thought from *Buddha*'s teachings, Tagore asserts that: "It is through the heightening of our consciousness into love, and extending it all over the world, that we can attain *Brahma-vihara*, communion with this infinite joy" (321). In the name of civilization, man indulges in cannibalism that deadens consciousness and results in a kind of spiritual suicide. Probably Tagore here refers to the imperial British who deprived nations like India of self-government and self-defense. As he rightly points out,

> *"...we never can have a true view of man unless we have a love for him. Civilization must be judged and prized, not by the amount of power it has developed, but by how much it has evolved and given expression to, by its laws and institutions, the love of humanity." (323)*

When love becomes the *modus operandi* among races and peoples, freedom, fair play and justice will replace then treating of people as slaves or instruments of power. Tagore discuses at length the quality of love adding that the world is born out of love, that it is sustained in love, that it moves towards love, and finally enters into love. It is love that enables man to transcend all limitations, as at the same time it is his love of life that urges him to continue his relation with this great world. Only love can harmonize the opposing principles of creation that of unity and diversity, loss and gain, personal and impersonal, bondage and liberation. It is the poet's strong perception, hence, that: "It is the high function of love to welcome all limitations and to transcend them. For nothing is more independent than love, and where else, again, shall we find so much of dependence?" (325). Love is not a product of compulsion but of joy. And this joy which is manifest in creation, "is the realization of truth of oneness, the oneness of our soul with the world and of the world-soul with the supreme lover" (325). Tagore, therefore, equates love to joy that in turn is equated to God.

Rabindranath Tagore's concept about the function of action is well extrapolated in the discourse on 'Realization in Action', wherein the poet philosopher appears to be speaking from his own experience. According to Tagore, a recluse who shuns the society and lives a life of seclusion can never attain God apart from the world of action. As he says aptly:

> *"The more man acts and makes actual what was latent in him, the nearer does he bring the distant Yet-to-be. In that, actualization man is ever making himself more and yet more distinct, and seeing himself clearly under newer and newer aspects in the midst of varied activities, in the state, in society. This vision makes for freedom."(326)*

The soul of man seeks freedom from ignorance or darkness, and in order to realize itself distinctly with the world soul, it creates fresh fields of action so as to set itself free in action. He critiques those sanyasins who believe that they can find *Brahma* outside of humanity or society. Tagore stresses the idea that "activity is the play of joy" (331), for just as the *Brahma* finds joy in creation/action so does man need to realize *Brahma* through his everyday action – a two way process. He is of the opinion that one must work to live, and simultaneously live to work; hence, that life and activity are inseparably inter-connected. In quoting the *Upanishad*, Tagore emphasizes that God's nature itself lies in knowledge, power and action. Therefore, one must learn to find joy in work and give oneself entirely to work rather than allow it to overpower us. *Radhakrishnan* points out that Tagore is vehemently against both the Western idea of the importance of the body/flesh/materialism that neglects the soul, as opposed to the Eastern faith in the significance of the soul that neglects the body. According to him, Tagore staunchly propounds the fact that a good balance between the two attitudes towards life is much more fruitful for humanity. Tagore believes in the integration of contemplation and work in the world, and as *Radhakrishnan* wonders about this belief of Tagore, posits the view that: "To live the life of man, both the calm and stress of life, the joy and self-abandonment and the pride of creativity should be chosen …random busyness as well as complete renunciation is a failure to live the life of man"[12]. Tagore ends this lecture on a prayerful note as when he says, "Let us once for all dislodge from our minds the feeble fancy that would make out thy joy to be a thing apart from action, thin, formless, and unsustained" (Tagore 333).

In his teachings on 'The Realization of Beauty', Tagore echoes a simple but universal truth, that unless we take joy in our work or action, it ends up being burdensome. As already specified by Tagore, everything in the universe is created and sustained in love and joy. In order to comprehend this principle in creation, man has divided the whole of creation as either beautiful or non-beautiful. However man has understood the idea of beauty differently at every stage of his growth in history, when there was a time in ancient India the beauty cult belonged to a chosen few. Then came a time, when in the history of aesthetics, people believed that beauty existed in things great and small. Beauty was recognized in common objects and so on. However Tagore attributes this kind of attitude to the narrowness of perception which sharply divides the field of aesthetic consciousness into ugliness and beauty. He says:

> *"When he has the power to see things detached from self-interest and from the insistent claims of the lust of the senses, then alone can he have the true vision of the beauty that is everywhere. Then only can he see that what is unpleasant to us is not necessarily unbeautiful, but has its beauty in truth." (335)*

Tagore also links beauty with truth and posits the view that it is through our sense of truth that we realize order in creation while our sense of beauty helps us recognize harmony in the universe (335). The more we become conscious of this harmony in creation both within (our soul) and without (the physical world), then our life is in itself an expression of beauty that inclines towards the *Brahma*. In other words, as Tagore quotes the words of John Keats, we understand that the aim of our existence is to obtain knowledge that beauty is truth, and truth beauty. It is music, according to Tagore, which is the most direct expression of beauty in art and at the same time the most finite form of the manifestation of the Divine. It is the poets who are the best seers who reflect the beauty of the infinite through the song of their hearts. In every movement of Nature, Tagore identifies the music and harmony of creation, as in the fall of rain, the child's first utterance, and the starry constellation etc. he sums up beautifully the music of his body at night when he is fast asleep-"the heart will throb, the blood will leap in the veins, and the millions of living atoms of my body will vibrate in tune with the note of the harp-string that thrills at the touch of the master" (337).

In his last discourse on 'The Realization of The Infinite', Tagore speaks about the nature of attainment of God. At the outset, he categorically states that God is not a material possession like money, or house or car. All these earthly objects manifest but one truth and that is they have their meaning not in themselves but only in their relation with the infinite. Desire for man is endless but once he realizes that worldly possessions are not the end, but he has to outgrow his desire for them, then that very moment his soul takes to the path of the eternal. He puts forward the proposition that God cannot be possessed; rather, He is to be experienced. In the finite world man is to fulfill his necessities of food, clothing etc, that satisfies a particular need of his. But once his self seeks joy and freedom beyond the finite existence, and then he no longer wants to get but only to be one with the *Brahma*. Tagore draws the analogy of the river, which joins the larger body of water, the ocean, but cannot become the ocean. Similarly man's soul though yearns to become one with the Infinite, however cannot become the *Brahma* Himself:

> *"Brahma is Brahma, he is the infinite ideal of perfection but we are not what we truly are; we are ever to become true, ever to become Brahma. There is the eternal play of love in relation between this being and the becoming; and in the depth of this mystery is the source of all truth and beauty that sustains the endless march of creation." (341)*

Tagore also uses the analogy of the poem to speak about the progress of the soul, which once it realizes the Infinite, is filled with joy and meaning, like a perfect poem. Another important factor regarding the nature of realization is that it can happen not through intellectual knowledge but only through joy and love. *Brahma* can be known only by the soul, "by her joy in him, by her love" (343). Man comes into relation with Him only by union of the whole being. The soul is likened to a bride by the poet and hence the union is a marriage of the *atman* with the *paramatman*:

> *"When the soul-bride understands this well, her heart is blissful and at rest. She knows that she, like a river, has attained the ocean of her fulfillment ...she knows the world as*

her own household by the right of knowing the master of the world as her own lord. Then all her services become services of love". (344)

But when the soul fails to recognize her lover then she is the handmaid that is swayed by dejection and sorrow. It is in the very heart of his activities that man seeks to unite with the lord, not from being relieved of all his works or responsibilities of life. Tagore appropriately ends by saying "therefore in the midst of our home and our work, the prayer rises, "lead me across!" for here rolls the sea, and even here lies the other shore waiting to be reached-yes, here is this everlasting present, not distant, not anywhere else". (345)

The philosophy of Tagore, as he presents in his work *Sadhana*, thus, is a comprehensive one that at once includes the idea of a happy reconcilement between service and renunciation, action and seclusion, between self and soul, the finite and the infinite, the individual and the world. As S. *Radhakrishnan* rightly says: "Tagore gives an eloquent expression to his thirst for social betterment. Man as a member of society has to offer himself entirely and exhaustively to the service of one's fellows"[13]. The soul filled with the infinite love spends itself in the service of man, which otherwise would be an abstract barren negative. To quote *Radhakrishnan*:

> *"The philosophy of Rabindranath is an absolute idealism of the concrete type... Rabindranath's is a wholeness of vision, which cannot tolerate absolute divisions between body and mind, matter and life, individual and society, community and nation, empire and the world."*[14]

Though *Sadhana* is a collection of discourses offered at various times it still represents the fine thread of Tagore's philosophy that forms the connecting link between all these lectures – that of the purpose of human life i.e., the realization of *Brahma* in our every thought, our every word and our every action on this earth, this universe which is but a manifestation of the Infinite, in terms of joy and love. *Sadhana,* means rigorous practice, and the subtitle being *Realization of Life* clearly states the mission of Tagore, that the poet-saint has been striving endlessly to realize his purpose in life in all its glory. Tagore himself is a fine example of this philosophy, for he has truly been a man of the world in fulfilling his worldly duties as a family man on the one hand and on the other he has been a man of the world in his service to society at large as a poet who rendered his work in joy and love, in propagating the oneness of Being, so as to be united with the *Paramatman.*[15]

References

1. Rabindranath Tagore, *Sadhana*, in The English Writings of Rabindranath Tagore, Vol.2, Ed. By Sisir Kumar Das (New Delhi: Sahitya Akademi, 2012), p. 278.

2. Rabindranath Tagore, The Religion of man, in The English Writings of Rabindranath Tagore, Vol. 3, Ed. By Sisir Kumar Das (New Delhi: Sahitya Akademi, 2012), p.120.
3. Quoted from S. *Radhakrishnan*, "Most Dear to All the Muses", in Humanistic Philosophy of Tagore at http://www.kritike.org/journal/issue 11/sarma june2012.pdf
4. P. Gopichand and P. Nagasuseela, Rabindranath Tagore: A Retrospection, Jaipur, 2011, p. 209.
5. Quoted from S. *Radhakrishnan*, "The Philosophy of Rabindranath Tagore", in Tagore's Philosophy of Life, at http://rupkatha.com/V2/n4/11Tagorephilosophy.pdf
6. K.S. RamaswamiSastri, Sir Rabindranath Tagore, His life, Personality and Genius, Madras, p. 398.
7. Quoted from K.S. *Radhakrishnan*, "The Philosophy of Rabindranath Tagore", in "Tagore's Philosophy of life, p. 505.
8. Sadhana in English Writings of Tagore, Vol. 2, p. 289.
9. *Ibid.,* p. 290.
10. *Ibid.,* p. 297.
11. Quoted from S. *Radhakrishnan*, "The philosophy of Tagore" in "Tagore's Philosophy of life", p. 508.
12. *Ibid.,* p. 509.
13. Quoted from S. *Radhakrishnan*, "The Philosophy of Tagore", in "Tagore's Philosophy of Life, p. 511.
14. *Ibid.,* p. 511.
15. *Ibid.,* p. 512.

Bibliography

Aruna, M.J. (2010). Tagore's Philosophy of life. *Rupkatha Journal, Vol 2, No 4, http://rupkatha.com/V2/n4/11Tagorephilosophy.pdf.*

P. Nagasuseela, P. Gopichand. (2011). *Rabindranath Tagore: A Retrospection.* Jaipur.

Sarma, A.J. (2012). Humanistic Philosophy of Tagore. *KRITIK, Vol 6, http://www.kritik.org/journal/issue11/sarma june2012.pdf.*

Sastri, K. (Undated). *Sir Rabindranath Tagore: His Life, Personality and Genius.* Madras.

Tagore, R. (2012). *The English Writings of Rabindranath Tagore.* Vol. 2,3, New Delhi: Sahitya Akadmi.

PART— IV
MUSIC, POETRY AND SPIRITUAL TRADITIONS

1

Interrelation between Peace Education and Music With Special Reference To Rabindrasangeet

Susmita Bhattacharyya

Abstract

Today most of the societies of the world are disturbed by various kinds of conflict oriented activities. These kinds of problems are associated with not only with societal level but these will ultimately affect individual on personal level also. To get rid of those troubles people need conscious efforts of searching the lost mental equilibrium. As a consequence of seeking equilibrium, it is revealed that peace is the most coveted means to attain this goal. Previously peace prevails in societies normally but during course of time peace as a concept disappears from regular way of life. Hence peace education becomes a necessity for normal operation of societies in modern societies. Peace education means to educate every new generation of the children and youth of the world with the help of their parents, guardians and teachers to become peacemakers. Thus peace education is linked with a culture of peace, healing and excellence. Like all other processes there are some agents of peace education. Family, school, community and so on are some examples of agents in this aspect. Music can also be treated as agents for this purpose. Music is the lyrical expression of some meaningful words. In this connection a link can be established between music and peace education. The objectives of peace education will be executed with the presence of music in general. Music has an internal capacity of unification. This force can be utilized in peace education for attaining proper harmony within society. This link can be interpreted theoretically. Music can act as an agent of pattern maintenance in society. Thus music can surely linked with peace education. Music functions in an integrative mode to attain solidarity. So through music a harmonious aspect can be traced in peace education. Music can be utilized as a remedy in several situations where conflict is very much commonplace. Symbolic interactionist perspective treats music as the sum total of meaningful words and tune. Thus music will enhance the capability of peace education for destroying unwanted conflicts. Music performs the role of bridge in connecting several societies in harmonious ways. Rabindrasangeet is an excellent genre of music on the aspect of its great link with peace education. Textual analysis of Rabindrasangeet with respect to meaning will reveal a clear orientation of peace education. The linkage is sometimes direct; sometimes this is indirect in application. Rabindrasangeet can establish its direct and indirect link with peace education undoubtedly and spontaneously. Thus social implication of Rabindrasangeet can be discussed in this connection theoretically and empirically with respect to peace education.

Keywords: **Peace education, music, Rabindrasangeet**

Whole world is now going through a phase of unstable conditions of several kinds. This kind of instability ultimately takes shape of severe conflict. In macro level by and large societies are filled with conflict prone activities. But this large scale troubles are not delimited within societal sphere alone. It obviously affects personal level of the individuals. So in micro level people are highly disturbed by this kind of external situation. In the words of Dalai Lama it can be said that 'when we rise in the morning and listen to the radio or read the newspaper, we are confronted with the same news: violence, crime, wars and disasters. It is ironic that the more serious problems emanate from the more industrially advanced societies. Science and technology have worked wonders in many fields, but the basic human problems remain. There is no doubt about the increase in our material progress and technology, but somehow this is not sufficient as we have not yet succeeded in bringing about peace and happiness or in overcoming suffering. We can only conclude that there must be something seriously wrong with our progress and development, and if we do not check it in time there could be disastrous consequences for the future of humanity.' [Dalai Lama: 2014] Hence people need stability in mental condition to combat all these kinds of uncertainties. Actually to get rid of those troubles people need conscious efforts of searching the lost mental equilibrium. As a consequence of seeking equilibrium, it is revealed that peace is the most coveted means to attain this goal. Previously peace prevails in societies normally but during course of time peace as a concept disappears from regular way of life. Hence peace education becomes a necessity for normal operation of societies in modern societies. In this paper present researcher tries to establish a linkage between peace education and music in the context of contemporary world.

Conceptualization

Peace Education (PE) is a discipline that focuses on concepts as human rights, freedom, democracy, and environmental protection, as well as informing them about the negative consequences of conflict and violence. This is currently the most common approach to inclusion of peace in common parlance. On the basis of conceptual features there are some basic tenants of Peace education:

First, humanity is one; second, the oneness of humanity is expressed in diversity; third, the greatest opportunity before humanity is to safeguard its oneness and protect its diversity; and fourth, the greatest challenge before humanity is to accomplish this task through peaceful means, with a particular focus on educating every new generation of children and youth according to these principles. The main objective of peace education is to create an environment of peace and stability with the help of teachers, staff, parents, guardians, students, youth, adult, old and all others in the society. In a broader way peace education can be equated with a culture of peace, a culture of healing and a culture of excellence. Actually these three are related components for proper execution of peace education in society.

Music is sum total of different meaningful words which are linked with proper lyrical connotation. Musical presentation is performance based. Music actually has a direct impact upon the mind of the individual. It helps to create mental stability of individual. In this context the ideas of individual consciousness as well as collective consciousness can be applied. Music singularly and collectively affects people. So music has eternal impact in the maintenance of peace in society. Rabindrasangeet is a specific genre of Bengali music. This sector of song is linked with the golden touch of Rabindranath Tagore. These songs are subjected to mental equilibrium of the individual. In most of Tagore songs psychological conditions are highlighted. Hence a close relation between peace and Rabindrasangeet can be established logically and literally.

Agents

Several agents are there for proper execution of peace education. Formal agents like family, education, work place, mass media, religion and so on are playing significant role here. Informal agents like recreation, literary fact, music and other artistic activities have considerable functions in this sphere. Among all other agents the role of music is worth mentioning.

Study

A project 'Music Works' was done in West Africa and Ghana. The aim of the project is to promote peace by music education. Here the basic assumption is that music helps to give joy and happiness to human soul. Music has the force to break down the boundaries of all kinds of differences. It narrows down the distinction between different people. Music can be utilized as medium of self-expression for school students. Music inspires the learners to know about different cultures of the society. Thus the horizon will be wider enough to have a feeling of peace within the mind of individuals. Actually music has the potential to develop on many levels of mental conditions of individuals. Hence a link between peace education and music can be established.

Process

Like all other aspects of education peace education incorporates several related concepts. External learning is referred a specific style in relation to environment and its link in observance of people's manifest behaviour. But no interrelation is obligatory between perspectives of people and actual behavior patterns. Music can be applied as a tool for this kind of external learning aspect of peace education. 'Aanondodhara bohiche bhubane' of Tagore can be taken as an example of this genre. Here the main connotation is beauty of external world. The philosophy of the song is dealt with how small is the existence of individual in comparison to the whole universe. If each and every individual is quite habituated with this thought process the theme of peace education can be realized easily to all. Another aspect of peace education is relational learning. This takes place within the context of love.

This aspect includes all kinds of human relationships which are linked with love. Learning environment plays significant role here. Home, educational institutions, community, media – all are components of learning environment. Various kinds of relations emerge from this environmental sphere. This sector focuses on power of human love and its healthy as well as creative expression of life. An example will be 'Aay tobe sohochori'. Here main theme is centred on relations of friend circle and its role in maintaining unity among the group. Next aspect is internal learning. It is linked with psychological process from the core of heart. Here a basic assumption is highlighted that is the tripartite power of thinking, feeling and decision making of individual. In application level the process leads to collective level.

In this aspect a relation can be established between powers of human soul, emotive and conative capacities with respect to cognitive knowledge of individual. 'Antoro momo bikoshito koro' of Tagore can be taken as an example. This is a prayer song focusing on the issue of potentialities of human soul. The main aim of maximization of human power is to attain inner harmony and peace to create a condition of stability in society.

In advocating peace education cultural factors like theatre, literature, cinema, music and so on play important role. Through music thoughtful and interactive actions can be easily achievable. Music as a medium of peace education can be related with activity based learning.

This is also known as 'discovery learning'. In emphasizing the process of peace education through music a clear procedure should be maintained. The process requires skill, attitudes and values which are linked with target population as a whole. Sometimes training programmes and meetings will be parts of the procedure. For the purpose of proper execution of the programmes holistic understanding involving entire society becomes necessity.

Act of listening is somewhat related to a pyramid of communication. It can help to analyse the way of spreading music from individual level to society wide process.

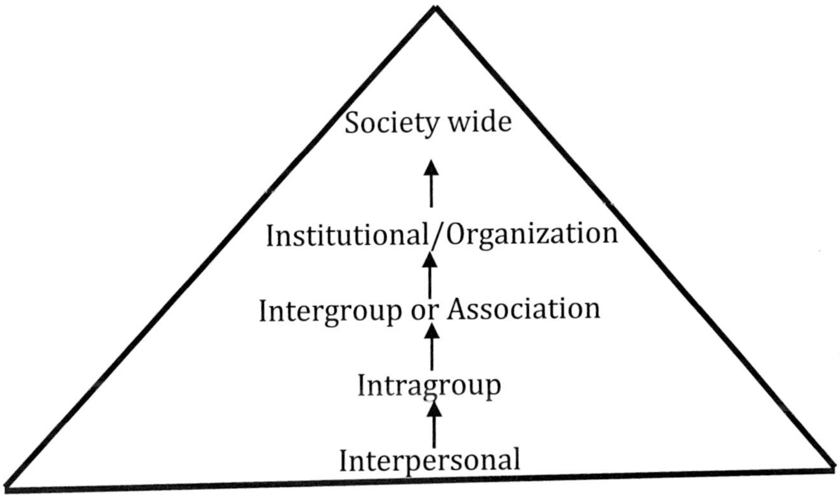

Whole society is involved in the process of spreading music. At a level below that of the whole society, there are several different kinds of musical network. One type duplicates the larger society at the level of region, city or town. Another is represented by work organization. It may not have a single location. But it should be integrated within its own organizational boundaries. Another variety is represented by institution. Below this level there are varied types of communication level. This level is based on some shared features of daily life. At this level the key questions concern attachment and identity, co-operation and norm formation. At the inter group and inter personal levels, attention has emphasized on forms of conversation pattern of interaction, influence, affiliation (degree of attachment) and normative control. At the interpersonal level, processing information deserves attention. The process of globalization makes communication a complicated factor. Music as an object of communication is not limited to a specific region now. It crosses the national boundary also. So the members of listening group increases day by day. in this way music can be used as a kit or tool for peace education.

Theoretical Linkage

The behavioral approach (Mcquail: 1994:296) has its root in social psychology. The main focus is individual behaviour in this context. Individual needs, motives and circumstances are the central features of this approach. The sociological variant focuses on the behaviour of members of socially defined population and favours the multi variate analysis of naturally collected data. Individuals are classified according to relevant variables of social position, disposition and behaviour. The variables can be statistically manipulated. On the basis of this perspective it can be said that behaviour of individual should be taken as unit of analysis. Every listener can't be treated as a potential target of peace education through music. This kind of ability depends upon the nature of individual. The capability is subjective; it varies from one individual to others.

Socio cultural approach (Mcquail: 1994:297) deals with the particular social context of the listeners. According to this, the musical preferences of the listeners depend on the pattern of family and the process of socialization. Family helps to grow the musical tastes of the listeners. For that purpose peace education through music is linked with culture of a particular society. Societal formation is the determinant factor of the nature of music used in peace education. So, cultural diversity becomes an important factor in this context.

As a theory functionalism (Turner: 1995:37) explains social institutions in terms of the 'needs' of the society and of individuals. In case of music the needs are mainly associated with continuity, order, integration, motivation, socialization, adaptation etc. Here music can be treated as an expression of need in the sphere of peace education. Through proper utilization music is considered as a weapon for establishing peace in society. Society is a totality of interlinked subsystems of which music is a part. Following Lasswell and Wright, McQuail pointed out the main functions of media as surveillance of environment, correlation of the parts of the society in responding to its environment, transmission of the cultural heritage and entertainment. All of these functions are related directly with music. Entertainment provides individual reward, relaxation and reduction of tension. It helps people to cope with real life problems. In this context Parsonian concept (Turner: 1995:57) of latency and pattern maintenance of AGIL model can be used by the researchers. Undoubtedly music diverts listeners from tension. Thus pattern of society and internal harmony of the listeners can be maintained easily. It socializes the listeners with the idea of building consensus. As a whole, music contributes in peace education not only on general basis but on specific aspect also.

According to conflict theory (Turner: 1995:129), conflict of interest is the striking factor. Need for peace becomes an imperative in the society today. Actually modern conflict theory deals with competition, structural inequality, revolution and war. All these are linked with the requirement of peace education in society. So, conflict is functional prerequisite of peace education. From interactionist perspective the act of listening to music is interplay between the creator and the receiver of music. Hence music can be treated as symbol. Through the process of interaction music related meaning is expressed to the individuals. For this function music is recognized as the significant medium of peace education. Exchange theory focuses on interplay of material as well as non-material sources. In the sphere of music this kind of give and take is very common. Music is an important source of cultural exchange undoubtedly. This source can be used as a medium for maintaining peace in society.

Music has a great role in representing national interest. Rabindrasangeet is particularly concerned with nationalistic aspiration. This kind of sentiment upholds the feeling of unity in society which ultimately leads to maintenance of peace in a broader sense. In elaborating the role of Rabindrasangeet in maintaining harmony and peace the focus can be given to the national anthem of two countries. National anthem of India and Bangladesh were Rabindrasangeet. These are examples of cultural integration as well as cultural assimilation. These are the steps towards attaining peace within and outside society. 'Janaganamana adhinayaka jaya he' [power of mass and unification amidst various diversity] and 'Aamar sonar Bangla' [love for motherland Bengal emphasizing positive qualities of Bengal and feeling of possessiveness] actually are linked with inner feeling of the citizen of the country. If they become assembled in a platform then peace will prevail in its fullest form in the society. These songs can build a notion of solidarity especially within multi-cultural communities like India. The function of these songs is related with negotiation and contestation between several groups. Thus patriotism is expressed in some Rabindrasangeet. There the emotion is centred on reconciliation of national identification.

This feeing of identification is excellently presented in several songs of Tagore. These can be also considered in the perspective of unity creating principles. Through the feeling of unity within people peace will persist in society. Ethos of internationalism is also expressed in Rabindrasangeet. 'Bishwosathe joge jethay biharo'. [trans national identity and interconnectedness of individuals] There the global identity and link are highlighted. At the same time this kind of song has the power of transcending the boundary. Hence focus should be given to the boundarilessness of society. This feature is ultimately gone to overwhelming process of creation of peace. This global unity is presented in the expression of peace education. Sometimes unity centric Rabindrasangeet is mentioned here as a tool of peace education. Example can be cited as 'Ak sutre badhiaachi sahosroti mon' [unity of mind functionally and structurally]. This kind of bonding within group actually helps to have a feeling of peace. This song can be taken as an expression of enthusiasm. This genre of song says something in against the feeling of protest, alleged discrimination, injustice and similar negative mental aspects. Through peace education all these kinds of expression come to an end.

A small survey is done by the present researcher to establish a link between music and peace education. Methodologically it can be said that 100 respondents are selected for this purpose. They are residents of south Kolkata. Their age group starts from 18 and ends with 75 years. Face to face interview is used for data collection. Purposive sampling method is adopted in this context. Collected data can be represented in the following tabular form.

Relation Between Peace Education and Music

Positive	***Negative***	***Neutral***
70	25	5

The individuals with positive opinion say that music is linked with inner harmony. Music has an anti-depression motive. Music helps to de stress people with their specific healing touch. Music creates a feeling of personal integrity within the self. As a whole, music must be considered as a significant tool of peace education. Those who are of negative opinion, say that music creates undoubtedly a positive feeling immediately. But, this feeling has no long-lasting impact. It has no far reaching impact.

Relation Between Peace Education and Rabindrasangeet

Positive	***Negative***	***Neutral***
80	18	2

Most of the respondents (80%) are of the opinion that Rabindrasangeet has tremendous power of unification and creation of peace. Actually they have an emotional bonding with this specific genre of music. So, according to their opinion Rabindrasangeet must be utilized as medium as well as agent of peace education. 18% of the respondents think there is no relation between Rabindrasangeet and peace education. They say that informal agents like Rabindrasangeet can't be used as a medium of peace education.

Education as an institution has a role in cultural transmission. Peace education performs the function of maintaining peace, unity and harmony in society. Peace education is also linked with cultural assimilation with a holistic impulse of its own. Music operates the role performance relating to the motive of peace education. Rabindrasangeet has a close interconnection with connotation of peace. Hence an impact of Rabindrasangeet in peace education can easily be discernable. Inner worth of Rabindrasangeet has its effect in the minds of individuals as well as collectivity. Thereafter peace education can be done with respect to Rabindrasangeet to get assured result. Ethos of Rabindrasangeet can do wonder in this sector like all other applications also.

References

Giddens A. (2004). Sociology, Polity.

Lama Dalai, (2014). A Human Approach to World Peace, Business Economics, Spirituality to Humanity,

McQuail D. (1994), 3rd Edition – Mass Communication Theory – An Introduction, Sage Publication.

Tagore Rabindranath (1982). Gitabitan, Bishwabharati Granthon Bibhag.

Turner, J.H., (1995). The Structure of Sociological Theory, Rawat Publications.

Turner, J.H., (2003). The Structure of Sociological Theory, Thomson Wadsworth.

2

A Discussion on Utilitarianism and Renunciation: A Sufi Perspective

Mohammad Israr Khan

Abstract

Utilitarianism is the generalized guide of economic behavior. However, it becomes a value loaded and normative dogma when the supposed 'positive' character of self-interest overtakes an empiricist character to reign over everything, including the humankind itself, put in a commodity frame. At its extreme utilitarian ethics becomes an end in itself, searching for the self and meaning of self in a narcissist frame of consumerism, unconscious of the sufferings of the toiling man and nature as well. Such a state of affairs is precarious to long term peace and sustainability of an integrated self and the world around of living and non-living dimensions forming total ecology. The way out of such an obscurantist enclosure is to search for the eternal and eternity which transcendent the contemporary. Tasawwuf or spiritual tradition of Asiatic Sufism provides one such frame of reference which relies upon 'will-less-ness', instead of consumerist 'will-ness', to enjoy the bliss or a sort of it which is not much dependent upon material abundance but which is internally caring and sharing. The article attempts to provide a critique of utilitarianism and consumerism, evaluates the efficacy of 'voluntary austerity', and puts forward the Sufis' construct of 'renunciation of will', in place of a self-defeating will of consumer-self.

Keywords: *Utilitarianism, consumerism, narcissist-self, rational constraints, voluntary renunciation, tasawwuf, renunciation of will, ordained necessity.*

Introduction

Modern economics rests upon the foundation of 'utilitarianism', which is an ideological conceptualization of 'self-interest' manifested through utility maximization. So termed, it is the balance of calculations, of the 'pains' of sacrifices of any kind like putting labor, spending money or parting with the wealth at one end, and of the 'pleasures' of consumption, and accumulation etc. on the other. It is taken by the economists of all hues to be the behavioral guide of all actions of an individual, permeating to all spheres of life- economic, political and social-cultural as well. This paradigm of human behavior so constructed, was advanced by the classical political-economists of great wisdom. Though inseminated, explained and elaborated by many, the largest credit for 'utilitarianism' goes to Jeremy Bentham (1789). It is firmly planted in the economic writing of classical philosophers, say David Hume and JS Mill, to the recent ones like John Rawls, the strand of rational 'calculations' being the same; though there were minor variations of concern regarding the components, feasibility and optimality of the common good.

Utilitarianism is a faith system believing that "Nature has placed mankind under the governance of two sovereign masters, *pain* and *pleasure*. It is for them alone to point out what we ought to do, as well as to determine what we shall do. ... they govern us in all we do, in all we say, in all we think: every effort we can make to throw off our subjection, will serve but to demonstrate and confirm it. ... By utility is meant that property in any object, whereby it tends to produce benefit, advantage, pleasure, good, or happiness..., or... to prevent the happening of mischief, pain, evil, or unhappiness..." (Bentham, 1789: 183). The political counterpart of economic 'utilitarian optimality' is the public policy concern for striving to attain the *greatest happiness for the greatest numbers* i.e. making of the policies which ascertain greatest common good compatible with the least interference to liaises faire.

The 'utilitarian' approach to economic actions, very easily and simply, translates itself into what is variously known as 'consumerism' or the 'enlightened consumerism'. Economic actions and efforts, then, based upon utility relationship, gather around two broad categories- utility enhancers (pleasures) and utility reducers (pains); the former being the desired one. However, the pleasures cannot be attained without being preceded by the pains. The rational economic agent therefore makes a calculation by balancing the indexes of pleasures and pains, and settles down for maximization and optimization of utility function via any form of present and future consumption or accumulation. The utility thus understood and achieved becomes the purpose, the means and the ends of individual life, then and there.

The classical formation of economic man- its rationality, its obsession with sensual pains and pleasures, its utilitarianism, its maximization, its self-interest all sum up to infinity of material abundance, luxuries, desires, instinctive gratifications etc., epitomized by the very emergence of a consumerist outlook. It is nothing but the smoking away of all that is absolute and abstract there in man and nature. Frustration and non-sustainability at a larger long-term plane are its twin offspring. It is the *idealized statue of economic man* reinforced into the human society through the paradigm of *conditioned-response-stimulation* which turned all the wisdom of the past upside down. The simple task of a Smithian economic system is to expose the historical existence into fragments. Stipulate the ideal of economic man. Indoctrinate and intoxicate these fragments with the rationality of that economic man. Everything is done. The incarnation of economic deity has taken place. The rest of the story is the perpetuation and fine tuning of the 'myth' of the paradise on earth to be brought about by this economic angel.

Strict observance of the rules of economic rationality which is qualified by circumscribed self-interest, leads not to 'rational behavior'. Rather, it fails to be "sensitive to the heterogeneous interests" (ibid: 67) of the diverse populations. In the beautiful words of Amartya Sen (2006: 70):

> *"Bentham's concern and that of utilitarianism in general was with the total utility of a community. This was irrespective of the distribution of that total, and in this there is an informational limitation of considerable ethical and political importance. For example, a person who is unlucky enough to have a uniformly lower capability to generate employment and utility out of income (say, because of a handicap) would also be given, in the utilitarian ideal world, a lower share of a given total. This is a consequence of a single minded pursuit of maximizing the sum-total of utilities."*

Consumerism

Consumerism is an extension and outcome of the conceptualization of *economic man* and its *self-interest* manifested by *utilitarian* matrix of *pain* and *pleasure* residing in material *commodities*. Utilitarianism is assumed to be both a public and a personal behavioral guide (Bentham, 1789).It can be defined as an excessive and obsessive preoccupation of consumption and accumulation of consumables. It is perhaps the most critical factor in natural resource depletion, environmental degradation and climate change. The world of global markets is said to follow the sovereign commandments and dictates of the consumer king. But the market has a personality of its own. It has a fascination and fetish as well. It writes and underwrites the self-serving maxims of utility to make it reside in commodities, both consumable and storable. The more one has the more she is happy, and vice versa. Conspicuous consumerism and corporatized market as well have less to do with usefulness and more to do with creation of commodity fetish and buying appetite. Consumerist persona is a product of utilitarian reduction of the '*man*' a whole into the '*economic man*' a compartment.

Consumerism has been described variously by the people belonging to different fields. It is like *narcissist* consumer self which is false and void; it arises out of distortion of authentic human needs and desires (Kanner, 1995). Cosumerism creates an addiction of ever increasing wealth like that created by drugs (Wachtel, 1989). It also creates an illusion of 'prosperity and prestige' centered around the exchange value as a commodity's capacity to confer prestige (Lasch, 1979: 72). Consumerism has been considered as an economic imperative for employment and growth in the affluent first world (McKibben, 1989; Suzuki, 1997; Cohen, 2003). The history of modernity and the contemporary history of economic development suggest that the 'paradigm' of 'utility' residing in material commodities and comforts had led to a rush towards 'consumerism' coining epithets like 'consumer satisfaction', 'consumer delight', 'consumer sovereignty', 'consumer is the king', 'killing instinct' and so on. Consumerism has spiral effects. It is unending and unrelenting. It feeds upon and feeds the false narcissist-self. It becomes unbearable when deprivation, destitution, poverty and hunger assume conspicuous co-existence. It bereaves the humanity of social and civilizational concerns. It produces extreme inequalities and perpetuates exploitation.

Instead of want-on-ness of obsessive and possessive consumerist rationality it is much more necessary to move towards non-excessive and non-accumulative forms of utility and alternate versions of consumer rationality. The invisible visibility of economic sufferings, hand in hand with conspicuous consumption, then juxtaposes dangers to societal organization and social peace. Degrading levels of inequity and inequality coupled with absence of distributive and redistributive justice create friction and cracks in society which cannot wait for a very long time.

Voluntary Restraints and Renunciation

Serious challenge to consumerism comes from institutional, psychological, environmental and welfare paradigms of economic analysis. The consumption ethics of affluent and leisure class is looked upon as an institutional factor in rich societies. Therein it is difficult to be dethroned. Psychological studies suggest that commodity fetish cannot provide long term satisfaction (Scitovsky, 1992), and it has to be supplemented by a vibrant way of living which enjoys multiple forms of utility; not alone the mono-utility of a Benthamite description. Utility equilibrium to that extent requires modifications.

It is in this tradition that we find an iota of 'voluntary simplicity' (Etzioni, 1999: 1-26). The processes of simplification can be ctegorized as 'down shifting', 'status inversion', 'strong simplification' and 'holistic simplification' at individual level, as well as at 'societal simplicity'. In the strata of voluntary simplifiers 'Downshifters' are termed those rich people who "voluntarily give up some consumer goods they could readily afford, but basically maintain their rather rich and consumption-oriented life style" (Etzioni, 1999: 4). 'Status inversion' refers to the simplicity action of those affluent people using moore primitive or natural substitutes for modern conveniences (ibid: 5),whereby conveying the impression of wealth becomes suddenly unfashionable (Brooks, 1997). 'Strong simplifiers' are the people who voluntarily opt for significant downward restructuring of their income and consumption patterns (Etzioni, 1999: 6). The strongest category of American simplifiers may be termed as the 'holistic simplifiers'. They are the people "who adjust their whole life pattern according to the ethos of voluntary simplicity"... "motivated by a cohehrent articulated philosophy" (Etzioni, 1999: 8).

The movement for volutary simplcity got intellectual inspiration from Duane Elgin (1993) who emulated various indegenous practices and world religions for a simple life. Consumerism could be denounced for the evils it creates and leads to e.g. excssive shopping, indebtedness, stress, depletion of nature etc. Abraham Maslow (1986) had earlier presented a well-articulated hierarchy of different needs, wherein commodity based needs ceased to be motivators after a certain stage and intrinsic motivations for self-esteem and self-actualization set in as powerful satisfiers leading to non-material based happiness. His need hierarchy provides an internal criticism of consumerist corporate agenda. Irreversible environmental degradation and non-sustainability of a modern development paradigm have also been seriously challenged across the world, especially in the background of the Report of World Commission on Environment and Development (Brundtland Commision, 1987) and after the earth summit in 1992 at Rio de Janeiro, Brazil. Scientific community is unanimous on one thing: a 'rational restraint' on the use of nature and natural resources for economic gratifications.

Generalized abundance is neither quite feasible nor desirable; it is a non-solution as well. Restraints imposed due to shortages lead to penury. Commanded restraints yield, if any, the suppressed psychic which can bounce back anytime, as it has been observed in case of Soviet-Bloc economies. 'Self-imposed' (Sen, 2006) 'voluntary simplicity' (Elgin, 1993) and 'voluntary renunciation' (Etzioni, 1999) discuss a feasible and desirable course of internal social response towards a rich and fulfilled life; far happier doing with far less consumption articles. However, the forms of voluntary renunciation of consumption seem to work at higher levels of income. It is not the general consumerist who opts for restraints. Rather, the wealthier and the richer bring forth their 'conspicuous presence' via 'status inversion' and displayed asymmetry. So what is there is neither the presence of non-consumption utilities, nor the absence of consumerist ethics and consumer self. Rather a part of the observed simplicity might be a re-channelization and re-shaping of preferences, to be visibly different from others. Barring the case of 'strong and holistic simplifiers' who tend to change their course of action to a lower economic affluence, voluntary simplicity remains a sub-part of larger consumerist approach following the same hedonist code of conduct.

There is strong need for all good reasons to go, beyond the approach of voluntary scaling down of consumerist conduct where what is reduced is the consumption, not the will to consume, to a paradigm where what is renunciated is the 'will' guided by mere pains and pleasures to consume. The most rational course of action from the viewpoint of human beings and the nature would be an act of the renunciation not only of non-ethical consumption, but also the *renunciation of the 'will' to consume*, voluntary of course. Guided and guarded by the better senses of historical ethics and morality, the renunciation of the desires, instincts and psychological floats, or the renunciation of that rather 'industrial ethics' which looks for a mundane paradise as a substitute to heavenly paradise, provides a way towards constant solutions.

Tark-e-Ikhtiyar: Sufi's Renunciation of Will

In contrast with the *accumulation of will* and desires, the notion of *renunciation of will* and volition to possess, accumulate and enjoy is inspired from the tradition which believes in the unity of existence. It looks upon worldly pleasures and consequential chaos as destructive and void of meanings. It lives in communion with all that is there in existence. Obligations are duly to be honored to fellow existence. No pain, no inconvenience, no barrier be put upon others for the sake of the self. Shirking from the evils and sharing of the goodness is desired. One is on a course of heavenly voyage and bliss; the mundane is void of true purpose. It can be easily observed that the higher is the degree of renunciation and sacrifice, the higher is the social and humanitarian relevance unbounded by time and place. It is equivalent to reiterate that the excellence of a man's work is proportional to the excellence of his ideas for "man is what he loves" (Augustine as quoted in Nicholson, 1898: 253). Maulana Rumi[1] has said:

خامُش که همان ارزد ای خواجه که میجوي ؟ د

"Peace! For it is worth, O master, just that which it seeks"
(Nicholson, 1898: 74-75).

In the present context, by renunciation of 'will' we mean a self-imposed, self-disciplined, considered, convinced, conscious and voluntary application of will to renunciate the 'will' relating to that part of will which acts upon uncontrolled, influenced and self-created fascinations, passions, instincts, urges, lusts, desires, angers, illusions, material hallucinations and so on. Thus renunciation of 'will' may refer to the application of willingness to contain certain components of willingness itself. It is a state where the will controls the will; where the will directs the will; and where the will renunciates the will of the self to attain actualization of free-will. The person, who has no personal wills and realizes the renunciation of will, simply follows the supreme 'will', by performing at his part the ordained necessity and by not claiming that he is the performer. What we have here is the action part in its live role but the 'will' to act upon, hence also the action acted upon, has been qualified by an element of renunciation. The result is the renunciator who takes on the role of acted upon in contrast to being the actor, becomes detached from the worldly actions, and remains conscious of actionable and non-actionable variables in the given situation till he attains the stage of total submission and renunciation.

The Sufis (صوفى) emanate from Islam and are eclectic to adopt Semitic tradition. They are adherents and followers of Islam. Nicholson (1898: xxxi) has attributed conceptual similarities between Sufist and 'neo-platonic' ideas. Notwithstanding any limiting argument, Sufis belong to a larger tradition. They follow, like many others, at different times, and different places, "that mystic religion which, though it has nothing in it but that same spirit, that same truth, and that same life, which always was and always must be the religion of all God's holy angels and saints in heaven, is by the wisdom of this world accounted to be madness." (Law, 1871 as quoted in Nicholson, 1898: v). It is quite remarkable that the Upnishad's idea of 'Ekatm' (unity of created and the creator) is fairly comparable to 'Wahadatul Wajood' (unity of existence) of Sufism.

Sufism, per se, is regarded as Islamic mysticism. But it is also regarded as an extreme viewpoint of Islam. Some Islamic scholars and sects regard the practice of *Tasawwuf* as an innovation over Islam. Therefore they delegitimize the very idea of Tasawwuf itself. There are many scholars of Islam, especially post-renaissance scholars like Sir Iqbal who find fault with the foundational idea of Sufism i.e. the idea of *wahadatul wujood* (unity of existence) and *wahadatulshuhood* (unity of forms). Apart from abstractness Sufism has a cultural context. It originated in West Asia, followed the Semitic symbols, practiced the religion of Islam and adopted a very eclectic approach. However the threads of mysticism connect Sufism with various ascetic traditions. Indian philosophy also holds the concept of 'unity' in the form of 'ekatmvaad', though it subscribes to an unmanageable multitude of deities and allows a virtual liberty to anybody claiming godhood. Christian ascetics, too, followed a mysticism. But the semblance and presence of more mystical traditions does not enable generalization and de-contextualization of Sufis' postulates and behavioral and inspirational appeal.

Sufi, the true seeker and lover of divine Beloved and a benefactor of His men, was regarded the highest place in the society, though he did not claim the same. Materialism was downwardly looked upon by the Sufis. Social organization was supposed to be virtue centric. Deeds were categorized, and accordingly rewarded, into virtues and vices. Morality both social and individual was an ethical component of life. Compare this scenario with the formulation of economic rationality. The positivism took over the voice of the inner and the normative morality. Dehumanized cause and effect substituted the scale of virtue and vice. The wealth creator took charge of affairs. Materialism became the behaviour guide. Self-interest became its progeny. Economic morality occupied monopoly of morals, if any. Now compare the inevitable presence of exercisable 'will' of an enterprising economy with the idea of *renunciation of 'will'* (تركِ اِختيار) of a Sufi practitioner, ideologue and follower. We have to look for what the possibilities and possible forms of renunciation might be there.

With a little relaxation of orthodoxies, we can have very meaningful and valuable insights for an alternate paradigm. The exercise of *renunciation of will* is an attribute of a true Sufi. However, though desirable, everyone cannot attain that level. So at a lower level the renunciation of will might cover that order of economic activities which is neither performed willfully, nor against the will (because of absence of will) but as an ordained necessity, '*subordinate to eternal law*' and '*not surrendering to the compulsion of passions*'. This way the soul, though a part of nature, has her 'foot in the ideal world' (Nicholson, 1898: xxxv). It can still move upwards from the many to the One (*ibid:* 260). The term '*ordained* necessity' is immensely important for our purpose. At the same time it is much difficult to be precisely identified. Only the soul of a righteous one can determine it reliably.

Renunciation of will does not relate to itself the passions of attachment or detachment, as is generally argued in Brahmanic and Budhist states of renunciation. The idea of the 'soul' of the person diluted to the personal being can be read as the person itself. The soul [read the person] is neither attached, nor detached, with worldly actions which bear ordained necessity, for example breathing. The soul will not break the will of God or the Universal 'will' reflected via the manifestation of creation (كُن فيكُون: God wills and it becomes). The soul cannot have a self-interest other than its upward movement and the ordained necessity, both of which are not but the will of God. The soul says, writes Rumi:

كار من سر بخشى و بيخويشى است

كارِ ما سر بخشى است

'Tis my business to yield up life unselfishly,
To bestow life is the business of our king of kings. (Nicholson, 1898: 278)

مرغ باغ م ؟ ل ؟كوتم نيم از عالمِ خاك

دو سِه روزی قفسی ساخته اند از بدنم

I am a bird of heavenly gardens; I belong not to the earthly sphere;
They have made, for two or three days, a cage of my body. (ibid: 278).

The will to have material embodiments is befalling. A man is intimately related with what he seeks and what he loves, and his work is proportional to the excellence of his ideas:

خامُش که همان ارزد ای خواجه که میجوي ؟ د

"Peace! For it is worth, O master, just that which it seeks." (Ibid: 74-75).

Where the place for worldly desires, the soul is wary of the empyrean and the sky!

چه جایِ هواهایِ عرش و ف ؟ ل ؟ ك

بگُلزار و؟ صلست سیرانِ ما

"What place here for aspirations toward the empyrean and the sky?
Our journey is to the rose-garden of union." (Ibid: 11-12).

The soul is from nowhere save from God. It belongs to none else. It does not know the discrimination between people of different faiths. It has to be universally benevolent:

چه تدبیر ای مُس ؟ لمانان که من خ ؟ ود را نمیدانم

نه ترسا نه یهودم من نه گُبرم نه مُس ؟ لمانم

"What is to be done, O Moslems? for I do not recognize myself.
I am neither Christian, nor Jew, nor Gabr, nor Moslem." (Ibid: 124-125).

The soul is universally benevolent. It prays for universal grace of God:

گُفتا ز من چه خواهی گفتم که لطفِ عامت

"He said: 'What do you want?' Said I: 'Thy universal grace." (Ibid: 54-55).

Two worlds do not accomplished. Duality does not work. The two worlds are but the one:

دوئي از خ ؟ ود ب ؟ د ؟ ر کردم یکی دیدم دو عال ؟ م

یکی جویم   یکی دانم   یکی بینم   یکی خوانم

"I have put duality away. I have seen that the two worlds are one;

One I seek, One I know, One I see, One I call." (Ibid: 126-127).

The duality is untenable. Whether it is of phenomenal world or it is of the personal world. A person must be one to maintain consistency. A squinted seer cannot find the right path. Personal unity can occur when the senses and the eternal are in unity. How a person who thinks otherwise talks otherwise, heeds to otherwise and listens to otherwise and so, can achieve unity within and outside. The personal fragmentation and fragmented sight are due to lust and anger.

مرد احو ؟ ل گردد از میلان و خشم

"Tis is lust and anger that make a man see double" (Ibid: 267, from Mathnavi 12.14).

A consumerist personality, by virtue of lust and desires, is a broken one and a dual like the one discussed above.

مردانِ خُدا گرچه هزارند یکی اند

مستانِ هوا گرچه یکانست دوگانست

"Those drunk with God, tho' they be thousands, are yet one;

Those drunk with lust – tho' it be a single one, he is a double." (Ibid: 60-61).

The operative definition of the term 'renunciation of will' is to be deciphered from the relationship between the lover and the Beloved. What is there between the two? Verily the love! What is Love? The Renunciation of will! So Hazrat Maulana (RA) provides the meaning of both in terms of each-other. 'Freewill is the absence of self-will':

گویند عشق چیست بگو ترکِ اِختِیار

هر کاو ز اِختِیار ن ؟ رست اِختِیار نیست

*"They say, '**What is love?**' Say '**Renunciation of will.**'*

Whoso has not escaped from will, no will hath he." (Ibid: 51, emphasis added).

Nothing can fall out contrary to the desires of him who desires nothing; he may fare as one by whose majestic will the world revolves. “The Sufi must live in the present, regarding neither yesterday nor to-morrow, but absorbed in the ‘eternal Now’ of divine energy.” (Ibid: 234). He has neither the will nor the wish to wait for, thereby:

نظّاره گر مباش درین راه مُنتظِر

والل?ّه که هیچ مرگ ب ? ت ? ر ز اِنتِظار نیست

“Be not an expectant looker in this path;
By God, there is no death worse than by expectancy.” (Ibid: 50-51).

And will-less-ness is not a void; it is a virtue which attains realization of the will of wills:

هر کس که بی مُراد شُد او چون مُریدِ تُست

بی صورتِ مُراد مْرادش مّيِ ? سّ ? رست

“Every one that is without object is thy disciple:
His object is gained without the semblance of object.” (Ibid: 44-45).

Economic dimensions of Tasawwuf, however, might have a very complex characterization. At the very first sight it may seem to be non-relevant from economic viewpoint. After all what is the role of spirituality and non-economic prudence in an economic world? This point is also raised by Nicholson (1898) in his description of early [read classical] Sufis of Persia:

> *“... free thinkers ... ... admitting no guidance but the pole-star of divine illumination, they press in wild career to the very brink of madness. As citizens they are undeniably a grave scandal and a useless burden to the state; they sap the national prosperity and demoralize the national character; but if a country’s literature is righty reckoned among its noblest heirlooms the debt which Persia owes to the Sufis may balance and perhaps overpay, these injuries” (ibid: xxix).*

But this is a simplified reading of the obvious. The other aspect is also important. Sufis have not renunciated the world as a heretic. They disconnect from the world only when the soul has disconnected it from the physical self. But then, too, they do not lose their relevance is guiding and comforting the society.

The paradigm of ‘renunciation of will’ suggests and supposes modifications in our understanding of consumer behavior. Thus conventional assumptions are confronted fundamentally. The maxims of an economic man and rationality defined by preference to more quantities in comparison to less become compromised at the very beginning if we are to allow consideration of renunciation as an economic input. Our economic man transliterates itself into a universal entity. His ideal is not the maximization of utility by means of commodities. His objective is to derive a source of satisfaction and contentment which is less dependent upon consumables and accumulation. He also breaks down the usual budget constraint. The resources may be greater by any degree but his preferences are not ever increasing.

Pedagogical Relevance

Contemporary world is obsessed with materialism. It is flatly besieged by everything or anything termed as developmental and progressive. The underlying motivations of utilitarian and consumerism as discussed above, have become predominantly overarching over the horizon. The global world under economic management of Bretton Woods Institutions, mainly the World Bank, International Monetary Fund and World Trade organization, is exhausted in the parody of economic growth. Neo-liberal and neo-classical political-economic gospel has made nations preoccupied with gross domestic product (GDP) and other fascinating figures. In such a scenario the very first casualty is the sustainability of civilizational, environmental and ecological factors. Sharpened division of humanity into haves and have-nots is another serious concern. Forty eight percent wealth of the world is reported to be in the hands of just one percent of population (Hardoon, 2015: 2). Eighty percent of global population (5.6 billion people) has to do with just five and a half percent of global riches. Inequality is more debilitating and more intensified at bottom lines. Apart from starvation and other deprivations for billions of people, this sharp divide is both increasing the power of the state and the role of the state as a policeman to protect the rich ones' interests from any kind of encroachment by the toiling and tattering people.

The fact of political-economic divide and dominance has far reaching implications for social, cultural, educational and civilizational contours. Mainstream patterns everywhere seem to have visibly subsumed the non-stream and sub-altern structures in every field of social existence. Education is also not immune from these devastating transformations; its mainstream has overtaken the mirror image of global materialism. It is a well-recognized prerequisite of education and pedagogy that these be based upon a strong philosophic and social footings. But a simple look into our educational system right from primary to higher education provides us with a pessimism and a vacuum. We have a leviathan and gigantic system of education in India. However its only preoccupation is nominal literacy, examination and degrees. Its only philosophy is 'for money'. Its only guidance is political-economic utilitarianism. It inculcates intense sense of 'self-interest' and produces an excessively consumerist narcissist-self. Instead of a humanitarian and integral personality, our educational system creates obsessive and disintegrated selves. There is, therefore, nothing to be surprised for large scale practice and common acceptance of corruption in public and private life, more particularly among the educated segments. One can only feel sorry for a perceivably strong relationship between education and corruption in India in personal and national life!

Most of the social problems including behavioural distortions and generalized corruption are, most probably, because of something seriously wrong with education. If educated persons adopt corrupt means, and if education cannot modify their behavioural modes, what sort of intrinsic value does it possess? Our humble submission is that education is not merely another production function. Rather, it is something that is intrinsic and eternal, and an internal factor of ethical modification of behavioural modes, too. No doubt education carries a burden of diverse demands. It is subjected to a tremendous agenda of various dimensions like social, cultural, political, economic etc. It is supposed to accomplish various things at the same time. So it has every possibility of sitting squeezed under its own weight. However, to make it internally consistence and strong, education must be allowed to possess an 'intrinsic' value and an inclusive character of its own,

Apart from its content, context and technology, mainstream education obviates and obliterates all other traditional and historical modes of instruction and personality formation. Thereby it surpasses a great treasure of historical wisdom as well as meaningful and diverse pedagogical experiences, the most important being the Asiatic spiritual traditions which have historically been great benefactors of humanity. Right from Mahatma Buddha to *Advaitvad* and *Kabirpanth*, there is a lot of humanism and universalism to guide the humanity, provided that it is read in right perspective.

In the same spirit *Tasawwuf* has been the most splendid, and superbly humane and humanitarian, tradition of spiritual guidance for a very large number of people across national frontiers. If the inferences are not wholly unjustified, then *Tasawwuf* has been a via media between Islam and the world outside Islam. A radical Islam sans *Tasawwuf* is 'unwelcome' and unkind to the world, as witnessed by the contemporary allegations of Islamists' fundamentalism.

There is an immense need for inclusion of the spiritual value of *Tasawwuf* into the pedagogical content of our educational system. Inculcation of a *renunciationist* and *will-less-ness*out look, in contrast to a utilitarian-consumerist one, would be a desirable variable keeping in view the peaceful and sharing coexistence of human civilization, and sustainability of live-able ecology and environment.

Footnotes

1. Hazrat Maulana Jalaluddin Rumi was born at Balkh on 30th September, 1207. He lived up to 16th December 1273. He is said to have instituted the order of Maulavi dervishes who have their special dress, the Indian garb of mourning and whirling dance, *sama'a*. (Nicholson, 1898: xxv). Diwani Shamsi Tabriz, Feihe Ma Feihe and Mathnavi Ma'anvi are his classical, of all times, creations. Maulana Rumi put forth the idea of renunciation of 'will' of the self so that the will of the Universal Sovereign, the God, reigns supreme. And this is the attainment of freewill, the will which moves the nature, the world and the universe.

Bibliography

Bentham, J. (1789). *An Introduction to the Principles of Morals and Legislation.* As quoted in Medema S.G. and Samuels W.J. (ed.), (2003). The History of Economic Thought: A Reader. New York. Routledge, pp. 183-85.

Brooks, D. (1997). The Libral Gentry. *The weekly Standard (December 30-Januuary 06, 1996-97), as quoted in Amitai Etzioni (1999); Essys in Volutary Simplicity. Springr: Berlag, pp. 24.*

Brundtland Commision (1987). *Report of The World Commission on Environment and Development: Our Common Future.* UNDP.

Cohen, L. (2003). *A Consumer's Republlic: The Politics of Mass Cosumption in Postwar America.* New York: Vintage Books.

Elgin, D. (1993). *Voluntary Simplicity.* New York: Willium Morrow.

Etzioni, A. (1999). *Essays in Socio-Economics.* Berlin: Springer.

Hardoon, D. (2015, January 19). *Wealth: Having It All and Wanting More (Oxfam Issue Briefing).* Retrieved from www.oxfam.org: 26.1.2015.

Kanner, A.D. (1995). *The All-Consuming Self, in Roszak T., Gomes M.E., and Kanner A.D. (eds), Ecopsychology: Restoring The Earth - Healing The Mind.* San Francisco: Sierra Club Books.

Lasch, C. (1979). *The Culture of Narcissism: American Life in an Age of Diminishing Expectations.* New York: W.W. Nortan and Company. As quoted in Emerald, N.D. (2004, Nov.). Consumerism, Nature, and The Human Spirit. USA: Virginia Polytechnic Institute and State University. http://scholar.lib.vt.edu/theses/available/etd-12272004-133514.

Law, W. (1871). *The Spirit of Love; as quoted in Nicholson, R. (1898) Diwani Shamsi Tabriz reprinted by Kitab Bhavan, New Delhi in 2006.* London.

Maslow, A. (1986). *Towards A Psychology of Being.* Von Nostrand: Princeton.

McKibben, B. (1989). *The End of Nature.* New York: Anchor Books. As quoted in Emerald, N. D. (2004, Nov.). Consumerism, Nature, and The Human Spirit. USA: Virginia Polytechnic Institute and State University. http://scholar.lib.vt.edu/theses/available/etd-12272004-133514.

Mehta, J.K. (1962). *A Philosophical Interpretation of Economics.* London: George Allen and Unwin.

Nicholson, R.A. (1898). Selected Poems From The Diwani Shamsi Tabrez (reprint). New Delhi: Kitab Bhavan.

Rumi, J. (2000). *Malfoozate Rumi (Urdu translation of Feihe Maa Feihe by Shams Barelvi).* New Delhi: Adabi Duniya.

Scitovsky, T. (1992). *The Joyless economy: The Psychology of Human Satisfaction.* New York: Oxford University Press.

Sen, A. (2006). The Possibility of Social Choice. In A. Sen, *Rationality and Freedom* (pp. 65-118). New Delhi: Oxford University press.

Suzuki, D. (1997). *The Sacred Balance: Rediscovering Our Role in Nature.* Vancouver: Greystone Books. As quoted in Emerald, N. D. (2004, Nov.). Consumerism, Nature, and The Human Spirit. USA: Virginia Polytechnic Institute and State University. http://scholar.lib.vt.edu/theses/available/etd-12272004-133514.

Wachtel, P. L. (1989). *The Poverty of Affluence.* Philadelphia: New Society Publisher. As quoted in Emerald, N. D. (2004, Nov.). *Consumerism, Nature, and The Human Spirit.* USA: Virginia Polytechnic Institute and State University. http://scholar. lib.vt.edu/theses/available/etd-12272004-133514.

3

Envisioning the Role of Song-Texts (Padas) as A Reinforcement Towards Spiritual Realization and Moral Values (With Special Reference to The North Indian Classical, Semi-Classical And Bajan Styles)

Sangeeta Pandit

The textual tradition of Indian classical music are replete with the value based principles which were set by the ancient scholars in the field of music. Sangeet Ratnkar by Sharung dev 12th Century A.D. depict the guide-lines for the essential qualities for the music performers, teachers, learners and even for the audience (prekshak). The "Purva Rang" tradition mentioned in "Natyashastra" is another symbol of submission to the divine for every pursuit of art. In Indian tradition, the two streams of classical music "Margi" and "Deshi" Sangeet are the two parallel ways. One "Sadhya" - "Music as God" the another as "sadhan" "communication medium for social benefit". Through the ages, music is being used as a medium for social reform. As per historical reviews Indian social and cultural scenario has been affected by many social evils at times giving birth to the degradation in social and moral values. In the course of time many social reformers like saint poets, artists, spiritual gurus have enlightened the hearts of common man of the society through their writings, which had a wide range of issues related to social problems. They taught values very easily through music. This paper is an attempt to explore the role of song-texts in spiritual realization with special reference to the North Indian Classical, Semi Classical and Bhajan Styles.

Keywords: Dharma' prakrit, 'padas, spiritualism

Taking a glance at the gradual development of the culture of India we find that the core of Indian culture was innately patterned with spiritual philosophy. The oneness with the almighty was the ultimate goal of life. The orientation of the ancients leaned towards the submission to the almighty for every persuit of life which guided the society to set high moral and spiritual values. The *Puran* texts are replete with numerous instances depicting the importance of human values.

What we consider today as moral or human values, "*Bhagwad Geeta*" mentions it as *'Prakriti' or 'Sampad'*.In the sixteenth Adhyay of *'Geeta'*, two kinds of 'Sampad' are mentioned as *'Daivi Sampad'* and *'Aasuri Sampad'*. Further *Shankaracharya* defines it as the nature of human being.

"Daivi Aasuri Rakhshasi Ca iti praninam Prakritiya": The moral and immoral qualities will determine the character of an individual.[1]

If we analyse then we observe that, values are psychological objects which carry commitment and determination too. They are deeply related to other concepts such as- morality and ethics (The motivation based on ideas of right and wrong) thus resulting in improvement of social and cultural conditions of a nation and moves the society towards progress.[2]

Values are of two types- intrinsic value and extrinsic value or instrumental value. Intrinsic value is ethical and philosophical quality and an object with this value, may be regarded as end in itself. In contrast the extrinsic value is that which depends on how much it generates intrinsic value.

According to *peter singer*, something is of intrinsic value if it is good or desirable in itself; the contrast is with extrinsic is that, is value as a means to some other end or purpose.[3]

Decline in moral values is a global phenomena. Changing social norms are creating yet another problems. In this modern age of economic and material development, the rise of violence all around is phenomenal. For a well balanced and well oraganised society, eigther the society can establish discipline with the help of law or with the help of education and socialization. These disciplines can be inculcated only by following the moral and ethical rules. So the society needs a role model or ideal which can discriminate between right and wrong.

The rules for discipline which we carry are called *'Dharma'- 'Dharanat iti Dharma'* means the good qualities which can be possesed by a individual is *'Dharma'*.[4] Absence of this *Dharma* creates imbalance in society which is reflected in individual behavior. Changing social norms are creating social imbalance resulting in violence, discrimination, lie, enimity, etc. Different thinkers have mentioned different characteristic of *'Dharma'* or "*moral qualities*" naturally inherent in the form of *'Neetis'*. Every society has certain moral environment which are probably perfect blending of spirituality, morality and ethical values. Though societies may differ but these values are universal. The code of conduct maintains the society.

Indian culture is based on the eternal human values and places these values, most important for the moral and spiritual upliftment. *Dhairya, Kshama, Akrodh, Dhee, Vidya, Satya, Indriya-Nigraha Shuddhi* are such desirable moral qualities. These universal principle of harmony and love exhibits itself through values of *goodness, selflessness, tolerance, respect* and so on.

Moral values, ethical values and submission to the divine is the perfect blending which promotes spiritual realization in an individual. Attitudinal transformation is therefore necessary to enlarge the focus of consideration to which, education, specially *music education* can contribute substantially. In Indian tradition the teacher or the 'Guru' has a pivotal role in the process of teaching and learning. He is considered as guide,philosopher, architect and role model.Education is all problems in the society. Through education it is easy to inculcate values in students and people of society. Without human values we cannot establish a peaceful society.

The levels of Indian insight into the spiritual world of quest for the unknown, deserve a serious review by every young Indian today.[5]

Today, the indegenous knowledge traditions are often ignored though it's significance is realized globally.The value it creates, contribute to strengthen the moral fibres of the society more effectively.

From the times immortal music has been a integral part of human culture. It has been visualized as a spiritual force towards self-realization and *'Moksha'*. The *"Veda"* place great emphasis on the syllable *'OM'* and the audible sound *(Nada)* is said to be the manifestation of the *'cosmic sound'* itself. *'Nada'* is considered to be capable to transform the states of mind and body, literally influencing the whole world. So music *(Nada)* too is the most effective way of attaining spiritual enlightment and realization. "*Yagyabalka Smriti"* depicts "*Talagyashcha Prayasen Moksha Marg Nigachhati"*.[6] The person who is expert in *Veena Vadan, Jati & Taal attains moksha* very easily without extra effort and *Tapasya.*

The textual tradition of Indian classical music are replete with the value based principles which were set by the ancient scholars in the field of music. *Sangeet Ratnkar by Sharung dev 12th Century A.D.* depict the guidelines for the essential qualities for the music performers, teachers, learners and even for the audience *(prekshak)*. The "*Purva Rang"* tradition mentioned in "*Natyashastra"* is another symbol of submission to the divine for every pursuit of art. In Indian tradition, the two streams of classical music "*Margi" and "Deshi"* Sangeet are the two parallel ways. One "*Sadhya" - "Music as God"* the another as "*sadhan" "communication medium for social benefit*". Through the ages, music is being used as a medium for social reform. As per historical reviews Indian social and cultural scenario has been affected by many social evils at times giving birth to the degradation in social and moral values.

In the course of time many social reformers like saint poets, artists, spiritual gurus have enlightened the hearts of common man of the society through their writings, which had a wide range of issues related to social problems. They taught values very easily through music.

In common terms music denotes any kind of dance, vocal and instrumental performance may it be classical or light music or folk. When we discuss about classical music, then it requires a certain rules to be followed in terms of *Swar, Tala, Pada* while at the same time classical music is a beautiful blending of rules and freeness (Improvisation scope within rules of Ragas) for tonal movement.

All the charcteristics essential for having moral values are equally needed in classical musical tradition also. *Dhairya, Kshma, Dhee, Vidya (quest for knowledge) Akrodh, attention, purity, hard work,* is equally necessary for teaching and practicing of music. The general tendency of human being is to attain everything in a shortcut method but according to the quotation – "*Shanirvidya Shanairbrittam*"[7] gaining knowledge and mastery over anything *(Siddhi)* is a gradual process.

So mastery in *Swar* and *Tal* (the basic component of music) needs patience *(Dhairya).* For this, one has to practice regularly. For regularity, one has to withdraw oneself from external attractions and anger.

Thus, keeping the mind and body truly clean, one can achieve knowledge of *Sangeet Shastra* and intricacies of *Swar, Tal, and Pada*. This practice leads to self-realization.

Any kind of art is capable of melting out the emotions from the heart of the musician through the musical expression and convey it to the listener and affect him at the realm of heart and mind.

Music is the most effective means of communicating the expression. It doubles, when it is joined with *text (Pada) and* affects more meaningfully. Any kind of moral teaching could be possible through means of such compositions, set in *Swar, Tal and Pada.* That is why social reformers such as the saint poets, musicians and scholars used song texts (padas) of spiritual values set in music for wider communication for the benefit of the common people.

These pad composers had felt the degradation in the moral human, cultural, spiritual values in their contemporary ages and contributed to a large extent in the social and cultural transformation through their writings. The music was considered as a strong means of communication between these great saints, artists and the common people we can observe or wide range of moral education in their compositions.

The composers of these song texts were well acquinted with traditional classical ragas, talas and styles. The Saint poets namely *Surdas. Tulsidas, Kabirdas, Meerabai, Raidas, Brahmanand, Nanak, Musicians like Swami-Haridas, Tansen, Nayak-Baizu, Sadarang, Adarang, Har-rang, Amir khusro*, and parallely *sufi saints like Baba Bulle Shah, Peer Baba Farid* gave unparallel contribution with their moral teachings through *padas* set in *ragas & talas,* which are still relevant and capable to mould and transform the minds and lead towards the true essence of life that is spiritual realisation of the oneness of individual with the Almighty.

In the medieval period of musical history, the *shringaric bandishes* were in vogue, but in a parallel stream, the song texts (Padas) full of spiritual contents inspired and encouraged the musicians to perform their social duties too. These song texts (Padas) were written and composed *by saint poets, artists, bandishkars*, (famous and unknown both) for last six hundred years.

In the modern period of musical history, *Pandit Vishnu Digambar Paluskar jee and Pandit Vishnu Narayan Bhatkhande jee* contributed at large scale. They started composing and propagating the 'Padas' of spiritual relevance and high moral values and evoked the sense in common people of the society that music is not mere a means of entertainment. It is not a subject to be seen as degraded. At the contrary, it is a channel to develop moral qualities and spiritual realization. This great tradition was imbibed in their disciples also, who were greatly inspired by the philosophy of their *'Guru'* and they also contributed with numerous song texts (Padas) for propagating the awareness regarding humanity, human values, emotional and spiritual development. Some of the composers (vaggeyakars) of these song texts are Pt. Omkarnath Thakur (Pranav Rang), Pt. Balwant Rai Bhatt (Bhav-Rang), Vinayk Rao Patwardhan, Apart from this, many other modern composers are Pt. Ramashray Jha (Ram Rang), Pt. Lakshman Narayan Gune, Pt. Ritwik Sanyal (Dhrupad song texts) and so on can be enlisted for their contribution.

While tracing the emergence of different singing styles in north Indian classical music like *Dhrupad, Khyal, Thumri, Bhajan* and many more. We observe that the flourishment of Dhrupad style was at its peak during the period of *Raja Mansingh Tomar* who contributed a lot in the field of Dhrupad. With gradual development, *Raja Mansingh Tomer* developed the song texts (Padas) in *Madhya-Deshi bhasha* and the artist compsers like *Nayak Baiju, Nayak Bakshu, MiyanTansen* composed numerous song texts *(Padas)* which gave emphasis on higher moral qualities and evoked the sense of self-realisaton.

Some of the selected *'Padas'* by different composers are discussed here, which are set in different *Ragas* and *Talas.* These *Padas* set as different *Bandishes in different ragas* have a wide range of moral teachings. These teaching are addressed to the human being to have a sense of realisation that –" *Almighty is the ultimate.*

Sub mission to the almighty is essential. This world is not the reality only reality is almighty. Every kind of proud regarding beauti, skill, knowledge is the sign of ignorance. Sacredness of soul can be attained only through following truth, forgiveness, love, pity and harmony". Some selcted *'Padas'* are being mentioned here, which cover and showcase the different moral teachings.

The famous *Pada in Rag Bhupali*

"Tero man me ketno gun re jo tu teto prakash kar re,

'Pada' by Nayak Baizu (Late.15 century)[8]

it symbolizes-encouragement for *Riyaz* and *Tapasya* for attaining self-confidence and self-realization.

Another modern composition by Pt. Ritwik Sanyal (2013) depicts *Nad sadhana* as '*Sadhya'* itself.

"Anand lok me Rahat Magan sab
Niraker Nirankar howe. Amurta ko murta kare
Aseem rup ko Aahat Anhad ko Shruti gyan ko bhaye"[9].

It makes to realize the value of music *to be self-less, it indicates the abstract and intangible art of music gives eternal bliss. Music has limit less powers.*

Teaching and caution *(Seekh and Chetawani)* oriented Padas

"Taja Re Abhiman Jan Gunijan ko
gun ki sewa na maan awaman"[10]
(Rag-Bilaskhani Todi)

"Sanchi kahat hai adarangNdi nav sanjog".[11]*(Rag – Deshi)*
"Pariye Pay na wa ke Sajani
Jo na mane guniyan ki seekh"[12]
(Rag – Jaunpuri)
"Gunan ko chit dhariye"[13]
(Rag – Marwa)

"Gyan na pawe Guru bin Gyani"[14]
(Rag – Shree)
Nad – Mahima
"Sadhat guni saras Nad"[15] – Rag Patdeep

Submission to almighty oriented Padas

"Prabhu data saban ko"[16]

(Rag – Bhairav)

"Jap re mana puneet prabhu nam"[17]

(Rag – Ahir Bhairav)

"Hari nam kar gan" [18"]

(Rag – Bhatiyar)

"Prabhu ke charan kamal"[19]

(Rag – Shree)

Apart from these, numerous *Padas* in form of *Bandishes* are there which can be sung and taught. Some examples are—

"Kar yad prabhu ko aj" (Maligaura)[20] *"Hari Hari Kar man" (Shreetank)*[21] *"Kalas Jyoti lagi rahe" (Jait)*[22] *"Rab ko nam sumar mana" (Bibhas)*[23] *"Ram nam bhajan karo" (Kalingra)*[24] *"Guru charan sharan kar manuja" (Sohini)*[25] *"Kareem nam tero" (Miya malhar)*[26] *"Murh abudh Nar Taj Abhiman" (adana)*[27] *"Karna ho so kar le pyare" (Shankura)*[28] *"Bahu gun kam na aawe sajani" (Bageshri)*[29] *"Nad bheda aparampar" (Hindol)*[30] *"Soch samaj man meet piyarawa" (Kedar)*[31] *"Pratham adi shivashakti" (Sohini)*[32] *"Nitya suddha buddha mukta" (Multani)*[33] *"Dhar re man dheer dha" (Shuddha Kalyan)*[34] *"Kahe sochat tu more man" (Kamod)*[35] *"Le saheb ko nam" (Ramkali)*[36] *"Manush Janam atul payo" (Lalit)*[37] *"Samjhat na man tu mera" (Darbari)*[38] *"Mai tohe dhyaun ab peer Jalaluddin haider" (Bibhas)*[39] *"Soch samajh ab man le pyare" (Barwa)*[40] *"Ap hi hot adi anta" (Malgunji)*[41] *"Karta so pandit mano" (Hanskinkini)*[42] *"Gyan gun data rab mata vidhata" (Sindh Bhairavi)*[43] *"Papi Hari mukh bol re" (Nayakikanhra)44 "Anhat shabda upjyo"(Bilaskhani Todi)*[45] *"Narayan tu hi kartar" (Gurjari Todi)*[46] *"Gori jobanwa ye rahiye sada nahi" (Sarang)*[47] *"Mo malin deh sang" (Sarang)*[48] *"Mane sukh dukh aur harakh shok" (Tilang)*[49] *"Deh dhare vividh rup" (Durga)* [50]*"Sansar ko sar" (Bhupal Todi)*[51]

Not only the classical *Bandishes* are the source of self-realization. The semi classical compositions also have wide variety of *padas* of *Nirgun bhakti subjects*. Some of the famous *Thumri, Dadra and Chaitis* are appropriate examples like :

"Ye sundar Saari mori maike maile bhai[52]*"*

Denotes the caution about maintaining the purity of the soul.

"Nahak laye gawanwa ho ram"[53]

depicts the lack of knowledge about the almighty.

"Mora Saiyan bulawe wohi par"[54.]

It denotes the attractions of the earthily matter restricts us to unite with the almighty. A Pada by Meerabai

"Soch Samajh Nadan"[55]

it give caution to self-realization that nothing lasts but the truth. Another composition by Shankaracharya

"Ab sudh lo more Ram"[56]

and "Ab more naiya kaise lage par" [57]

and another one by

Kabir das jee "Tadpe bin balam mora jiya"[58]

"Sowat nindiya Jagawe ho Rama bhor hi bhore"[59]

depicts the craving of the Atma to meet with almighty.

These all are the treasure from Indian Literature which were the ultimate means for creating spiritual awareness during the ages. The *Padas* by saint poets set in different *Ragas* and *Talas* in form of Bhajans were the another source for inspiration for common man who were not so capable of following or attending classical traditions. Such *Bhajans* were very deep in meaning and were very easy to absorb by the common man of the society. Still such Padas are having very deep rooted meaning whereas pleasant to ears for their tunes set in *Kirtan* style or *Bhajan.* They are capable of transmitting the teachings of these *Padas* very easily and effectively. Such as—

Man lago mero yar phakiri me[60]*(Kabirdas), Sadho ye tan thata tambure ka*[61] *(Kabridas), So ka jane peer parai* [62]*(Raidas), Sadho rachana sram banai*[63] *(Nanak), Prabhu ji tum chandan hum pani*[64] *(Raidas), Sanware rang ranchi,*[65] *Mhari surat suha gun nar,*[66] *Payo ji maine ram ratan dhan payo*[67] *(Meera bai), Prabhu more avagun chit na dharo*[68]*(Surdas), Mamta tu na gai mere man te*[69] *(TulsiDas), Musafir kya sowe ab jag,*[70]*Kahe soch kare nar man me* [71]*(Bhrahmanand), Vishnav jan to tene kahiye je*[72] *(Narsi Mehta), Chaap tilak sab linhi re mose naina mila ke* [73]*(Amir Khushro), Na Twaham Kamaye Rajyam*[74]*(Madan Mohan Malviya).*

So concluding at the point that in the basic philosophy of "*Vedanta*", *"Brahma"* has been accepted as a *"Chetan satta"* which is transcended in everything. So in every art form, the contents of the art and knowledge is also accepted as *Brhama (Chetan).* The basic content of music is *'Nad'*, so It has been labelled as "*Nad Brhama"*. The consciousness of the almighty "*Brhama*"is everywhere in this universe so the earthily matters may be dynamic or static are considered capable of *Lokranjan and Vyavhar* so music is also considered as *'Sadhya'* and *'Sadhan'* both. We can achieve every goal by worshiping music as *'Brhama'* and we can take it as a *'upadan'* to achieve *Brhama (God).* So the contents of song texts *(Padas)* can mould our consciousness towards the spiritual realization of the self very effectively. Indian classical music tradition has a rich and wide range of such song texts (Padas), traditional and contemporary both so the need is to use these compositions on a wide scale for teaching and performance so that the moral values in these texts can be propagated amongst the society and create a society enriched with high moral values and establish a society loaded with universal principles of love, speace and harmony.

References

1. Pradhan Awadhesh, *"Geeta me pratipadit Daivi aur Aasuri samppatiyon ka mulyaparah vivechan."* Pragya – Ank-56, p. 45.
2. Nirmal, Arati, *"An evaluation of the value at the values"*, Pragya, Vol.-56, p. 245.
3. Singer Peter, "The environmental challenge" environmental values. Tan Marsh (ed.) Melbourne, australia, Longman Cheshire (1991)
4. Srivastava Jyotsna *"Vartaman Sandarbhon me Naitikata ki Upadeyata"*, Pragya, Vol. 56, p. 83.
5. Meena R.S., *"Need for moral values to Indian Youth",* Pragya, Vol. 56, p. 218.
6. Yagyavalkya, Yagyavalkya smriti, Prayaschittaddhya, Shlok 115, Ref. *"Manviya Mulya evam Shastriya Sangeet"*, Sharma, Swar Vandana, Pragya, Vol. 56, p. 92
7. Subhasit, Ratna Bhandagar, Nirnay sagar press, Mumbai, 1952, 156/126, Ref. Sharma Swar Vandana, *"Manaviya Mulya aur Shastriya Sangeet",* Pragya, Vol.-56, part-1, Year 2010-11, p. 92
8. Traditional badish of Dagur Gharana in Rag Bhupali Ref. Oral tradiation from Pandit Ritwik Sanyal Senior most desciple of Ustad Zia Mohiuddin Dagur – Farduddin Dagur.
9. Oral Tradation from Dhrupad Maestro Pandit Ritwik Sanyal's composition.
10. Traditional badish of Rag Bilaskhani Todi Set in Teen tal, Ref. oral tradition from Prof. Sarayu R. Sonni, Deptt. of Vocal musci, F.O.P.A., B.H.U.
11. Traditional, 'Ada rang' composed, Ref. Kramik Pustak Malika Vol.-IV. by pt. Vishnu Narayan Bhatkhnde, Edited by Milan Debnath, 2003, p. 478
12. Traditional 'Daras' Ref. Bhatkhande Karmik Pustak Malika, part-III, Edited by Milan Debnath, 2003, p. 184

13. Bandish in Rag Marwa set in Drat Ektaal. Ref. Oral tradition, pt. Balwant Rai Bhatt, Bhavrang Lahri, part-I, p. 170.
14. Traditional Bandish in Rag Shree, Edited by Ramashray Jha Ramrang, Ref. Rag Shastra, by Dr. Geeta Banerjee, p. 218
15. Bandish in Rag Patdeep, set in Drut Ektaal, pt. Balwant Rai Bhatt, Bhavrang Lahri, Part-I, p. 60
16. Traditional Bandish in Rag Bhairav, Ref. Bhatkhande Kramik Pustak Malika, Part-II by V.N. Bhatkhande, p. 181
17. Bandish in Rag Ahir Bhairav, Part-II, Set in teental by Pt. Balwant Rai Bhatt, Ref. Bhavrang Lahri, p. 59
18. Bandish in Rag Bhatiyar, Set in Jhaptal by Pt. Balwant Rai Bhatt, Ref. Bhavrang Lahri, part-III, p. 317
19. Bandish in Rag Shree, Set in Jhaptaal, Ref. Bhatkhande KramikPustak Malika, Part-III, IV, Edited by Milan Debnath, p. 104
20. Karamik Pustak Malika, Part-VI, p. 293, Edited by Milan Debnath, 2003
21. *ibid,* p. 260
22. *ibid,* p. 303
23. *ibid,* p. 309
24. *ibid,* Part-III, IV, p. 86
25. *ibid,* Part-III, IV, p. 110
26. *ibid,* Part-III, IV, p. 316
27. *ibid,* Part-III, IV, p. 339
28. *ibid,* Part-III, IV, p. 245
29. *ibid,* Part-III, IV, p. 135
30. *ibid,* Part-III, IV, p. 272
31. *ibid,* Part-III, IV, p. 47
32. *ibid,* Part-III, IV, p. 120
33. *ibid,* Part-III, IV, p. 514
34. *ibid,* Part-III, IV, p. 360
35. *ibid,* Part-III, IV, p. 366
36. *ibid,* Part-III, IV, p. 413
37. *ibid,* Part-III, IV, p. 456
38. *ibid,* Part-III, IV, p. 478
39. *ibid,* Part-III, IV, p. 312
40. *ibid,* Part-V, VI, p. 346
41. *ibid,* Part-V, VI, p. 473
42. *ibid,* Part-V, VI, p. 364
43. *ibid,* Part-V, VI, p. 512

44. *ibid,* Part-V, VI, p. 413
45. *ibid,* Part-V, VI, p. 516
46. *ibid,* Part-V, VI, p. 530
47. Sangeetanjali part 1, Pandit Omkar Nath Thakur, Edited by Premlata Sharma, Suhadra Choudhary, p. 43
48. Sangeetanjali Part-I, Pt.Omkan Nath Thakur, Edited by Premlata Sharma, Subhadra Chaudhery, p. 44
49. do, p. 58
50. do, p. 32
51. Bhav Rang Lahri, Part II by Pandit Balwant Rai Bhatt, p. 126.

52 – 59. Bandishes from Oral Tradation of Pandit Surendra Mohan Mishra (Mohan Ji), Banaras Gharana.

60 – 72. Bhajan Sangrah, Published by Geeta Press, Gorakhpur.

73. Tradational Sufi Pad by Hazrat Amir Khusro
74. Shlok written by Bharat Ratna Pandit Madan Mohan Malviya Ji.

4

Analytical Approach to *Masnavi* Ideology of Jalaluddin Rumi

Feroz Haidry

Abstract

Thirteenth Century in which Maulana Jalaluddin Rumi was born and lived (1207 - 73 AH) the Islamic world was in economic and political turmoil. Tartars that rose like a strong current of wind not only subjugated many an established sultanates but also destroyed centers of learning in Iran and Iraq, which were considered to be think-tank of Islamic world along with Syria and Egypt. Repeated changes of political power in new hands, some of whom indulged in the plunder of common people in order to collect resources to sustain their power and trust that came with it, were taking place. The elite who were hitherto living a luxurious life became pamper overnight being target of plunder. The Crisis Continued for Longer period than ever witnessed in the history. This caused a change in the people's perception of life. Having lost worldly comfort they were now trying to find solace in spiritual from active life. They were increasingly drawing towards Fakirs and their Khanqahs where they found peace and tranquility. Sheikh Najmuddin Kubra, Sheikh Shahabuddin Saharwardi, Sheikh Akbar, Ibn-e- Arabi, Khwaja Fariduddin Attar, Sadruddin Qunvi and many others were there in response to the demand from the frustrated people.

Keywords: Masnavi, gnosism, huma oost, sokhtam

Maulana Rumi's father, Mohammed Burhanuddin Walad, who lived in Balkh, was a highly reputed man. For some reasons he had to leave his home-town and migrate. At that time Maulana Rumi was six years old. After moving around for some years and performing Haj he finally settled down at Qunia, where he died in 1231 AD. Maulana Rumi received education under the guidance of his father. After his death one of his father's followers, Syed Burhanuddin Mohaqiq took the responsibility of educating the Maulana. In his Practical life Maulana marched on the foot-steps of his father and resumed teaching and preaching through discourses. This continued till he happened to meet Shams Tibriz in 1244. This meeting had changed the life of Maulana, who abandoned teaching and preaching and spent all his time in the company of Shams Tibriz discussing secrets of gnesis.

This was resented by Rumi's disciples and followers. But still Maulana continued to be in the company of Shams then Maulana's followers started harassing and even insulting him. Irked by such behavior Shams left Qunia without informing Maulana about his act in 1246 AD. and according to some sources he was murdered in 1247 AD. The separation caused Maulana restlessness. However after some times he found some solace in the Company of Sheikh Salahuddin Zarkoob. After his death Hassmuddin took his place. He wrote the Masnavi at the instance of Hassmuddin.

The critical edition of the Masnavi was edited by Prof. Arnold Nicholson (1924-1940 AD) Ghazals and Rubais of Rumi were compiled and edited by Prof. Badiuzzaman Farozan Far in 1336-38 AH.

Maulana's misson was to propagate spiritual and ethical values. So he sung the song of analysis of soul; purification of thought and Love of God. These are the themes that are spread all over the Masnavi. Besides Gnosticism he has also explained many problems of Shariah by allegorical stories and events. At this plan the Masnavi can be termed as an encyclopedia of Sharia and Tariqah (Dr. Sy. Naimuddin)1. All the stages of issues like seeking God and Later spiritual integration with Him has been explained through these stories and events.

Khush-tar aan bashad ke sirr-e dilbaran
Gufta aayad dar hadis-e-digaran

What is the secret of beloved? Rumi thinks that the secret of beloved is hidden in one's soul. That is why he has emphasized in the Masnavi, Diwan and Fih-ma-Fih that the real human is not his body. Body is no more than a mere handful of dust. Under the body flows a strong current of soul. If our limited soul enjoins the Unlimited it will not stay in the body and will become immortal. And this can be possible by love alone. One can attain this immortality by first of purifying his heart from all pollutants and whole heartedly concentrating on his search of God. Rumi says, in this way, one can gain such knowledge which is out of the reach of mind. He says that in the path of gnosism worldly reason is as ineffective as a wooden foot in a body. Without giving any importance to reason one can march forward in his search for God through the path of devotion and Love. And as Holy Quran says : " and that to you Lord is the goal (Qur'an 50 : 42) And also for seekers He is nearer to you than your own vein."

Many interpreters expound the Masnavi in terms of the pantheistic system associated with *Sheikh Mohiuddin Akbar Ibn-e Arabi*. Being convinced that the poem was deeply influenced from that quarter, they hold that it cannot be made intelligible without reference to those ideas. Such a mode of explanation is apt to mislead us. In a poem that consists of thousands of verses only at two or three passages some verses are there which given this impression. For example in **Daftar 1** there is a verse:

Jumla ma'shooq ast wa a'shiq parda-i
Zinda ma'shooq ast was a'shiq murda-i (2)

The idea that whole creation is beloved leads one to think of pantheistic doctrine ***(Huma Oost)***. But such verses are very few in comparison to that ***(Huma az oost).*** We must remember that Rumi is a poet and mystic, not a philosopher and logician. He has no system; he creates an aesthetic atmosphere which defies analysis (Nicholson).

Rumi was worried because people's behavior towards Shams Tibrizi was not good, they also envied Salahuddin Zarkoob (on the ground that he was an ordinary goldsmith and did not deserve the honor Rumi was bestowing on him) and finally they also envied Hassmuddin Chelebi. Rumi told people again and again that one's status is decided by his knowledge and piety and not by his worldly riches. To emphasize his pointed he also praised Hassmuddin in the Masnavi, He held Tibrizi, Zarkoob and Hassmmuddin as real worshipers of Unity. For Rumi Unity meant burning oneself to brighten his life like day-light.

Chist tawhid-e Khuda aamokhtan
Khweshtan ra pesh-e wahid sokhtan
Gar hami khwahi ke befrozi choo roz
Hasti-e hamchoo shab-e khud ra besoz

For Rumi one who completely devotes himself to the will of Allah, rises above the worldly sense of bad and good and he does not differentiates between sugar & poison.

Ta zaher wa az shakar too naguzri
Az gul-e wahdat kuja boo-e bari

Rumi's Masnavi begins with the complaint of separation;

Bishunaw az nay choon shikayat mi kunad
Az judai ha hikayat mi kunad

Rumi does not hesitate even cursing those who do not burn themselves in the fire of love for God;

Har ke een aatish na darad nist baad
(Prof. Aatish)

Rumi had surpassed in love of God from the stage of "**Pukhta Shudam**"and reached the higher stage of **"Sokhtam"**. As a result a sense of spiritual courage flows in his poem which is a distinct deviation from his predecessors, who showed a feeling of helplessness.

The Masnavi was hailed by not only the Rumi's disciples and later members of the great brotherhood of which he was the founder, but all Persian speaking Sufis as a unique revelation of truth long before Jami called it: "the Qur'an in Persian (***Hast Qur'an dar zaban-e Pahlawi***) and said of Jalaluddin himself: "though he is not a prophet, he has a book (***neest payghambar vali darad Kitab***). Sufis boast of many inspired books of this kind, but none has been so carefully studied and copiously expounded in all the principal languages of Islamic world. The oldest exegesis dates from the 15th Century, *Kamaluddin Husain Ibn Hasan at Khwarizmi al-kubravi*, a disciple of *Khwaja Abul Wafa* discussed and explained the Masnavi in two works which he entitled respectively *Kunzu-l Baqaiq fi Rumuzi-l Daqaiq* and *Jawahiru-l Asrar wa Zawahiru-l Anwar*; and his example was followed by a younger contemporary, *Nizamuddin Mahmood Ibnul Hasan al-Husain of Shiraz*. Though Iran led the way but first complete and systematic commentaries were produced in Turkey. For these we are indebted to *Muslaehuddin Ibn Mustafa Sururi*, who died in 969 AH, and *Ismail Anqirawi* (1041 AH).

The Masnavi was, and still is, equally popular in India. Well known Sufi of the 16th Century Abdul Quddus Gangohi (1538 AD) quoted verses both from the Masnavi and the Diwan-e-Tibrizi in letters to his disciples and followers. During 17th and 18th Centuries the Masnavi was read with keen interest by almost all Persian knowing households in the country as it was prescribed in the syllabus of madrasas; religious preachers also quoted verses from the Masnavi in their discourses. *Miftahul Ma'anvi by Abdul Fatah* (1049 AH), dataful Masnavi by Abdul Latif Abbasi (1048 AH) and *Mukashifat-e Razvi* are the popular explanatory works of the 17th Century. Abbasi also compiled and edited an authentic Volume of the Masnavi, entitled *Nushkha-e Nasekha wa Masnaviyat-i Suqimah*, after deleting verses, from it, supposed to be inserted by others. During this period *Rasukhi Ismail Dadah Anqrawi* (1631 AD) expounded the Masnavi from the point of view of *Ibn Arabi*. Explanatory work by Baharul Uloom's "*Sharah-e Masnavi* (1877 AD) gained much popularity in India.

All these works form a part of an immense mass of exegetical materials which no modern commentator can afford to ignore, though a great deal of it yields no or bitter fruit. But in the beginning of the past century *Allama Shibli No'mani* in his *"Sawaneh Maulana Rum*", reviewed the Masnavi and *Diwan-e Shams* in such a way that it gave new meanings to the verses of the Masnavi, which hitherto remained hidden. He put forward such verses which exposed the courage and deep knowledge of *Rumi*, who wanted his followers to be active in life;

Zin ham-rhan-e sust unasir dilam girift
sher-e khuda wa Rustam-e dastanam aar zi-dast
Choo ghulam-e aaftabam ham az-aaftab goyam
Na Shabam no Shab parastam ke hadis-e khwab goyam

5

Mystic Fervour and Similarities in the Poetry of Rumi and Kabir

Shamenaz Bano

Rumi and Kabir are the two mystical legendry philosopher poets unanimously recognized and respected around the world for their mysticism, love, devotion and humanity. Their works are considered as best poetical works inspiring people from generations to live peacefully with all the ethnic groups residing in the world. A brief knowledge of the order or tradition to which they belonged is imperative in the understanding of these two poetic geniuses. While Kabir was a follower of Bhakti cult, Rumi belonged to the Sufi tradition.

Sufism is a concept in Islam as defined by many scholars, intellectualas the inner, mystical dimension in Islam. There are many interpretations and meaning regarding Sufism as a word or a practise. It is one of the most popular religious orders of the world. Sufism is still practised around the globe especially in India, Pakistan and Bangladesh.

'Many classical Sufi scholars have defined Sufism as, "a science whose objective in the reparation of the heart and turning it away from else but God." Another Sufi teacher, Ahmad Ibn Ajiba defines Sufism in the following words:

"*a science through which one can know how to travel into the presence of the Divine, purify one's inner self from filth, and beautify it with a variety of praiseworthy traits.*"(Ahmad Ibn Ajiba)

Sufism is believed to be universal in nature that is the reason for which it is amalgamated in all the other ethnic societies of the world. As author Idries Shah had opined that, 'Sufi philosophy is universal in nature, its roots predating the rise of Islam and Christianity. (279–281)

There are many schools of Sufism around the world including Western countries who allow non-Muslims to receive, "instructions on following the Sufi paths." However with the rise of radicalization in Islam, some Muslim scholars have become opponents to Sufism declaring it outside the sphere of Islam. But still the influence of Sufism is beyond the boundaries and expanding day by day and has spanned several continents and cultures over a millennium. The belief of Sufism was originally expressed in Arabic but it expanded to Persian, Turkish, Indian languages and many other languages of the world.

The word, 'sufi' as believed by Abu RayhamAlbiruni, a medieval scholar is derived from the Greek word 'sofia' meaning wisdom which is quite complimentary for Sufi saints who devout their entire life acquiring wisdom. There are different Sufi orders and their teachings varies from each other but Sufism as whole primarily believe in direct personal experience and hence sometimes it is compared with other ethnic forms of mysticism resulting in bringing harmony with other forms (e.g., as in the books of Hossein Nasr).

There are various Islamic Institutes around the world promulgating tolerance, peace and brotherhood among different ethnic groups. The Islamic Institute in Mannheim, Germany is working towards the integration of Europe and Muslims. The Institute views Sufism as particularly suited for interreligious dialogue and intercultural harmonisation in democratic and pluralist societies. It believes Sufism as a symbol of tolerance and humanism–non-dogmatic, flexible and nonviolent (25). Philips Jenkins, a Professor at Baylor University speaks about Sufism:

"The Sufis are much more than tactical allies for the West: they are, potentially, the greatest hope for pluralism and democracy within Muslim nations." So Sufism is a path which promotes peace, non-violence and harmony around the world. In the same way,Bhakti movement also follows the same doctrine.

Bhakti movement was the religious movement of India in Hinduism during medieval period. The movement believed in 'moksh' which can attainable by all. Moksha refers to the liberation there is remarakable difference in the 'bhakti' in the two places. The Southern movement favoured devotion to Shiva, Vishnu and his avatars, the Northern paid their devotion to Rama and Krishna, and both of them are believed to be incarnations of Vishnu. However, the devotion towards Shiva and Vishnu also existed in North India. The Bhakti movement co-existed peacefully with the other movements in Hinduism. The Bhakti saints were against the division of caste in Indian society. They disregarded Brahmanic rituals and did not consider it necessary for spiritual salvation. As it was against the superstitions and orthodox belief existing in the society, it gained immense popularity among the masses. But with the passage of time, due to its popularity and royal patronage by many rulers it became orthodox. However it is still considered as one of most important modes of religious expression in modern India.

Some very influential saints of 19th century of Bhakti movement were Sant Kabir, Namdev, Raidas and Pipaji. They paths they carved out was easy for common people to follow. I also brought reforms in the society. The most important reform which they tried to do is that bringing equality in the class and caste ridden society.

These two movements Sufi and Bhakti movements were closely related to each other. They were like two sides of a same coin. They almost appeared at the same time. Both the movements advocated that a personal expression of devotion to God is the way to become at one with Him. There are many other values and belief which are very similar to each other advocated by both the movements. Even Saints and Philosophers associated with Sufi and Bhakti movements had same thoughts. Jalaluddin Rumi and Saint Kabir are two such saints belonging to Bhakti and Sufi traditions. They preached the quite identical as reflected by their poetry reflects. Jalaluddin Rumi and Saint Kabir are the two mystical masters and poets who have laid their lives giving message of peace, brotherhood and humanity. For these reasons they both are ranked among the world's greatest poet of all times, and their couplet are widely read and translated in all the languages of the world. They are mostly united in their broader outlook towards religion, love for mankind, mystic and spiritual approach to reach the almighty God.

Kabir is recognized as a soul of India and perhaps the most quoted author, with the exception of Tulsidas.He is a mystic poet and one of the most famous saints of India who greatly influenced the Bhakti movement. His date of birth is a little uncertain and is believed to be perhaps in 1398-1448 and thought to have lived longer than 100 years. His works are critique of almost all the existing sects in India, whether Hindu or Muslims or others but is still mentioned with respect by even orthodox writers. His influence on Indian philosophy and Hindi poetry is immense and can still be seen.

The name Kabir is derived from Arabic al-Kabir meaning 'The Great' is the 37th name of God in Islam. Today Kabir's greatness and legacy has lead to a path known as 'Kabir Panth' (Path of Kabir). It is a religious community which recognises him as its founder and is one of the Sant Mat sects. Kabir has shown his belief in both Bhakti and Sufi ideas.He has greatly contributed to the Indian mystical writing, his works include: *Bijak*, *SakhiGranth*, *Kabir Granthawali* and *Anurag Sagar*. *Songs of Kabir* is a collection of his poems by KshitimohanSen from mendicants across India, which has been translated by Rabindranath Tagore.

He wrote many poetry and songs which are still recited and sung in the Indian household. These writings are renowned in literary scenario as well. His recorded verses are in Hindi and are characterised by a free use of the vernacular. It is unfettered by the grammatical bonds of his day. This is the quality of Kabir's philosophy which has made it easy accessible the Indians since generations and people love to read his poetry even now.

Jalauddin Mohammad Rumi was born in 1207 in Wakhsh (Tajikistan) to a family of theologians; he founded the Mawlawi Sufi order which is a leading mystical brotherhood of Islam. He is called as Mevlana or Mawlana meaning 'master.' A leading mystic poet of all times, he was initiated into the mystical path by a wandering dervish, Shamsuddin of Tabriz.Throughout his life, he has composed many Persian poems (ghazals) which have been collected in the *DivaniKabir* or *Diwan Shams Tabrizi*. His influence transcends national borders and ethnic divisions: Iranians, Turks, Cappadocian Greeks, Afghans, Tajiks, other. Central Asian Muslims of South Asia have greatly appreciated his spiritual legacy for the past seven centuries. Today he isthe most widely read poet and best seller in America.

In his lifetime, Rumi was greatly inspired by dervish Shamse Tabrizi who changed his life and from an accomplished teacher and jurist, transformed him into an ascetic. He was encouraged by his companion, Salahuddin Zarkub and later by his favourite student and companion, Hussame Chalabi who inspired him to write. By Hussam imploration, Rumi began dictating the six volumes of his masterpiece work, the *Masnavi* to him in Anatolia and completed in twelve years. His Masnavi are the fables with events from everyday life, Quranic revelations and exegesis and also metaphysics into a vast and intricate tapestry.

Rumi believed in Sufism and so like other mystic and Sufi poets of Persian literature, his general theme is the concept of union with his beloved (the primal root) from which/whom he has been cut off and become aloof—and his longing and desire to restore it, which is the concept of *tawhid*. He had a great admiration for poetry, music and dance and believed passionately that they are a path to reach God. Rumi believed that music helps devotees to focus their whole being on the divine and in the intense practise of music the soul was both destroyed and resurrected. All these ideas became the base of the practice of whirling Dervishes which later developed into a ritual form. His teachings paved the way for Mevlevi order, which was further carried by his son, sultan Walad. Rumi favoured Sama, listening to sacred music or performing the sacred dance. *Sama* is a part of Mevlevi tradition, representing a mystical journey of spiritual ascent through mind and love to the Perfect One. This is the journey, in which the seeker symbolically turns towards the truth, develops through love, forsakes ego, searches truth and arrives at the Perfect. Hence the seeker returns from a mystical or spiritual voyage, with profound maturity, to love and to be of service to the whole of creation without discrimination with regard to belief, races, classes and nations. As Rumi gives the universal message of love in his verses in *Masnavi*, he speaks in one of his verse:

The lover's cause is separate from all other causes
Love is the astrolabe of God's mysteries.

His poetic works include: Matnawiye Manawi, which are *Spiritual Couplets*, a six volume containing approximately 27, 000 lines of Persian poetry. It is believed by many scholars, intellectuals and poets to be one of the greatest works of mystical poetry. His other major work is the *Diwane Kabir* or *Diwane Shamse Tabrizi* containing 35000 Persian couplets, 2000 Persian quatrains, 90 Ghazals, 19 quatrains and 19 quatrains and a couple of dozen or so couplets in Turkish and 14 couplets in Greek. He has also has some prose work in Persian to his credit like*Fihi Ma Fihi* (*In It What's in It*) providing a record of seventy one talks and lectures given by Rumi to his disciples on various occasions. The second is *Majalese Saba* (*Seven Sessions*) and as the name implies it contains seven Persian sermons given by him in seven different assemblies. And the last is *Makatib* (*The Letters*), a book containing his letters to his disciples, family members, men of state and of influence.

Rumi's writings have universal appeal like Kabir, they are considered as ecumenical in nature. For him, religion was mostly a personal experience, not confining to logical arguments or perceptions of the senses. His creativity was based on love, or the urge to rejoin the spirit to divinity, the goal towards which everything moves. He believed that, the dignity of life particularly human life (which is conscious of its divine origin and goal) was important. It can be summed up in the following statement: 'The nation of Love has a different religion of all religions—For lovers, God alone is their religion. He had a spiritual vision whose abstruseness is much wider and is beyond narrow sectarian concerns. In one of his rubaiyat, he says:

On the seeker's path, wise men/fools are one.
In his love, brothers and strangers are one.
Go on! Drink the wine of the beloved!
In that faith, Muslims and pagans are one. (3)

In the above stanza, poet is referring God as his beloved, which is a fine example of 'Ishq-e-haqiqi.' Kabir also gave the message of love to all humans, irrespective of caste and religion, as in one of his dohas, '*Looking at the grindingstone*' he speaks his emotions:

Kabira in the market place, wishes welfare of all
Neither friendship nor enmity with anyone at all

Reading books everyone died, none became any wise
One who reads the words of Love, only becomes wise

Rumi and Kabir, both believed in same ideology and were against superstitions, idol-worship and blind faith followed by people. For them a pure heart was the centre of all pilgrimage. In one of his poem, *Going to Mecca*, Rumi is addressing the pilgrims who visitsthe Holy land to free themselves from all sins:

O! pilgrim who visits the Holy Land
I'll show you heaven in a grain of sand.
Why traverse deserts, why confronts the storm,
If within you, resides the formless form.
Of the Beloved? If he's in your heart,
Your pilgrimage has ended where you start.

This is the height of his purity of his thought poured down in the form of poem reflecting his true vision detached from worldly forms. In a similar way Kabir also expresses his views in one of his Sakhi, 'Where do you Search me':

Moko Kahan Dhundhere Bande
Mein To TerePaas Mein
Na Teerath Mein, Na Moorat Mein
Na EkantNiwas Mein
Na Mandir Mein, Na Masjid Mein
Na Kabe Kailas Mein

If these lines are translated in English, it means the following:

Where do you search me?
I am with you
Not in pilgrimage, nor in icons
Neither in solitudes
Not in temples, nor in mosques
Neither in Kaba nor in Kailash

They both had the opinion that God resides in our hearts and one should find Him in it means making our hearts pure free from any malice and prejudices.

Kabir's philosophy has a great impact on social and practical manifestation on people since ages irrespective of caste, creed and religion. It is so because he represented a synthesis of both Hindu and Muslim faith. He accepted virtues from both the religion as he believed in the concept of reincarnation and law of Karma from Hinduism. He rejected the caste system and idolatry and practice single God which is the doctrine of Islam. He propounded the simplicity of religion. According to Kabir, all life is interplay of two spiritual principles. One is the personal soul (Jivatma) and the other is God (Paramatma). He believed that salvation is the process of bringing into unison these two divine principles of soul and God.Kabir believes that whatever one possess belongs to God and human has:

Mera mujhme kuchh nahin, jo kuchh hai sab tor
Tera tujhko sab saunp de, kya laagat hai mor.

(Referring to God he says:

Nothing that is mine belong to me, all that I have is yours.
To give all that belongs to you, it costs me nothing.
In the same way Rumi says inone of his couplet, 'By His Will':
Only by His will do atoms move
The beat of every wing He must approve
No one can explain this and none should try
The infinite can never answer 'why?'
Even though we strive to know the 'how?'
Through science, before Him we have to bow
And give ourselves, our lives and will to God
With no thought of a blessing or reward.

Rumi thus reflects the same spirit towards God as it was later believed by Kabir.

Kabir has a great impact on Indian history and society. He equally holds relevance for Hindus, Muslims and Sikhs alike. He openly criticised superstitions and idol worship existing in all sects and gave a new direction to the Indian philosophy. He touches the soul, the conscience, and the sense of awareness and the vitality of existence in a manner that is unequalled in both simplicity and style. It is for this reason that Kabir acquires high esteem in the hearts of million around the world.

They both respected Prophets, saints and philosophers of all religions. As it is obvious in one of the poem by Rumi, *In Voices* when he says:

All Prophets are but windows to the light,
You can't say one was wrong and one was right.
They are the same, their message is but one,
To crave the light, is to accept the sun.

Kabir also believed in the same ideologyas in none of his couplets he has criticised any Prophets, saints and philosophers of any religion.

Rumi believed in simplicity of life which is away from material desires and longing, as his views can be summed up in the following lines of the poem '*The Will to Drown*':

Desire and your longings will bring you to a fall,
Why fear falling, my friend, isn't it after all.
Like willing yourself to drown in God and go to paradise,
To a haven under the waters or a garden in the skies?

In a similar vein Kabir says in one of his couplet, 'The Last Flight':

The Swan will fly away all alone,
Spectacle of the world will be a mere fair
As the leaf falls from the tree
Is difficult to find?
Who know where it will fall?
Once it is struck with a gust of wind
When life span is complete
Then listening to orders, following others, will be over.

Both Rumi and Kabir have lived a simple life not depending upon any material desires and longing. Kabir is held in high esteem around the world because his poetry touches the soul, the conscience, and the sense of awareness and the vitality of existence in a manner that is unequalled in both simplicity and style. Another beauty of his poetry is that he derives his inspiration from the situations of daily lives. In the present scenario also his poetry are importance and helpful in both social as well as spiritual context. People follow him as he is not only considered as poet but also a spiritual master. Following Kabir means understanding one's inner self, realizing oneself, accepting oneself as is and becoming harmonious with one's surroundings.

Both Rumi and Kabir are mystical poets giving message of peace and brotherhood to the world. They believed in love and devotion to the Lord, love of fellowmen, compassion for all beings, and the moral principles of good and noble living. It is their greatness that after so many centuries have passed since their existence but they are still being loved, praised and respected, not only by the lover of poetry but also by the common people as well around the world.

References

Ahmed Zarruq, ZainebIstrabadi, Hamza Yusuf Hanson. *The Principles of Sufism*. Amal Press. 2008.

An English translation of Ahmad ibn Ajiba's biography has been published by Fons Vitae.

Munn, Richard C. (January–March 1969). "Reviewed work (s): The Sufis by Idries Shah". *Journal of the American Oriental Society* (American Oriental Society) 89 (1): 279–281. (https://www.jstor.org/stable/598339).

"Sufism, Sufis, and Sufi Orders: Sufism's Many Paths" (http://www.uga.edu/islam/sufismwest.html). Uga.edu.

Idries Shah, *The Sufis*, ISBN 0385079664

Alan Godlas, University of Georgia, *Sufism's Many Paths*, 2000, University of Georgia(http://www.uga.edu/islam/Sufism.html)

Michael Sells, Early Islamic Mysticism, p. 1

Albiruni: commemorative volume, Hakim Mohammad Said, Pakistan. Ministry of Education, Unesco, Hamdard National Foundation, Pakistan, 2010.

The memoirs of Sufis written in India: reference to Kashafulmahjub, Siyarulauliya,and Siyarularifin, Mahmud Husain Siddiqui, Dept. of Persian, Urdu, and Arabic, Faculty of Arts, Maharaja Sayajirao University of Baroda, 2009.

Introduction to Sufi Doctrine, p. 3, Titus Burckhardt, KaziPublications, 1976.

Sufism, Sufis, and Sufi Orders: Sufism's Many Paths (http://www.uga.edu/islam / sufismintro.html)

Ron Geaves, Theodore Gabriel, Yvonne Haddad, Jane Idleman Smith: *Islam and the West Post 9/11*, Ashgate Publishing Ltd., p. 67

Jamal Malik, John R. Hinnells: *Sufism in the West*, Routledge, p. 25

Philip Jenkins (January 25, 2009). "Mystical power"(http://www.boston.com/bostonglobe/ideas/articles/2009/01/25/mystical_power/?page=full).Globe Newspaper Company.

Jagadeeshan, N., *The Life and Mission of KaraikkalAmmaiyar*, Bhattacharya, N. N. (ed) *Medieval Bhakti Movements in India*, MunishiramManoharlal, New Delhi, (1989), pages 149-161.

Schome, Karine; McLeod, W. H., eds. (1987), The Saints: Studies in a Devotional Tradition of India, Motilal Banarsidass.

H. Ritter, 1991, *Jalaluddin Rumi, The Encyclopaedia of Islam* (Volume II: CG), 393.

Jalaluddin Rumi (Maulana), Ibrahim Gamard, "Rumi and Islam: Selections from His Stories, Poems, and Discourses, Annotated & Explained", Sky Light Paths Publishing, Feb 1, 2004.

Grousset, Rene, The Empire of the Steppes: A History of Central Asia, (Rutgers University Press, 2002), 157~"...the Seljuk court at Konya adopted Persian as its official language."

Barks, Coleman, *Rumi: The Book of Love: Poems of Ecstasy and Longing*, HarperCollins, 2005, p. Xxv.

MaulanaRumi (25 May 2011). *The Masnavi I Ma'navi of Rumi: Complete 6 Books* (http://books.google.com/books? Retrieved 28 September 2011.

Naini, Majid. *The Mysteries of the Universe and Rumi's Discoveries on the Majestic Path of Love.*

Franklin Lewis, Rumi Past and Present, East and West, Oneworld Publications, 2008 (revised edition). p. 306.

Franklin D. Lewis, Rumi: Past and Present, East and West: The Life, Teaching, and Poetry of Jalaluddin Rumi, rev. ed. (2008). p. 314.

Khalifah Abdul Hakim, "Jalalal Din Rumi" in M.M. Sharif, ed., A History of Muslim Philosophy, Vol II.

Rumi: 53 Secrets from the Tavern of Love, trans. by Amin Banani and Anthony A. Lee, p. 3.

http://www.poemhunter.com/poem

PART — V
EDUCATIONAL PERSPECTIVES

1

Education and its Role in Promoting Communal Harmony

Arpana Singh

Abstract

The 21st century has witnessed various discoveries, innovations and breakthroughs in every field across the world. The Indian society has also been developing very rapidly. Since it is one of the fastest developing countries of the world, the developments and advancements taking place in the country in every sphere have been enormous. However, we can see that in this technologically advanced age the importance given to moral, spiritual, aesthetic and civic values have been negligible. The education system also has not been able to do much in this area. If the education system fails to instil such values in the children they cannot understand and appreciate the true essence of the Indian culture. India is a multi-cultural, multi-lingual and multi-racial country. Being a secular country, India practices religious tolerance. People belonging to different communities, religions and races live in India. Every state in India has different cultures and traditions. All these cultures and traditions collectively have made their contribution in making India a country with a rich cultural heritage. In recent times, the forces of disintegration in India have been very powerful. Too much of fondness for one's own religion and community leads to fanaticism. This in turn results in violence and activities of terror which ultimately lead to disintegration of the country. In the post-modern era, communal harmony has become the need of the hour. Education being one of the most important sub-systems of the society has a pivotal role to play in developing communal harmony and national integration.

Education moulds the very character and personality of an individual. Therefore, if at an early stage of education, cultural, social, moral and spiritual values are instilled in the students, it would help them in understanding the cultural background of the nation. Children who are the future of the nation should be given adequate opportunities to know about the rich cultural heritage of the country. They should be made aware of the existence of the diverse languages, religions, castes, traditions and cultures of India. Only then can the nation function as a whole towards growth and development. With these points in view this paper attempts to explain the concept of communal harmony and how education can be employed as an important instrument in achieving it.

Keywords: *Communal harmony, cultural heritage, education, national integration.*

Introduction

India is a country where people belonging to many different castes and communities live. They have varied ethnic origins. India is a multi-lingual and multi-racial nation. The culture and traditions of the various communities differ widely from each other. In spite of such variations in the population of the nation, people have been living in harmony with each other since ages. However, in recent times, as a result of modernization and growing emphasis on globalization and the development of the nation, the forces of disintegration tend to become active. India is one of the fastest developing countries of the world. In order to ensure the steady growth of the nation, all round development of the nation is essential. The Government should be able to take preventive measures against the forces of disintegration and every care should be taken to promote harmony among the people of the nation. India has a rich cultural heritage. In order to pass on this cultural heritage from one generation to the other it is of utmost importance for the young people to know their own customs and traditions and also of other communities so that they can understand and appreciate the diverse nature of the Indian culture. The country can move towards development as a single, united, integrated and cohesive nation only if the people live in harmony with each other. In order to rise above trivial issues and conflicts related to religion, races and communities, it is essential that the countrymen become aware of the diverse differences in communities, races, castes and religions existent in the nation. Communal harmony is the need of the hour for India in order to remain integrated and fight internal and external disintegrating factors.

Communal Harmony – A Prerequisite for National Integration

Communal harmony means the harmony, acceptance and love among the people of various communities belonging to different castes, races and religion.

Shinde (2014) writes, every religion, culture, society provides for living in harmony with everything surrounding us since ages. Harmony is the fundamental law of creation; it is the law that continues to govern our life. But etymologically harmony means 'joint'. Harmony is understood as binding together and being in concord with one another and the cosmos. From a sociological perspective, harmony can be understood as a mode of social existence. Social harmony means living with unity, mutual reciprocity, beyond class, creed and gender barriers. Sin or violence emerges whenever this harmony is disturbed. Harmony by itself cannot be disturbed. It needs an agent. Religious and communal harmony, economic harmony, political harmony and ecological harmony are increasingly necessary today. No human being enjoys disharmony or violence.

'Communal' means:

(i) For common use or benefit shared;
(ii) Of or relating to a commune;
(iii) Of or relating to the community and
(iv) Between different communities.

During the post-independence period, there has been a rise in the rigid and narrow communal and religious sentiments. These feelings eventually lead to violence, bloodshed and chaos and also create misunderstanding among the different communities. National integration is the creation of a feeling of oneness where the diversities are recognised and respected by imbibing a sense of nationhood. In India, 19th November, the birthday of former Prime Minister, Smt. Indira Gandhi, is observed as National Integration Day. The main objective of National integration is to encounter all fissiparous forces. It also aims at spreading unity, peace, affection and brotherhood among the people. It is a complex concept and has social, political, religious and regional and economic dimensions. The three basic factors of National Integration:

- Structural equality - equal opportunity must be provided for all especially those who are socially and economically backward.
- Cultural unity – Caste discriminations like untouchability and inapproachability should be eradicated.
- Ideological unity – Awareness about 'national objectives' should be created among the people who hold divergent views on political and religious and similar other fields.

For National integration it is essential for the citizens of the nation to become aware of the rich cultural heritage of the country. Only if they understand the multifarious dimensions of the cultures and traditions of their countrymen can they stop indulging in conflicts and violence. Communal harmony is the most important element which contributes towards National Integration and unity of the nation. National integration and communal harmony revolve around secularism, national unity and integrity, which are the characteristics of our polity. However, in recent times there have been many incidents which have threatened the unity and integrity of the nation.

Education for National Integration and Communal Harmony

Education plays a significant role in shaping the future of the nation. It is one of the most influential factors which helps in nation building and it also acts as the unifying and integrating element of the nation.

It is mentioned in the Report of the Education Commission 1964-66 that, even more important is the role of education in achieving social and national integration. Indian society is hierarchical, stratified and deficient in vertical mobility. The social distance between the different classes, particularly between the rich and the poor, the educated and the uneducated, is large and is tending to widen. Our people profess a number of different religions; and the picture becomes even more complicated because of caste, an undemocratic institution which is still powerful and which, strangely enough, seems to have extended its sphere of influence under the very democratic process of the Constitution itself. The situation, complex as it was, has been made critical by recent developments which threaten both national unity and social progress. As education is not rooted in the traditions of the people, the educated persons tend to be alienated from their own culture. The growth of local, regional, linguistic and state loyalties tends to make the people forget 'India'. The old values, which held society together, are disappearing, and as there is no effective programme to replace them by a new sense of social responsibility, innumerable signs of social disorganization are evident everywhere and are continually on the increase. These include strikes, increasing lawlessness and a disregard for public property, corruption in public life, and communal tensions and troubles. Student unrest, of which so much is written, is only one, and probably a minor one, of these symptoms. Against this background, the task to be attempted-the creation of an integrated and egalitarian society-is indeed extremely difficult and challenging.

In such circumstances, the system of education should be designed in such a way which would sensitize children and inculcate values of brotherhood, oneness and generate 'we feeling' among them. The Education Commission 1964-66 has given the following recommendations in order to achieve social and national integration.

The Common School – In a situation of the type we have in India, it is the responsibility of the educational system to bring the different social classes and groups together and thus promote the emergence of an egalitarian and integrated society. But at present instead of doing so, education itself is tending to increase social segregation and to perpetuate and widen class distinctions. If these evils are to be eliminated and the educational system is to become a powerful instrument of national development in general, and social and national integration in particular, we must move towards the goal of a common school system of public education:

- Which will be open to all children, irrespective of caste, creed, community, religion, economic conditions or social status;
- Where access to good education will depend not on wealth or class but on talent;
- Which will maintain adequate standards in all schools and provide at least a reasonable proportion of quality institutions;
- In which no tuition fee will be charged; and
- Which would meet the needs of the average parent so that he would not ordinarily feel the need to send his children to expensive schools outside the system.

Social and National Service - The intelligentsia should try to become a real service-group striving to uplift the masses and should resist the temptation to become a parasitical group living for itself and perpetuating its own privileged position. Some form of social and national service should be made obligatory for all students and should form an integral part of education at all stages. This can become an instrument to build character, improve discipline, inculcate a faith in the dignity of manual labour and develop a sense of social responsibility.

Community Living in Schools and Colleges – Every educational institution should try to develop a rich community life of its own and provide adequate and satisfying opportunities for students to participate in it and help in organising it.

Participation in Programmes of Community Development – It is essential to make participation in meaningful programmes of community service an integral part of all education from the primary to the undergraduate stage. Such participation can help to create positive attitudes towards social service and to develop closer ties between the educated persons and the rest of the people. It can also help in building up a sense of social purpose and self-confidence and giving students a sense of participation in community life and activities.

Evolution of a Language Policy – Of the many problems, which the country has faced since Independence, the language question has been one of the most complex and intractable, and it still continues to be so. Its early and satisfactory solution is imperative for a variety of reasons – educational, cultural and political.

Development of Modern Indian Languages – It can make scientific and technical knowledge more easily accessible to the people in their own languages and thus help not only in the progress of industrialization but also in the wider dissemination of science and the scientific outlook. Energetic action is needed to produce books and literature, particularly scientific and technical, in the regional languages.

Channels of Internal Communication – Hindi (or any other Indian language for that matter) must be greatly developed and enriched before it can attain the status of a library language, that is, a language which can serve as a vehicle for acquiring a substantial part of the current and rapidly expanding stock of world knowledge. This has to be taken into account fully in determining our language policy.

Promoting National Consciousness– The deepening of national consciousness can be fostered specially by two programmes: (1) the understanding and re-evaluation of our cultural heritage and (2) the creation of a strong driving faith in the future towards which we aspire.

In addition to the above recommendations made by the Education Commission 1964-66, there are some other important factors through which education can help in promoting communal harmony and national integration, in contemporary India.

Education for inculcating ethical values – According to Narendran (2012), education should instil ethical values in society. Education should make us understand that most aspirations are common to mankind. Education should instil an awareness and appreciation of the cultural heritage of the 'Others'. Education should give us knowledge of ourselves as individuals and by extension of those around us. Education should produce 'thinking' persons. Education should produce cultured and wise persons. Education should produce persons who understand their limitations and can learn from those who transcend these limitations. Education should produce persons with respect for 'Others'. Education should produce persons who seek to learn the 'Wisdom' distilled from previous generations and from those of learning and wisdom in their society and the world at large. Education should help understand the distinction between rhetoric and truth/facts. Education should help us reconcile the duality we see in everything around us and appreciate the whole – the concept of reconciling the opposites. Education is the key to achieving harmony in any society. Education should transform us into an 'Ethical nation', from one that is built on expediency.

Formal and Non-Formal Education – Since the population of our country has been on the rise since decades, the formal system of learning sometimes becomes insufficient to educate the masses. A large number of people due to inevitable reasons cannot enrol themselves in the formal system of learning. In order to provide education to the whole nation the formal system of education should be made less rigid and utmost importance should be given to the non - formal institutions of learning, so that people become aware of the whereabouts of their own country and of the world as well. Educating the masses through different forms of education would help the nation to progress as a united one.

Women as teachers for promoting communal harmony – The role of women as teachers also could pave the way for development of communal harmony and national integration in the society. The influence of teachers on children is very strong next to the influence of family especially that of mother. The value education along with scientific education both are desirable in making a future citizen who can resist pressures and temptations from various divisive groups and take decisions based upon the facts of the situation and on that of his or her own secular values rather than basing them upon narrow parochial interests of religious groups. The aim of education is to develop a scientific temper and the ability to see the situation from different perspectives. Education could also provide a check on the development of prejudices and biases among the people. Therefore, women as teachers could provide the desired education to the children for enabling them to develop as responsible citizens of the country contributing to the harmonious and integrated development.

Promoting communal harmony through the teaching of History and Culture – While teaching various subjects in schools and colleges History and Culture should be given special emphasis. They should not be taught with the aim of just passing on facts. This is because History as a subject holds great stories and legends of the times that have gone by. India has a very rich and unique history. The various customs, traditions and cultures of the various communities have given India a very pleasant cultural heritage. These instances should be related to the new generation and the generations to come, so that they can understand, appreciate and learn from the glorious past to live in harmony with each other.

Kaur (2013), writes that there is urgent need to rethink about our basic political and cultural concepts, reinterpret them, and be bold to emphasize them through educational system, political behaviour and social environment. At the same time socio-economic and cultural differences are to be avoided also. Caste discriminations should be eradicated. We must realize that we have the strong bond of same cultural heritage and must not let ourselves fall apart and disintegrate. We must show to the world that a country with as old a tradition as ours can hold back personal differences for the sake of higher interest of the country. Toleration, co-operation and feeling of brotherhood should guide us in maintaining the national unity of our country. Let us echo what Pandit Nehru said, "There is no division between North and South, East and West of India. There is only one India of which all of us are inheritors; it belongs to all of us."

Conclusion

In order to ensure national integration, promoting communal harmony is indispensable. However, achieving communal harmony is not the only necessary condition, as there may be various conflicts in the nation based on race, gender, class, etc. Nevertheless, communal harmony to a great extent helps in uniting the nation. Education is a very useful instrument for promoting communal harmony. In the present state of the nation if the prevalent system of education is reformed in some aspects India can achieve its glorious past, where people in spite of their diversities were united and lived in harmony with each other.

References

Kaur, G. (2013). *Understanding National Integration and Challenges in its ways.* Retrieved from http://www.confabjournals.com/confabjournals/images/810201381117.pdf on 20-12-2014.

Kumar, G.S.J. & Muralidhar, B.V. (Eds.). (1997). *Achieving Communal Harmony and National Integration: A Dream for Every Indian.* M.D. Publications Private Limited: New Delhi.

Mann, B.S. (Ed.). (2004). *National Integration and Communal Harmony.* Publishing Bureau Punjabi University.

Mohanty, T.K. (2006). *National Integration and Communal Harmony.* Orissa Review January,2006. Retrieved from http://www.orissa.gov.in/e-magazine/orissareview/jan2006/engpdf/National_Integration.pdf on 20-12-2014.

Narendran, R. (2012). *Role of Education in Building a Harmonious Society: Challenges and Opportunities.* Retrieved from http://dbsjeyaraj.com/dbsj/archieves/4669 on 22-12-2014.

National Integration (2009). Retrieved from http://www.scert.kerala.gov.in/images/text_books/unit%2009.pdf on 17-12-2014.

Report of the Education Commission 1964-1966. Vol. 1.

Role of Women in Creating Communal Harmony and National Integration. (2010). Retrieved from http://womenandharmony.blogspot.in/2010/11/role-of-women-in-creating-communal.html on 17-12-2014.

Shinde, D. (2014). Proactive Policing for Maintaining Communal Harmony with the help of Journalism. *Indian Journal of Applied Research.* Vol. 4.

2

Faithful Superstitions – An Enigma Towards Education

Biswajit Chatterjee

Abstract

Faith means being sure of the things we hope for and knowing that something is real even if we do not see it. Faith is the confidence or trust in a person, thing, deity, in the doctrines or teachings of a religion, or view even without empirical evidence. It makes us sure of the things we hope for and that assurance is itself proof of these things. But superstitions, unlike faith, have no substantial basis; nor are its conclusions reached by logical deductions. Actually superstitions originate in the diseased brains of fallible men, and upon no subject are they as prevalent as upon religious subjects. Superstition can be defined as the irrational belief in the existence of unseen forces controlling people's fates or the outcomes of events, usually with negative effects, unless particular actions are taken to prevent the ill effects or to produce the desired good effects; this may involve a person's behaviors and actions, avoidance of actions, places, etc., or the use of amulets, etc. Many educated, intelligent people still hold on to a variety of superstitions, almost as though they are cherished traditions of a sort. If you ask them, when it gets right down to the nitty-gritty, they don't actually believe in something, yet they still act upon the belief. No doubt, superstitions and irrational beliefs arise due to ignorance but it is also a fact that ignorance arises due to carelessness of the parents regarding their child. Children are like wet cement; whatever falls on them makes an impression. Only knowledge can remove the darkness of ignorance and according to the Encyclopedia of Philosophy (Vol.4, page 347), "Knowledge is justified true belief". It means only true knowledge has the power to change conception into conviction. So, if children are fed with such knowledge, it will lead them to compatible faiths. Such nourished minds can self-differentiate between rational and irrational beliefs. Now we have smart phones, tablets, 4G connections, but somewhere we have a leaning towards supernatural things, and normally we go to a priest for an amulet. Traditional beliefs and illusion of knowledge with ignorance is the factor. We are responsible for not using common sense, logic and conscience. Of course education is a must but it is very difficult to change the thoughts of one's mind with normal education. We need to apply our common sense also with it.

Keywords:

Introduction

"Superstition makes a man fool and Skepticism makes him mad"

—Henry Fielding

In our country, there exists a curious mixture of superstition and faith mostly arising out of ignorance. Superstition involves beliefs, practices and procedures based upon assumptions usually concerned with nature of cause and effects and mysteriously connects unrelated incidents and coincidence with each other (Jayapalan, 2001). Superstition destroys one's peace of mind creating insecurity. Many times we hear about blind faith in spirits and other things. All these things are a manifestation of ignorance, which we see in the villages and sometimes in cities also. Sometimes people don't even try to rationally analyze a superstition because of laziness or because they are scared of losing their illusions (Glanville, 2011). Superstitions and irrational beliefs mislead and are a sign of weakness. People are not aware of these things due to lack of education. No doubt, superstitions and irrational beliefs arise due to ignorance but it is also a fact that ignorance arises due to carelessness of the parents regarding their child. Children are like wet cement; whatever falls on them makes an impression. Only knowledge can remove the darkness of ignorance and according to the Encyclopedia of Philosophy (Vol.4, page 347), "Knowledge is justified true belief". It means only true knowledge has the power to change conception into conviction. So, if children are fed with such knowledge, it will lead them to compatible faiths. Such nourished minds can self-differentiate between rational and irrational beliefs (Das, 2008).

Faith and Superstitions

"When you believe in things that you don't understand,
Then you suffer,
Superstition isn't the way."

— Stevie Wonder, Superstition (1972)

Faith is in general the persuasion of the mind that a certain statement is true. Its primary idea is trust. A thing is true, and therefore it is worthy of trust. It admits of much degree up to full assurance of faith, in accordance with the evidence on which it rests. In many times, faith is the result of teaching. Knowledge is an essential element in all faith, and is sometimes spoken of as an equivalent to faith. Yet the two are distinguished in this respect that faith includes in it assent, which is an act of the will to the act of the understanding. Assent to the truth is of the essence of faith, and the ultimate ground on which our assent to any revealed truth is the veracity of God.

Superstition can be defined as the irrational belief in the existence of unseen forces controlling people's fates or the outcomes of events, usually with negative effects, unless particular actions are taken to prevent the ill effects or to produce the desired good effects; this may involve a person's behaviors and actions, avoidance of actions, places, etc., or the use of amulets, etc. A superstition is an irrational belief basically arising from ignorance. Superstitions are based on a belief that future events are influenced by specific behaviors, without having a casual relationship (Pickering, 2003). Many superstitions deal with important events in a person's life such as birth, entering adulthood, marriage, pregnancy and death. Most of superstitions involve ensuring good luck, avoiding bad luck or making good things happen. Some superstitions are blatantly obvious to us while some are subtler, more deeply ingrained in our daily life (Potter, 1991).. There are so many of our daily activities which are affected by inherited superstitions. There are endless numbers of superstitions. Some are bad and some are nothing but neutral. Some of these superstitions have originated from our cities or villages, while others have their origins in foreign lands and have been adopted without any reason or barriers. Either way, one thing is for certain, superstitions do have quite a significant power over us. One does not need to believe in magic or negative karma in order to fall prey to superstitions (Radford, 2003).

Superstitions and Students

> *"One for sorrow, Two for joy, Three for a letter, Four for a boy,*
> *Five for silver, Six for Gold, Seven for a secret never to be told."*
>
> — **Anonymous**

This is a popular rhyme which is usually drilled in some of our houses. And you can't imagine that these One, Two, Three, Four.....are not related with any academic affair but very strangely these are related with the number of sneezes. If in this way normal people believe in superstitions then how can students escape such irrational illogic beliefs. Even though the students live in an age of advance technology and science and have an endless supply scientific information at our fingertips, they still believe in some or the other superstitions as a way of explaining and dealing with the unknown (Sokal, 2010). Many students think that some superstitions are scientific but few of them realize that those are unscientific. On the other hand, millions of students still believe in astrology and base important decisions on the position of the sun, moon, planets and stars (Smith, 2008). Even the students who do not believe in those tend to get caught up in the complex web of superstitions, one way or the other. It is a common belief that the Indians, compare to the other countries, are very rigorous in superstitions and it is somehow true also. The advancement of knowledge and intellectual integrity is prompted by all educational institutes and yet many college students routinely put themselves in the hands of fate. Superstitious beliefs and behavior are common among different groups of high schools and universities. It is frequently observed that superstitiousness is more prevalent among females and arts students than male and science students (Das, 2008).

Some Common Superstitions among Students

The most common and the most ancient superstition are related with black cat. It is typically considered a bad luck if black cat crosses their path. According to the superstition if a black cat crosses their path, it creates some evil in the near future.

On the other hand, totally opposite is observed for the case of black dog. If a black dog crosses their path it is treated as good luck.

Crossing their fingers before the start of the exam or before the declaration of the results is the most common superstitions among the students.

The number 13 is also being treated an evil number. Many of the students are trying to avoid that number in any form, whether is it is a class rolls number or it be a serial number in any form.

Added with that the combo 'Friday the 13th' is the most phobic one. Actually 'Friday the 13th' is diagnosed as a particular phobia called Paraskevidekatriaphobics.

Eating curd or getting a '*Tika*' in the forehead before going out for any exam or good work brings good luck.

If someone sneezes right before you are about to start or do something is considered a bad omen.

If your eye lid pulsates, it can be a sign of upcoming good or bad luck depending on whether it is your left or right eye.

If the first paper goes well one shouldn't change anything about his or her look.

There are also certain exam clothes. Wearing same pair of jeans in all exams or the same shirt helps in getting good results. Using same pen in exams is another popular belief.

Not shaving during exam time is considered another charm.

Some believe that a coin in the left sock, touching the sole of the foot, will help to reduce tension before an exam.

Red is the favorite color for many of the superstitions. There are more than 100 good or bad luck follows to only this particular color.

Entering the school or college from the same entrance, establishes a good flow of good luck. Entering from any other entrance will bring bad luck.

The horseshoe and the four-leaf clover are also among many lucky charms for the superstitions.

Causes and Effects of Superstitions among Students

Causes

Fear of Examinations: With the semester exams are in full swing, students are not just indulging in last-minute cramming and borrowing notes, but also they are turning to rituals and superstitions expecting to pass the exams smoothly. Examination season brings about a series of strange behavior amongst them. They are always in very much anxious about the fear of unknown.

Lucky Experiences: Most of the superstitions are based on indulging in a certain pattern of behavior which is a result experiencing success while indulging in them on earlier occasions. These are totally baseless but the ultimate result, experienced by them, diverts their feelings towards those superstitions.

Obsessive Compulsive Disorder: It is type of mental disorder characterized by intrusive thoughts that produce anxiety, by repetitive behavior aimed at reducing anxiety, or by combination of such thoughts (obsessions) and behaviors (compulsions). These behaviors have also been found a remedy to beat exam blues by the students.

Study of Tradition and Culture: Our traditions and cultures are full of irrational and abstract stories that they create a long lasting impact on minds which have been exposed to such beliefs since childhood. Certain stories are just made up by parents in order to make their children obedient towards them.

Personal Anecdotes: People from the earlier times were little uneducated and created their own lucky charms and tales of horrors and bad luck merely out of the lack of education and improper understanding of things around them. Our grandparents' beliefs have been passed onto the next generations and most of us not only remember them but also believe in them.

Novels and Literatures: Similar in the case of tons of literature and books which form the basis of existence of superstitions in our society. These are rooted very deeply in our mind from the childhood only. While the publishers and the authors are making money from that, at the same time they are also making a certain section of the society to believe in their fictions.

Effects

Loss of Concentration: Indulging in activities in superstition can have negative impact on the study of students. A mind which waiver towards beliefs and curriculum lacks concentration. One may not be able to give his full output or may fail in his or her exams.

Mental Disorders: When a person's personal experience in superstitions leads to strong beliefs, it becomes a tough task to make him or her realize the real truth. The foundation of a personal experience is closer to one's intellect than other's fact based realities. It can results in paranoia and other mental conditions which may inhibit unnatural behavior and unknown fear.

One's Belief Strengthens Another's: Just like a communicable disease superstitions can manifest itself through the words of mouth. For a teenager who has a slight inclination towards such beliefs, a casual conversation with superstitious adults can spread and strengthens his or her own personal beliefs in such matter.

Hampering the Development of Personality: Change of focus amongst the students hampers the development of one's personality. Instead of acquiring virtues necessary for an individual to live in a society, the individual is seeking in seemingly beneficial task.

How Faith and Superstitions are Mingled

Faith always has a good, sound, reasonable basis. It is simply an established confidence. You have faith in your friend because, you say, you have known him for years: you have observed and mentally noted his principles of action, and have found them uniformly the same; he has always been just, true, benevolent and kind; for many years and under many tests you have observed his steady faithfulness to these principles, and so your confidence or faith has been so established that you never think of doubting him. You know, judging from the past, that he will always be true to these principles, and hence can often tell just what his future course will be in various contingencies that may arise wherein these principles may be involved.

But superstitions, unlike faith, have no substantial basis; nor are its conclusions reached by logical deductions. Actually superstitions originate in the diseased brains of fallible men, and upon no subject are they as prevalent as upon religious subjects. Here they are legion. They are in direct opposition to true faith and should be carefully avoided by every sincere person. And not only should we avoid the superstitions themselves, but we should be careful to so frame our conversation that our true faith, minus all superstition, may be apparent to all (O'Sullivan, 2010).

We have seen so many being taken for a ride by unscrupulous godmen, priests and witch-doctors, who claim to be agents of God (*Babas*) and fool people. They use ordinary tricks that are passed off as miracles and they claim those as the faith towards God (Kovoor, 2009). The common faithfully superstitious people are very dare to unfollow or disobey them. Even the educated people in India are willing to accept them as faithful miracles and fall easy prey (Copeman & Ikegame, 2012). The only solution is to make young students develop a scientific temper in school. It has to be started early, for by the time a student leaves school, his beliefs and ideas have taken root. We can hold demonstrations to expose the tricks commonly used by those godmen. But unlike other rationalists' bodies, we can work actually on the field, catching godmen, exposing them and even handing them over to the police (The Telegraph. 27 May 2012). It can involve a lot of risk, for devotees don't always accept it easily. But we can proceed in this case very sympathetically, because those devotees are also the prey of faithful superstitions under those godmen (Kovoor, 2003).

Role of Education

Superstitions are usually attributed to the lack of education. But, in India educated people have also been observed following beliefs that may be considered superstitious. The literacy rate of India, according to the 2011 census is at 74%. (Live Mint, 2011) But this number is totally useless when still many of the Indians follow the age-old faithful superstitions. In today's scientific world, it is necessary that we do not blindly follow all the superstitions that were handed over to us by our ancestors. We are modern, both in our outlook and the age we are in. Therefore we should have a judicious look for some logical reason behind every superstition before accepting it. We would then be able to give up those superstitions which have no rationality and applications in today's life. It is only in this way that we can lead or normal lives. Experiments are on to find out that man has the soul which leaves the man when he dies. People are said to have confirmed ghosts and premonitions at several places. But it remains to be proved that ghosts do exists and posses the power they are supposed to exhibit. Dogs are very sensitive to changes around them; they become sexless before the onset of a natural calamity and wait to inform their masters of the impending doom. So, one cannot just simply reject this superstition. In south India people bath early in the morning and apply sandalwood on their forehead. People have now realized that sandalwood keeps the forehead cool and soothes the brain and hence the practice has been there since time immemorial. No doubt, superstitions are an undesirable part of our life. Ignorant people have faith in something unseen. Even educated people are doing the same thing. We have got all this from our evolution from dark ages. The only cure for unnecessary superstitions is education and awareness. We should develop our reasoning power. We must have a scientific mind; we should try to analyze the things in logical way. Only then we may be free from unnecessary superstitions of mind.

Role of Teachers or Educators

Teachers in a society impart knowledge on day-to-day facts and reason out things which are observed and provide the students the power to question and interpret their knowledge and suggestions. A teacher's role involves more than simply standing in front of a classroom and lecturing. In fact, even though a teacher spends the majority of the day in the classroom, the actual teaching component is only part of the job. An effective teacher understands that teaching involves wearing multiple hats to ensure that the school day runs smoothly and all students receive a quality education (Srivastava & Bhandari, 2006). Teachers by making the students work with materials found in their environment and solving problems stimulate the curiosity of the students and ensure that the students do not get satisfied with vague explanations of things. Teachers can inculcate scientific attitudes, temper and habits in the students. Inculcation of scientific attitudes into the students encourages them to view facts objectively and free themselves from superstitions, thus developing an ability to think, imagine and be creative. Science teachers provide students the necessary information and explanation which science teaches about these beliefs and superstitions. Science teachers motivate students to understand, analyze and think scientifically against such beliefs. Every teacher should give explanations for most of the belief which is obtained from scientific studies and helps students to acquire knowledge against superstitious practices and beliefs.

Conclusion

Superstition is referred to as any belief which is unexplained, which is in contradiction to modern science and that cannot be proved. They are merely assumptions based on personal opinion, which may become popular. These beliefs arise out of fear and sometimes from helplessness. These beliefs have existed since the earliest days of mankind. William Shakespeare, the world's most celebrated poet said, "Ignorance is the curse of God; knowledge is the wing wherewith we fly to heaven." It is a matter of grave pain that having broken the shackles of slavery sixty-five years ago, we have still not been able to unfetter ourselves from the clutches of superstitions and irrational beliefs. Nearly every household adheres to some myth like black cat crossing ones path, sneezing as illomen, hiccups as being remembered by dear ones, and many more (Vyse, 2000). These irrational thoughts are funny but sometimes they may prove to be fatal. In rural areas, due to lack of sound knowledge and scientific temperament, adults are killed in the name of witch-hunt, innocent infants are sacrificed to please God, and unwell patients are placed in the dungeon of tantriks. Aren't these myths baseless? If that were the case, the entire traffic would have been brought to a standstill if a cat were to cross the road. Besides, Anna Hazare, being the talk of the country and loved by millions would have complained of perpetual hiccups!! These irrational beliefs do not find space anywhere in this scientific world. We have to prevent the clouds of superstition from harming our people by educating them and encouraging study of science in the schools, from the rudimentary level. One who is educated believes in logic and does not believe in superstitions. With the advent of knowledge today's superstition could well become tomorrow's science if we follow the right theoretical developments. Modern men know that advancement of knowledge has explained the mysteries of the past by analyzing the happenings logically, scientifically and technically. Tackling an age-old superstition is a strenuous process and demands a lot of dedication and dogged patience. What is needed to end such practices is a multi-pronged campaign by the media and also by teachers, doctors and scientists.

References

Das, P. K. (2008). Protection of Women from Domestic Violence. Universal Law Publishing. p. 116. ISBN 978-81-7534-951-3. Retrieved on 31 December 2014.

Glanville, J. (2011). Privacy Is Dead. Sage. pp. 155–. ISBN 978-1-4462-0910-3. Retrieved on 30 December 2014.

Copeman, J & Ikcgame, A (2012). The Guru in South Asia: New Interdisciplinary Perspectives. Routledge. p. 87. ISBN 978-1-136-29806-6. Retrieved on 30 December 2014.

Joanne O'Sullivan (2010). Book of Superstitious Stuff. Charlesbridge Publishing. p. 119. ISBN 978-1-60734-367-7. Retrieved on 3 January 2015.

Kolhatkar, R. V. Vastu Nijaanijalu (Vaastu Myths) (in Telugu). Hyderabad Book Trust.

Kovoor, A. (2003). Begone Godmen. Jaico Publishing House. ISBN 978-81-7224-331-9.

Kovoor, A (2009). Gods, Demons & Spirits. Jaico Publishing House. ISBN 978-81-7224-216.

N. Jayapalan (2001). Problems of Indian Education. Atlantic Publishers & Dist. p. 155. ISBN 978-81-7156-973-1. Retrieved 3 January 2015.

Pickering, D (2003). The Dictionary of Superstitions. Cassels, 2003. http://www.amazon.com/exec/obidos/ASIN/0304365610/sanguinarius.

Potter, C. (1991). Knock On Wood: An Encyclopedia of Superstition, Longmeadow Press, 1991. http://www.amazon.com/exec/obidos/ASIN/0681410884/sanguinarius.

Radford, E. (2003). The Encyclopedia of Superstitions, MetroBooks, 2003. http://www.amazon.com/exec/obidos/ASIN/1586636170/sanguinarius.

Smith, D. (2008). Hinduism and Modernity. John Wiley & Sons. p. 3. ISBN 978-0-470-77685.

Sokal, A. (2010). Beyond the Hoax : Science, Philosophy and Culture: Science, Philosophy and Culture. Oxford University Press. p. 382. ISBN 978-0-19-162334-9. Retrieved on 29 December 2014.

Srivastava, R.S. & Bhandari, M. (2006). Teacher in Emerging Indian Society. A.P.H. Publishing Corporation. New Delhi. p. 111. ISBN 81-313-0008-0. Retrieved on 4 January 2015.

Vyse, S.A. (2000). Believing in Magic: The Psychology of Superstition. Oxford University Press. p. 20. ISBN 978-0-19-513634-0. Retrieved on 1 January 2015.

"India's literacy rate rises to 74%: Census". Live Mint. 31 March 2011. Retrieved on 30 December 2014.

"The God busters". The Telegraph. 27 May 2012. Retrieved on 30 December 2014.

http://www.bartleby.com/349/517.html Retrieved on 4 January 2015

http://www.thehindu.com/todays-paper/tp-national/tp-newdelhi/education-can-help-remove-superstitions/article5122531.ece Retrieved on 4 January 2015

http://www.economist.com/news/international/21623712-how-education-makes-people-less-religiousand-less-superstitious-too-falling-away Retrieved on 4 January 2015

http://timesofindia.indiatimes.com/city/kolkata/Teacher-on-crusade-against-superstition/articleshow/17907458.cms Retrieved on 4 January 2015

http://sabarishedn.blogspot.in/2014/11/science-teacher-and-society.html Retrieved on 4 January 2015.

3

An Attempt to Revizualise the True Spirit of Teacher Education by Young Teacher Educators

Minati Saha

Abstract

A well educated population is equipped with the relevant knowledge, attitude and skill and these are indispensible for building an equitable and just society. Teachers are the persons behind the process of man-making. Teacher education is one of the areas in higher education which trains student-teachers in pedagogy, which in turn helps them to train the young minds in educational institutions. In a multi-cultural country like India teacher education programme should be planned, formulated and implemented much more judiciously. The overall quality in education definitely depends on the quality of teachers and a sound programme of professional preparation of teachers is essential for imparting quality teacher education. In the fast changing world of the 21st century, role of teachers, schools and education has undergone transformation. Now educational institutions are the agencies and teachers are the agents of this change. NCF 2005 has emphasized on the development of the soft qualities along with professional skills. But NCFTE 2009 has laid equal emphasis on creating professional and humane teachers. 'Creating Humane Teachers' is the special need of hour. None other than the teacher can shoulder this responsibility well and it goes without saying that humane teachers can be developed only by humane teacher educators. Creating humane teachers is one such area which requires most attention in the present educational scenario. In this study data has been collected from aspirant teacher educators of different teacher education institutions of West Bengal who are serving in these institutes for only a few years. The items are framed to assess the professional as well as soft qualities of the young teacher educators. This study has two significant objectives firstly to enlist the desired qualities expected to be present in teacher educators on the basis of educational commissions, committees and policies and secondly to find out how the teacher educators rate themselves on these qualities. This study will help young teacher educators to understand their own status in terms of expected teacher competencies and qualities and will try to inculcate these qualities within him/her.

Keywords: *Teacher education, humane qualities*

Introduction

Education uplifts the standards, promotes co-operation and maintains harmony in the society. It makes every individual an intellectual citizen of the nation. Education is the parameter that prepares a man in the true sense of the term. Any country can expect its growth and development on the basis its 'Education', only if the education system is fair and good enough to move the country in a right direction. In the Republic, Plato uses the phrase 'better and more complete education', suggesting that there is education of different levels of quality, not merely different kinds of education (Hamilton and Cairns, 1961; p. 752). In the same way Gautam Buddha's discourse indicates the significance of correctness in the choice of knowledge and ways of teaching it, for an incorrect choice could be dangerous (Hanh, 1996). This idea impels us to conceptualize the concept of quality in education.

Education system in India is one of the finest in the world but there are certain impediments that still hinder its move towards perfection. Filtering our education system of these impediments is very much significant in present context. This is a major challenge for the teachers, especially the teacher educators. With humane qualities and professional expertise they will definitely be able to refine and improve the existing educational situation.

Factors like economic depression, unemployment problem, youth unrest, political instability, social decadence are directly affecting the quality of life. Unlimited human demand is leading to such problems which we could not even think of before two decades. Unfortunately, Education is also not out of this. As it has become a profitable sector to invest like Media and Health, nobody is bothered about the real purpose of education and one ends up paying more in donation and not getting any real education, leading to a both ways loss. Still this critical condition can be harnessed only through proper education. Teachers are the torch bearers of our society who can show the right direction by setting examples of their own lives. Here the role of the teacher educator is of immense importance, since they are blessed with the opportunity of moulding the minds of trainee teachers by inculcating humanitarian values in them. Only humane education can create better students, compassionate citizens and contributors to the greater community and foster a sense of responsibility for children to act upon their personal beliefs.

Teaching is a very difficult job irrespective of the place where teaching is conducted and the person being taught. Expectations from the teachers are different to different people. Some experts expresses that the characteristic features of teachers shine through their content knowledge and determine the quality of teaching. While other experts and researchers summarised their expectations towards future teachers and they claimed that future teachers need to be open towards the needs of the learners and they should also be innovative and creative. But teaching becomes more difficult when we speak of Indian schools. At home parents know very well how difficult it is to bring up even two children. In a classroom consisting of 40-60 students coming from almost the same number of backgrounds are managed by a single teacher. Many students come from poverty stricken families and are expected to listen to the teacher, study well and behave in a disciplined way in hungry stomachs. Gifted children need content of study, activity, assignment at par with their level, lack of which make them disinterested and in disciplined in class.

Humanity is a quality characterized by tenderness, compassion, and sympathy for people. Teaching is the act, practice, occupation, or profession of a teacher. Creating humane teacher implies preparing teacher who are tender to their students, compassionate to their own peers and have sympathy towards people, society including the whole environment. These qualities are the most desirable qualities for persons in any profession that may be doctors, engineers, policy makers, industrialists, teachers, business men etc. These qualities are not only desirable but a must in a teacher educator. As it is the mother profession and teachers are the creators of all other professions in the world. Good teachers use a variety of techniques. Unfortunately, search for objective standards by which to measure quality teaching has overlooked the fact that the root of teaching lies not in simple methodology, but in the messy business of human relationships. The inclusion of "intangibles," like trust and warmth, in program assessments hints at the deepening knowledge of the ways teachers' qualities influence their student's success (Dress, 2012).

Objectives of The Study

1. To enlist the desired qualities expected to be developed in students on the basis of national educational commissions and policies.
2. To find out how the teacher educators rate themselves on the desired humane qualities.

3. To find out how the teacher educators rate themselves on the desired professional qualities for teachers.
4. To justify the essentiality of these (humane and professional) qualities in teacher educators in the present social scenario.

Development of Humane Qualities In Students As Emphasised In National Educational Commissions And Policies

Radha Krishnan Commission (1948-49) recommended that the aim of university education should be to prepare students for citizenship and also for leadership who can take up national responsibilities successfully in various fields like politics, administration, education, industry and commerce in the best interest of the nation. Universities should preserve the culture and civilization of the country, as on the basis of one's culture one may acquire self-confidence, self-respect and self-dependence. Education has the power to discover the innate qualities of a person and develop them through training. To be civilized, we should sympathise with the poor, respect women, love peace and independence, and hate tyranny and injustice and university education should be able to infuse these ideals into the youths. Secondary education should develop qualities like discipline, tolerance, patriotism, co-operation, equal opportunities for thought, speech and writing, and the essence of the global citizenship in the students. "A special function of the secondary school, in this context, is to train persons who will be able to assume the responsibility of leadership in social, political, industrial or cultural fields - in their own small groups of community or locality" *(Mudaliar Commission, 1952-53).*

Kothari commission mentions, social and national integration is an important objective of a national system of education. The commission made the following recommendations for strengthening social and national integration through education.

Suitable provisions should be made for teaching mother tongue in schools since language is a firm adhesive for social and national integration.

The national system of education should emphasise on the cultivation of social, moral and spiritual values among students. Some periods should be provided in the school time table In order to achieve this *(Kothari Commission, 1964-66).*

"The status of the teacher reflects the social-cultural ethos of a society; it is said that no people can rise above the level of its teachers. Teachers should have the freedom to innovate, liberty to devise appropriate methods of communication and engage in activities relevant to the needs and capabilities of individual and the concerns of the community" *(National Policy on Education, 1986).*

The content of teacher preparation programme should be restructured to ensure its relevance to the changing needs of school education. The emphasis in these programmes should be on enabling the trainees to acquire the ability for self-learning and independent thinking *(Yaspal Committee Report, 1993).*

The major educational commissions, committees and policies of the country emphasise inculcation of humanitarian values in students. Radhakrishnan commission strongly mentions the importance of moral values to preserve the cultural heritage. It also admits that through training the innate qualities of a person can be discovered and developed. Effective training of the young minds is the most important concern of all these education commissions. Now who are entrusted with the responsibility of these young and budding minds? None other than the teachers are entrusted with this noble task. And teacher educators equip teacher to perform this noble mission.

Now the inevitable questions are - Can the teachers cultivate the desired qualities in the future generations? Are they suitably equipped to train the children? How the teachers can make themselves professionally sound? Two most significant documents in this area are the National Curriculum Framework 2005 and National Curriculum Framework for Teacher Education 2009. NCFTE has pointed the right thing at the right timc. India needs human being with humane qualities in all spheres. Teaching profession being the mother profession of all professions, only teacher educators can shoulder this responsibility of developing the young aspiring teachers as honest, responsible, and compassionate.

I personally feel that to achieve these, the humane component should be made a major element of teacher education programme especially in the present socio-economic condition. This study will make the teacher educators conscious about the essential qualities to be present in them. Rating themselves on these qualities will also help them assess their own position regarding these qualities. On the basis of the recommendations made by the educational commissions, committees and policies the following humane qualities are considered for the present study. These are Trustworthiness, Honesty & Faithfulness, Tolerance & Patience, Gentleness, Defenselessness, Generosity & Open-mindedness, Caring attitude, Love for teaching, Compassionate, Justice and ethics, Accountability, Mercy & Forgiveness, Discipline & Punctuality. Along with this some professional competencies are also considered in this study, those are Knowledge of Content, Skill of communication, Understanding students understanding, Using variety of media, Proactive rather than reactive, Using scientific methodology of teaching and Knowledge of Information Communication Technology.

SAMPLE:

The sample consists of 65 teacher educators who are teaching in different teacher training institutes of West Bengal. During selection of samples one important thing was kept in mind that all these teacher educators are teaching in these institutions for not more than five years to maintain the homogeneity of the sample. All the teacher educators are female.

TOOL:

A self-constructed questionnaire was administered on the teacher educators. The questionnaire consists of two sections. First section consists of 13 items indicating the Humanitarian values and the second section consists of 7 items denoting professional competencies. Altogether there were 20 items. The teacher trainees were supposed to rate themselves on a five point scale (1=best, 2=good, 3=moderate, 4=low & 5=very low), considering 1 as the best and 5 as the worst.

Collection of Data:

The blank questionnaire was sent to the teacher trainees individually and the filled in questionnaire was collected from them. Since the items are in the questionnaire are meant for self-rating, teacher educators are requested to rate themselves honestly.

Analysis of data:

In a table all the data regarding humane qualities were entered. In another table all the data regarding professional competencies were entered. Total number of best preferences to worst preferences was summed up. Best preference or rating herself 1, indicated that the subject thinks she is best in that quality. While the worst preference or rating herself 5, indicated that presence of the quality in the subject is minimum. After summing up all the categories percentage of 1, 2, 3, 4 & 5 were calculated. The same process was repeated for the second set that is the professional qualities.

Results:

Table 1. Percentage of responses in each of the five categories of Humane qualities and its graphical representation for items 1 to 13.

Categories of responses	*Percentage*
1	39%
2	43.33%
3	6.92%
4	4.60%
5	6.15%
Total	**100**

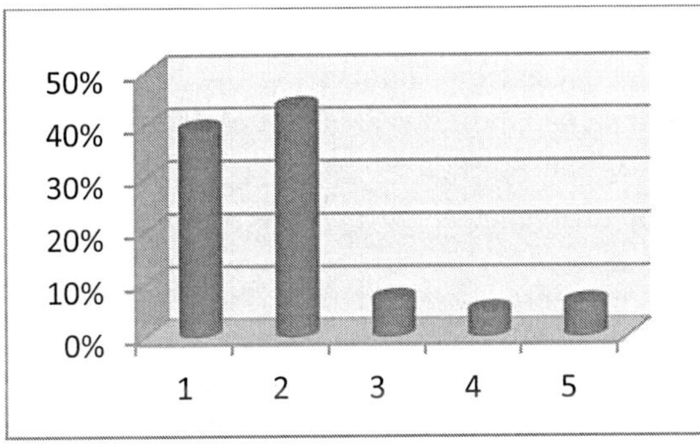

Table 2. Percentage of responses in each of the five categories of Professional competencies and graphical representation of data for items 14 to 20.

Categories of responses	*Percentage*
1	32.85%
2	37.14%
3	21.34%
4	7.14%
5	1.53%
Total	**100**

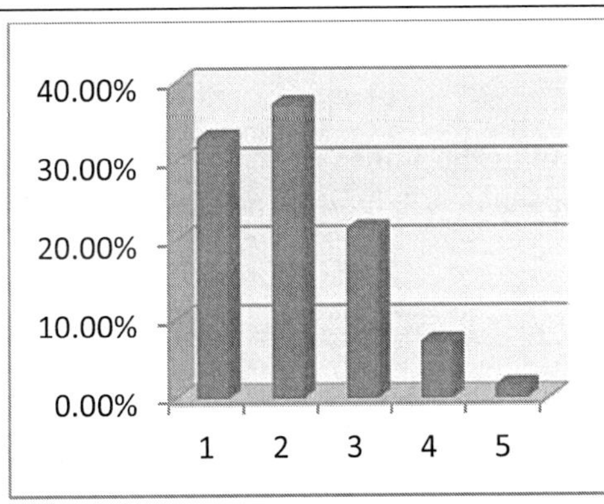

Interpretation of results

- Most of the teacher educators have rated themselves 1 or 2 on both the humane and professional quality, which implies they think themselves to be best or good.
- When the two dimensions i.e. the humane and professional qualities are considered, there is a similarity in the pattern of responses. This indicates a positive correlation between both the dimensions.

- Minimum possible score for these items is 20 and maximum is 100. A score near 20 indicates presence of humane and professional qualities in the best form while nearing 100 indicates presence of the qualities in lesser amount. In the study the range of score is 31-36.
- Thus intra group difference is low and this implies homogeneity of the group.

Conclusions

Professional and humanitarian qualities both are essential in teacher education. Professionalism equips teacher for their job and humane qualities helps to do their job well. The teachers in this study are equipped in both professional and humane qualities.

At present teachers are very much interested of increasing their API (Academic Performance Indicators) scores, so teachers in-service are also conscious about their professional development. But this study shows teacher educators are well aware of the soft qualities too.

Humane Education is an approach to teaching and learning that addresses the global consequences of our behaviour, lifestyle, and teaches students to use the power that they have to make a profound difference in the world through their individual choices, their work, and their activities. Efficient teacher educators enriched in humane qualities and professional qualities can only shoulder this responsibility.

Teacher educators should realise that they help shape the future of so many, hence they are also shaping the future of our society. Teacher educators should know very well their own potency, authority and energy then only they can illuminate the lives their trainees.

Limitations of the study

This study is conducted on the basis of self-rating. Teacher educators are grown up adults, so they are very well aware of the social desirability of the humanitarian and professional qualities. Hence their reponses may be biased to some extent.

Data was collected from only female teacher educators. So gender difference if any was not explored in this study. The sample size for this study was not so large. A larger sample may have revealed some other issues regarding the desirable qualities in teacher educators.

References

Dress, A. (2012). Reimagining Teacher Development: Cultivating Spirit. Exchange: The Early Childhood Leaders' Magazine Since 1978, pp. 28-31.

Education and National Development, Report of The Education Commission, (1964-66). Ministry of Education, Government of India.

Hamilton, E. and Cairns, H. (Eds.) 1961. *The Collected Dialogues of Plato* (Princeton: Princeton University Press).

Hanh, P.N. (1998). *The Heart of the Buddha's Teaching* (New York: Broadway).

National Policy on Education, (1986). MHRD, Government of India.

NCF (2005). National Curriculum Framework, New Delhi: NCTE.

NCTE (2009). National Curriculum Framework for Teacher Education: Towards preparing a Professional and Humane Teacher, New Delhi: NCTE.

Report of the Secondary Education Commission, (Mudaliar commission), Ministry of Education, Government of India. (1952-53)

University Education Commission (Radhakrishnan Commission) (1948-49).

Yaspal Committee Report, (1993).

4

Annette Susannah Akroyd Beveridge: An Authoritative Translator of Medieval Indian Texts And Women's Educational Reformer In Bengal

Moumita Gayen

Empowerment with education of the women is an essential parameter of judging the standard of a civilised society. The growth and development of a community or civil society depends upon the growth and development of its individuals in general and the women in particular. There is no doubt about the fact that men and women are equal, but women have a vital role in the over-all development of the society and the nation. Women are equal partners in the overall growth and development of the family, community, society and humanity. Women almost in every social set-up play an important role either it is economic or political or cultural life of nation. Women have been given a position of pride in every religion. So, it is true that to pave a way towards an egalitarian society which based on gender quality, female education should be equalised with male education.[1]

In the nineteenth and early twentieth century, due to the influences of the modern thoughts and culture and in harmony with other developments, a great social revolution began in Bengal. The most remarkable event was the women's educational reform when the Socio-religious obstacles were the main cause for this very socio-disregard in a male dominated society. In 19th century and the early of 20th century a big change has been seen in Bengal history, the 'weaker sex' becomes more active for their minimum needs of education and other activities. But the attempt of these changes has been started from the early 18th century by the Christian missionaries of European countries.

A remarkable activist from India and its sub-continent of Bengal and outside of India came forward for reforming the women's education and the right of equality with the men. Among them Annette Susannah Akroyd Beveridge was more eminent because of being a citizen of England she become women's educational reformer of Bengal and other hand she was an outstanding Persian scholar who translated the famous Indian biographical books: *Humayun Nama*, and *Babur Nama.*

Beveridge's Life

William Beveridge's mother, Annette Susannah Akroyd Beveridge was born in a business family in Mount Street, Stourbridge, Worcestershire, London on 13 December 1842, the third child and daughter surviving to adulthood of William Akroyd (d. 1869), a currier, and his wife, Sarah, née Walford, a daughter of the local livery stable owner. Beveridge's mother passed away when she was young but though her father re-married, her relation with him remained extremely close. She was educated at Bedford College and received as much education as a girl could receive in England at that time.[2] After graduating from Bedford College, she started teaching in the College for Working Women in London, and she also became a member of the *Kensington Society*, which was one of the earliest feminist groups in England. Both her parents were Unitarians and so, it is not surprising that Beveridge also joined the Unitarians.

After finishing her education and working for a while, she, inspired by Keshub Chandra Sen's speeches in England, decided to sail for India in 1873 to promote female education in Bengal, knowing the present condition of women in Bengal.

In India she got marriage to Henry Beveridge, a judge in the Indian Civil Service in 1875. They had four children, two of whom died before reaching adulthood. The two surviving children, were their son, Lord William Beveridge and a daughter, Annette Jeanie (later Mrs. R H Tawney).

Annette left India in 1890 and returned to Britain. She died in 1929, just months before her husband death.

Beveridge's View for Brahmo Samaj and Journey to India

Sometimes in the early 1860s Beveridge had met a Brahmo, Monomohun Ghose, in England, with whom she formed an abiding friendship. She thus had a fair idea of the social reform program of the Brahmo Samaj even before she met Sen or had decided to sail to India. At last she arrived in India in 1873 by inspiring of Keshub

Chandra Sen's speeches in England, and promotes female education in Bengal, knowing the present condition of women in Bengal. After arriving in India, she was the house guest of Monmohan Ghosh and his wife. All sections of *Brahmos* welcomed her. While she was highly impressed by Monmohan Ghosh and his wife (who were allied with the "conservative" faction). The link between Beveridge and Brahmo Samaj was made by the 'Kensington Society', which was one of the earliest feminist groups in England. The Unitarians were associated with the Brahmo Samaj in Bengal, India. Beveridge's links with the Unitarians exposed her to Brahmo Samaj.[3] However; she later fell out with the famous Bengal Brahma reformer and retired from public life.

The possible motive that amazes Beveridge to come in Bengal was her worried for women education and their social progress. But it's true that Annette Akroyd Beveridge came to India of her own agreement as an architect. William, Beveridge's son thinks there was no clear career path for her at home.[4] Another reason, Keshab Chandra Sen, on many occasions pleaded in his lectures for English women to come to India to educate Indian women.[5] Sen's pleas did have their appeal. Beveridge was always interested in the cause of women's education and feminism.

Though Beveridge is more important for the wide-ranging images of nineteenth century Bengal. She portrayed in her writings, she stands out as the first public example of a British women's limitations in understanding Bengal and its culture, a trend that, though marginally diminished, was not entirely missing in the twentieth century. "Nineteenth century British imperialism." As her biographer Martha A. Scherer Puts it, 'she earned that reputation'.[6]

As A Women's Educational Reformer of Bengal

Annette Susannah Akroyd Beveridge was one of the best examples who fought for women's educational reform in Bengal. After Beveridge meetings and discussions with Keshub Chunder Sen, she shocked about the women condition of Bengal. On the other hand, Sen maintained that while he was progressive he wanted to "go slow" as he wanted to give women the inner strength with which to protect themselves. Sen had started a female and adult normal school on 1 February, 1871. The school supplied teachers to Bethune's school and other schools later on.[7] Amongst those involved with Sen in the field of education only Umesh Chandra Dutta (who later split from Sen in 1878) appeared progressive to her. Others such as Bijoy Krishna Goswami, Aghore Nath Gupta and Gour Govinda Ray were traditionally Hindu in educational background.

In November 1873, due to the efforts of Annette Akroyd a girals school was stublished located at 22 Beniapukur Lane, Entally, Kolkata, India, namely the *Hindu Mahila Bidyalaya* with 12 students. Under Annette's strict supervision the school was run along western lines. After the marriage of Annette Akroyd, The school, shut down for a while, was reopened on 1 June in 1876 as the first women's liberal arts college in India named Bangla Mahila Bidyalaya (Bengali Women's College).[8]

The school made a break with the idea of less taxing curricula for girls, and provided the same kind of learning for its students as was available for boys.[9] Sources record different dates for the establishment of the school. While Jogesh C. Bagal, records the date of establishment as 18 November 1873.[10] David Kopf mentions it as 18 September 1873.[11] Under Annette's strict supervision the school was run along western lines. She even taught the students how to use cutlery, something not in vogue in India (even in 21st century).

Dwarkanath Ganguly was the headmaster.[12] Ananda Mohan Bose and Durga Mohan Das bore the expenses of the institution.[13] Others involved in the school were Sivanath Sastri and Monomohun Ghose. Mrs. J. B. Phear was an honorary teacher.[14]

On 1 August, 1878, this institution was merged with Bethune's institution as *Bethune College*, and immediately it won the recognition and financial support of the Government.

Bethune's school went through a rough time till the above amalgamation. Annette Akroyd's attempt was at a higher English boarding school for girls; among the students were Kadambini Basu, Sarala Das, Abala Das and Subarnaprava Basu.[15]

Beveridge as a Persian Scholar and Translator

She was one of the excellent Persian scholars and translator of the early twentieth century Bengal. Beveridge had leaned Bengali and Persian and began a new career as a translator.

Annette's lasting contribution was her authoritative translations of medieval Indian texts into English. Late in life she began to learn Persian and Turki and turned to the world of oriental scholarship, in which her husband was also a comrade and companion. She is an acknowledged orientalist and translator of Persian and Turki texts. Among these are *Gulbadan Begum's Humayun Nama*, and a fresh translation of *Babur Nama*, the autobiographical memoir of the first Mughal emperor, published in 1922 by the Royal Asiatic Society. It was the first English translation from the *Chaghatai Turki* in which Babur wrote his famous account. A monumental work of scholarship, it is all the more remarkable for having been completed at a time when *Chaghatai* language studies were in their infancy. The translation is characterized by utter reliability and precision, exhaustive footnotes and numerous appendices

Politically a conservative, Annette was opposed to the Women's Suffrage Movement gaining ground in England at the time. She was, in fact, the local secretary from Pitford, of the National anti-women's suffrage league. Annette died a peaceful death at the ripe age of 87, in the London home of her illustrious son Lord William Beveridge. Lord Beveridge paid lasting tribute to the memory of Annette and Henry in a biography of his parents, India called them based on a rich collection of their private correspondence.

Beside the above, Mrs. Beveridge is the author of a large number of articles on Oriental subjects, published in Royal Asiatic Society.[16]

References

Acharya, Poromesh, "Education in Old Calcutta", in "Calcutta, the Living City", Vol I, edited by Sukanta Chaudhuri. Oxford University Press, ISBN 0195636961, pp. 86-87.

Amin, Sonia. "Beveridge, Annette Susannah Akroyd". Banglapedia. Asiatic Society of Bangladesh. Retrieved 2007-04-18.

Amin, Sonia. "Beveridge, Annette Susannah Akroyd". Banglapedia. Asiatic Society of Bangladesh. Retrieved 2007-04-18.

Bagal, Jogesh Chandra, (1949). "History of the Bethune School and College (1849-1949)" in "Bethune College and School Centenary Volume", edited by Dr. Kalidas Nag, p. 33.

Bagal, Jogesh Chandra, (1949). "History of the Bethune School and College (1849-1949)" in "Bethune College and School Centenary Volume", edited by Dr. Kalidas Nag, p. 33.

Bagal, Jogesh Chandra, (1949). "History of the Bethune School and College (1849-1949)" in "Bethune College and School Centenary Volume", edited by Dr. Kalidas Nag, p. 33.

Beveridge, India Called Them, 211.

Beveridge, India Called Them, 211.

Beveridge. India Called Them, 88. (Letter to Fanny, Beveridge's sister.)

Bhattacharjee, Dharitri. (2007). British Women's Views of Twentieth-Century India: An Examination of Obstacles to Cross-Cultural Understandings. A Thesis Submitted to the Faculty of Miami University, Department of History, Miami University Oxford, Ohio.

Karlekar, Malavika. (4 February 2007). "Lessons in a Sari Did women's education in India change the way they dressed?" The Telegraph. Retrieved 2007-04-18.

Kopf, David. (1979). The Brahmo Samaj and the Shaping of the Modern Indian Mind, Princeton University Press, ISBN 0-691-03125-8., pp. 34-39.

Kopf, David. (1979). *The Brahmo Samaj and the Shaping of the Modern Indian Mind.* Princeton University Press, ISBN 0-691-03125-8, pp. 34-39.

M.A. Scherer. (1995). Annette Akroyd Beveridge: Victorian Reformer, Oriental Scholar. (Dissertation. Ohio State Committee.

Sarwar, Firoj High. (Nov. - Dec. 2012). Christian Missionaries and Female Education in Bengal during East India Company's Rule: a Discourse between Christianised Colonial Domination versus Women Emancipation. IOSR Journal of Humanities and Social Science (JHSS). ISSN: 2279-0837, ISBN: 2279-0845. Volume 4. Issue 1, pp. 37-47.

Sastri, Sivanath, History of the Brahmo Samaj, 1911-12/1993. Sadharan Brahmo Samaj. p. 164.

5

Indoctrination and Education: The Curious Case of Dinanath Batra

Navneet Sharma and Harikrishnan Bhaskaran

Abstract

In this paper, I wish to appreciate Batra's attempt of writing and re-writing the history of India. His attempt for re-constitution of the moral fabric of India is also worth appreciation and analysis. For this, we would undertake the analysis of some 'texts' written by Dinanath Batra. At the conclusive end, we might suggest, if that is not blasphemy, why is the 'teaching-learning' attempt undertaken by him in his texts a source of indoctrination rather than education. Reading Batra, one may presume that there are 'scientific' narratives about foetus trans-plant, sex change operations, creating LoCs, missiles, aphrodisiacs, helicopters, human flying, satellite transmissions, body implants when 'Hindu' texts refer to the 'mythical' transfer of Balaram, Shikhandi, Lakshman Rekha, Agni Baan, Dhritrashtra having 100 sons, Pushpak Viman, Hanuman crossing sea, Akashvanis, Ganesh getting a trunk face and many more. Comprehending Batra one may conclude that modern science and technology is nothing but footnotes to the works of fiction. The above may be a different 'perspective' on education or 'indianisation' of education catering to the whims, fancies and fantasy of Batra, but it attracts attention and scrutiny when this is made part of the curriculum and textbooks. The learners with 'impressionable' minds are given to 'indoctri-nation' rather than education, and in turn what we get is the 'dedicated' citizenry or blind-folded followers rather than 'conscientised' people for the country.

Keywords: *Indoctrination, scientific' narratives, mythical' transfer, hindu texts*

Indoctrination and education are so intricately stitched together that one cannot be differentiated with the other. The earnest question that what is education or 'good' education or good schooling carries the inherent texts and practices of indoctrination. The objective of 'shaping'/ 'making'/ 'constructing'/ 'altering' the 'behaviour'/ 'knowledge' of the learner/ student is shared with equal zeal by both education and indoctrination. Both have agenda guided by the political economy of the time and their founders or promoters, both need an efficient teacher both need text and curriculum, evaluation, peer group, home-tasks, reward and punishment for their success.

Whether education can be distinguished from indoctrination is a question that has been very much disguised. Usually indoctrination refers to the moulding of minds. If indoctrination means simply influencing other people, there is really no ground for debate as to whether it can be distinguished from education; it cannot, for any teacher can exert an influence upon students.

Indoctrination as a word immediately passes negative vibes and is something that is usually associated with condemnation. Oxford dictionary defines the verb 'indoctrinate' as 'to teach (a person or group) to accept a set of beliefs uncritically'. According to Barrow and Woods, indoctrination involves teaching unverifiable propositions as unquestionable truths.

In this paper, we wish to examine Batra's attempt of writing and re-writing the history of India. His attempt for re-constitution of the moral fabric of India is also worth appreciation and analysis. For this, we would undertake the analysis of some 'texts' written by Dinanath Batra. At the conclusive end, we might suggest, why is the 'teaching-learning' attempt undertaken by him in his texts are a source of indoctrination rather than education.

Being a student or being a teacher would not be easy in the times of Batra. One can be 'guru' or 'disciple' only. One would need not reason with the unreason perpetuated by the 'texts' written by Batra. The only problem, seemingly to Batra, is that Indians have grown too 'Marxist' and 'Macaulayvian'. Somehow, Batra pushes for his agenda forcibly, when there is a Rightist Government at the helm, raises more problems for the 'liberal' agenda of his 'own' government. The problem with Batra's approach is that it stands in contrast to Modi's plank of development on which he won the massive mandate.

Indoctrination is a process of inculcating certain beliefs, attitude or set of ideas in any individual. But the major difference between indoctrination and education is that indoctrination doesn't allow people to questions the beliefs imparted whereas education guides the pupil logically and rationally to construct their own knowledge based on reasonable evidence and science. But we can't call every time if a certain belief or ideas being imparted to young children as indoctrinatory. The classic example will be the case of educating young child who have not crossed a developmental stage where they can pursue logic and rationality. The parents most of time tell their child about the moral conduct like respecting elders, not eating junk food and most time they might use authority to do that but this case cannot be indoctrinatory because a child is allowed to questions it when he grows up and examine evidences in support or against it. Teaching scientific and mathematics facts can't be called indoctrinatory because all the facts has been rationally proven and can be examined and verified whereas case of indoctrination is imparting certain belied which can't be proved or examined or verified or lack of general agreement on it.

Barrow and Woods (1988) state certain features or conditions to be present in case of indoctrinatory teaching. Barrow and woods take Catholicism as an undisputed example of indoctrination. Indoctrination involves passing on of certain beliefs, the nature or content of these beliefs is important to consider. In case of these beliefs, there is no agreement as to the sort of evidence that would count to prove them true or false. These propositions by their very nature are not verifiable or falsifiable and serve rather as guiding principles for interpreting the world. For example, 'God exists', to the person who is committed to this proposition, nothing counts as evidence against it, whereas for those who are not o committed, quite a lot of evidence counts against it.

According to Barrow and Woods (1988), one may take indoctrination to involve the imparting of doctrinal beliefs as a necessary condition but not as a sufficient one. A second necessary condition of indoctrination is that the indoctrinator should cause someone to have unshakable belief or commitment in the proposition or the doctrine. These doctrines are presented as truths and the indoctrinated person has a closed mind when it comes to the question of truth or falsehood of the doctrine. Barrow and Woods (1988), maintain that students in a catholic school are told that God exists; it not left for them to decide for themselves if they feel drawn to adopt this set of beliefs.

Barrow and Woods (1988), next points to the importance of method used to impart such beliefs. In order to cause someone to have unshakable belief in a set of propositions that cannot be demonstrated to be true rationally, non-rational methods have to be used. Therefore, some sort of non- rational persuasion is used.

Intention is logically necessary to the concept of indoctrination, for it does not make sense to talk about implanting an unshakable belief without taking into account the intentions of the person doing so (Barrow and Woods, 1988). They further maintain that it is important to make the distinction between avowed and real intention, as the indoctrinator might not admit to having it.

Reading Batra, one may presume that there are 'scientific' narratives about foetus trans-plant, sex change operations, creating LoCs, missiles, aphrodisiacs, helicopters, human flying, satellite transmissions, body implants when 'Hindu' texts refer to the 'mythical' transfer of Balaram, Shikhandi, Lakshman Rekha, Agni Baan, Dhritrashtra having 100 sons, Pushpak Viman, Hanuman crossing sea, Akashvanis, Ganesh getting a trunk face and many more. Comprehending Batra one may conclude that modern science and technology is nothing but footnotes to the works of fiction. The above may be a different 'perspective' on education or 'indianisation' of education catering to the whims, fancies and fantasy of Batra, but it attracts attention and scrutiny when this is made part of the curriculum and textbooks. The learners with 'impressionable' minds are given to 'indoctrination' rather than education, and in turn what we get is the 'dedicated' citizenry or blind-folded followers rather than 'conscientised' people for the country.

Usually, indoctrination refers to the moulding of children in somewhat the same way that propaganda refers to the moulding of adults. Sometimes it simply means influencing the immature; sometimes it means influencing them in a particular way, as by a play upon their feelings; and sometimes it means dealing with them in such a manner as to hinder their freedom of thought in a certain area. The RSS and people like Batra and their ilk have always followed the 'catch-them-young' policy for the above reason only.

Barrow and Woods have effectively conveyed the essential difference when they say that education becomes indoctrination: "When the teacher ceases to present the various views held by different people on the controversial… issue under discussion and becomes intent on getting his own views on the issue taken as gospel by his students, an intent which will.., necessarily involve the overriding of the rationality of those same students."

This refusal to acknowledge and respect the rationality of the students is what lies at the heart of indoctrination. When an attempt is made to impose a doctrine on a student and every effort is made to silence his conscience and reasoning abilities it is tantamount to refusing to treat the person in front as a human being. The very purpose of education gets defeated in such an exercise.

Indoctrination, in that it necessarily involves lack of respect for an individual's rationality, is morally unacceptable and hence fails to rate as education. And not only does it fail to rate as education, but to say that it is morally unacceptable is to say that it ought not to be indulged in. It would be appropriate to invoke the German Philosopher Immanuel Kant who opined that human beings are rational creatures and must always be treated as ends in themselves and not as mere means.

Indoctrinators violate this principle in that essentially they treat their audience as means. People are to be got to believe the preferred doctrines and there is to be no detached consideration of them.

Effective education appeals to the rationality of individuals and lets students discover for themselves. It does not preach but offers an invitation to explore. Thus it would be appropriate to term indoctrination as anti-educational in not only its aims but also in its methods.

Batra and fundamentalists like him do the same and disguise it in the name of education. For example, when Batra opposes the idea of blowing off candles on birthdays, he argues that this is not 'Indian'. Batra might not appreciate that his idea of being an 'Indian' confines it to the 'fair, dwija, north Indian male'. Though the beginning of the custom of putting candles on birthday cakes stays obscure, it is widely believed that it has Greek origins. The Greek used to present offerings to the Moon God with candles. There are mentions about the tradition of putting candles along with birthday cakes from 18th century Germany as well. Though it is not very clear who started putting the candles on the cake and blowing them off, there are assumptions that this started as part of the practical wisdom of not to get the melting wax mixed with the cake. Anyway, as the birthday cakes got popular, so do the custom of blowing candles.

However, the murmurs against blowing candles are not new. The RSS had always taken this particular stand against this custom. The RSS leaders made a lot fuss when Atal Behari Vajpayee cut the cake after blowing off candles on his 71st birthday when he was the prime ministerial candidate for the NDA. For Batra, cakes and candles are more an extension of the White Christian invaders and their culture, not to mention blowing off the candles. Anyway, it was not just the RSS which were anti-cake in history. Religious hardliners like Puritans have opposed it, extending their protests against religious festivals, even to family occasions like birthday celebrations. On this, other religious fundamentalists like the 'Islamists' might come close to sharing Batra's Hindu fairy-tale aka 'parikatha'.

If indoctrination means influencing unfairly, as by a biased presentation of the evidence, or by a premature appeal to authority, or by immediate resort to emotional appeal, or by the other tricks employed among adults by unscrupulous propagandists, the use of indoctrination in school is subject to all the criticisms levelled at the use of propaganda outside of school plus the indictment that advantage is being taken of immaturity.

It is akin to Batra's love (others, fundamentalists included) for the 'cow' or 'gomata'. Cows have been more than just bovine in the Indian political cow pen. Time and again cows are being dragged into the sacred realm no matter what they do. It is obviously up to the practitioners of the religion to consider it as a sacred animal as part of their religious beliefs, but when the sacredness is pushed to the primary school students in the form of supplementary knowledge, cows just turn out to be unquestionable holy cows.

In this reference, indoctrination is defined as any kind of teaching which hampers independent thinking in a given field, or any effort to secure acceptance of an idea in such a fashion as does not thereby help, as best as possible, to make the learner an independent judge in such matters.

The teachers' intention in the teaching process will be an important consideration to determine effective teaching and its distinguishing features from indoctrination. There might be a very thin line between the two sometimes. It would solely depend on how the curriculum has been designed, how much autonomy the teacher has and with the autonomy how much critical thinking the teacher facilitates in the classroom. If the authority of the teacher and the decision to communicate only some specific information undermines the contribution to a child's rational development, the intention to indoctrinate children not only into particular beliefs but also in ways of thinking would be there. Somewhere this would be different from conditioning of children. Unlike conditioning, the will of the person is not over-ridden in the in indoctrination process. The FARE Report 1991 states that 'indoctrination occurs when a person is given one view of the world in such a way that they cannot see the other' (Copley, 2005).

While education actually aims at enabling the learner to understand different perspectives and to approach them critically, the holy cows in the holy supplementary reader starts indoctrinating, not educating. Obviously, when the cow is sacred, counting it as bovine or as part of diet becomes sacrilegious. Though Hindu scriptures have conflicting accounts which suggest that people belonging to the higher strata of the society were also beef-eaters, the alleged sacredness of the cow now cuts off the present beef-eaters to be anti-Hindu and may be anti-nationals. Well, the same reasons which make the cow sacred can also be applied to Water Buffalo, then why is it not counted sacred?

With globalisation and advances in communication technologies, the world is slated to shrink as a global village. But ethnic and cultural strife across the world is giving birth to new nations on a day-to-day basis. However, Batra still strolls in the idea of large expansionist campaigns with which rulers like Alexander wanted to extend the geographical boundaries of their empire. As per Batra, the real India—Akhand Bharat—actually exists scattered into different countries, including all the immediate neighbours like India, Pakistan, Afghanistan, Nepal, Bhutan, Tibet, Bangladesh, Sri Lanka and Myanmar.

Thinking on the same line, countries which were part of the ancient Gondwanaland should be brought under a monolithic Gondwanaland, which will make us a much bigger and richer nation indeed. People who are intolerant about India's present diversity, dreaming about adding more number of culturally and ethnically different communities under an undivided India could be a good example of irony for upper primary students. But when Batra's book tries to supplement the knowledge gained in the learning process, the call for Akhand Bharat turns out to be a 'historically' supported fact, not irony, for facts are sacred and not to be challenged.

Education as contrasted with indoctrination is said to be a process of teaching the pupil how to think rather than what to think. Its object is not to secure the acceptance of any doctrine whatever, but to assist the learner to choose or develop his own doctrines. Any teacher who transmits ready-made conclusions is abandoning teaching for indoctrination if the process is of such a type as to restrict the pupil's ability to reach his own conclusions. The learner in this case is not supposed to visualise the idea of India but to abide by the idea of larger 'Hindu' Rashtra, the nation where the majoritarian Hindu benevolently accommodates other religionists for the sake of genial and 'Hindutva'-guided cultural nationalism.

Education and indoctrination are two very different processes wherein one can say that indoctrination is a counter-process of education. Education has some aims associated with it which are not in consonance with the objectives of any kind of indoctrination. Indoctrination is against many educational aims.

According to Barrow and Woods (1988), effective teaching encourages rational debate and sometimes may involve or require influencing the child toward acceptance of certain patterns of behaviour. The teacher should ultimately bring the students to examine the values or notions they conform to. This is exactly the opposite of indoctrination where the whole idea is to keep the students from engaging themselves in any kind of scrutiny.

Barrow and Woods (1988) maintain that in case of effective teaching, rationality always supersedes authority. For effective teaching to take place, the knowledge of the teachers should surpass their subjects, it essential that the teachers have a sense of overall aims and objectives. Along with the pedagogical aspect they also need to take into account and pay attention to the logical nature of their subject matter.

Effective teaching should equip the student to engage critically in any fact or set of information and assess not just the evidence but also the authenticity of the source of such information. The student should also be taught about the importance of flexibility in ones beliefs and to appreciate and value diverse opinions as they help one reach a better and dynamic conclusion.

Indoctrination overrides rationality, the development of which is one of the important aims of education. Education should emphasise on developing a rational attitude in human being but indoctrination is intended to get one to accept the indoctrinator's views without any rational method. Education should emphasise on the development of values based on reason and understanding whereas indoctrination doesn't consider these aspects.

Education should be aimed at the independence of action and thought but indoctrination is about developing unshakable commitment through non-rational methods by changing the beliefs of a person. The beliefs formed through indoctrination can't be open to dialogue and scrutiny due to the unshakable commitment but education emphasises on the individual's independence for his/her own actions and thoughts, irrespective of any externally indoctrinated belief.

The above issues clearly demarcate Batra and his kind as 'indoctrinators' rather than 'educators'. We do not have any problem with whosoever makes a choice to submit or surrender to indoctrination, but this process must not be expressed as one of education and befool the people.

In this paper, we are aware that we have not asked enough questions, but limited to what a single conceptual paper can convincingly uphold. There is enough writing on the relationship between state, power, knowledge, pedagogy and schooling. The researchers do not intend to re-invent the wheel but just wish to emphasise that many attempts and efforts are made by ideology and ideologues to indoctrinate which is been passed off as 'indigenisation' of knowledge but is 'Majoritarianism' or Hinduvisation of native knowledge. We hardly have explored the nuances of hidden agenda of curriculum but there are hardly anything hidden, the kinds of DN Batra are hardly hiding their whims and fancies.

The question that what teachers should do to identify this and action plan post identification is also a tricky one and can be answered differently from different ideological vantage points and no knowledge exists or can be created which can be neutral or the question whether asking such questions contributes and betters our educational system is still worth exploring but as we know that intellect is sceptical and dogmas are confident, they overwhelm the educational process run by the state and more easily in the state which is been governed by a political party with a remote control in the hands of the religious-cultural organisation.

The above knowledge when taught in a shakha, is identified as 'ideology' but when this is taught in a school— 'state-run school'— it is perceived as 'knowledge'. Ideology as knowledge is more harmful than ideology and its hegemonic dominance. Batra stands guilty of the sin committed at the altar of knowledge. We as citizens can either take a call or wait for 'Saraswati' or 'Vidya'mata to punish him for this sacrilege.

References

Apple, M.W. (2013) Knowledge, Power, and Education, Routledge, London.

Barrow, R. and Woods, R. (1988) An Introduction to Philosophy to Education, Routledge, London.

Carr, W. (1997). Professing Education in a Postmodern Age. Journal of Philosophy of Education, **31** (2), 309-327.

Chambliss, J. (Ed.). (1996). Philosophy of Education: An Encyclopedia. London: Garland Publishing Inc.

Copley, T. (2005). *Religious education versus the injustice of secular indoctrination?*. [online] Retrieved from: http://old.religiouseducation.net/member/05_rea_papers/copley_2005.pdf [Accessed: 23 Dec 2014].

Freire, P. (1970). Pedagogy of the oppressed. USA: The Continum Publishing Company.

Freire, P. (1998). Teachers as Cultural Workers. USA: Westview Press.

Kellner, D. (n.d.). Toward a Critical Theory of Education. Retrieved from http://gseis.ucla.edu/faculty/kellner/essays/towardcriticaltheoryofed.pdf

Palmer, R.R. (1957) Education and Indoctrination in *Peabody Journal of Education*, Vol. 34, No. 4, pp. 224-228.

Peters, R. (Ed.). (1967). The Concept of Education. London: Routledge & Kegan Paul.Randall, C. (Ed.). (2006). A Companion to Philosophy of Education. USA: Blackwell Publishers.

Raven, J. (2005). Liberal Education and Liberalism in Modern Society. The Good Society-Journal of the Committee on the Political Economy of the Good Society, **14** (3), 29-37.

Batra, D. Shikshan Nu Bharatiyakaran.

Batra, D. Tejoymay Bharat.

6

Education of the Transgender in India: Exploring the Possibilities from a Sufi Perspective

Sujoy Paul

Abstract

Transgender is a term that describes individuals who are neither categorized as male nor as female along with the social category present in some societies who recognize three or more genders (Sharma, 2012). Although the term 'Transgender' is of recent origin, people of the 'third gender' have existed in every culture, race, and class since the early historical times of human civilization. In India, they are among the most marginalized classes who have so far been deprived of their basic rights of food, clothing, shelter, education and health. Among the mainstream societies, the people of the transgender community are looked upon as taboos- a 'sexless class', a set of tormented souls, whose 'curse' and 'abusive behaviour' are feared by almost everybody. This social stigma has reduced them from the once enjoyed highly respectable status in the society to the disgraceful position of beggars and sex workers (Kain, 2008). In such circumstances, education can play a key role in changing their social status in India and helping them in their material and spiritual upliftment.

Sufism, which is a mystical branch of Islam, is an exploration of the path of spiritual advancement and an urge to experience a dimension beyond the material world in order to know and return to a spiritual Essence or Truth. According to the Sufi saints, the urge toward mysticism is inherent within every human soul, irrespective of a person's religion, caste, creed or gender identities. In that sense, Sufism is an art of awakening the soul by allowing the lights of knowledge, wisdom and spirituality to enter the human heart and also the other faculties of perception. Moreover, Sufism has a different approach towards the gender issue as it argues that God is without gender (Kim, 2009). During 'Urs' festival, the participation of the socially marginalized groups such as women, transgender, and minorities are encouraged (Mokhtar, 2012). Thus, Sufism, the other name of which is Ihsan or 'sincerity' has a strong potential to embrace the transgender people by providing them education of the heart so that they can lead a social life of respect and reconciliation.

This analytical paper takes a critical look at the issue of transgender education that could be overcome with the help of a Sufi approach to looking at them. It presents the sorry state of the transgender people in India where they have been excluded from effectively participating in its prevailing social and cultural life. And it argues that a Sufi perspective, which tells us that it is possible to see beyond the veils of darkness that enclothe our perceptions and beliefs, is required to understand the problems of the transgender people. In fact, Sufism allows us to see things as they truly are. Therefore, it is possible to get rid of the taboos concerning the transgender by illuminating the ignorant mind through proper education.

Keywords: Transgender, education, sufism, sufi perspective

Introduction

The term 'transgender' refers to persons whose understanding of gender identification is somewhat different from the society's popular and polarized gender conformation. The dichotomized system of gender (i.e., male and female) prevalent in the mainstream society does not necessarily apply to them as they are categorized neither as male nor as female but a combination of the two popularly known as 'third gender'. Although the term 'Transgender' is of recent origin, people of the 'third gender' have existed in every culture, race, and class since the early historical times of human civilization. However, there is no one way to be 'transgender'. They are young and old, rich and poor, engaged in every human activity, and they belong to every race and every country in the world (Simmons & White, 2014). But everywhere they are subjected to manhandling and discrimination due to their gender identity or expression. They are the victims of physical and mental assault in every step of life. People regularly working with the transgender community have confronted the reality of their being evicted from house, bullied at school, fired from jobs, exposed to mistreatment and violence, and dismissed from having access to health care which they badly need (Grant, et. al., 2011).

In India, the transgender people are deprived of their basic rights of food, clothing, shelter, education and health care. Among the mainstream societies, the people of the transgender community are looked upon as taboos- a 'sexless class', a set of tormented souls, whose 'curse' and 'abusive behaviour' are feared by almost everybody. This sort of attitude to them has been built through conventional stories about them and the caricature versions presented in the popular movies (Ummeed Live, 2012). This social stigma has reduced them from the once enjoyed highly respectable status in the society to the disgraceful position of beggars and sex workers (Kain, 2008). In such circumstances, providing them educational opportunities can play a key role in changing their status and helping them in their material and spiritual upliftment.

This spiritual upliftment could be achieved through the teachings of Sufism, which is a mystical branch of Islam that inspires its followers to explore the path of spiritual advancement. It also develops an urge to experience a dimension beyond the material world in order to know and return to a spiritual Essence or Truth. And contrary to the formal religious beliefs, Sufism has a different approach to the issue of gender as it argues that God is without gender (Kim, 2009). As Sufism is an art of purifying the soul by allowing the light to enter our hearts and other faculties of perception, it leads to the development of our inner spiritual and intuitive abilities. Therefore, the message of Sufism addresses all people irrespective of their religious affiliation, caste, creed or gender identities. In this sense, the transgender people too have the right to be illuminated by the Sufi way of mysticism that runs through an individual to bring forth one's untapped potentials. This paper critically analyzes the issues related to the education of thc transgender people in India and an approach to overcoming them through a Sufi perspective.

The Transgender and Their Status in India

The word 'Transgender' in its contemporary usage has become an "umbrella" term that is used to describe a wide range of identities and experiences, including but not limited to transsexual people, male and female cross-dressers, intersexed individuals, along with men and women, regardless of sexual orientation, whose appearance or characteristics are perceived to be gender atypical. There are a host of transgender groups living in the Indian sub-continent like hijras/kinnars, jogtas, jogappas, Aradhis, Sakhis, etc. Howcver, there are transgender individuals who do not belong to any specific group as they live independently (Sathasivam, 2011). The action and behaviour of the transgender do not always conform to the existing norms in which men and women usually act and behave. As a result, they are considered as a set of deviated people who are mostly 'unacceptable' among the mainstream societies. Even the welfare schemes announced by the government are for men and women only, and the transgender people do not figure anywhere (Sharma, 2012). Thus, they have been excluded from effectively participating in the socio-cultural milieu of the nation because their participation in the political, economic matters and in the decision-making process has not been encouraged. However, in a landmark judgement in April 2014, the Supreme Court of India has recognized the people of the transgender community as a 'third gender'. This legal status is expected to reduce the amount of mistreatment that they have to face in their every day social life.

Although, the official data regarding the total number of transgender people living in India put them to 4.9 lakh (The Time of India, 2011), trans activists in India claim that the actual number is likely to be seven times higher (Senzee, 2014). That means the actual number of such people in India could be somewhat around 3.5 million. The Supreme Court judgement has paved the way for their being included as a distinct category in the electoral rolls of the country. So far, people of the transgender community had to enroll themselves either as male or as female, which was degrading and embarrassing for them. However, the scenario is changing since they have been recognized by the Nation Census Bureau; the voter and Aadhar IDs have an 'Other' gender option, and the National Aids Control Organisation is on its way to complete its estimation exercise of the transgender, making India the first country in the world to do so (Chowdhury, 2013). This recognition is regarded as the first step towards their inclusive development.

According to historical records, the transgender people once enjoyed a proud place in the Indian society as they gained trusted positions in royal courts protecting the nobility's 'harems' or 'zenanas', and many even rising to powerful court positions (Nelson, 2009). But today, India's transgender people have lost their past glory as they are often seen roaming around public places asking for 'bakshis' and threatening people to curse them or embarrass them by exposing their castrated genitals if they do no oblige. And, this dreaded form of begging is not their only source of income. There are others who make their livelihood by working as prostitutes, while some are found making money by blessing during childbirth, weddings and other auspicious occasions. In fact, the people of the transgender community, particularly the 'hijras' are believed to possess occult powers, and their blessings and curses are both considered to be very potent (Dutt, 2002). In response to a Writ Petition, The honourable Supreme Court of India (2013) has observed, "The transgender community, generally known as 'Hijras' in this country, are a section of Indian citizens who are treated by Society as unnaturals and generally as objects of ridicule and even fear on account of superstition. All human beings are born free and equal in dignity and ought to be entitled to enjoyment of human rights without discrimination on the basis of sexual orientation or gender identity" (p- 18). The Court also argues that the transgender people, like all other people of the country are part of the society and have the right to enjoy equal opportunities as are available to other persons of the society. Therefore, their right to education and empowerment has to be taken care of so that they are not deprived of availing the facilities the country offers to all its citizens.

Educational Opportunities of the Transgender

Education, as a fundamental human right, can expand the horizons of human mind by helping us to learn about ourselves and our world and build foundational skills for our working lives (Grant, et. al., 2011). Bu unfortunately, all do not get the opportunity to pursue education in a safe and supportive environment. This is more pertinent in case of the transgender and gender non-conforming people, who are unable to avail equal educational opportunities due to harassment, discrimination and violence in the educational institutions. Some young trans people are rejected even by their families leading them to drop out of school as they do not have funding support for them. And, their woes become manifold in their later life when they are rejected in the job market as most of the public and private companies cite several excuses to deny them employment. Therefore, the only solution to get rid of the numerous troubles faced by the transgender people is to educate them and accommodate them in the mainstream society. And most of them can be pulled out of the path of begging and prostitution by providing employment in any field as opted by them according to their qualification and efficiency (Kain, 2008).

Several steps are being taken to achieve universal literacy both at the primary and the secondary levels of education. Programmes like National Literacy Mission (NLM), Total Literacy Campaign (TLC), 'Saakshar Bharat', Sarva Siksha Abhiyan (SSA), and Rashtriya Madhyamik Siksha Abhiyan (RMSA) etc. are some of the major initiatives to impart education among all in the country. In the 'Report to the People on Education' (2011-12), the Ministry of Human Resource Development has said, "Literacy is an integral and indispensable element of educational development. Literacy can pave way for reduction in population growth, child mortality and poverty, and facilitate in attaining gender parity, sustainable and holistic growth. .... Literacy is all the more important to those sections of population, who have been historically neglected". (p-13). This shows the importance of providing educational opportunities to the transgender people who are 'historically neglected'. However, the most significant impetus has come in the form of the Right of Children to Free and Compulsory Education (RTE) Act, 2009, which says that every child in the age group of six to fourteen years shall have a right to free and compulsory education in a neighbourhood school. It further says that a child "belonging to disadvantaged group are not discriminated against and prevented from pursuing and completing elementary education on any grounds" (Chapter- III, Sec. 9c).

However, despite affirmative actions in providing equal rights and opportunities to the transgender people they still remain one of the marginalized and vulnerable communities in the country as they seriously lag behind on various human development indices including education. The National Expert Committee on Issues of Transgender Persons (2013) has presented some appalling facts regarding education of the transgender people. They are:

(i) Transgender persons face high level of stigma and physical, sexual, emotional violence, and violence in terms of neglect and discrimination in educational institutions leading to most of them dropping out of their studies.

(ii) Exclusion from society and family cause them to face hindrances for accessing education.

(iii) The apathy of the teachers and staff towards the community has adverse effect on the continuity of transgender people in educational institutes.

(iv) The low level of education either push them to other occupation like sex work making them vulnerable to HIV and other Sexual Transmitted Diseases (STDs), or force them to take socially degrading jobs like begging etc.

Therefore, the child, irrespective of its gender identity should be given the best possible facilities so that the fullest potential of the child is realized. With its stereotypical functions, education should be used as a vehicle to build one's character by inspiring the spirit of the child and rewarding the child's positive acts. According to Sufi philosopher Hazrat Inayat Khan, "To sow the seed of knowledge and righteousness in the heart of a child is the greatest and most blessed opportunity that life offers." And teachers should endeavour to bring out the best in the child- physically, mentally, morally, socially and spiritually by developing the qualities that are inherent in the spirit of the child (Corda, 2010). In fact, Sufism emphasizes on the realization of the spirit, commonly referred to as "I' Or the Self (described in Sufi terms as 'nafs') as a key function of education. And this 'I' is activated by mystical experiences, which like an electrical current runs through an individual, bringing forth the untapped potentials.

The Essence of Sufism

Sufism, regarded as a mystical branch of Islam, is aimed at paving the path for spiritual advancement through the purification of the soul. Central to the concept of Sufism is the love for God as the Sufis commonly express their quest for God through the language of love (Chittick, 2009). Sufism is compared to a tree with many branches, yet having four essential roots or principles. In her book 'The Principles of Sufism', A'ishah al-Ba'uniyyah, a sixteenth century Muslim scholar has identified them as repentance (tawbah), sincerity (ikhlas), recollection (dhikr), and love (mohabbah). On the basis of these four principles, Sufism informs us that it is possible to remove the darkness that veils our belief system by illuminating the heart.

Therefore, proper training in the Sufi teaching is required to reach the state of mind when one can see things as they truly appear.

However, for many people in the modern world it may seem that such spiritual teachings are alien to their culture or are a thing of the past – if indeed they ever existed. Others may vaguely recognize that their destiny lies in the unfolding of these teachings in their lives, but are faced with overwhelming difficulties in finding a trustworthy and authoritative teacher who can show them the way out of the darkness. So, it must be realized that Sufism is the path that leads to the gradual awakening of the heart and it enables one to witness realities which previously appeared obscure and mysterious. And it needs one to be increasingly sincere in following the path of Sufism, as the other name for Sufism is simply 'Ihsan' or sincerity. Therefore, spiritual enlightenment can be achieved even by an ordinary person who lives a sincere life devoted to the Supreme Being. In fact, one of the aims of the Sufi teaching is to make tried and tested methods of gaining enlightenment accessible to people who are living ordinary lives in the modern world.

Sufi Perspective to Transgender Education

As already stated, Sufism has a different approach towards the gender issue as it argues that God is beyond the stereotypical concept of gender. During 'Urs' festival (the celebration of death anniversary of a Sufi saint), the participation of the socially marginized groups such as women, transgender, and other minorities are encouraged (Mokhtar, 2012). In fact, contrary to some other religious beliefs, Sufism bears a radical view about gender issues. Some scholars who have translated the Verses contained in the Qur'an, the holy book of Islam from which Sufism also derives its essence, point to the gender issues contained in them. For example, Verses 42:49-42:50 are translated in the following way- "To God belongs the dominion over the heavens and the earth. It creates what it wills. It prepares for whom it wills females, and it prepares for whom it wills males. Or it marries together the males and the females, and it makes those whom it wills to be ineffectual".

It indicates that God is the creator of all forms of humans- men, women, and a combined form of men and women, known as third gender or transgender who are only 'ineffectual' in terms of the power of reproduction. In all other respect, they are just like the men and women of the mundane societies. If such is the case, then it is incorrect to think that the transgender people are different, bad or abnormal. Like everyone else, they have equal rights in all the resources of the world. Rejecting them from getting education and ignoring their demands for education and employment is absolutely undesirable. In fact, the transgender youths need a more welcoming approach from people of the mainstream societies for inclusive growth of a nation.

On its way to spiritual enlightenment Sufism provides one with the kind of knowledge and wisdom to embrace everyone with love, because it is love that frees one from the bonds of narrow-mindedness, material yearning, and selfishness. Sufism also talks about the combination of the inner and the outer selves to make the most of one's God-given potentials. Its teachings reflect the conviction that just as atoms having unlimited energy hidden within them, the human body is a reservoir of potentialities. And, the Sufi perspective encourages the student to search for this hidden treasure following a refined scientific approach and experimental method. The student strives to understand the essential nature of the human being, the universe, and humanity's relationship to the universe in ways that are relevant today and also tomorrow. Moreover, the libertine attitude of Sufism towards gender issues allows the people of the transgender community to live a life of honour. In today's troubled time, such attitude is really pertinent in lifting the status of this community.

Conclusion

Thus, Sufism, in its path of spiritual advancement tries to develop the innate spiritual and intuitive abilities by allowing the light of knowledge and wisdom enter our hearts and other faculties of perception. According to Sufi perspective, a person should practise Sufism in such a way that leads to the expansion of that person's consciousness. And gender identity of a person should not come in the way to awakening the unused but subtle centers of consciousness inherent in one's heart. In fact, the seekers of spiritual enlightenment should repent of selfishness and turn to a sincere life of love through the recollection of human limitations and God's limitless love (A'ishah, 16th Century A.D.). Following the Sufi path, the schools should reach out to the poor and marginalized communities for lifting the human potential.

Along with this, initiatives should be taken by schools to improve the diversity climate by teaching about gender and sexual diversity so that all including the transgender students get maximum opportunities for academic success (Meyer, 2010). Initially, carrying out conversations on gender issues may cause discomfort and disagreement for some members of the school community, but these conversations should be continued for the purpose of making a safe and supportive school environment for all students including the gender non-conforming learners so that they learn, grow, develop, and maximize their potential (Fisher, 2013). This spirit of accommodation and adaptation is, in fact, one of the pillars of Sufi teaching which is based on humanity and love. Moreover, Sufism allows us to see things as they truly are. It is a way of leading a humble and peaceful life. Therefore, it is possible to get rid of the taboos concerning the transgender by illuminating the ignorant mind through proper education. And in this way, the true nature and essence of Sufism could be realized.

References

A'ishah, A. (16th Century A. D.), The Principles of Sufism, translated in English by Th. Emile Homerin, New York University Press, New York and London.

Chittick, W.C. (2009). *Sufism: A Beginner's Guide*. Oxford: One-World Publications.

Chowdhury, A.M. (2013), NGOs, govt join ranks to empower transgender people, One World South Asia, accessed on Nov. 8, 2014 from southasia.oneworld.net/news

Corda, M.V. (2010), Holistic Child Development, Seed Centre Philosophy of Education, PDF e-book downloaded from www.lulu.com/shop

Dutt, N. (2002), Eunuchs- India's Third Gender, accessed on Dec. 22, 2014 from Things Asian @ http://www.thingsasian.com/stories-photos/2022

Fisher, E.S. (2013), Creating Safe and Supportive Learning Environments: A Guide for Working with Lesbian, Gay, Bisexual, Transgender, and Questioning Youth and Families, Routledge, New York and London.

Grant, Jaime M., Lisa A. Mottet, Justin Tanis, Jack Harrison, Jody L. Herman, and Mara Keisling (2011). *Injustice at Every Turn: A Report of the National Transgender Discrimination Survey.* Washington: National Center for Transgender Equality and National Gay and Lesbian Task Force.

Kain, S. (2008), Educational Challenges for Eunuchs in India, Education blog accessed on August 23, 2014 from education.sulekha.com/education_4_tag_page-781

Kim, S. (2009), A Sufi Approach to Issues of Gender and Reconciliation, St Francis Magazine Nr. 1 Vol. V (February 2009)

Meyer, E. J. (2010), Gender and Sexual Diversity in Schools- An Introduction, Springer, New York.

Mokhtar, S. (2012), Sacred Spaces and Expressive Bodies: At the *Urs* of Lal Shahbaz Qalandar, M. A. Thesis, School of Journalism and Communication, University of Oregon.

National Expert Committee on Issues of Transgender Persons (2013), Approach Paper on Education and Employment opportunities & Challenges for Transgender, Ministry of Social Justice and Empowerment, Government of India, New Dalhi.

Nelson, D. (2009), Indian eunuchs seek recognition as 'third sex', The Telegraph, accessed on July 3, 2014 from www.telegraph.co.uk/news/worldnews/asia/india

Report to the People on Education (2011-12), Ministry of Human Resource Development, Government of India, New Delhi.

Sathasivam, P. (2011), Rights of Transgender People – Sensitising Officers to Provide Access to Justice, *Lecture delivered on Refresher Course for Civil Judges (Junior Division)-I Batch at Tamil Nadu State Judicial Academy on 12.02.2011.*

Senzee, T. (2014), In Recent Election, India's Trans Population Counted for First Time, accessed on Dec 22, 2014 from www.advocate.com

Sharma, P. (2012), Historical Background and Legal Status of Third Gender in Indian Society, International Journal of Research in Economics & Social Sciences, Vol. 2, Issue 12, accessed on July 2, 2014 from http://www.euroasiapub.org

Simmons, H. & White, F. (2014). 'Our Many Selves' in the book 'Trans Bodies, Trans Selves: A Resource for the Transgender Community', Ed. Laura Erickson-Schroth, Oxford University Press, London.

The Gazette of India (2009), Extraordinary, Part-II; Section-1, The Right of Children to Free and Compulsory Education Act, 2009, New Delhi, Thursday, August 27, 2009.

The Supreme Court of India, Civil Original Jurisdiction, Writ Petition (Civil) No. 400 of 2012 Vs. Writ Petition (Civil) no. 604 of 2013.

The Times of India (2011), First Count of third gender in census: 4.9 lakh, accessed on Dec. 18, 2014 from www.timesofindia.com

Ummeed Live (2012), Final Report, Third Gender Leadership Development Project, Raipur, Chhattishgarh, UNDP India.

7

Rethinking Teacher Education: Engaging Souls

Debika Guha

Abstract

As the twenty-first century unfolds with its emphasis on global concerns and technology, we need to reconsider Teacher Education. Teaching has undergone a revolution over the past decade. Research into the role of the teacher has uncovered the true potential of the teacher to make a difference. Much of this research insight is captured in the notion of 'Quality Teaching', a perspective that speaks of intellectual depth, inter-relational capacity and self-reflection. However, 'Quality Teaching' cannot be achieved unless the 'Spiritual' aspect of the teacher's personality blossoms. To cultivate this through Teacher Education programmes is a challenge as it demands a shift in our thinking. No longer is the goal 'Technical Mastery' but an 'Inner Quality'. Teacher Education needs to emphasise the inner life of a teacher even believing that it should be ahead of other attributes. Traditional Teacher Education methods are significant but we cannot reduce the effectiveness of a teacher purely to her knowledge. The way to truly increase capacities and skills of teachers is to 'Engage Their Souls'. Teacher Education should include helping trainees to discover the spiritual qualities which is an integrating construct that works with our cognitive, emotional and social side (mind, heart and soul) to provide meaning and purpose. Spirituality emphasises the connectedness of all ideas, people, life-forms, nature and so on.

Keywords: *Spiritual Capital, spiritual reflectivity, Teacher Education, Life-changing, Engaging souls*

Spiritual qualities in a teacher would involve making ethical and compassionate choices, and is symbolized by a search deep within and a rising above our physical realities. It is the 'Spiritual Capital' which must be emphasised in Teacher Education. It indicates a degree of coherence in terms of shared values, ethics, belief and attitudes towards life, teaching-learning process as well as the strength of moral purpose in an organisation such as an educational institution with those in the wider community.

Inclusion of emphasis on 'Spiritual' qualities is inadequately explored in Teacher Education in India. In my teaching experience as a teacher educator for past sixteen years, I have witnessed the neglect of spiritual commitments in our Teacher Education programmes whether in the B.Ed. or the M.Ed. course. For me 'Spirituality' does not essentially have a religious connotation. I do not believe that one must necessarily have a religious allegiance in order to be vitally involved in the pursuit of spirituality. I believe 'Spirituality' is centred on the deepest values and meanings by which people live. It embraces the idea of an ultimate reality. It envisions an inner path enabling a person to discover the essence of his being. Not all modern notions of spirituality embrace transcendental ideas. Secular spirituality emphasises humanistic ideas on moral character, qualities such as love, compassion, patience, tolerance, forgiveness, contentment, responsibility, harmony and a concern for others. These are aspects of life and human experience which go beyond a purely materialist view of the world without necessarily accepting belief in a supernatural reality or divine being. I feel a teacher may believe in any religion but must imbibe universal values and foster them in students. As teachers we need to agree that everything and anything that is good is necessarily spiritual. Further, personal well-being both physical and psychological is an important aspect of modern spirituality. Contemporary authors suggest that spirituality develops inner peace and forms a foundation for happiness. Spirituality leads to positive health outcomes including morale, happiness and life satisfaction.

Therefore, spiritual impulse is psychologically and socially primary for people and it is existentially inauthentic to avoid such issues in the education of teachers. We must find ways to recognize, honour and cultivate that fact in order to foster profound forms of reflectivity. Teacher Education should make the trainees understand "our individual experiences of the sacred...provide as with reference points, both emotionally and intellectually, telling us that our lives have meaning and purpose (Wuthnow, 1994).

It is unfortunate yet persistent that the purpose of Teacher Education is the training and acculturation of teachers into what B.F. Skinner (1968) called "the technology of teaching" and into what Schon (1987) has termed the ethos of "technical rationality". Such behaviouristically- based approaches to teaching still prevail in institutions of Teacher Education in the form of competency- based teacher education curricula. In most of these curricula, one is trained to perform a prefabricated set of teaching skills and functions. Such programmes or courses tend to pay very little attention to the psychological, ethical or spiritual contexts of teaching. They ignore the deeper motivations and purposes of the teacher trainees. The efficiency-based, depersonalized vision of teachers and teaching is alive in Teacher Education courses in our country. Nevertheless, the view of teachers as moral agents whose commitment to teaching rests on foundational spiritual commitments has not disappeared. Many teacher educators persist in explaining to the trainees in seeing their role as primarily the emotional and moral nurturance of children in addition to nurturing the cognitive dimensions of the students. It is this role which provides those, psychic rewards which in some measure, compensate for the lack of financial rewards in teaching. For instance, Serrow et. al. (1992) studied students of Teacher Education at five public universities in the United States and found that over 90 percent of the respondents had chosen to be teachers because of a desire to serve and nurture others. Similarly, Pajak and Blaise (1989), in a study of 200 teachers concluded that:... teachers identified their own spiritual beliefs as having a beneficial effect on their professional lives. Most spoke generally of values and a belief in the inherent dignity of man. Their spiritual beliefs were a source of stability, meaning and direction in life. Teachers generally portrayed their relationship with students as caring, understanding, accepting, patient and trusting and said that this was the result of their spiritual commitments.

The question is 'How can we as teacher educators ignore the emphasis of spiritual qualities in a teacher to be? Why is this neglected in our Teacher Education courses?'. We need spiritual reflectivity in Teacher Education. In teacher reflectivity, the intending or practicing teacher reflects on the deeper pedagogical, emotional and moral forces that he has internalized and which both consciously and unconsciously shape his practice. In order to clarify the conscious assumptions and make the unconscious ones explicit, reflective Teacher Education should employ reflective journal keeping, seminars, dialogues and action research projects. Through these dialogic and empirical tools, the teacher to be or the trainee is able to uncover her hidden assumptions about teaching and when appropriate, change them. The goal is for him to practice to become more pedagogically effective, personally satisfying and sensitive to values.

The B.Ed. course of Calcutta University has introduced from 2013, reflective journal keeping, action research projects and paper on 'Teaching as a Profession'. This paper includes an analysis of Professionalism and Teaching, Professional Growth of teachers, Developing Competencies and related issues. What about the inherent qualities of a teacher? Why is the word 'Professional' being emphasized? Where is the role of spiritual commitments placed in the course? Although the new syllabus is far improved than the previous one, I believe that our present forms of scope for reflectivity is not deep enough in Teacher Education. The teachers to be must be provided opportunities to explore the motivations for becoming a teacher and they need to engage in spiritual reflectivity in order to better understand their desire to teach and elaborate on their images of good practice. By neglecting the development of spirituality in our intending teachers, we do not fully serve students and seriously compromise the depth and effectiveness of their reflectivity. In fact, I would argue that we actually do moral violence to such students by requiring that they "bracket off" the spiritual dimension of their existence as intellectually irrelevant or even institutionally unacceptable. Some rubrics that might serve as spring boards for teachers' spiritual reflectivity may be (1) The meaning of life (2) Values (3) Morality (4) The organization of the Universe (5) Suffering (6) Beliefs and attitudes. I would also like to suggest that critical reflectivity, which aims at sensitizing the teacher to implications and applications of his practice will often be incomplete if it does not take his spiritual commitments into account.

Teacher Education should

- Build where appropriate on the foundation of moral development
- Pay due attention to development of moral reasoning
- Encourage active involvement of students in community outreach programmes
- Aim for consistency in reinforcing the fundamental value as infused by schools
- Reflect on their own values and or the appropriateness of the example they set through their personal and professional conduct
- Include variety of activities which develop character
- Ensure that the learning that occurs through their relationship with their pupils is positive
- Explore different methods for developing values, attitudes and personal qualities.
- Help teachers to be to develop a sense of their own moral identity
- Include Value Education classes
- Provide opportunities to think through their own values and attitudes and to reflect critically on the place of values in education so that they are more confident to talk about values when they teach in classrooms in future
- Provide scope to observe, study, reflect on the ways in which children learn values and attitudes through the curriculum and through the life of the school.
- Include practical methods and strategies for teaching and assessing many aspects of value education
- Teacher Education should include what Vivekananda termed as 'Character Building'. This may be achieved not only through what has been discussed but also through:

- Teach by example: Teacher educators need to be role models themselves. They must be respected for their virtues.
- Direct Instruction: Direct instruction through value education classes, teaching and learning, problem solving, cooperative learning, experience based projects, integrated thematic learning and so on are essential.
- Learning Environment: The moral climate of Teacher Education Institutions must be consistent with the values promulgated.

Habituation: The teachers to be need to develop intrinsic motivation and need repeated opportunities to practice good behaviour until it becomes a habit, part of their personal narrative. Students need to develop practical understanding of the requirements of fairness, cooperation and respect.

The present Teacher Education in India holds schools and teachers more accountable for student learning as demonstrated by everyone's expectations for stronger student performances on standardized tests. Unfortunately, the increased emphasis on reading, mathematics, and science to prepare students for a global, technological, and information-based marketplace seems to relegate the general well-being of students. A virtue is socially valued, while moral virtues, such as honesty, is morally valued. Schools and teachers should educate for character, especially through teaching respect and responsibility. As teachers interact with students, it is vital for them to serve as role models of character by making professional judgments and decisions based on social and moral virtues. Therefore, this should be emphasized in Teacher Education along with academics and other activities. The erosion of virtuous behaviours should be of concern to teachers. The media reports on an unending stream of law-breaking actions. Young people read about and see dishonesty, corruption, lying, stealing and cheating as the way that many people in society have chosen to get ahead. What students need are lessons that teach and model just the opposite- spiritual qualities including moral virtues and character. According o Gough (1998), the ultimate goal of character development occurs when each person reaches the point where doing 'good' becomes automatic or habitual. Teacher Educators need to agree that students need to imitate teachers who are effortlessly honest, trusting, fair, respectful and responsible in their actions. Soloman (1997) asserts… "Unless character development is directly addressed, the moral maturation process will not likely occur".

The epitome of living a value-based life is the fulfillment of moral obligations with integrity. This is true regardless of religion, culture, race or ethnicity. Teachers need to teach students that integrity means consistently to choose to do what is right, even when it would be easier to do something that is personally more beneficial. Teachers who demonstrate integrity are accountable for providing academic programmes of quality and positive educational experiences. We need to expect educators to teach character and virtues that can help shape and mould young teachers into contributing members of society. Teacher Education courses have the potential to be life-changing if the spiritual dimension of a trainee's personality is blossomed. Teacher educators need to teach trainees to be role models by imbibing the following qualities.

Honesty: Teachers to be need to be taught that teachers display honesty by telling the truth and acting in an honourable way. Teacher Educators can explain and show that honesty means telling the truth about why an assignment was not submitted, being true to yourself in the quest to learn.

Trust: Trust is the belief in others that develops whenever people fulfill promises and commitments. Trust is nurtured for example when fear of failure of the student is transformed into an opportunity to learn. Trust is nurtured when students turn to their teachers because they feel they will be listened to when they are struggling with interpersonal relationships, academic issues or personal problems.

Fairness: Teachers should not discriminate among students and provide equal opportunity to all. However sometimes fairness may mean treating students differently because this is the right thing to do.

Respect: Teachers to be need to understand that developing respect is vitally important. He must show respect for each student as a unique individual regardless of their ethnicity, race, gender, socio-economic status or abilities. They must be unbiased in their responses.

Responsibility: Teachers demonstrate responsibility by being morally accountable for their actions and fulfilling their duties.

I feel Teacher Education courses should include opportunities to teach how to reason morally. Moral reasoning is the systematic process of evaluating personal virtues and developing a consistent and impartial set of moral principles by which to live (Lumpkin et. al., 2003). The first stage is moral knowing, which is the cognitive phase of learning about moral issues and how to resolve them. The second stage is moral valuing, which is the basis of what individuals believe about themselves and others. The third stage is moral acting, which is how people act based on what they know and value. Teacher educators should teach students to use the moral-reasoning process when making decisions. Through course content, during class activities and in one-on-one interactions with students I have continually emphasised their spiritual qualities for the past one and a half decade and have seen my students imbibe the qualities but the seed has to be planted by us and nurtured. We need to help students to interalize the spiritual qualities- moral values by continually reinforcing what is right and good. Moral reasoning does not promise behavourable change but it does promise individual soul searching and reflection on personal beliefs, values and principles.

Many educators feel that effectiveness as a teacher stems from a combination of knowledge, skills and personal characteristics. While aspiring teachers can increase their knowledge and develop their skills, their personal characteristics- which involve the socio-emotional and spiritual realms are more likely to be fixed when they enter Teacher Education courses. Teachers to be need to be helped to understand to be effective teachers they need to:

- Have a sound knowledge of subject matter
- Take personal interest in each student
- Establish a caring /warm atmosphere
- Show enthusiasm with students
- Reflect on spirituality –their own beliefs, values, attitude and positive health to benefit teaching-learning process.

If we need to 'engage their souls' we as teacher educators can do all that I have discussed and much more for instance, explain and show that the following personal qualities are significant: Passion (it is closer to drive), Perseverance (dedication, tenacity), Willingness to take risks (willing to go against the norm at times to benefit the child's education), Pragmatism (be realistic and understand that we at times need to settle for small wins and make gradual progress), Patience (self-control, ability to give time for things to work), Flexibility (adaptability, deal with change), Authenticity (integrity and conviction), love of learning (life-long learning), High Energy (intrinsic motivation translating into enthusiasm) and a sense of humour. Maria Montessori believed "It is my belief that the thing which we should cultivate in our teachers is more the spirit than the mechanical skill of the scientist". This quote by Montessori piques the imagination in today's educational field where we still struggle to find an answer to the question of quality. What makes a good teacher? How do we teach people to teach? To listen to the wisdom of Maria Montessori, among others, is to suggest the answer does not lie in training requirements. There are myriad techniques for teaching and no one method works for all teachers or all students. Indeed good teachers use a variety of techniques (Intrator and Kunzman, 2006). Unfortunately, our search for objective standards by which to measure quality teaching has overlooked the fact that the root of teaching lies not in methodology but in human relationships. Embracing this means recognizing that who we are and how we relate to the world around us makes a difference in our teaching.

Teacher educators need to remember that spirit cannot be taught in a traditional methodology. The quality we long for in teachers is not only for them to have to right technique, but for them to have the soul of a teacher. Teachers to be need to have a sense of having a calling-something that you do because you are uniquely suited for it, and therefore pursuing it throughout life. In Christian theology, this is known as a 'vocation'. To help teachers remain vital, we must recapture the deeper meaning of vocation:

- To be aware of one's vocation is to recognize that there is some mysterious combination of personal skill and passion
- To be convinced that they will be capable teachers
- The challenge is keeping the sense of purpose alive

Encouraging reflection that helps teachers to explore their reasons for teaching is one way of increasing vitality. The key to developing this kind of reflection is to make it a regular part of life, so that teachers to be can begin to internalize the process and develop their own means of self-reflection: engaging their souls.

Nurturing creativity may also be helping teachers to develop intrinsically. Creativity encourages vitality, engagement, sense of fulfillment and purpose. Good teaching can never be scripted. We need to encourage teachers to find their own creativity. Further, another inner quality that can be nurtured in teachers is a sense of wonder or awe. Wonder is not merely curiosity. Wonder is a deep desire to be present in the world, to witness the marvels of the children as they learn and grow and to be inspired to share this sense of wonder in the classroom.

I feel if education fails to feed the deeper-living forces then it represents not only the absence of good but becomes a source of ill. The body and soul needs nourishment. As I have argued earlier I feel spirituality envisions an inner path enabling a person to discover the essence of his being and is centered on the deepest values and meanings by which people live. As teachers, spiritual commitments are surely crucial in shaping one's world view and determining the existential space in which we live and teach. Thus as teacher educators and educational scholars we are on sound ground in including our spiritual commitments in our educational theory and practice.

We must spend less time telling teachers to be 'what to do' and more time showing them 'how to be' guiding trainees through processes of self-reflection with the hope of helping them to connect with their inner lives as teachers to be. The premise is that teaching requires more than knowledge, its relational nature draws on our souls, as our minds. We cannot afford to ignore the spiritual aspects of the personality in a Teacher Education programme. Teacher Education is ever evolving and dynamic. It must provide opportunities for understanding self and others including one's beliefs, assumptions, emotions, self-actualisation, adaptability, creativity, innovation and reflection. A personal vision is essential for students aspiring to be teachers to respond to complexities of life. Teachers are catalysts of change and models of inspiration which can only be achieved by 'engaging their souls'.

References

Da Ros-Voseles, D., & S. Fowler- Hangey. (2007). The role of dispositions in the education of future teachers. *Young Children* **62**(5): 90-98.

Gough, R.W. (1998). A practical strategy for emphasizing character development in sport and physical education. *Journal of Physical Education, Recreation & Dance,* **69**(2), 18-20,23.

Intrator, S., & Kunzman, R. (2006). The person in the profession. *Educational Forum,* 16-32.

Lumpkin, A., Stoll, S.K., & Beller, I.M. (2003). *Sport ethics: Applications for fair play* (3rd ed.). Boston: McGraw-Hill.

Pajak, E., & Blase, J. (1989). The impact of teacher's personal lives on professional role enactment: A qualitative analysis. *American Educational Research Jounal* 26 (2): 283-310.

Schon, D. (1987). *Educating the reflective practitioner.* San Francisco, CA: Jossey-Bass Publishers.

Serrow, R., Eaker, D., & J. Ciechalski. (1992). Calling, service, and legitimacy: Professional orientations and career commitment among prospective teachers. *Journal of Research and Development in Education* **25**(3): 136-141.

Skinner, B.F. (1968). *The technology of teaching.* Englewood Cliffs, NJ: Prentice Hall.

Solomon, G. (1997). Does physical education affect character development in students? *Journal of Physical Education, Recreation & Dance,* **68**(9), 38-41.

Wuthnow, R. (1994). *Producing the sacred: An essay on public religion. Chicago,* CA: University of Illinois Press.

8

Persian Influence in Bengal and Bengal's History Writing in Persian

Simanta Roy

Abstract

Among other region of India, Bengal was a vital place that can be considered as the most important centre for the foreign transaction. Consequently, Bengal came into contact with the Middle East and Iran. The Persian's Merchants and sailors used that Bengal ports for the commodities transaction. As a result a good relation made between Bengal and Iran and Along with Iranian merchants and commodities, soldiers and generals, engineers and craftsmen, Sufis and darwishes used to come to the Bengal. Persian language, literature and its culture actively came touch with Bengal from the establishment of Muslim Conquest in Bengal. From the beginning of Sultanate period to the end of the Mughal, in this Duration can be called the golden age of Persi culture in Bengal and also in India. Yet After the British invention in Bengal was influenced with the Persian language, as it was the Second language, After English. The Muslim rule was established in Bengal by the Turks. After the Turks successively came the Afghans and the Mughals as rulers of the country. Though Iran is neither contiguous to Bengal, nor did Iranians get a chance to establish their rule in this country, yet Iranian influence was consistently dominant in Bengal throughout the Muslim rule with their language, literature and culture. The compilation of numerous books on theology and mysticism by the Sufis, influenced the development of Persian language in Bengal. Thousands of books had written in Persian and hundreds of poets had been composed their poems in Persian. The excellent copies of these unique contributions have been preserved in different libraries of Bengal as well as in the sub-continent, either in books or in manuscript forms.

Keywords: *Persian language, Kulli people, Aryans, Sufis and darwishes*

Introduction

"Few people have been more closely related in origin and throughout history than the people of India and the people of Iran"

— Jawahar Lal Nehru

India has been always becoming familiar with the foreign languages and cultures and made them for Its very own. Knowing the other languages it does not mean, just to learn the grammar and pronunciation but it also shows the history, culture and literature of the part of the world from which the language comes. It gives a completely new perspective for viewing the world. Each language has its own peculiarity and there Persian holds a unique place.

The Turks established Muslim rule in Hindu Bengal. Though Iran is neither contiguous to Bengal, nor did Iranians get a chance to establish their rule in this country, yet Iranian influence was consistently dominant in Bengal throughout the Muslim rule; First the Turks, then the Afghans & Mughals. But people of Bengal welcomed Persian language by their heart for the sweetness of the language and its full-grown literatures.

Bengal is a large part of the former undivided India now divided into Bangladesh (former East Bengal) and the province of West Bengal in India. Bengali is the main language of both the parts. Persian language and culture was so rich and attractive that even the Turks and Afghans adopted Persian as the official language in Indian subcontinent under Muslim rule. Persian was the official language of Bengal throughout the Muslim Period and Persian literature enormously influenced Bengali literature. A countless Persian words entered into the Bengali language and literature and the official documents and the idiom of court circles. This was possible due to the immigration of many Iranians to Bengal in the train of Muslim conquest and in the service of the rulers. The Iranians came and engaged themselves either in peaceful pursuits or joined the army or the administration. Those of the first category included the *Ulama*, *teachers, poets* and those of the second category were the *subahdars, nazims*, and *diwans*. In the 18th century many *Shia* Muslims from Iran came and settled in the cities of Bengal: Hooghly, Murshidabad, Dhaka, etc. Whenever any Iranian officer came to Bengal he was accompanied by a number of his adherents and supporters. In this way people of Iranian origin increased, some made this country their home and settled and died here, while others left for their homes or for northern India.

And a significant contribution of Persian language is the books of Bengal's history, written in Persian: *Tabkat-i Nasari* in 1260 CE by *Minhaj-i-Siraj* in and *Riyaz-al-Salatin* in 1787-8 by *Ghulam Husaint Salim.*

Pre-Historical Background

Before knowing the Persian History with its contribution in Bengal, it is necessary to know about its pre-history and historical background in India and its sub-divisions. According to the historians in the pre-historical age the people of Persia and India were from same lineage, approximately they lived together in about 3000 to 2000 BC; their language, religion and the general life span were similar, therefore they are from one family. These two ancient neighboring civilizations had close historical links through the ages. They had a common homeland and shared a common linguistic and racial past. Over the several millennia, they interacted an enriched each other with the knowledge in fields of language, religion, arts, culture, food and other traditions.

The People of *Kulli*[i] culture of ancient India around 3000 BC had the inter-relation with Persia because of *Susa*[ii], an ancient city of Iran; some pieces of painted pottery were found which was made by the *Kulli* people before 3000 years BC. *Professor A.L. Basham* says: "During the pre-historic times (around 3000 BC), the people of *Kulli* culture (North West Indian borders) excelled in making small boxes of soft stone, delicately engraved with linear patterns. At *Susa* (west Iran) a few pieces of painted pottery have been found which appear to be similar to the wares of the *Kulli* people. In the hills of Baluchistan, where the people of *Nal*[iii] and *Zhob*[iv] cultures built their little villages, the *Barhuis*, though ethnically now predominantly Iranian, speak a Dravidian language (spoken in South India)".[1]

The people of Indo-Iranian family as Indian and Iranian people came from same source before the beginning of the Indo-Iranian civilization and on the other side they probably had the same tradition of culture, language and religion. They had been living equally about many centuries in the central Asia.

"It is believed that Indians and Iranians belonged to one single family before the beginning of the Indo-Aryan civilization and lived together with a common language for many centuries in pasturelands of Oxus valley in Central Asia (Tajikistan, Uzbekistan, Kyrgistan, Turkmenistan and Kazakstan)".[2]

It is believed that before 2000-3000 BC, the inhabitants of modern Iraq and southern Iran as also the people of west and north-west India came from the same region. Later, around 1500 BC, the Aryan tribes from north invaded and defeated these people and marched further to the parts of south Asia.[3]

The earliest invaders or settlers about whom anything at all definite is known were the people of the *Rig-Veda* hymns, who called themselves Aryans, and are conveniently designated as Indo-Aryans in order to distinguish them from their brethren who remained at the other side of the passes. They separated themselves sharply from the non-Aryan dark-skinned early inhabitants of India, and were no doubt tall and fair. They were akin to the Iranians or Persians, who also called themselves Aryans. It is certain that they slowly worked their way across the Punjab and down the courses of the Indus and Ganges. Probably they advanced as far as *Prayag*[v] at a tolerably early date.[4]

If we focus on the origin of the languages, the Bengali with some other Indian languages and Persian had came from the Indo-Iranian branch. And the Indo-Iranian is among one of the ten Indo-European branch of languages. Indo-Iranian is also called the Indo-Aryan but here the word *'Aryan'* is used in the narrow sense, and Indo-European as its broader meaning. The people of Indo-Iranian branch were proud to call themselves *'Aryan'*. Therefore the name Indo-Aryan came from this time. According to *Dr. Rameswer Shaw*, the sub-dialect of the main languages of Indo-European family, that entered India and Iran, is known as Indo-Iranian sub-dialect. The people of this branch of language is proud to call themselves '*Aryan*' as they were, but the word Aryan is understood here in a narrow sense.[5]

In Bengal Persian contribution started before the migration of Muslim. Unlike other sub-continent of India, Persia has come in contact with Bengal for their trade. The trade linked between the Indian ports of *Daybul, Nirun, Suparaka, Barygaza, Tagara, Muziris, Nelkynda, Ariake, Tamralipti, Gange, Saptagrama,* and *Sarandip* and the ports of *Ubulla, Omana, Eudaimon, Siraf, Qais,* and *Hormuz* along the *Persian Gulf*. Among them the ancient city ports of Bengal, *viz Tamralipti, Gange* and *Saptagram* or *Satgaon* were great centers of maritime trade and commerce in ancient days, attracting sailors and merchants from both the eastern and western seas. The importance of *Tamralipti* increased at the beginning of the Christian era due to the establishment of a brisk trade between Bengal, the Middle East and the *Greco-Roman* world.

Among other region of India Bengal was a vital place that can be considered as the most important centre for the foreign transaction. Consequently, Bengal came into contact with the Middle East and Iran. The Persian's Merchants and sailors used that Bengal ports for the commodities transaction. As a result a good relation made between Bengal and Iran and Along with Iranian merchants and commodities, soldiers and generals, engineers and craftsmen, *Sufis* and *darwishes* used to come to the Bengal, and began to culture each other language and tradition. The cultivation of the Persian language and the propagation of Islam started from before the establishment of the Muslim rule in Bengal. As people converted to Islam, they became acquainted with the Quran and *Sunnah* in Arabic, as well as in Persian, the language of the Sufi preacher. The compilation of numerous books on theology and mysticism by the Sufis, influenced the development of Persian language in Bengal.

Historical Background

History shows that the foreigners, who had been migrated from time to time to the fertile Indo-Gangetic plains and gradually moved to other parts of the country. The *Aryans, Semeiters, Mongoloids, Sakas, Kushans, Bactrians, Scythians,* and *Huns* in the ancient period and the *Uzbeks, Turkmans, Iranians* and *Afgahans* in the medieval period migrated to India, each bringing with them their beliefs, social customs, values and economic patterns, which contributed to forming the base of India's secular heritage. The most powerful elements have been the Dravidian and Indo-Aryan in the ancient times and the Indo-Muslim in the medieval period.[6]

Among other region of India, Bengal was a vital place that can be considered as the most important centre for the foreign transaction. Persian language, literature and its culture actively came close with Bengal from the establishment of Muslim Conquest in Bengal. From the beginning of Sultanate period to the end of the Mughal, in this Duration can be called the golden age of Farsi culture in Bengal and also in India. Yet After the British invention in Bengal was influenced with the Persian language, as it was the Second language, After English. The Muslim rule was established in Bengal by the Turks. After the Turks successively came the Afghans and the Mughals as rulers of the country.

In Sultanate period traders and mystics had contributed with a great extent to the spread of Persian language in the subcontinent as well as in Bengal, the language spread hastily throughout the subcontinent, and then Persian gained the status of court language.

During the Mughal period, Persian language and literature reached its uppermost stages of development in Bengal and greatly influenced the local language and literature. Contemporary and later chronicles and biographers have referred to the dignitaries of learning at the courts of the Mughal governors of Bengal: *Munim Khan, Islam Khan, Qasim Khan, Shah Shuja, Shayesta Khan and Mir Jumla.* These governors encouraged Persian poetry and offered asylums to many poets.

In 1757 AD, *Nawab Sirajuddaula* was defeated by the East India Company at the Battle of Plassey, ushering in British rule. Persian, however, continued to be the dominating language during the first century of British rule in Bengal. In 1765 *Mirza I'tesamuddin* accompanied Captain *Archibald Swinton* to Europe and wrote his travels in Persian under the title of *Shigurfnama-i-wilayat*. Among other Persian writings of this period are *Seir-al Motaakkherin* (1783 AD) of *Golam Hossein Tabatabai, Siraj-ussalatin* (1787 AD) of *Golam Hossein Selim, Tarikhe Bangalah* (1763 AD) of *Munshi Salimullah*. Considering the position of Persian in society, the British Government was obliged to continue Persian as an official language for eighty years (1757 to 1837 AD) after the establishment of its dominance in the region.

In 1882 AD, *Nawab Abdool Luteef*, highlighting the social importance of the study of Arabic and Persian, expressed his comments to the Hunter Education Commission as follows: 'Unless a Mohamedan is a Persian and Arabic scholar, he cannot attain a respectable position in Mohamedan society; he will not be regarded as a scholar. And unless he has such a position, he can have no influence in the Mohamedan community.

By the middle of the 19th century, however, the importance of Persian faded in Bengal. The use of Persian as an official language was prohibited by Act no. XXIX of 1837 passed by the president of the Council of India in Council, on the 20th November 1837 which read in part:

(I) It is hereby enacted, that from the First Day of December 1837, it shall be lawful for the Governor General of India in Council, by an Order in Council, to dispense, either generally, or within such local limits as may to him seem meet, with any provision of any Regulation of the Bengal Code which enjoins the use of the Persian language in any Judicial proceeding, or in any proceeding relating to the Revenue and to prescribe the language and character to be used in such proceedings.

(II) And it is hereby enacted, that from the said day it will be lawful for the said Governor General for India in Council, by an order in Council, to delegate all or any of the powers given to him by this Act, to any subordinate Authority, under such restrictions as may seem meet.

Influence of Persian in Bengali Language and Literature

We saw that there are close kinship between Persian and Bengali language, Many Persian wards appear in Bengali vocabulary and several Persian books were translated into Bengali and some Bengali books there also been translated in Persian during Sultan, Mughal and sometime in British, for more than 600 years, an age of cultural assimilation set in and continued. Except the language, there are strong illustrations that the correlation of the theme and thought between Perso-Bengsli literature. And the distinctive stream of medieval Bengali Literature, which was inspired by Sufism. The compilation of numerous books on theology and mysticism by the Sufis, influenced the development of Persian language in Bengal. Thousands of books had written in Persian and hundreds of poets had been composed their poems in Persian. The excellent copies of these unique contributions have been preserved in different libraries of Bengal as well as in the sub-continent, either in books or in manuscript forms.

Bengali Literature praises of Allah and the Prophet Muhammad

The tradition of Persian literature specially flows by praising of *Allah* and the

Prophet Muhammad. This was a consistent practice of the Iranian writers of epics and long narratives like *Ferdousi, Sadi*, and *Attar*. This tradition was followed by the Muslim poets of Bengali literature, when the *'Pondit Kobi' Alaol* wrote *Padmavati*, the story of a Hindu princess, or when *Daulat Qazi* wrote the story of *Sati Maina*, another Hindu princess, they started by hymning the praises of *Allah* and His Prophet.

The Sufis and the Mystic Literature in Bengal

The Sufis played a major role in preaching Islam in this country. Both the literary and folk traditions in Bengal were shaped by Sufi mysticism. The literary tradition fall into two categories: philosophical exposition of the theory and practice of mysticism, and the tradition of songs, mainly *padavalis*. The folk tradition consists mainly of the traditions of *Baul* and *Murshidi* songs, which describe the different stages that a disciple should pass through in order to reach the final stage of illumination and self-annihilation. Among the writers of the philosophic tradition are *Haji Muhammad* and *Syed Sultan*.

Haji Muhammad's Noor Jamal is more philosophical than *Syed Sultan's Jnan Pradip*. *Haji Muhammad* tells his readers about *Shariat*, and then goes deep into the philosophical expositions of different theories about *wahdatul wujud*, pantheism. He also discusses the different theories of *Ibn-ul-Arabi* and *Mujaddid-i-Alf-e-Sani*. The popular *Murshidi* and *Baul* songs are deeply philosophical. Most of the *Murshidi* songs found in Bengal are influenced by *Maulana Jalal Uddin Rumi's* Masnavi and *Shaikh Fariduddin Attar's Mantiq-ut-Tair*.[7]

'Dobhasi' Literature

Persian influenced what is known as *dobhasi* literature, literally literature of two languages. Even today the practice of using Arabic and Persian words in order to describe a typically Muslim context is very common. Thus, in *dobhasi* literature, if a Muslim court was described, a Muslim king addressed, Islamic thoughts and ideals and the Quran or the holy books referred to, Muslim saints and learned men mentioned, Arabic and Persian words were used. This was true of both Muslim and Hindu writers. *Shah Muhammad Sagir*, the great Bengali poet of the court of *Sultan Ghiasuddin Azam Shah* (1389-1410 AD), referred to holy books as *kitab*, learned men as *aliman*. *Zainuddin* (15th century AD) used a host of these prototypical phrases and words in his *Rasulbijay*: *taj* was used instead of *mukut*, *sawar* instead of *arohi*, *dada* instead of *pitamaha*. This becomes more conspicuous in a later poet like *Syed Sultan* (1550-1648 AD) who, in *Shab-i-Miraj*, used words such as *Allah, Rasule Khuda, Noore Muhammadi, peer paigambar,* in addition to *kitab, aliman, alim*.

Of the *dobhasi* puthi writers following this tradition, the most famous are *Gharibullah*, author of *Yusuf-Zulekha* and *Amir Hamza* (1st part) and *Hatem Tai*.

The traditional *dobhasi* love-story has certain common features: immutability in love, bravery and heroism. During the early eighteenth century, this tradition of writing got mixed up with the tradition of writing on the fantastic exploits of heroes in *Bijay Kavyas*. In most of the narratives of *dobhasi* literature there was a growing tradition of escapism, Fairy Tale, romance and fantastic adventures.

The first works in this tradition are *Yusuf-Zulekha* and Amir Hamza (1st part) of *Gharibullah.* The next important poet is *Syed Hamza* who wrote *Madhumalati* in the traditional linguistic style but resorted to *Persianized dobhasi* style in *Amir Hamza* (2nd part), *Jaiguner Puthi* and *Hatem Tai. Arif's Mrigavati* and *Shahnama* and *Janab Ali's Shaheede Karbala* can also be mentioned here. Moreover, the tales of the Arabian Nights were adapted in this linguistic and thematic style. There were at least three such versions: *Mafizuddin Ahmad's Keccha Alif-Laila, Raushan Ali's Alif Laila* and the third, and the most popular, version by *Syed Nasir Ali, Habibul Hossain* and *Aizuddin Ahmed.*[8]

There was substantial Persian influence on the different genres of Bengali Literature like Heroic Verse, Romantic Narratives, Historical Narratives and Religious Verse.

Zainuddin's Rasulbijay, Rasulbijay and *Hanifer Digbijay* of *Shah Barid (or Sabirid) Khan*, *Muhammad Khan's Hanifar Larai, Gharibullah's Janganama, Heyat Mahmud's Janganama* and *Syed Hamza's Amir Hamza* are the best examples of Heroic Verse. There the Romantic Narratives are also played an important role. Most significant writers in the field were *Shah Muhammad Sagir,* the author of *Yusuf-Zulekha, Daulat Qazi* of *Arakan,* author of *Chandrani* or *Sati Maina; Alaol*, the writer of Padmavati, Saiful Mulk Badiuzzamal, Haft Paikar and Sikander Nama; Abdul Hakim, author of Yusuf-*Zulekha; Quraishi Magan Thakur*, author of *Mrigavati; Abdul Nabi,* author of *Amir Hamza; Heyat Mamud*, author of *Janganama; Muhammad Mukim* writer of *Mrigavati* and etc.

The first important writer of historical narratives is *Syed Sultan,* in *Nabi Bangsha*; he narrates the life and history of the Prophet Muhammad. Other is *Muhammad K*han, he had written a book titled *Maqtul Hussain.* And in the genre of Religious Verse, *Muzammil* one of the earliest writers who wrote *Neeti-Shastravarta*. *Afzal Ali* preaches the rules and regulations of Islam in his *Nasihatnamah,* which follows the style of the *Mangalkavyas*. *Nasrullah Khan* In his *Shariatnamah*, tells Muslims what the orders of God are and warns them against doing what God has forbidden.

Writing the History of Bengal in Persian

Other hand it is also important that writing the history of Bengal in Persian. Mainly two great books were written in Persian language in Bengal. *Tabkat-i Nasari* in 1260 AD by *Minhaj-i-Siraj* and *Riyaz-al-Salatin* in 1787-8 AD by *Ghulam Husaint Salim.*

Tabkat-i Nasari; We have had so far about Bengal history are from different sources that have defined the Bengal history from different angles, but no attempts have so far been made to treat the history of Bengal in the light of some specific medieval sources dealing with politics, administration, society, and economics of Bengal. In this respect, *Tabaqat-i-Nasiri* of *Minhaj Uddin* us *Siraj* is of immense importance to know about the history of this region.[9]

Minhaj al-Siraj Juzjani, full name *Abu Osman Minhajuddin* bin *Sirajuddin* was born in *Ghur* in 1193 AD. In 1227, Minhaj Uddin us Siraj migrated to Ucch then to Delhi.[10] Juzjani was the principal historian for the *Mamluk Sultanate* of Delhi in northern India.[11] He started planning to leave in India in 1221 AD. Minhaj Uddin us Siraj left for India in 1227 AD and reached Uchch. His stayed at Lakhnauti, capital of Bengal for nearly 3 years (1241-1242 and 1243-1244 AD), enabled him to get accurate information about the outlying and he wrote Tabaqat-i Nasiri (1260 CE) for *Sultan Nasir ud din Mahmud* of Delhi.[12]

"Tabaqat-i-Nasiri's meaning calls for some explanation. Literally, the word means a "layer" but it is used for a class or order, race or generation. Its connotation concerns both space and time. Earlier, the term was used for the royal houses of Iran only, but latter on it was used for others also (*shuara, sufiya, fiqaha, attribute*). In *Hadist,* this terminology indicates those who transmit *Hadist* one generation to the others."[13]

He has given an eyewitness account of the conquests of Ikhtiar-uddin Muhammad Bakhtyar Khalji in Bengal. The entire chapter of this book goes through the military exploits of Bakhtyar Khalji in Bengal. But the significant approach was the thirteenth century Bengal history was kinness with which Minhaj Uddin us Siraj observed the contemporary social background. Besides giving the graphic description of every military encounter of Bakhtyar Khalji, Minhaj Uddin us Siraj always focused with curiosity on the social formation in Bengal. Minhaj Uddin us Siraj appeared to be particularly interested in describing military strategies. If one goes along the line of narration given by Minhaj Uddin us Siraj, it appears that Bakhtyar Khalji had used both military powers and strategic deception to conquer Nadia. Since Minhaj Uddin us Siraj stopped his narrative about Bengal with the incident of Bakhtiar Khalji's assassination, he did not mention any thing about the administration in Bengal. It is presumable that Bakhtiar Khalji did not get any time to organize his administration.[14]

Riyaz-al-Salatin: Riyaz-al-Salatin the first complete history of the Muslim rule in Bengal. Written in Persian language by Ghulam Husain Salim Zaidpuri.

Ghulam Husaint Salim was a historian who migrated to Bengal and was employed there as a post-master to the East India Company. Ghulam Husain Salim died in 1817 AD and lies buried at *Malda* town in the quarter known as *'Chak Qurban Ali'*.

Ghulam Husain Salim composed the book At George Udny's (a Commercial Resident of the East India Company) request and completed in 1787-8 AD. It covers the whole Muslim rule from Bakhtiyar's conquest of Nadia in 1204-05 AD to the battle of Palashi in 1757. He divided the introductory chapter into four sections: (i) boundaries, geographical and topographical features and population; (ii) characteristics of the country, origin of the people of Bengal and some features of the living condition; (iii) description of some cities; (iv) a brief sketch of the Hindu rule in Bengal. The rest he divided into four chapters; the first three are: (i) the sultans of Delhi and their governors, (ii) independent sultans of Bengal, and (iii) Mughal rule in Bengal. He divided the fourth chapter into two parts - the first part deals with the Christians, the Portuguese, the Dutch, the French etc. (other than the English) and the second part deals with the coming of the English and the establishment of their rule in Bengal.

Notes

(i) *The Kulli culture was a prehistoric culture in southern Balochistan (Gedrosia) in Pakistan ca. 2500 - 2000 BC. The pottery and other artifacts are similar to those of the Indus Valley Civilization and it is not clear whether the Kulli culture is a local variation of the Indus Valley Civilization or an own culture complex. The culture is named after an archaeological site discovered by Sir Aurel Stein. More than 100 settlement sites are known but very few are excavated. Some of them have the size of small towns and are similar to those of the Indus Valley Civilization. The houses are built of local stone along streets. The latter are sometimes paved. There are stairs on the street for getting access to higher levels. The settlements are often placed at important strategic positions on small hills overlooking the surrounding country side. Most settlements are close to dams. Murda Sang is one town, about 35 ha big. The latest occupation level belongs to the Kulli culture.*

(ii) *The modern Iranian town of Shush is located at the site of ancient Susa. Shush is the administrative capital of the Shush County of Iran's Khuzestan province*

(iii) *Nal culture, was one of the pre-historic culture of Asia, is located in western Pakistan and mostly in Khuzdar a district in Baluchistan, archaeological sites are very attractive for the archaeologists all over the world Nal culture site was excavated in 1925.*

(iv) *Zhob' is a valley in north Baluchistan, western Pakistan, with a number of sites of a Chalcolithic culture, Rana Ghundai, Periano Ghundai, and Moghul Ghundai are*

the best-known sites. The potterys have founded from this era, by the people lived over here arround c 4th-3rd millennia B.C, is painted black or red over a red slip; decoration may be stylized humped cattle and buck and groups of vertical lines linking narrow horizontal bands. Other artifacts include female figurines and copper. Buildings were of mudbrick and burials by cremation. Related material was found stratified beneath that of the Indus Civilization at Harappa, and there are similarities to the painted ware of Tepe Hissar in northern Iran. This phase was succeeded by the 'Incinerary Pot' phase, with burials placed in vessels under house floors, after disarticulation and some cremation.

(v) Prayag or Prayaga is the earlier name of the city Allahabad, Prayaga existed during the Vedic period, and is mentioned in the Veda as the location where Brahma, the Creator of the Universe according to Hindu mythology. Mughal Emperor Akbar in changed Prayag as Allahabad in 1583. The name in Indian languages generally is Ilahabad; ilah being Arabic for "Lord" or "God (Allah)" and -abad is Persian for "to construct or to create a garden", which explains the meaning of the name Allahabad as "Garden of Allah".

References

Basham, A.L. (1967). The Wonder that was India, p. 14.

Nafisi, Saeed. (1949). The Indo-Iranian relation. New Delhi, p. 349.

Jorfi, Abdul Amir. (Oct-Dec 1994). Iran and India: Age old Friendship'. India Quarterly, p. 69.

Vincent, A. Smit. (1919). The Oxford History of India: Oxford at the Clarendon Press. Book-I, Ancient India, Chapter –I, pp.6-7.

Shaw, Dr. Rameswer. (1996). General Linguistica and the Bengali Language (Sadharan Bhasavijnan O Banla Bhasa). Pustak Bipani. Calcutta. ISBN 81-85471-12-6.

Kapoor, Subodh. (2002). The Indian Encyclopaedia. Cosmo Publications. ISBN 81-7755-257-0. p. 6495.

Abu Musa Mohammad Arif Billah: http://www.banglapedia.org/HT/P_0166.htm.

Ibid.

Sarkar, Dr Anil Kumar. (October 2013). Tawarikh: International Journal for Historical Studies, **5**(1) C.E.

Bosworth. (1977). The Later Ghaznavids. Columbia University Press, p. 112.

Shafique, N. Virani. (2007). The Ismailis in the Middle Ages: A History of Survival, A Search for Salvation. Oxford University Press. 23; "Minhaj-i-Siraj Juzjani, the foremost historian of the Delhi Sultanate, wrote his "Nasirid Generations" (Tabaqat-i Nasiri)...."

Ali, Duad. (2012). Indian Historical Writing c.600-c.1400; The Oxford History of Historical Writing: Vol. 2: 400-1400. Oxford University Press. 94.

Sarkar, Dr Anil Kumar. (October 2013). Tawarikh: International Journal for Historical Studies, 5(1).

Ibid.

9

Peace Education—A Need of Hour

Neeti Trivedi

Abstract

In the 21st century we have reached the pinnacle of technological advancement yet along with the positive achievements, we are also confronted with depressing influences such as inequality, materialism, stress, overwork and social pressure. In many parts of the world, civil society suffers because of situations of violent conflicts and war. It is important to recognize the crucial role of education in contributing to building a culture of peace and condemning instances in which education is undermined in order to attack democracy and tolerance. Peace is the felt-need of the hour. Peace is the cherished goal of mankind. It cannot be achieved by peaceful measures and cannot be enjoyed by a group of people or a particular country exclusive of others. It can be realized only through mutual understanding, international harmony and world brotherhood. Education is the key to uniting nations, bringing human beings closely together. Education which promotes such international understanding, fellow-feeling and brotherhood is called Peace Education. It must enable the human being to be in peace irrespective of caste, creed, colour and geographical location. Peace education in an era of 21st century to bring down the stress level and flaring up and enable the people to enjoy their life peacefully in a meaningful way. Peace education play an important role in promoting the culture of peace, non-violence and tolerance by which human beings learns to live together with peace and harmony at individual level, which will intern effect at global level. Peace education aims to help students acquire skills for non-violent conflict resolution and to reinforce these skills, for active and responsible action in the society for the promotion of the values of peace. The aim of this paper to show lights on meaning of peace education, its importance in today's time and its role in conflict resolution.

Keywords: *Peace education, conflict resolution, succumbing*

'Peace is not merely the absence of war but the presence of justice, of law, of order- in short, of Government'

— **Albert Einstein**

Introduction

The significance of 21st century has been the emergency of information era, which has brought human kind into the age of universal communication by abolishing distance. Now the most accurate and up to date information can be made available to anyone in the world within the click of mouse. Today the world is shrinking to a global village on one hand there is growing intolerance violence, race, caste, sex creed discrimination and fanciticism. There is no denying fact that the crime is also becoming globalised. Easy with money information can now cross frontiers, has facilitated illegal trade of drugs, arms nuclear armaments and even human beings as well as encouraging terrorism and criminal networks. Arms race has touched a new high creating a world with dark and uncertain future sitting over a huge pile of dangerous and destructive nuclear weapons which is no longer simply a deterrent intended to ensure against the risk of war between the countries. The rise of conflict between the nations is marginalized.

As a result, many people are succumbing to negative emotions such as retaliation, intolerance, hatred etc. the results of such negative emotions is aggression at an individual level and violence, disharmony and eventually terrorism at the collective level. The recent incidents in various parts of the world and the resultant media coverage has brought to fore the necessity of peace in society and the world at large. Perhaps peace education thinkers think peace can be taught like war is taught, but the reality is that neither war nor peace can be taught since they are learning concepts. Violence and war are products of the mis-education of a privileged minority and the non-education of a poor majority in many parts of the world. Looking at the world today any sensible person feels disheartened and even horrified to see the kind of violent acts being committed by man against man and nature, women feel unsecured to move alone. It is sad to realize that we live in an era of unprecedented violence, in the form of terrorism where crime is just an operation and exploitation amidst a seemingly out world development enjoyed by a few, the majority of mankind lives in stark society, struggling for survival. In the modern shrinking world, one cannot keep himself aloof from others. All are interrelated and share the same destiny-sorrows and sufferings, happiness and prosperity. Mankind is threatened with nuclear holocaust and mass devastation today. Peace is the felt-need of the hour. It has been eulogized through ages. It has been desired by mankind most and the two world wars have cast shadow of despair in the living human memory. Peace is the cherished goal of mankind. It cannot be achieved by peaceful measures and cannot be enjoyed by a group of people or a particular country exclusive of others. It can be realized only through mutual understanding, international harmony and world brotherhood. Education which promotes such international understanding, fellow-feeling and brotherhood is called *Peace Education*. It must enable the human being to be in peace irrespective of caste, creed, colour and geographical location.

Meaning of Peace Education

In general, peace education may be defined as "the process of acquiring the values, the knowledge and developing the attitudes, skills and behaviours to live in harmony with oneself, with others and with the natural environment. Peace education is about helping students to understand and transform conflict in their own lives, in the community and in the world at large. It is part of all learning areas and is reinforced by people treating each other in positive ways in classrooms, playgrounds and in their families and communities.

Peace education is an essential component of quality basic education. It is concerned with helping learners to develop an awareness of the process and skills that are necessary for achieving understanding, tolerance and goodwill in the world today. Peace education is concerned with helping learners to develop and awareness of the process and skills that are necessary for achieving understanding, tolerance and goodwill in the world today.

Peace education encompasses the key concepts of education and peace. Peace education aims to help students acquire skills for non-violent conflict resolution and to reinforce these skills, for active and responsible action in the society for the promotion of the values of peace. Therefore, unlike the concept of conflict resolution, which can be considered retroactive, trying to solve a conflict after it has already occurred-peace education has a more proactive approach. Its aim is to prevent a conflict in advance or rather to educate individuals and a society for a peaceful existence on the basis of nonviolence, tolerance, equality, respect for differences, and social justice.

Peace education is a broader discipline, disarmament education, human rights education, environmental action, education for non-violence, education for international understanding and global education are the branches of peace education. Peace education concerned with the peace ideas, peace studies and peace activities. It deals with conflicts arising out of injustice or exploitation. Peace education is a science with studies the basic need of man and woman and the true nature of society in which these needs to be satisfied and aware the learners towards human rights and structurally violence and non-violence in creating a culture peace in building a non-violent and just society.

Importance of Peace Education

Peace is one way in which human betterment is interpreted, as the seventeenth century Czech educator Comeniu, first acknowledged peace educator, recognized. Peace to prevail peace education is significant and would be possible by sowing in the minds of the learners and the people in general the seeds of spirituality, human rights knowledge, and human values and by learning to live as well as to dismantle the present conflict and violence culture. Violence is emerging in an unprecedented manner in human society. Looking at the world today any sensible person feels disheartened and even horrified to see the kind of violent acts being committed by man against man and nature. It is sad to realize that we live in an era of unprecedented violence in the forms of terrorism, war, crimes, injustice and oppression and exploitation amidst a seemingly outward development enjoyed by a few. The majority of mankind lives in stark poverty, struggling for bare survival. There is so much disorder and confusion in the society man has built for himself.

The saddest part of the story is that this state of disorder and confusion in the society is affecting the children's innocent minds. Children naturally absorb the spirit of violence in the atmosphere and will soon grow to be the next generation of perpetuators of violence. Therefore the need to nurture peace in the hearts of children has arisen as urgent issues to be addressed.

Peace education is a remedial measure to protect children from falling into the way of violence in society. It aims at the total development of the child. It tries to inculcate higher human and social values in the mind of the child. In essence it attempts to develop a set of behavioural skills necessary for peaceful living and peace building from which the whole of humanity will benefit.

Importance of Peace

Peace is important because it precisely means human life. Amongst the basic rights of mankind the first one is protecting life. This rights infringed around the world today. The most important factor that reflects the importance of peace is psychological comfort. If you don't have psychological comfort at first you are stressed then depressed and then may go crazy and have a suicide. Because if a person doesn't have this psychological comfort and living with the fear of death, he cannot do anything correctly; he cannot go anywhere and in the end begin to lose the control of himself, his logic and his brain. Even he cannot eat because of that fear, so the importance of our psychological balance is the most important so no-one can say "if peace is permanent like all other goods, the services of health care and education work continually. By this way people gather around a specific aim. Human learns to have respect for other's ideas, religions, points of views and most importantly learns to have respect for other's freedom. Finally, importance of peace is seen clearly and opposite of peace "war" is understood to be end of existence of every kind of creature. *One can easily see that peace is necessity but why it cannot be provided? Answer of this question is up to you. Does anyone have one?*

Aims of Peace Education

Peace education is about helping students to understand and transfer conflict in their own lives, in the community, and in the world at large. It is part of all learning areas and is reinforced by people treating each other in positive ways in classrooms, playgrounds and in their families and communities are cultural dialogue as a body of common and shared values for guiding peaceful conduct and relations among peoples, come education for peace should promote key values in various faiths and ethnic national groups that have been recognized through interfaith and nations, such as peace, compassion, justice, love, respect, kindness, freedom, tolerance, empathy, responsibility, discipline, patience, mercy, honor, benevolence, fairness, equity, diversity, forgiveness, sincerity, acceptance, truthfulness, harmony, truth, hope.

Need of Peace Education

All over the world, a great deal of emphasis is currently being placed upon peace education, as the quest for peace necessitates extensive knowledge and unfailing assiduity. The widespread interest in preparing individuals for peace on earth makes us resort to the teaching-learning process. The inevitability of this emphasis upon education for peace has arisen not only from the need to educate the public opinion of the scourges of war, its prodigality or the danger of total annihilation etc., but also from the necessity to promote understanding, acceptance and friendship among all peoples and nations, and to strengthen respect for human rights and fundamental freedoms.

Learning to make a living is not the sole reason for getting education, there is another, equally important byproduct: learning to make a life, life that is beneficial, useful and peaceful. After all, humans are social animals, their success in life is largely a matter of successful social relations. Quite evidently, student age is the crucially important period which enriches one's personal life, nurtures social adjustments, fosters friendship and affects one's whole life pattern. *Peace Begins in the Minds of Children*

Most people recognize instinctively the role of education in preventing conflict and in building peace. Education is also part of the social and political landscape, and contributes directly to growth, peace and stability. The benefits of education are lasting because the children who acquire them will transfer them to the next generation.

Mahatma Gandhi once stated, "If we are to reach real peace in this world we shall have to begin with the children." Lasting peace may depend on educating future generations into the competencies, perspectives, attitudes, values, and behavioral patterns that will enable them to build and maintain peace.

Education is the key to uniting nations, bringing human beings closely together. In many parts of the world, civil society suffers because of situations of violent conflicts and war. It is important to recognize the crucial role of education in contributing to building a culture of peace and condemning instances in which education is undermined in order to attack democracy and tolerance.

Humanity faces challenges of unprecedented proportions such as the continued development of weapons of mass destruction, conflicts between states and ethnic groups, the spread of racism, community violence, the huge widening gap between the rich and the poor throughout the globalised economy, massive violation of human rights and the degradation of the environment. These issues are a stumbling block to the attainment of world order. In order to tackle these complex and interwoven problems, there is need to make the preventive measures and solutions to these problems deeply routed in the minds of the populations. This justifies the need for peace education, which should focus on human security and how to live in a world infested with diversity.

Conclusion

We need peace education for ourselves, our relationship with other human beings to promote respect for oneself and respect for others on individual level as a prerequisite for the prevention of violence and conflict at society level and to raise people's consciousness about their rights whilst promoting international understanding between the people of different worlds.

Peace education as a formal subject must be said has arisen primarily in the western world and the developing world is in pursuit. This hardly means that peace education was cultivated only in the west, but it does mean that the mainstream peace education field has cultivated assumptions that are grounded in western traditions, examples being, peace education approaches centering on school children and yet in poor African (Ugandan) settings, children drop out of school often in the early formal education process.

References

Harris, L.M. (2013). Conflict Resolution and Peace Education: Transformations across disciplines. *Journal of Peace Education*. Retrieved on 1st December 2014. www.tandfonline.com

Kumar, R. (2014). Education and Peace: A Gandhian Perspectives. Retrieved on 15th December 2014. http://www.mkgandhi.org/articles/education_peace.htm

Manoharan, P.K. (2009). *Higher Education*. A.P.H Publishing Coropration. New Delhi.

Mayor, F. (2014). What is Peace Education. Retrieved on 15th December 2014. http://www.ncte-india.org/pub/unesco/ch1.htm

Mohanty, J. (2004). *Modern Trends in Indian Education*. Deep and Deep Publications Pvt. Ltd. New Delhi.

Mishra, L. (2010). *Encyclopedia of Peace Education.* APH Publishing Corporation. New Delhi.

10

Peace Education in Indian Schools

Nasrin

This paper highlights the following points :

1. What is Peace Education ?
2. Indian Society and Peace Education
3. Peace Education; need of the time
4. Peace Education and School Curriculum
5. Conclusion

The word education has been derived from the latin word 'educare', 'to draw' or 'lead out'. Peace education draws out from people their instincts to live peacefully with others and emphasizes peaceful values upon which society should be based. Peace education is the process of acquiring the values, the knowledge and developing the attitudes, skills, and behaviors to live in harmony with oneself, with others and with the natural environment. Peace education has both short and long term goals. Peace educators address the sources of immediate conflicts and give their students knowledge about strategies they can use to stop the violence. In the long term they hope to build in student's minds a commitment to nonviolence and provide knowledge about non-violent alternatives, so that when faced with conflicts they will choose to behave peacefully. In this way peace education tries to build peace into the minds of the students.

Letus look at some of the outstanding characteristics of our Indian society to see wherein they represent strength and wherein weaknesses, and to discover the major lines of improvement that need to be undertaken. One of the chief characteristic is that our society is democratic. Speaking generally and noting certain exceptions, we are free to worship as we want; we speak and write freely, we can engage in business and industry; we can seek employment in our chosen work; we can change from one employer to another; we can move freely in any part, of the country without social or political restrictions, etc. But at present we are living in turbulent times. We have weathered the crisis and continue to be confronted with formidable problems of poverty, illiteracy, malnutrition and disease. Terrorism has become major challenge of our times. It has assumed new forms. Violent groups use modern communications and the media to dramatize their demands. Their contempt for human life borders on barbarism. Violent acts by individuals or groups are indefensible-at the national and international level. Under such circumstances, we must show consideration to one another, under all circumstances and at all times. One may be permitted to add that it might constitute the prime consideration governing all human social action. Individuals; do indeed have rights - rights to self-realization and self-fulfillment, but they have, at the same time, obligations too to meet. The principal such obligation is to respect similar rights of others. This would be true of each and every conglomeration of individuals if a just and mutually beneficial workable order is to be established. Man is a social animal functioning in a complex network of multifarious human relationships, ranging from a family commune to international intercourse of diverse kinds between nations.

The disregarding of this fundamental feature of an orderly society, would inevitably lead to conflict, discord, anti-social activities, disruption and disintegration of the social fabric be it the relationship between nations in their dealing with one another. To spell out some of its operational features, it may be stated that an enlightened social outlook would require that the rights, of the weaker sections of the society-the economically and socially backward be given over-riding consideration because of their disadvantaged position and plight and their inability to help themselves adequately. It should be open to all' citizens, irrespective of their race, caste, colour, or creed to participate in the political, economic, social and cultural life of a nation in accordance with their aptitude and be duly tolerant and respectful towards each other's sub-cultures.

It would not be out of place to quote Pandit Nehru, who spoke many years ago about developing a scientific temper. A scientific temper does not mean just using high technology seeing to it that things work properly. We have to seek peace to pursue our development. Prevailing tensions pose a threat to our progress and prosperity. We have to make a conscious effort to remain outside the vertex of these tensions. These tensions have brought about changes in the entire scene, of democracy and democratic way of life.

Now this is a time for people in Education to accept this challenge and to provide 'Education for peace' in the context of present circumstances. The basic questions are what is peace in relation to school education? how can education contribute to peace? What can the school do in this regard?

The first question is what is peace? There is an oft quoted maxim, "If you want peace prepare for war. It is an advice to bear yourself whether you are in quarrel or not so that all possible opposers may beware of thee". After the sequel to the storm Noah sent out a dove which returned with a no live branch. The dove now is a symbol of peace. Surprising though in some cases the dove is dovetailed with war. In a society torn by terrorism industrialism, exploitation; injustice, mankind is faced with problem of offering the olive branch to avert violence which threatens to destroy the edifice of such a civilization.

Regarding the second question we all agree that the school must teach the 'methods of intelligence'; or the 'what', 'why' and 'when' of schooling are found 'in the potential of individual learner'; or the task of the learning must be organized around thc 'significant problems of a changing society' with a broad objective, i.e. to educate the students, to develop caring and understanding of others, and that they are to participate at different avenues in a democracy in a peaceful manner.

Education for peace should not be included as a separate subject in the school curriculum, but its notions should be integrated in the total school curriculum especially in social studies, languages, moral education and community studies. The following are the peace notions:

- Economic and social justice
- Religions and their basic principles.
- International organizations i.e. U.N. its character on human rights.
- Peace through country's constitutional rights
- Feeling of universal brotherhood
- Non-aggressive interaction within family, school, community and society.

The following ideas could be introduced and discussed as clements of concepts:

- thc pupil's self respect should be developed.
- Pupils should be conscious of being members of a family, a community with rights and certain duties. Each individual is a part of a whole, and there is interdependence and exchange through constant interaction.
- Friendly exchange of ideas is necessary
- Pupils should be a conscious of the fact that a human being is one among many living beings.
- Pupils should develop an ability to learn from event which take place in society and from other members.

Thus an ability to observe, study and resolve conflicts may emerge. Peace Education should be considered with both cognitive and moral values, and should lead to action.

The following topics can be included in the social studies curriculum at the middle school level.

1. Non-Violence - meaning and importance, Gandhiji's philosophy of Ahimsa
2. Conflicts within society - religious, political, lingual etc.
3. Human aggression, devoid self-understanding, and good- will towards humanity.
4. The struggle for survival of national interests.
5. Respect and regards to others. The concept of human dignity
6. Universality.

At the high school level the basic concepts of Peace Education shall be:

- Personal Violence
- Structural Violence
- Negative and Positive Peace

Core topics shall be:

- Conceptual clarification
- Human aggression
- Internal conflicts
- Non-Violence
- International organizations and their role.

The great advantage of including peace notions in school curriculum is to provide an opportunity to the school students to view our problems in broader perspective context and with a sense of consciousness. We normally think of these problems keeping in our mind our own socio-economic and geographical set up. As we view the problems for a better social order here, we must apply our minds to its national as well as international aspect. So far as the first one is concerned problems will differ from country to country but with many common features, there are no great differences in the aims and objectives for which educationists of vision and goodwill are serving in different countries. We conceive of good life not merely in terms of the satisfaction of our material needs but also in terms of our socio-cultural and spiritual needs.

I am sure in our discussion we will have an opportunity to discuss the common problems and solution to these problems, and we will eventually find that basic human identities are more important than the differences and that a rightly conceived program of peace education can inculcate Attitudes and values which, are as applicable as vitally important for the preservation and improvement of our democracy.

At the end I would like to quote what Jesus said and pray that we all remember it while we are struggling to bring peace and goodness in all the societies of the world.

"Do your best, add goodness to your faith; to your faith add knowledge; to your knowledge add self-control, to your self-control add endurance to your endurance add Godliness, to your Godliness add brotherly love, to your brotherly love add love. These are the qualities you need, and if you love them in abundance they will make you active and effective".

References

Banta, B. (1993). *Peaceful Peoples: An Annotated Bibliography* (Metuchen, N.J.: Scarecrow Press).

Boulding, E. (2000). *Cultures of Peace: The Hidden Side of History*. Syracuse, NY: Syracuse University Press.

Brocke-Utne, B. (1985). *Educating for Peace: A Feminist Perspective*. New York: Pergamon Press.

Diaz, J.C. (1979). "Reflections on Education for Justice and Peace". *Bulletin of Peace Proposals*, Vol. 10, No. 4, 374-381.

Harris, I. (1988). *Peace Education*. Jefferson, NC: McFarland & Co.

Heater, D. (1984). *Peace through Education*. London: Falmer Press.

Johnson, D. and Johnson, R. (1991).*Teaching Students to be Peacemakers*. Edina, MN: Interaction Press.

Mushakoji, K. (1974). "Peace Research and education in a Global Perspective". In Christolph Wulf, ed. *Handbook on Peace Education* (pp. 300-314). Germany: Frankfurt/Main: International Peace Research Association.

Renna, T. (1980). "Peace Education: An Historical Review", *Peace and Change*, Vol. VI, nos. 1 and 2, Winter: 61-65.

World Health Organization (2002). *World Report on Violence and Health*. www.who.int/ volence injury_prevention.

11

Sufi, Their Traits and Its Demand in Modern Education

Mohammad Shafi Ahmed

In our education system education not brings humanity. Different education institution i.e. schools, colleges and universities and different kind of degrees provide us knowledge information to became doctor, engineer and professor but not teach us to became a real human being which is and should be the basic aim education. An example what we are getting from this education system. . . . . . .

A car mistakenly knocked a boy who injured seriously, with the major injuries in his head. The car owner took him to a nearby hospital where he has had to meet the countries famous nerve specialist doctor for his operation. The doctor demanded his fees first. He told the doctor he doesn't have anything right now but he will pay the fees after the operation. Doctor told fees first then only the operation, car owner gave his key and told keep it but start the treatment.

After that doctor saw the boy and gone mad. . . . . The boy was the only son of the doctor who died.

Who a Sufi is and why their teachings are important in our modern education system?

Sufism itself is nothing but the perfect following of the way of Muhammad, both inner and outer.

Therefore, Sufism, can in no way be divorced from the teachings of the Prophet Muhammad (peace be upon him). Anyone who acts contrary to the principles of Islam cannot be considered a Sufi, in spite of their claims.

According to Quran "unquestionably there will be no fear concerning them, nor will they grieve—Those who believed and were fearing Allah. For them are good tidings in the worldly life and hereafter no change is there in the words (i.e. decrees) of Allah. That is the great attainment.

The Sufi strove in the manner of Prophet with piety, austerity, discipline, self-sacrifice and giving preference to others. Their love and hatred was for the sake of Allah, they have deep compassion, mercy and kindness for all creation of Allah.

Importance of Sufi Teachings in Modern Age

Followings are some extracts from Islamic classics and life of the companions of the Prophet S.A.W. Each incident has some relevance to the modification of heart.

Feeding the Guest in Darkness

One came to the prophet (sallallaho a' laihi wasallam) and complained of hunger. Just then the Prophet had nothing in hand or in his home to feed him. He asked the Sahabah. Would anybody entertain this person tonight on my behalf? One of the Ansar "O, Prophet of Allah I will do that".

The Ansar took the person in his house and instructed his wife.

Look here, this man is a guest of the prophet. We will entertain him as best as we can and won't spare anything in doing so.

The wife replied: by Allah I have got no food in the house except a very little-something just enough for the children.

The Ansari said: "you lull children to sleep without feeding them while I sit with the guest over the meager meal, when we start eating you put out the lamp pretending to set it right, so that the guest may not know my not sharing the meal with him"

The scheme worked nicely, and the whole family including the children stayed hungry to enable the guest to eat to his fill.

It was over this incident that Allah revealed the verse

(Yusiruna Aalaa Anfosihim wa Ao Kana bi him Khasa Sa)

"They prefer others above themselves though poverty becomes their lot."

Sahabah Dying Thirsty for Others

Abu-jahm-bin-Huzaifah (radhiallaho anho R.A.) narrates: "During the battle of Yarmuk I went out in search of my cousin, who was in the forefront of the fight. I also took some water with me for him.I found him in the very thick of battle in the last throes of life. I advanced to help him with the little water I had. But, soon, another sorely wounded soldier beside him gave a sigh, and my cousin averted his face, and beckoned me to take the water to that person first. I went to this other person with the water. He turned out to be Hisham-bin-Abilas. But I had hardly reached him, when there was heard the groan of yet another person lying not very far off. Hisham too motioned me in his direction. Alas, before I could approach him, he had breathed his last. I made all haste back to hisham and found him dead as well. There upon, I hurried as fast as I could to my cousin, and in the meantime he had also joined the other two.

U'mar's Wife As a Midwife

Amir ul-mominin U'mar (R.A.) during the time of his Khilafat used to patrol the streets and suburbs of Medina himself to keep a look out for the welfare of the citizens. During one of his night patrol he noticed a camel–hair tent pitched in an open space. He has never seen this particular tent before. Approaching the tent, he found an individual sitting outside, and heard a continuous groan coming out of the tent. U'mar (radhiallah anho) greeted the stanger with "*Assalamu-alaikum*" and sat down beside him.

U'mar: "whence brother?"

The person: I am from the desert; and a stanger to this place. I have come to request Amir-ul-Mominin for some help iin my need.

U'mar: "Who is there groaning like this inside the tent?"

The person: "Please mind your own business."

U'mar: "Do tell me please. May be that I can help you".

The person: If you must know, inside there is my wife groaning with labour pain.

U'mar: "Is there anybody else to attend her".

The person: "None".

U'mar (radhiallah anho), thereupon, got up hurried homewards. He the subject to his wife ummu-kulsum (radhiallah anho) thus:

"ALLAH has brought an opportunity of great merit in your path."

Wife: what is it, O, Amir-ul-Mominin?"

U'mar: "a poor woman of the desert is in child birth with none to attend her".

Wife: "I am ready to attend her if it may please you so."

Umme kulsum (Radhiallaho anha) was after all the daughter of Fatima (Radhidallaho anha), and the granddaughter of the Prophet; how could she hesitate at the time of such a need of a forlon sister, and neglect a service which is the very essence of all that is human and the central point of all religions conceptions—a devotion which ALLAH loves best?

U'mar: then you should make all due haste. Also take a kettle, some butter, provisions and other things that needed during confinement."

Umme kulsum (Radhiallaho anha) did as she was bidden and left for the place where the tent was pithed. U'mar followed her close. She entered the tent,while made a fire occupied himself with something which those people can eat. After some time Umme kulsum (Radhiallaho anha) called out from inside the tent,

Amir-ul-Mominin congratulates your friend on the birth of a son".

The person was much embarrassed when he heard the address of 'Amir-ul-mominin' and realizing the position of the person who had been serving him. But U'mar (Radhiallaho anha) put all these fear s to rest, saing:

"That is all right, there e is nothing to worry about".

He then placed the kettle near the tentasking his wife to take it and feed the woman. She fed her and returned the kettle then U'mar (Radhiallaho anha) bade farewale to the person:

"Come to me tomorrow, and I can see what can I do for you.

Having rendered (RAW) returned home with his wife. Is there any king, nay a petty chief even an ordinary middle class persin of our time who will thus take his wife out at dead of night and out in the wilderness to attend a poor stranger woman, while he himself gladly engages in making a fire and cooking food. Leave the worldly rich aside, how many of clergy would do that? We should realize that unless we really follow in the footsteps of those God –fearing people whom we profess to look up to as our models we cannot deserve and wish for the special blessings which ALLAH bestowed on them.

Role of a Teacher

Teachers play most important and vital role in steering inner peace in the society beginning from the tender hearts. Teachers are required to be utmost careful about their behavior, deeds and words. The holy Qur'an also says, "*You preach others but forget your own self.*" (Sura Baqr). Sheikh Imam Ghazali writes in *Ihya-ul-uloom*, that the Prophet S.A.W. was asked by the companions-

"Which people are called more learned"

The Prophet replied,

"Those who make you aware of the Anger of Allah."

The 'Sahaba' (companions) again asked.

"Who among us are the best, kindly tell us so that we may get the company of them."

The Prophet told them,

"Those are the best among people, when you see them, you remember Allah."

Again he was asked,

"Who are the worst among the people?"

The Prophet said,

"I Seek refuge of Allah, May Allah forgive them."

The Sahaba requested earnestly to tell the name of those people, then the Prophet said softly-

"Those are the learned people (Ulema) of a community if they go corrupted."

Empathy for Others' Sorrow

It is the 'self-realization' of other's sufferings. The greatest example of this strategy is the personality and modality of the Prophet S.A.W. himself. He used to sit on mat, knit of date leaves, instead of a royal throne. He never ate food alone. Always he shared his food with other companions (Sahaba) whom he called specially to feed (knowing their poverty). He never wore costly clothes. His sheet was patched. He spent his whole life in poverty and sufferings in spite of being the undisputed authority in the whole Arab, in later period of his life. In one battle a follower (sahabi) told the Prophet that he was hungry since last 2 days and in order to lessen the feeling of hunger he had bound 2 stones on his stomach. Then the Prophet, raised his clothe from the belly and shown to him, 'There were 4 stones bound on the stomach of the Prophet and he had not eaten food since 4 days.

Hazrat Fatima Zahra, the blessed daughter of the Prophet was cooking food. There was not much material in the house. Flour was limited, only for 4 chapatis. When she cooked one, a beggar came at door and asked for food, Fatima gave him one chapati. She cooked second, then another beggar came. She gave him next chapatti. The other two chapattis were also given to other beggars and that night Hazrat Ali, Hasan, Husain and Hazrat Fatma slept empty belly. Next day the Prophet said to Fatima, "You are declared by Allah, the chief of all the women in Jannah do you agree with it?"

Thus this is the feel of other's sorrow and sufferings, that bring prosperity in our state and spirituality. A number of Sufi masters adopted this strategy to teach their pupils. They inspire pupils to feel others distress and helplessness. This creates in us, the real intention to help others and a strong desire for philanthropic deeds. 'Roza (fasts) during the month of Ramzan convey also this message i.e. to feel others' need so that you may help the needy heart and soul.

To attain the highest level of spiritual qualities they have followed the teachings of Prophet (SAW) which are as follows ....

Nawwas ibne-Saman Al-Ansari narrates: I asked Rasulullah (SAW) about righteousness and sin. He replied: Righteousness is good character, and sin is that which revolves in your heart about which you do not want people to know. (Muslim)

Anas (RA) narrates: I served Rasulullah (SAW) for ten years in Madina. I was an adolscent. Therefore all my services were not according to the desire of my master (because of my tender age, many lapses were committed during these ten years). However, he never said a word of displeasure to me; neither "why did you do this?" Nor "why did you not do that?"

Abu Sa'id Al-Khudri (RA) narrates that Rasulullah (SAW) said: He who had three daughters or three sisters, or two daughters or two sisters, and treated them well, and feared Allah towards them, for him is paradise.

Anas Ibne-Malik (RAW) that Rasulullah (SAW) said: He who wishes that his life span be prolonged and his provisions increased should treat his parents well and maintain his bonds of kinship. (Musnad Ahmad).

Ma'rur Rahimullah narrates: I met Abu Dhar (RAW) at Rabadhah; who was wearing a cloak and, his slave was also wearing a simular one, I asked him the reason for this. He replied: I abused a person by calling his mother with bad names. Nabi (SAW) said to me: O Abu Dhar! Did you abuse him by calling his mother with bad names? You still have some characteristics of ignorance of pre Islamic times. Your slaves are your brothers and Allah has put them under your command. So whosoever has a brother under his command should feed him with what he eats and dress him with what he wears. Do not ask them (slaves) to do things beyond their capacity (power) and if you do so, then help them. (Bukhari)

Abu Hurairah (RA) narrates in a Hadith Qursi that Rasulullah (SAW) said: Indeed Allah will say on the day of Resurrection: O son of Adam! I was sick and you did not visit me; to which he will reply: O my Rabb! How could I visit You? You are the Rabb of the worlds. Allah will say: Did you not know that my such slave was sick, and you did not visit him? Did you not know that if you had visited him, you would have found Me with him? O son of Adam! I asked you for food, but you did not feed Me; to which he will say: O my Rabb! How could I feed You. You are the Rabb of the worlds? Allah will say: Did you not know My such slave asked you for food, and you did not feed him. Did you not know if you had fed him, you would have surely found him near Me? O son of Adam! I asked you to give Me water, but you did not give Me water to drink; to which he will reply: O my Rabb! How could I give you the water to drink, You are the Rabb of the worlds? Alllah will say: My such slave asked you for water, but you did not give him water to drink. If you had given him water to drink, you would surely have found him near Me? (Muslim)

Jabir (RA) narrates that Rasulullah (SAW) said: Any Muslim who plants a tree, then whatever is eaten from it, is Sadaqah for him;; what is stolen from it is Sadaqah for him; what breasts eat is Sadaqah for him; what birds eat is Sadaqah for him; whosoever takes anything from the tree (fruit etc) is Sadaqah (for the planter). (Muslim)

Abu Dhar (RA) narrates that Nabi (SAW) said: there will be nothing heavier on the scale than good conduct.

Abu Dhar (RA) narrate that Nabi (SAW) ordered me seven things: (1) He ordered me to love the poor, and be close to them, (2) He ordered to look at those inferior to me and not to look at those who are superior, (3) He ordered me to bind ties of kinship; even if they turn away from me, (4) He ordered me not to ask anyone for anything, (5) He ordered me to speak the truth, though it may be bitter, (6) He ordered me not to reproach of anyone in respect to the orders of ALLAH., (7) And he ordered me to recite frequently, (La haula wala quwata illah billah). There is no might to resist evil, no power to do well, except through ALLAH, for these words are undoubtly from the treasure under the throne.

Some Qualities of Great People to Bring Humanity in Modern Education System:

1. Be kind to all even the smallest creature.
2. Do not hurt anyone and give love and affection to everyone.
3. Keep on eyes inferior to you.
4. Don't look to your superior.
5. Listen the first voice of your heart.
6. If heart not allows in some matter means it's wrong.
7. Share the things with others.
8. Don't be jealous about anything.
9. Give to everyone but don't ask from anyone.
10. Don't fill your stomach too much.

References

Haqqani, Abdul Qayyum. Bees Bade Auliya, ed.Wajid, Sajidul., Zam Zam Book Depot, c. Nov 1997.

Haqqani, Muhammad Palan. Shariat –Ya-Jahalat, ed. Hasan, Mahmudul., Delhi: Shaiba Offset Press, c.2000.

Kandhalwi, M. Zakarya. The Teachings of Islam, New Delhi: Idara Ishaat-e-Diniyat, c.1980.

Kandhalwi, Muhammad Yousuf. Muntakhab Ahadith, ed. Kandhalwi, Muhammad Saad., Rodgaran, Delhi: Yaseen book depot, c. 2009.

Rahmani, Minatullah, Muslim Personal Law And Uniform Civil Code, ed. Qasmi, Nizamuddin., Pataudi House, Darya Ganj, New Delhi: Farid Book Depot, c. 2004.

Usmani, Muhammad Taqi. Akabir Deoband Kya The?, Deoband: Zam Zam Book Depot, c. May 1995.

Zakarya, Muhammad. Fazail Aamal Part I, Lalita Park, Laxmi Nagar, Delhi., c. 2009.

PART-VI
EPITOMES OF INDIAN CULTURE

1

भारतीय आध्यात्मिक परम्परा

योगेश प्रवीन

भारतीय दर्शन में अपने आप की खोज को अध्यात्म कहा गया है। हम हैं तो हमारा आदि है, हमारा अन्त है और वहीं ईश्वर है। वह ईश्वर जो बिंदु भी है सिंधु भी है। ऊँ सर्वशक्तिमान ईश्वर का संक्षिप्त प्रतीक है। हिन्दू धर्म के अनुसार ज्ञान उपार्जन अर्थात ज्ञान प्राप्त करने के सभी अधिकारी हैं। ज्ञान की तलाश ही जीवन का उपक्रम है इस तरह हिन्दुत्व और विज्ञान एक ही सिक्के के दो पहलू हैं। भारतीय अध्यात्म के अनुसार मानव जीवन साधना एवं मोक्ष के लिए ही निहित है आत्मा अजर अमर है तथा जन्म मरण से रहित है। सच्चा जीवन हिंसा का नहीं अहिंसा का पक्षपाती होता है और यह शरीर, भव सिंधु को पार करने के लिए प्राप्त नौका के समान है।

भारतीय परम्परा में प्रार्थना का बड़ा महत्व है, वेद की रिचाएं इसी सन्दर्भ को रेखांकित करती हैं वहां प्रार्थना परमेश्वर को पाने के लिए शाब्दिक यंत्र है और वो भी जो अदृश्य यन्त्र है जो मनुष्य को साहस, सामर्थ्य प्रदान करते हुए अवसाद का निराकरण करता है।

हिन्दू दर्शन में ईश्वर से मिलने का जो अभिलाषी होता है ईश्वर भी उससे मिलने का अभिलाषी होता है।

ये यथा माँ प्रपध्यन्ते
तास्तथैव भजाम्यहम

भगवान कृष्ण गीता में भक्तों का आवाहन स्वयं करते हैं।

एकं सदविप्रा बहुधा वदोन्ति कह कर भारतीय दर्शन ने सारे संसार के सभी धर्मों, सम्प्रदायों, महजबों, मतों के महत्व को प्रतिपादित कर दिया है।

स्वामी विवेकानन्द गर्व से कहते हैं उपनिषद के हर पृष्ठ से मुझे साहस की शिक्षा

प्राप्त हुई है। भारतीय ग्रन्थों में भी विश्व के अन्य धर्मग्रन्थों की तरह स्वर्ग और नर्क की परिकल्पना है लेकिन इस के भी ऊपर धर्म और मोक्ष को रखा गया है। हिन्दू दर्शन की अवधारणा ''पुरूषार्थ चतुष्टय'' के बहाने से दुनिया के सर्वांगीण महत्व को जीवन में निहित कर दिया गया है। यहां धर्म, अर्थ, काम, मोक्ष चारों को एक ही पंक्ति में रख कर संसार को पूरी प्रतिष्ठा दी गयी है। और फिर जब गोस्वामी तुलसीदास जी इन चारों सम्पदाओं को अपने आराध्य भगवान राम पर निछावर करते हैं तो वहीं प्रेम की पराकाष्ठा प्राप्त होती है। जिसे हम इश्क़ की इन्तहा कह सकते हैं।

अरथ न धरम न कामरूचि पद न चहहुं निर्वान
जनम जनम रति राम पद यह बरदान न आन(रामचरितमानस)

भारत के प्रधान धर्म सनातन आर्य धर्म, जैन धर्म और बौद्ध धर्म है। हिन्दू आत्मा, परमात्मा तथा जीव–जगत तीनों को मानता है। जैन आत्मा और जगत दो को स्वीकार कते हैं परन्तु बुद्ध तीनों को ही नही मानते।

फ्रांस के दार्शनिक बर्गसां और जर्मनी के विद्वान कांट ने महात्मा बुद्ध के उपदेशों को समस्त मानवता के लिए उपयोगी कहा है।

जगद्गुरू शंकराचार्य ने कहा है कि जैसा जीवन्त जगदीश सनातन धर्मी के पास होता है वैसा विश्व में अन्यत्र दुर्लभ है। भारतीय सन्त परम्परा में आत्मीय समानता और न्याय का उपदेश ही सर्वोपरि है

आग लगी आकाश में झरझर पड़े अंगार
सन्त न होते जगत में जल जाता संसार

सच तो यह है कि महात्मा कबीर के सारे आग्रह मनुष्य जीवन और जगत को संवारने के रहे हैं। इसी प्रेमपंथ के पथिक नज़र आते हैं जो प्रेमी भाव से अपने प्रिय की प्रतीक्षा करते हैं।

नयना अन्तर आव तूं नयन ढांपि तोहि लेहुं
ना मैं देखूं और को ना तोहि देखन देहुं

उसी निर्मम प्रियतम के लिए अवध के शयर मुन्नू लाल सफ़ी सीतापुरी कहते हैं

अर्श का कब ये सलीक़ा है सितमगारी में
कोई माशूक है इस परदए जंगारी में

फारस देश के सूफी विचार जलालुद्दीन रूमी के रंग में यूं नज़र आते हैं

तू पस्तियों में आलमे रूबरू है
बना तू हर इक फूल में रंगो बू है
और आईना देखा तो रूबरू तू है
निगाह जिस तरफ उठ गई तू ही तू है

और फिर भारतीय संत कवि यही कहते मिलते हैं
प्रियतम हम तुम एक हैं कहन सुनन को दोय
मन से मन को तौलिए दो मन कबहुं न होय

प्रेम से परमेश्वर को प्राप्त करने की यह परम्परा हमारे देश में बहुत पुराने समय से विद्यमान रही है। भगवान कृष्ण के लिए जड़ चेतन, पशु पक्षी, ग्वाले गोपी सभी के पास एक तड़प है।

दिवस न भूख, नींद नहीं रैना प्रान विकल भए, प्रान अधारे
दरसन देना प्रान पियारे नन्दलाल मेरी आँखों के तारे

चित्तौड़गढ़ की राजरानी मीरा हों या दक्षिण की आलवार परम्परा की आण्डाल हो सब परमेश्वर के ही किसी स्वरूप पर दिलो जान से कुर्बान मिलती है।

अमीर खुसरो भी अपने पीरों मुर्शिद के लिए उसी रंग में डूबते नज़र आते हैं

खुसरो रैन सुहाग की जागी पी के संग
तन मेरो मन पीउ को दोऊ भए एक रंग

प्रेममार्गी भक्ति परम्परा में मलिक मोहम्मद जायसी भी ईश्वर को प्राप्त करने का प्रमुख साधन प्रेम को ही मानते हैं। राजा रतन सेन और राजकुमारी पद्मिनी के प्रेम प्रसंग(गुरू सुओ जेहि पंथ दिखावा) का प्रेरक यहाँ हीरामन तोता है।

भक्ति युग में कृष्ण के प्रति अविरल प्रेम सूफ़ी परम्परा का ही एक प्राचीन बिम्ब है, जहाँ हृदय की व्याकुलता प्रेम की एकाग्रता, विरह की तड़प और मिलन की चाह एकदम अनूठी है

इश्क है वो फल कि जिसके तुख़्म हैं ये अश्क सुर्ख
बेखुदी है मगज़ इसका और छिलका इज़्तराब

2

उत्तर भारत की विभिन्न धार्मिक परम्पराओं में सूफी संगीत परम्परा : एक अवलोकन

रितु सिंह

भारत एक धर्म प्रधान देश है। यहाँ जन सामान्य से जुड़े सभी सामाजिक कर्म व्यवहार एवं लोकाचार सम्बन्धी नियम किसी न किसी प्रकार धार्मिक मान्यताओं के साथ गुंथे हुए हैं। हमारे भारतीय संगीत में प्रत्येक विद्या का उद्भव, विकास तथा प्रचार–प्रसार इन्ही धार्मिक परम्पराओं से सुरक्षित रहा है।परम्पराओं के संरक्षण में ही हमारा संगीत वंशानुक्रम से एक पीढ़ी से दूसरे पीढ़ी को हस्तांतरित किया जाता रहा है।

मानव जीवन का चरम ल़क्ष्य परमात्मा का साक्षात्कार माना गया है, और इस लक्ष्य का सर्वोतम साधन संगीत ही है। साधक की अहंता का प्रेमास्वाद की दिव्य प्रीति में रूपान्तरित हो जाना अथवा यों कहें कि दिव्य प्रीति में विलीनीकरण हो जाना ही भक्ति का वास्तविक स्वरूप है। भक्त का चित्त संसार–आकर्षण एवं कामनाओं के लिए विभक्त नहीं होता, उसका एक मात्र अपने आराध्य से ही दृढ़ योग बना रहता है, प्रेमास्पद प्रभु ही उसके एकमात्र आधार बल और विश्वास बल होते हैं–

"एक भरोसे, एक बल
एक आस, एक विश्वास"

हमारे देश में भक्ति का विकास वैदिक काल से होता आया है। मध्य काल में इस्लाम के आगमन तथा प्रसार ने इस देश के जनमानस में भक्ति की पुर्नस्थापना की एक पृष्ठभूमि तैयार कर दी और यहीं से सूफी परम्परा का आर्विभाव हुआ।

सूफी संगीत का स्थान मध्य काल की सांस्कृतिक एवं धार्मिक परम्पराओं में उल्लेखनीय है। मध्य काल की अनेक सांस्कृतिक एवं धार्मिक परम्पराओं में सूफी परम्परा अत्यन्त महत्वपूर्ण

है।यह परम्परा 8वीं 9वीं शताब्दी से विकसित होने लगी थी तथा मध्य काल तक आते–आते अपने उत्कर्ष पर थी। यह परम्परा भारतीय द्वैतवाद तथा विशिष्टाद्वैतवाद आदि दर्शनों से साम्य रखती है एवं रहस्यावाद के निकट है। भारतीय संस्कृति, साहित्य तथा विशेषतः यहाँ की संगीत सूफी परम्परा से बहुत ही ज्यादा प्रभावित है। इस परम्परा के संतों ने विशेषतः हिन्दू–मुस्लिम एकता एवं भाईचारे पर बहुत बल दिया है।सूफीवाद इस्लाम के धार्मिक जीवन की वह अवस्था है, जिसमें बाह्य क्रियाओं की अपेक्षा आन्तरिक क्रियाओं पर विशेष बल दिया जाता है।

वस्तुतः भारत में सूफी साहित्य तथा संगीत अपने युग की चेतना और जन–जीवन की संस्कृति का अमुल्य कोश है। भारत में सूफी संत कवियों तथा संगीतज्ञों ने लोक–विश्वास, लोक–परम्परा, लोक–धर्मकी अभिव्यक्ति ही नहीं की अपितु व्यापक अर्थ में मानव मुल्यों की रक्षा करने का भी श्रेय प्राप्त किया। यह शास्त्र तथा साहित्य युग विशेष के जन–जीवन का दर्पण ही नहीं है, बल्कि सही मायने में जीवन का व्याख्या तथा रचनात्मक समीक्षा भी है।

सूफी शब्द का सर्वप्रथम प्रयोग हजरत मोहम्मद साहब के देहावसान के लगभग दो सौ वर्ष पश्चात 9वीं शताब्दी के मध्य बसरा के अरबी लेखक जाहिज ने किया था। जामी के अनुसार इसका सर्वप्रथम प्रयोग कूफा के अबू हासिम के लिए हुआ। तत्पश्चात् पचास वर्ष के अन्दर इराक तथा दो सौ वर्ष में सभी मुस्लिम रहस्यवादियों के लिए इसका व्यवहार होने लगा। ये सभी लोग उज्जवल जीवन व्यतीत करते थे।

इस शब्द की भिन्न–भिन्न व्युत्पत्तियाँ भी इस तथ्य की स्थापना करती है किवे व्यक्ति जो पवित्र जीवन व्यतीत करते हुए धर्माचरण में संलग्न रहते थे, सूफी कहलाए।

एन्साइक्लोपीडिया ऑफ रिलीजन एण्ड ईथिक्स के अनुसार "सूफी" शब्द की व्युत्पत्ति "सफा" शब्द में मानी गयी है। कतिपय विद्वानों का विचार है कि मदीना में मोहम्मद साहब द्वारा बनाई गई। मस्जिद के बाहर 'सुफ्क' अर्थात् चबूतरे पर जिन गृह–विहीन व्यक्तियों ने आकर शरण ली थी और जो पवित्र जीवन–मुल्यों तथा नियमों का पालन करते थे, वे सूफी कहलाए। कुछ विद्वानों ने इसकी व्युत्पत्ति ग्रीक शब्द 'सोफिया' (ज्ञान) से मानी है। अर्थात् सूफी वे व्यक्ति थे जिनके हृदय में ईश्वरीय ज्ञान का प्रकाश हो गया था। अबू नस्र अल सर्राज का कथन है कि जो यती या सन्यासी 'सूफ'अर्थात् उन के वस्त्र धारण करते थे, वे सूफी नाम से अभिहित हुए।

सूफी शब्द की उपरोक्त व्युत्पत्तियों से यही निष्कर्ष निकलता है कि जो व्यक्ति संत थे, जिनकी मनोवृत्तियों उज्जवल थीं, जो धर्माचरण करतें थे, जिनके अन्तस्तल में ज्ञान का प्रकाश हो गया था और जो सादा जीवन व्यतीत करते थे, वे मुस्लिम सूफी संत कहलाए।

सूफी–दर्शन में प्रतिपदित सिद्धान्तों के अनुसार फरीदुद्दीन अत्तार ने 'वहदतुलवजूद' (केवलत्ववाद) के सिद्धान्त का प्रतिपादन किया जिसके अनुसार परमसत्ता समस्त दृश्यमान जगत का आदि –स्त्रोत है और अविभाज्य होते हुए भी एक है। 'अलवजूद अलमुतलक अस्ल

कुल्ल वजूद' अर्थात् परम सत्ता के अतिरिक्त जो कुछ भी है, उसका कोई अलग अस्तित्व नहीं है, बल्कि मन की उपज है। जब जीवात्मा में द्वैत होता है तो मौलाना रूपी विरहिणी आत्मा की उपमा बाँसुरी से देते हुए लिखते हैं–

बहनों अज नै चूं हिकायत भी कुनद।
बज जुहाईया शिकायत भी कुनद।
कज नमस्तां ता मरा बबुरीद : अन्द।
अज नफीरम मर्दोजन नालीदा अन्द।
सीना खाहम शरह शरह अज फिराक्।।
ता बगोयम शरहे दर्दे इश्तियाक।
हर कसे कुदुर अज वस्ले खेश।
बाज जोयद रोजगारे वस्ले खेश।

अर्थात् बाँसुरी जो कथा सुनाती है, उसे सुनो। वह वियोग की शिकायत करती है। जबसे मुझे (बाँसुरी को) जंगल से काटा गया है, तब से मेरे माध्यम से स्त्रियों एवं पुरूषों में ओहो नाला किया है। मैं चाहती हूँ कि मेरा हृदय विरह से टुकड़े–टुकड़े हो जाए जिससे मैं ज्ञान और जिज्ञासा के दर्द की व्याख्या कर सकूं।

सूफी परम्परा मूलतः प्रेम दर्शन पर आधारित थी। प्रेम ही इस परम्परा का मूल सिद्धान्त था। इस परम्परा में प्रेम को 'इश्क' संज्ञा से अभिहित किया गया। इश्क के दो प्रकार बताए गए हैं–"इश्के मिजाजी"(सांसारिक प्रेम) और "इश्के हकीकी"(ईश्वरीय प्रेम)। सांसारिक या लौकिक प्रेम के माध्यम से ईश्वरीय प्रेम तक पहुँचने का सूफी परम्परा अनुमोदन करती है।

सूफीयों ने ईश्वर प्राप्ति के लिए चार प्रकार की साधनावस्थाओं को निश्चित किया है– शरीफत, तरीफत, हकीकत और मारीफत। मारीफत के अन्तर्गत दो अवस्थाएँ है– हाली और इल्मी। हाली के अन्तर्गत सात साधक 'मुकमात' होते हैं। इसी 'मुकमात' शब्द से 'मुकाम' शब्द बना। जो सुफीयों के आध्यात्मिक परम्परा के प्रमाणस्वरूप उपलब्ध है। आध्यात्मिक परिप्रेक्ष्य से ही अमीर खूसरों ने ईरानी मुकाम सिद्धान्त का भारतीय संगीत जगत से परिचय कराया था। बाद में इसी मुकाम पद्धति से रागों का वर्गीकरण किया गया। अब 'मुकाम' का अर्थ राग अथवा राग– प्रयोज्य स्वरसमूह, संस्थान, मेल या ठाठ के पर्यायवाची शब्द हैं। परन्तु मुकाम के शाब्दिक अर्थ की व्याख्या और अनंतता की पृष्ठभूमि मध्यकालीन संगीत ग्रन्थों में विशद रूप से वर्णित किया गया है।

मध्य काल की अनेक सांस्कृतिक एवं धार्मिक परम्पराओं में सूफी परम्परा अत्यन्त महत्वपूर्ण है। सूफीयों की मूलतः चार परम्पराएँ थीं– (1) चिश्ती परम्परा (2) कादरी परम्परा (3) नक्शबन्दी परम्परा (4) सुहरावर्दी परम्परा। इनमें से मुख्यतः चिश्ती परम्परा और सुहरावर्दी परम्परा ही अधिक प्रचलित हुई। चिश्ती परम्परा का प्रचार सबसे अधिक हुआ। चिश्ती परम्परा के प्रसिद्ध सूफी संत हजरत मुईनुद्दीन चिश्ती, बाबा फरीद, सलीम चिश्ती, निजामुद्दीन

औलिया आदि थे। चिश्ती परम्परा के सूफीयों ने भारतीय संगीत को आधार मानकर उसमें अरबी संगीत का मिश्रण करके नए प्रयोग किए। जबकि सुहरावर्दी परम्परा के सूफियों ने अरबी संगीत को आधार मानकर उसमें भारतीय संगीत का समिश्रण किया। यही कारण है कि चिश्ती परम्परा के सुफीयाना कलाम आज भी जिन्दा है। जबकि सुहरावर्दी परम्परा का प्रचार अधिक नहीं है। चिश्ती परम्परा में संगीत को एकाग्रता का साधन भी माना गया।

सूफी दर्शन मूलतः जीवात्मा और परमात्मा के प्रेम पर आधारित था। इस दर्शन में जीवात्मा को नायिका तथा परमात्मा को नायक माना गया है। नायक (परमात्मा) तथा नायिका (जीवात्मा) के मिलन, परिणय या अभिसार का इस दर्शन में स्थान–स्थान पर चित्रण है। अमीर खूसरों द्वारा रचित यह रचना देखिए–

छाप तिलक सब छीनी रे मोसे नैना मिलाय के
प्रेमभटी का मधवा पिलाय के।
मतवाली कर लिन्ही रे, मोसे नैना मिलाय के।
बलि–बलि जाँउ मै तोरे रंगरेजवा,
अपनी सी कर लिन्ही रे, मोसे नैना मिलाय के।

सूफी संगीतज्ञों ने भारतीय संगीत के शास्त्रीय पक्ष को भलि–भाँति समझकर उन्होने इसमें अरबी–फारसी संगीत का समिश्रण कर अनेक गायन शैलियों को निर्मित किया जो इस प्रकार हैं–

कव्वाली–कव्वालीके विन्यास का श्रेय अमीर खूसरों को जाता है। कव्वाली का विशेषता यह है कि उसमें अरबी, फारसी, इरानी तथा उत्तर भातीय संगीत का अच्छा मिश्रण हुआ है। कव्वाली में श्रोता एक क्षण लोक धुन सुन सकता है तो दूसरे क्षण शास्त्रीय ढ़ंग का आलाप। अमीर खूसरों का एक पद यहाँ द्रष्टव्य है –

बहुत कठिन है डगर पनघट की
कैसे मैं भर लाउँ मधवा से मटकी
पनिया भरन को जो मैं गई थी
दौरझपट मोरी मटकी पटकी
खुसरों निजाम की बलि बलि जैइये
लज रखों मोरे घूँघट पट की।

कौल–इसका वास्तविक नाम कोहल है। इसमें अरबी शब्दों के साथ–साथ कुछ टुकड़े तरानों के बोलों के भी होते हैं। इसके स्थायी, अन्तरा दो भाग होते है।

कल्वाना–कल्वाना की असल "कल्बहु" है। यह गाना अरबी और हिन्दी शब्दों को मिलाकर बना है। इसमें कई– कई तालें शमिल होती है। इसमें हर टुकड़े के साथ इसकी ताल भी बदल जाती है। इसी कारण 'कल्वाना' को कुछ विद्वान 'ताल–सागर' भी कहते हैं।

नक्श और गुल–फारसी भाषा का सिर्फ एक शेर हो, उसको नक्श और जिसमें फारसी

की रूबाई हो उसको गुल कहते हैं। ये गाने मौसमी होते है।

नक्श–निगार–इसमें फारसी का एक शेर या रूबाई होता है। नक्श–निगार मल्हार ऋतु के रागों में गाए जाते हैं।

बसीत–यह चतुरंग का एक रश्म है। बसीत के हर टुकड़े में अलग–अलग राग बंदिश की सूरत में होते हैं। विद्वानों ने इसे राग–सागर कहा है।

ख्याल–ख्यालफारसी भाषा का एक शब्द है, जिसका अर्थ है विचार या कल्पना। कुछ लोग अमीर खूसरों को इस गायकी का जन्मदाता मानते हैं। ख्याल शैली के दो भाग स्थाई और अन्तरा होते हैं तथा ख्याल दो प्रकार के माने जाते हैं– विलम्बित ख्याल तथा द्रुत ख्याल। वर्तमान समय में ख्याल शैली भारतीय संगीत की सर्वाधिक लोकप्रिय शैली है।

गुर्जरी तोड़ी का छोटा ख्याल का एक उदाहरण यहाँ प्रस्तुत है–

स्थायी– माने ना मोरा जिया उन बिन री।
कैसे समझाउँ समझत नाही।।

अन्तरा– बहुत दिन बीते नहीं आए।
रामरंग पिया घर नैना नीर बरसाए।।

सूफीयों के संगीत में मूलतः गेय संगीत का बहुत अत्यधिक महत्व था। अनेक विद्वानों का मानना है कि ख्याल गायन शैली का उद्भव भी सूफियों के कव्वाली से हुआ है। सूफी परम्परा में कव्वाली और ख्याल दोनों ही गाने की परम्परा रही है।

अतः उपरोक्त विवेचन से स्पष्ट है कि सूफी संगीत परम्परा निश्चित रूप से एक आस्था अथवा दार्शनिकों, विद्वानों, लेखकों एवं रहस्यवादियों के लिए कट्टरता एवं रूढ़ीवादी तत्वों से मुक्त एक बुद्धिवादी एवं भावनात्मक निधि रहा है तथा भारतीय संगीत के विकास एवं पुनरोत्थान में सूफी संगीतज्ञों का अतुलनीय एवं अविस्मरणीययोगदान रहा है।

संदर्भ ग्रन्थ सूची

1. मिश्रा, डॉ. ज्योति, मध्य युगीन संगीत समग्र, अनुभव पब्लिशिंग हाउस, इलाहाबाद, प्रथम संस्करण– 2013
2. शर्मा, डॉ. सुनिता, भारतीय संगीत का इतिहास आध्यात्मिक एवं दार्शनिक, संजय प्रकाशन, दिल्ली, प्रथम संस्करण–1996
3. वही
4. सचदेव, डॉ. रेनू, धार्मिक परम्परायें एवं हिन्दुस्तानी संगीत, राधा पब्लिकेशन, नई दिल्ली, प्रथम संस्करण–1999
5. शर्मा, डॉ. सुनिता, भारतीय संगीत का इतिहास आध्यात्मिक एवं दार्शनिक, संजय प्रकाशन, दिल्ली, प्रथम संस्करण–1996
6. सिहं, डॉ. श्रीमती राजबाला, मध्यकालीन भारत में सूफी मत का उद्भव और विकास, राष्ट्रीय कला एवं शोध संस्थान, वाराणसी, प्रथम संसकरण–1985
7. श्रीवास्तव, डॉ. संगीता, उत्तर भारत की विभिन्न धार्मिक परम्पराओं में संगीत, समवेत प्रकाशन, कानपुर, प्रथम संस्करण–201

3

संगीत की उपासना स्थली–सूफी दरग़ाह खानक़ाहे–नियाज़िया

रूचि गुप्ता

दिल्ली और लखनऊ के मध्य स्थित इनका दिल बरेली उत्तर प्रदेश का एक महत्वपूर्ण और समृद्धशाली महानगर है। प्राचीनकाल से लेकर आज तक भौगोलिक, सामरिक एवं आर्थिक दृष्टि से अत्यन्त महत्वपूर्ण नगर है। बरेली जिसके आस–पास है, प्राचीन नगर ''अहिच्छत्र'' के अवशेष, बौद्धस्तूप, हजारों वर्ष पूर्व महाभारत कालीन ''महाराज द्रुपद'' की राजधानी ''पांचाल''। इस क्षेत्र में जमींदोज पुरातत्व सम्पदा को अब भारत ही नहीं पूरा विश्व जानना चाहता है। अफगानिस्तान के रोह क्षेत्र से आये रूहेला पठानों के कारण इस क्षेत्र को ''रूहेलखण्ड'' नाम से भी जाना जाता है। इस पूरे इलाके पर कब्जा करने के लिये अंग्रेजों को सबसे ज्यादा पापड़ बेलने पड़े थे। इस बरेली ने कौमी एकता और सलीके से जीने का संदेश पूरे देश को दिया। ''आइनेअकबरी'' में ''अबुलफजल'' ने लिखा कि अकबर ने जब इस क्षेत्र की यात्रा की तो हिन्दू मुस्लिम एकता के लिये काम करने की प्रेरणा उसे यहीं से मिली। इसी क्षेत्र की वैभव और समृद्धि का वर्णन अपने यात्रावृतान्तों में चीनीयात्री ''ह्वेनसांग और ''फाहियान'' ने भी किया।

हिन्दू–मुस्लिम एकता की नगरी इस बरेली में ख्वाजा कुतुब मौहल्ले की पेंचदार गालियाँ में स्थित खानकाहे नियाजिया पूरी दुनिया के करोड़ों हिन्दू–मुसलमानों का श्रद्धा का केन्द्र है। सवा दो सौ साल पुराना श्रद्धा का यह केन्द्र प्रसिद्ध सूफी शाह नियाज अहमद द्वारा स्थापित किया गया, जो कि ''ख्वाजा गरीबनवाज'' के रूहानी जानशीन माने जाते हैं। नियाज साहब के पूर्वज ''बुखारा'' (उजबेकिस्तान) के शासक थे। नियाज साहब सभी सूफी सिलसिलों का संगम थे। वे अध्यात्म से सराबोर इस्लाम के प्रकाण्ड विद्वान तो थे ही,

योग, ज्योतिष, गणित, फिजिक्स, हकीमी और संगीत के महारथी भी थे। ज्ञान–विज्ञान की सभी शाखाओं के विद्वान थे आप। उर्दू भाषा के अतिरिक्त अरबी, फारसी, पश्तो, हिन्दी, ब्रज भाषाओं पर आपका पूर्ण अधिकार था।

नियाज साहब चार भाषाओं के विद्वान कवि थे। उन्होंने 'नियाज बेनियाज' उपनाम से उच्च कोटि की शायरी की जिनमें फारसी मिश्रित उर्दू भाषा का प्रयोग किया। अरबी भाषा के शब्दों का भी काफी प्रयोग उनकी शायरी में मिलता है। उनकी शायरी आध्यात्मिकता में सराबोर है। आपका क़लाम अजमेर में ख्वाजा गरीब नवाज, दिल्ली में ''निजामुद्दीन औलिया'', ''ख्वाजा बख्तियार काकी'' की दरगाह में बड़े सम्मान के साथ पढ़ा जाता है। साथ ही यहां उर्स का समापन भी आपकी गज़ल से होता है। यहीं नही पाकिस्तान और अफगानिस्तान में भी उनके क़लाम से उर्स का समापन होता है। तमाम दुनिया में आपके क़लाम की धूम है।

लगभग पौने दो सौ साल पुरानी शायरी आज भी बहुत प्रासंगिक है, ऐसा लगता है जैसे आज के दौर के लिये यह लिखी गई हो। जायसी और खुसरो के पद और नियाज साहब के लिखे ब्रज भाषा के पदों में अंतर कर पाना मुश्किल लगता है क्योंकि इनमें बहुत अधिक समानता है। नियाज साहब की रचनायें चाहें वे किसी भी भाषा में हो लगता है गायकी के हिसाब से ही लिखी गई है मतलब कि वे सभी गेय हैं। उर्दू, फारसी, अरबी की रचनायें गज़ल रूप में है तो ब्रज में रचित पद रूप में हैं। उनके अलावा यहाँ के अन्य सूफी संत ''अज़ीज मियाँ साहब'' ने 'राज' उपनाम से शायरी की है। ''नसीर नियाजी साहब'' ने भी सूफियाना शायरी की है। ये सभी रचनायें उच्च श्रेणी की हैं एवं गायकी के हिसाब की हैं।

चिष्तिया सिलसिले से जुड़ी बरेली सूफी दरगाह खानकाहे नियाजिया का संगीत से विशेष जुड़ाव प्रारम्भ से लेकर अब तक बना हुआ है। यहां संगीत की दीक्षा एवं शिक्षा का प्रबन्ध होता है। खानकाहे नियाजिया भले ही किसी धर्म विशेष से जुड़ी है किन्तु यहां का मूल संदेश ही है कि इंसानियत धर्म से ऊपर है। यही कारण है कि सभी धर्मों के लोग यहां से जुड़े हुये हैं और हर धर्म मजहब का इंसान यहाँ अपना सिर झुकाता है। यहां पर समाजसेवा, कौमीएकता, भाईचारा, दोस्ती व मानवसेवा बिना किसी धार्मिक भेदभाव के पलती–बढ़ती हैं। संगीत के कलाकारों और संगीत के लिये यह जगह बहुत खास है क्योंकि विभिन्न कलाओं के विशेषज्ञों के लिये यह पवित्र स्थल कुछ कर गुजरने की प्रेरणा देता है। देश–विदेश से संगीतकार और विश्वविख्यात पद्मपुरूस्कारों से सम्मानित अपनी–अपनी विधाओं के महारथी कलाकार यहां अपनी हाजिरी देने आते हैं और वे यहां के मुरीद हैं। मुख्य कलाकारों में जैसे उस्ताद बड़े गुलाम अली खां, उस्ताद मुश्ताक हुसैन खां, उस्ताद अहमद जान थिरकवा, उस्ताद अलाउद्दीन खां, उस्ताद विस्मिल्ला खां, उस्ताद विलायत खां, पंड़ित शम्भू महाराज, पंड़ित लच्छू महाराज, बेगम अख्तर, पंड़ित बी.जी. जोग, उस्ताद अमजद अली खां, पंड़ित अजय चक्रवर्ती, उस्ताद राशिद खां, उस्ताद शुजात खां, पंड़ित बिरजू महाराज डागरबन्धु, पंड़ित राजन मिश्रा साजन मिश्र, नैना देवी, पंड़ित राजेन्द्र प्रसन्ना, गिरिजा देवी, पंड़ित शिव कुमार शर्मा जैसे दिग्गज कलाकार प्रमुख है। सभी कलाकारों की यह दिली तमन्ना

रहती है कि वे खानकाह में आकर अपनी कला का प्रदर्षन करें। यहां समय–समय पर इन कलाकारों के लिये बड़े–बड़े संगीत समारोह यहां के प्रबन्धक श्री शब्बूमियाँ साहब द्वारा आयोजित किये जाते हैं। पिछले दस–पन्द्रह सालों में लगभग 500 से ज्यादा कलाकारों ने अपने यहां कार्यक्रम दिये हैं जो एक कीर्तिमान जैसा लगता है। यहाँ के सभी गद्दीनशीन संगीत के पूर्णज्ञाता और पारखी है और संगीत की बारीकियों से परिचित है और स्वयं भी संगीत की किसी न किसी विधा के पारंगत भी हैं। यह बरेली का सौभाग्य है कि इस सूफी पवित्रस्थली के कारण अन्तर्राष्ट्रीय ख्याति प्राप्त कलाकारों का प्रदर्शन बरेलीवासी देख–सुन पाते हैं। यहां की महफिलों का स्वरूप देखकर कलाकार खुद अचंभित रह जाते है। उनके अनुसार ऐसी कलापारखी महफिलें तो दिल्ली में भी नही होती। दृढ़ीभूत आस्था के इस केन्द्र में आकर कलाकार स्वयं को धन्य मानते है। संगीत के ऐसे महायज्ञ में कलाकारों द्वारा स्वरसमिधा समर्पित करना सौभाग्य की ही बात है। यद्यपि खानकाह में पर्याप्त स्थान का अभाव है तथापि कलाकारों का दबाव रहता है कि वे अपनी कला का प्रदर्शन इसी खानकाह में करेंगे। कारण उनका मानना है कि उनके कला शिखर तक पहुँचने में खानकाह के इन सूफी संतों की दुआओं का ही असर है।

संगीत यहां के कण–कण में बसता है। सही मायनों में यह संगीत की साधना स्थली और आराधना स्थल है और संगीत के कलाकारों के लिये तो प्रेरणा स्थली भी है यह पवित्र स्थल क्योंकि कलाकारों को कुछ नया करने की प्रेरणा भी उन्हें यहां से मिलती है जिसे उनके अनुसार शब्दों में बयान नहीं किया जा सकता। अलग–अलग बानी, सुरों और विभिन्न वाद्यों के माध्यम से नादब्रह्म के साधक कलाकार इस पवित्र स्थली में आकर अपनी स्वराजंली से ईश प्रार्थना और आराधना करते हैं। यही कारण है कि यहाँ प्रदर्शित कला में सच्चाई एवं सादगी होती है। अपनी कला द्वारा समर्पण का भाव यहां के अतिरिक्त उन्हें अन्यत्र कहीं और प्राप्त नहीं होता। कानों को स्पर्ष करते, दिलों में उतरते स्वर, लय पर थिरकते पाँव और एक के बाद एक अलग–अलग साजों से उभरती स्वरलहरियां इन सबका मिला जुला माहौल यहां का एक आम माहौल है। संगीत के माध्यम से हिन्दू–मुस्लिम एकता की मशाल को जलाये रखने में खानकाहे नियाजिया के योगदान को भुलाया नहीं जा सकता। आज के बिगड़ते माहौल ओर अलगाववाद के दौर में यहां के सरकार यह चाहते है कि इस खानकाह से संगीत के सुरों के माध्यम से प्यार–मौहब्बत, खुलूस और अपनेपन का पैगाम पूरी दुनिया में अपने पैर पसारें। यहाँ बसन्त और होली का त्यौहार सभी एक साथ मनाते है।खानकाहे नियाजिया के सूफी संतों ने सांगीतिक महत्व की बेशकीमती रचनायें बनाई है। जिनका मूल्य आंका जाये तो वे अमीर खुसरों की रचनाओं से कहीं भी कमतर नही हैं। उर्दू, अरबी, फारसी भाषाओं में तो यह हैं ही लेकिन ब्रज भाषा में बहुत सी रचनायें यहां के सूफी संतों ने रची है यहीं नहीं उनके राग एवं तालों का निर्धारण भी उन्होंने स्वयं किया है जिससे यह स्वतः सिद्ध होता है कि वे कितने बड़े संगीतज्ञाता और वाग्येकार रहे हैं। शारंगदेव के वाग्येकार की परिभाषा में ये सूफी संत पूरी तरह समाविष्ट नजर आते है।

इस प्रकार खानकाहे–नियाजिया वह साधना और उपासना स्थली है जहां संगीत बसता है, गूंजता है, पलता है और पल्लवित–संबर्द्धित होता है और जहाँ कलाकार स्वराञजलि द्वारा प्रार्थना और आराधना कर उस परम शक्ति से एकाकार होता है।

4

संगीत शिक्षा के सामाजिक सारोकार

अमित कुमार वर्मा

सारांश

संगीत के सामाजिक सारोकार बड़े गहरे हैं। उच्चतम् जीवन मूल्यों की प्राप्ति हेतु विभिन्न विद्वानों ने शिक्षा में संगीत विषय की अनिवार्यता व महत्ता को स्वीकारा है। विभिन्न संगीत सम्मेलन व संगीत उत्सव भी समाज को संगीत के संस्कारों से संस्कारित कराते है। संगीत सम्मेलन सैंकड़ों देशी–विदेशी श्रोताओं व दर्शकों को आकर्शित करते हैं, जिससे सांगीतिक पर्यटन को भी बढ़ावा मिलता है। संगीत शिक्षा के अन्य पहलुओं के अंतर्गत– वर्तमान में संगीत एक चिकित्सा पद्धति के रूप में समाज को स्वास्थ्य लाभ दे रहा है साथ ही रोजगार के अवसर भी उपलब्ध करा रहा है। सीमापार के देशों के साथ सौहार्दपूर्ण संबंध बनाने में संगीत की महत्वपूर्ण भूमिका रही है। अंतर्राष्ट्रीय स्तर पर विभिन्न देशों के संगीतकारों का एक–दूसरे के देशों में आवागमन से तथा एक–दूसरे को सम्मानित किये जाने से सांस्कृतिक भाई–चारे की भावना को बल मिलता है। संगीत के अंतर्राष्ट्रीय मंच पर भारतीय संगीतकारों ने विभिन्न देशों के संगीतकारों के साथ मिलकर संगीत की दो भिन्न धाराओं की जो जुगलबंदी प्रस्तुत की, वह संगीत के वैश्वीकरण के साथ–साथ अंतर्राष्ट्रीय मंच पर विभिन्न देशों के मध्य सांगीतिक एवं सांस्कृतिक एकता को भी दर्शाती है। प्रस्तुत शोध पत्र में उपरोक्त बिन्दुओं की विस्तार से चर्चा की गई है।

संगीत आनंददायक होने के कारण ऐन्द्रिय सुख के साथ–साथ मानसिक, भावनात्मक और आध्यात्मिक सुख भी प्रदान करता है साथ ही मानवीय जीवन को संस्कारित भी करता है। संगीत एक ऐसी शिक्षा पद्धति है, जिसमें ज्ञान व अनुभव तो मिलता ही है साथ ही हमारी

चेतना शक्ति भी उद्दीपित होती है। जब शाश्वत शान्ति और अखण्ड आनंद के प्रश्न पर विज्ञान मौन हो जाता है तब संगीत चुनौती को स्वीकार करता है। कवि गुरू रवीन्द्रनाथ टैगोर ने कहा है–''सुख–दुख की प्रयोगशाला में संगीत यंत्र द्वारा जब आत्मा को उपचार रूप में पा लिया जाता है, तब परमानंद की स्थिति स्वयं आ जाती है।''

संगीत के सामाजिक सारोकार बड़े गहरे हैं। ब्रिटिश काल में जब राजाओं–नवाबों की रियासतें समाप्त हो गई तो संगीतकार, जिन्हें इन रियासतों मे संरक्षण मिला था, सड़क पर आ गये। पेट की भूख उन्हें कोठे पर ले गई। कोठियों की शान समझा जाने वाला संगीत अब कोठों की रौनक बन चुका था। जिस कारण संगीत सभ्रांत समाज से दूर हो गया। अच्छे घर के लड़के–लड़कियों के लिये नाचने–गाने की सख्त मनाही थी। ऐसे समय में पं0 विष्णु दिगम्बर पलुस्कर तथा पं0 विष्णु नारायण भातखण्डे ने संगीत को कोठों से निकालकर उसे सभ्रांत समाज में स्थापित करने का अविस्मरणीय कार्य किया। संगीत विद्यालय खोलने का उद्देश्य समाज को संगीत के संस्कारों से संस्कारित करना था। वह संगीत जो सैकड़ों वर्शों से घरानों की चार–दीवारी में कैद था, अब उसका लोकतंत्रीकरण हो चुका था। अब संगीत 'सर्वजन हिताय सर्वजन सुखाय' के लिये हो गया था।

उच्चतम् जीवन मूल्यों की प्राप्ति हेतु समय–समय पर विभिन्न विद्वानों ने शिक्षा में संगीत विशय की अनिवार्यता व महत्ता को स्वीकारा तथा उसके उदात्त स्वरूप के प्रति नई पीढ़ी में जागरुकता लाने का प्रयास किया। इसी क्रम में पं0 विष्णु दिगम्बर पलुस्कर ने वर्ष 1901 ई0 में लाहौर में गांधर्व संगीत महाविद्यालय की स्थापना की। उसी वर्ष कवि गुरू रवीन्द्रनाथ टैगोर ने शान्ति निकेतन में 'ब्रह्मचर्य विद्यालय' की स्थापना की तथा उसमें संगीत को एक अनिवार्य विशय के रूप में स्थान दिया। 1906 ई0 में बनारस में भातखण्डे जी के सहयोग से ''श्री काशी संगीत समाज'' की स्थापना हुई तो इसी वर्ष डॉ0 ऐनीबेसेन्ट के द्वारा 'थियोसोफिकल विद्यालय' की स्थापना बनारस में की गई। जिसमें संगीत को एक विषय के रूप में पढ़ाया जाना आरम्भ किया गया। भातखण्डे जी द्वारा ही 1926 ई0 में लखनऊ में 'मैरिस कालेज ऑफ हिन्दुस्तानी म्यूजिक' की स्थापना की गई तथा इसी वर्ष इलाहाबाद में 'प्रयाग संगीत समिति' नामक संगीत संस्था का शुभारम्भ हुआ। पं0 मदन मोहन मालवीय जी ने भी अपने नवसृजित 'काशी हिन्दू विश्वविद्यालय' में विज्ञान व आधुनिक विषयों के साथ–साथ कला व संगीत विषयों की अनिवार्यता को समझा। इसी उद्देश्य से 1950 ई0 में ''श्री कला संगीत भारती'' नामक संस्था स्थापित की गई। इस प्रकार नई पीढ़ी में नैतिक एवं सांस्कृतिक मूल्यों के हस्तांतरण में संगीत की विद्यालयीन शिक्षा का महत्व समझा गया। महात्मा गांधी भी बच्चों को संगीत शिक्षा दिये जाने के पक्षधर थे।

V. Hornerds अनुसार–"Music education is concerned with musical literacy, ear training, creating of musicAnd the emotionalAndAesthetic growth of the pupil as wellAs the enjoyment of music." डॉ. सम्पूर्णानन्द ने संगीत के आध्यात्मिक महत्व को बताते हुये लिखा है-"Music, Art and Literature lead a person from the lower level of physical existence to an existence to a higher spiritual plane and in this way help in self purification."

केवल संगीत विद्यालय ही समाज को संगीत की शिक्षा नही देते बल्कि विभिन्न संगीत सम्मेलन व संगीत उत्सव भी समाज को संगीत के संस्कारों से संस्कारित कराते है। स्वामी हरिवल्लभ संगीत सम्मेलन, जालंधर; तानसेन संगीत सम्मेलन, ग्वालियर; हरिदास संगीत सम्मेलन, मथुरा; खजुराहो नृत्य महोत्सव, खजुराहो; आदि संगीत सम्मेलन एक ओर नई पीढ़ी में संगीत के प्रति रुचि, आकर्षण व हमारी संगीत परम्परा के प्रति श्रद्धाभाव पैदा करते है तो दूसरी ओर पर्यटन को भी बढ़ावा देते हैं। विभिन्न राज्यों में होने वाले संगीत सम्मेलन सैंकड़ों देशी–विदेशी श्रोताओं व दर्शकों को आकर्षित करते हैं, जिससे सांगीतिक पर्यटन को भी बढ़ावा मिलता है।

वर्तमान में संगीत एक चिकित्सा पद्धति के रूप में मानसिक रोगों के निवारण में भी महत्वपूर्ण भूमिका निभा रही है। जीवशास्त्री व मनोवैज्ञानिक मानते हैं कि स्वस्थ मानव शरीर में जैव विद्युत धाराओं का प्रवाह निरंतर बना रहता है। इन जैव विद्युत धाराओं में अवरोध उत्पन्न होने पर विभिन्न प्रकार की शारीरिक व मानसिक व्याधियां उत्पन्न हो जाती हैं। संगीत उपचार में इस विधि में संगीत की सात्विक व ऊर्जावान ध्वनियां शरीर के भीतर की विद्युत धाराओं को अवरोधमुक्त कर देती हैं। जिससे शारीरिक व मानसिक स्वास्थ्य की प्राप्ति होती है। वर्तमान में विभिन्न रागों का मनुष्य के मानसिक स्वास्थ्य पर क्या प्रभाव पड़ता है, इस संबंध में काफी शोध हुये है और सकारात्मक परिणाम प्राप्त हुये हैं। 'राग पूरिया' से अनिद्रा तथा राग 'सारंग' से सिरदर्द जैसे रोगों का शमन होता है। 'राग मल्हार' व 'जयजयवंती' शरीर की ऊर्जा को बढ़ाते हैं तथा मस्तिष्क को शांत कर क्रोध को दूर करते हैं। इस प्रकार संगीत एक चिकित्सा पद्धति के रूप में लोगों को स्वास्थ्य लाभ दे रहा है साथ ही रोजगार के अवसर भी उपलब्ध करा रहा है।

सीमापार के देशों के साथ सौहार्दपूर्ण संबंध बनाने में संगीत की भूमिका को नकारा नही जा सकता। इतिहास इस बात का साक्षी है कि प्राचीनकाल से ही भारत विश्व के विभिन्न देशों के साथ सांस्कृतिक व सांगीतिक संबंध स्थापित कर विश्व शांति व विश्व बंधुत्व की परिकल्पना को यथार्थ में परिणित करता आया है। विभिन्न कालों में भारतीय संगीत का प्रचार–प्रसार धार्मिक एवं शिक्षण संस्थाओं, व्यापारियों, युद्ध के सिपाहियों, वैवाहिक संबंधों आदि के माध्यम से होता रहा है। वर्तमान में भारत सरकार ने सीमापार के देशों साथ सांस्कृतिक संबंध स्थापित करने के लिये 1950 में भारतीय सांस्कृतिक संबंध परिषद, 1953 में संगीत नाटक अकादमी जैसी कई संस्थायें स्थापित की। इनके अंतर्गत भारत सरकार द्वारा संगीत एवं लोक कला के कलाकारों, विद्वानों व प्रशिक्षकों को विदेशों में संबंधित कला के अध्ययन व प्रचार–प्रसार के लिये भेजा जाता है।

अन्तर्राष्ट्रीय स्तर पर सांगीतिक संबंधों को दृढ़ता प्रदान करने के लिये विभिन्न देशों की सरकारें तथा निजी संस्थायें समय–समय पर एक–दूसरे के संगीत कलाकारों को सम्मानित करती रहती हैं, जिससे सांस्कृतिक भाई–चारे की भावना को बल मिलता है। पाकिस्तान के अनेक कलाकार उस्ताद गुलाम अली, उस्ताद नुसरत फतेह अली खाँ, आबिदा परवीन

आदि फनकार भारत में सम्मानित हो चुके हैं। विदेशी संगीतकारों में विश्व प्रसिद्ध वायलिन वादक लार्ड यहूदी मेन्यूहिन को केन्द्रीय संगीत नाटक अकादमी द्वारा रत्न सदस्यता से सम्मानित किया जा चुका है। इसके अतिरिक्त संगीत के अंतर्राष्ट्रीय मंच पर विश्व के तमाम देशों ने भारतीय संगीत कलाकारों को उच्च सम्मानों वा पुरस्कारों से सम्मानित किया है। जिसके अंतर्गत पं. रविशंकर को संगीत जगत के सर्वोच्च अंतर्राष्ट्रीय सम्मान 'ग्रैमी अवार्ड' से दो बार सम्मानित किया जा चुका है। कैलिफोर्निया विश्वविद्यालय सहित दुनिया के 14 विश्वविद्यालयों ने उन्हें डाक्टरेट की उपाधि से सम्मानित किया है।

संगीत के अंतर्राष्ट्रीय मंच पर भारतीय संगीतकारों ने विभिन्न देशों के संगीतकारों के साथ मिलकर संगीत की दो भिन्न धाराओं की जो जुगलबंदी प्रस्तुत की, वह संगीत के वैश्वीकरण के साथ–साथ अंतर्राष्ट्रीय मंच पर विभिन्न देशों के मध्य सांगीतिक एवं सांस्कृतिक एकता को दर्शाती है। पं. रविशंकर, उस्ताद अली अकबर, पं. वी.जी. जोग और डॉ. एल. सुब्राह्मण्यम् जैसे दिग्गज भारतीय संगीतकारों ने वायलिन वादक लार्ड यहूदी मेन्यूहिन के साथ मिलकर अनेक कालजयी रचनाओं का सृजन और प्रस्तुतीकरण किया, जो संगीत के इतिहास की धरोहर है। यहूदी मेन्यूहिन ने भारतीय धुनों को अमेरिका व ब्रिटेन की जनता के सामने प्रदर्शित कर जो लोकप्रियता हासिल की, उसके लिये उन्होनें स्वयं को भारतीय संगीत का ऋणी माना।

पिछले कुछ दशकों में अंतर्राष्ट्रीय स्तर पर भारतीय संगीत की शिक्षा का काफी प्रचार हुआ है। यूरोप सहित पश्चिम के कई देशों के विश्वविद्यालयों ने भारतीय संगीत की शिक्षा को अपने शैक्षणिक पाठ्यक्रम में शामिल किया है। यूनिवर्सिटी ऑफ वाशिंगटन, कैलिफोर्नियो इन्स्टीट्यूट और फाइन आर्टस् जैसे पश्चिम देशों के विश्वविद्यालयों में भारतीय संगीत की शिक्षा दी जा रही है। जबकि भारत में सन् 1901 में तमिलनाडु में स्थापित 'कोडैकनाल इंटरनेशनल स्कूल' (के0आई0एस0) पिछले 100 से अधिक वर्षों से अंतर्राष्ट्रीय स्तर पर संगीत की शिक्षा दे रहा है। लगभग 30 से अधिक देशों के संगीतार्थी यहाँ पश्चिमी संगीत की शिक्षा ग्रहण कर रहे हैं। के0आई0एस0 बैण्ड यूरोप के इंटरनेशनल आनर्स बैण्ड और क्वायर फेस्टिवल समेत भारत तथा दूसरे देशों में कई कार्यक्रम पेश कर चुका है।

आज सभ्य मानव समाज के सामने आतंकवाद की समस्या गंभीर रूप धारण करती जा रही है। पूँजीवाद और उपभोक्तावादी संस्कृति के कारण विश्व के तमाम देशों के मध्य अधिक से अधिक आर्थिक लाभ कमाने की होड़ मची हुई है, जिसके कारण विभिन्न देशों के मध्य संबंध बनते बिगड़ते रहते हैं। भारत विभिन्न देशों के साथ मधुर संबंध बनाये रखने के लिये शुरुआत से ही सांगीतिक आदान–प्रदान की नीतियों का प्रयोग करता रहा है। चूँकि संगीत मानवतावाद का पोषक है तथा संगीत से प्रेम, सहिष्णुता विश्व बंधुत्व की भावना का सहज ही विकास होता है। इसलिये विश्व को आतंकवाद की समस्या से उबारने तथा उपभोक्तावादी संस्कृति के कारण नई पीढ़ी में हुये नैतिक मूल्यों के ह्रास की पूर्ति के लिये संगीत की शिक्षा को बढ़ावा दिया जाना समय की आवश्यकता है। संगीत शिक्षा के माध्यम

से जहाँ एक ओर नैतिक मूल्यों का संरक्षण होगा वहीं विश्व–शान्ति, विश्व–बंधुत्व तथा वसुधैव कुटुम्बकम् की भावना साकार होगी।

संदर्भ

1. मिश्र, विजय शंकर, (2004) अँतर्नादः सुर और साज, नई दिल्लीः कनिश्क प्रकाशन
2. पलनीटकर, अलका (2004) –शास्त्रीय संगीत शिक्षा, समस्या एवं समाधान,
3. संवाद' स्मारिका, संगीत एवं मंच कला संकाय, काशी हिन्दू विश्वविद्यालय द्वारा प्रकाशित
4. वर्मा, अमित कुमार –संगीत के माध्यम से नई पीढ़ी में नैतिक एवं सांस्कृतिक मूल्यों का पुनर्जागरण, कुसुम मिश्रा एवं स्वरवंदना शर्मा; संपादक, संगीत संचेतना, बसंत कन्या महाविद्यालय, वाराणसी, वर्ष 2007,
5. वर्मा, अमित कुमार –भारत के अंतर्राष्ट्रीय सांगीतिक संबंध, संगीत पत्रिका, जून 2009, पृ. 3–5.

5

भारतीय संगीत : आध्यात्मिक दृष्टि

विशाल जैन

संगीत-परंपरा

भारतीय संस्कृति धर्म एवं अध्यात्म से अनुप्राणित रही है। इस संस्कृति में आचार–विचार, जीवन चर्या, आहार विहार की परिपाटी सहित सम्पूर्ण मानव जीवन को अध्यात्मोन्मुख माना गया है। भारतीय संस्कृति व दर्शन में संगीत कला का स्थान 64 कलाओं में सर्वश्रेष्ठ माना गया है। संगीत न केवल कला है, वह शास्त्र है तथा विद्या भी है। भारतीय संस्कृति में किसी भी कला को ईश्वर प्राप्ति के मार्ग से जोड़कर उसे उच्च स्थान दिया गया है। जिनमें संगीत कला सर्वोपरि होने के साथ–साथ जनमानस में विशिष्ट स्थान रखती है। जीवन के प्रारम्भ से अन्त तक यह कला उसके साथ रहती है।

भारतीय परम्परा के अनुसार सभी शास्त्रीय विषयों का उद्गम वेदों से माना जाता है, और उनका संबंध देवों से जोड़ा जाता है। संभव है, कि दैवी शक्तियों के आशीर्वादों की परिकल्पना अथवा उसकी पवित्रता प्रमाणित करने की दृष्टि से उसका सम्बन्ध देवों से स्थापित किया जाता रहा हो, नाटयशास्त्र में उपलब्ध नाटयोत्पत्ति का इतिहास संभवतः विश्व में प्राप्त नाटयकला के उद्गम का सर्वाधिक प्राचीन विवरण है। नाटयशास्त्र के अनुसार वैवस्वत मन्वन्तर के त्रेतायुग के प्रारम्भ में जब लोग काम, क्रोध, मोह, लोभ, ईर्ष्या और सुख–दुखादि से अभिभूत हो गये थे, तब उस समय इन्द्र आदि देवताओं ने ब्रम्हा जी के पास जाकर कहा कि भगवन हम लोग ऐसा क्रीडनीयक (मनोरंजन) चाहते हैं, जो दृश्य–श्रव्य दोनों हो। तब ब्रम्हा ने योग का आश्रय लेकर चारों वेदों का स्मरण कर यह संकल्प किया कि "मैं इतिहास सहित एक ऐसे नाटय नामक पंचम वेद की रचना करता हूँ, जो धर्म एवं अर्थ की प्राप्ति करने वाला हो, यशस्य हो, उपदेश एवं ज्ञान संग्रह से युक्त हो, समस्त शास्त्रों के

अर्थों से युक्त हो तथा सभी शिल्पकलाओं को प्रदर्शित करने वाला हो" इस प्रकार विचार करके ऋग्वेद से पाठय, सामवेद से गान, यजुर्वेद से अभिनय और अथर्ववेद से रसों को ग्रहण करके नाटयवेद की रचना की, जो सभी वर्णों के लिए ज्ञेय था।[1]

इसी नाटयशास्त्र को 'सामवेद' के पश्चात संगीत का महत्वपूर्ण ग्रन्थ माना जाता है, क्योंकि इसके 28 से 33 वे अध्याय में संगीत संबंधी प्रचुर सामग्री प्राप्त होती है। 'नाटयशास्त्र' को 'पंचमवेद' की संज्ञा प्राप्त है व इसके पश्चात संगीत शास्त्रों की वृहद परम्परा पाई जाती है।

संगीत एवं दर्शन

संगीत के जिन शास्त्रीय ग्रन्थों में प्राचीन परम्परा जीवित है, वे सभी दर्शन से प्रभावित हैं, विशेश रूप से संगीत के तत्वनिरूपण में यथा–नाद, श्रुति, स्वर, पिण्डोत्पत्ति ताल आदि विशय प्रतिपादन शैली भी दर्शन से प्रभावित है, यथा पदार्थसंग्रह, प्रतिज्ञा, अनुबंध–चतुश्टय, पुरूशार्थ चतुश्टय, खण्डन–मण्डन आदि, नादब्रम्ह, प्राणाग्नि–संयोग से नाद की उत्पत्ति, ब्रम्ह का स्थान ब्रम्हग्रन्थि, दृश्टा दृश्टफल, ध्वनि को परायोनि यानि मूल कारण बताना, पिण्डोत्पत्ति– निरूपण भौतिक या वैज्ञानिक आधार पर नहीं बल्कि वेदान्त के दर्शन के आधार पर होना, श्रुतियों की बाईस संख्या के कारण का निरूपण, श्रुतियों के नाम, श्रुति जातियों की सार्थकता, स्वरों के वर्ण, ऋषि, छन्द, देवता, देवादिकुल इत्यादि स्थलों को देखने पर यह भावना दृढ़ होती है, कि भारतीय संगीत शास्त्र, दर्शनों से पूर्णतया प्रभावित है। ये सभी तथ्य यह स्पष्ट इंगित करते हैं, कि हमारे संगीत शास्त्रकार इन सभी परम्पराओं में जी रहे थे और उनसे परम्पराएँ जीवन्त थीं।[2] दर्शन की इस भावना से ही संगीत का पुष्ट विकास कालान्तर में हुआ, तथा अद्यतन यह विकास प्रवाहित है।

संगीतः भक्ति मार्ग

भक्तों के लिए संगीत अपने लालित्य, प्रवाह और सम्पूर्ण ब्रह्मण्ड में व्याप्त नाद और लय से अनुप्राणित होने के कारण अपने किसी भी रूप में आत्मविस्मृति की अवस्था तक पहुँचने का उत्कृष्ट साधन माना जाता है। संगीत साधन में 'नाद' को उपास्य तत्व एवं उपासना का साधन स्वीकार करते हुए उसे ब्रह्मस्वरूप माना गया है। केवल 'ओम' का उच्चारण हो या भजन, कीर्तन के रूप में प्रयुक्त संगीतात्मक विधायें–यदि अपने किसी भी रूप के भगवदोपासना के लिए प्रयुक्त संगीत अपने सम्पूर्ण रूप में पूरी निष्ठा, साधना तथा ईशवन्दना के लिए अपेक्षित भावना से सम्पन्न किया जाए तो ऐसा भक्ति संगीत मोक्ष प्राप्ति के मार्ग का श्रेष्ठतम साधन बन जाता है।[3]

भक्ति मार्ग के साधकों में अष्टछाप कवि, तुलसी, सूर, मीरा, कबीर, रैदास आदि ने संगीत को ही भक्तिमार्ग में माध्यम बनाया, जो आज तक प्रासंगिक है।

संगीत महिमा

वीणावादनतत्वज्ञः श्रुतिजातिविशारदः तालज्ञश्चाप्रयासेन मोक्ष मार्गं निगच्छति,
गीतज्ञो यदि गीतेन नाप्नोति परमं पदम रूद्रस्यानुचरो भूत्वा तेनैव सह मोदते,
याज्ञ0 स्मृति– 3–4–115, 116

जो वीणा वादन के तत्व या सार को जानता है जो श्रुतियों और जातियों के प्रयोग में कुशल है, जो ताल का ज्ञाता है वह मोक्ष मार्ग को प्राप्त होता है। गीतज्ञ यदि गीत के द्वारा परमपद को प्राप्त नहीं होता तो वह रूद्र का अनुचर बनकर उनके संग में आनन्द पाता रहता है।

एक विख्यात पौराणिक उक्ति इस प्रकार है–

अर्चनादधिकं ध्यानं ध्यानात कोटिगुणम जपः,
जपात् कोटिगुणं गानं गानात् परतरं नहि।,

ध्यान पूजा से अधिक है, जप ध्यान से अधिक है, गान जप से अधिक है और गान से अधिक कुछ भी नहीं है।[4]

ऐसे अनेको श्लोकों व उद्धरणों से भारतीय ज्ञान संपदा भरी पड़ी है, जिसमें संगीत को महत्वपूर्ण साधन माना गया है।

संगीत-व्याप्ति

हमारे देश के विभिन्न प्रान्तों में प्रवचन, गीत, नृत्य, नाट्य के स्वतन्त्र अथवा मिले–जुले प्रयोग की परम्पराएं चली आई हैं, बंगाल और महाराश्ट्र के कीर्तन में व्याख्यान, गायन के एकल और समवेत रूप, कहीं–कहीं नृत्य का भी मिला–जुला रूप दिखाई देता है, दक्षिण की हरिकथा का भी इसी प्रकार मिला–जुला रूप है। मणिपुरी नट–संकीर्तन और आसाम के बड़गीत में गान व सहकृत नृत्य है। पंजाब के शब्द में एकल व समवेत गायन का रूप है। नाम संकीर्तन तो पूरे देश में व्याप्त है।

ब्रज की रासलीला, रामलीला के विविध रूप, आसाम का अंकिया नाट और भावना, बंगाल की जात्रा, छत्तीसगढ़ का पण्डवानी गीत, नृत्य नाट्य के मिले जुले प्रयोगों का उत्कृष्ट उदाहरण है।[5]

शारंगदेव ने 'संगीत रत्नाकर' (12वीं शताब्दी) में गीत, वाद्य, नृत्य के समावेश को संगीत कहा है, समस्त कलाओं के लिए मार्गदर्शक संगीत कला भारतीय जनमानस के मन–प्राण में पूर्णतया व्याप्त है।

संगीत-साधना

प्रसिद्ध तबलावादक पं. छोटेलाल मिश्र के अनुसार– संगीत की कठोर साधना से संगीत की प्राप्ति होती है और साधना पूर्ण होने पर सिद्धि प्राप्त हो जाती है। संगीत मनोरंजन

का साधन है, परन्तु इसके साधको के चार वर्ग हैं साधारण, मध्यम, उत्तम एवं सर्वोत्तम। साधारण वर्ग के संगीतकार का संगीत साधारण होता है। जिसका श्रोता आम जनसमुदाय होता है, मध्यम वर्ग के संगीतकार का संगीत नियमित और शास्त्रानुकूल होता है, जिसके प्रयोक्ता मैं में लिप्त होते है, मैं गा रहा हूँ, मैं बजा रहा हूँ, मेरे शब्द हैं, मेरा संगीत है आदि रूपों में आत्मविज्ञापन करते रहते है। उत्तम वर्ग के संगीतकार निर्लिप्त भाव से साधना करने वाले संगीत के समर्पित साधक होते है। वे संगीत के लिए ही अवतरित होते हैं और संगीत में ही चिर समाधिस्थ हो जाते है, ऐसे संगीतकार अमर हैं, जैसे विष्णु दिगम्बर पलुस्कर, गुलाम अली खाँ, रविशंकर, विलायत खाँ, कण्ठे महाराज, अनोखेलाल मिश्र। सर्वोत्तम वर्ग के संगीतकार का ध्येय संगीत नहीं होता, उनका ध्येय ईश्वर प्राप्ति है, वे संगीत को ईश्वर प्राप्ति का माध्यम मानते है, जैसे– स्वामी हरिदास, स्वामी त्यागराज, जब भी संगीत में लीन हुए, उनके आराध्य देव उनके सम्मुख होते थे।[6] सभी वर्गो के संगीतकारों का अपना महत्व है।

भारतीय संगीत के विविध आयाम

भारतीय शास्त्रीय संगीत का ध्रुपद–धमार पूर्णतः ईश्वरोपासना का प्रतीक हैं। ध्रुपद के साथ पखावज व वीणा की संगति उसे ईश्वरीय व भव्य विधा बनाती है। ध्रुपद गायन के उन्नायक स्वामी हरिदास, बैजू, बक्शू, तानसेन इत्यादि रहे जिन्होंने इस विधा को भारतीय संगीत की सर्वोच्च विधा बनाया। ध्रुपद गायन के दो प्रमुख आश्रय स्थल रहे, वैशणव मंदिर और राजदरबार, ये दो धारायें साथ–साथ प्रवाहित होती रही और अनेक ध्रुपद एक से दूसरे में ग्रहण किये गये।

मंदिरों में देवदासी व नृत्यांगनाओं की प्रथा से सब परिचित है, ये मंदिरों के इश्टदेव के प्रति समर्पित होती थी और वहाँ गाये जाने वाले पदों के साथ नृत्य व अभिनय करती थी, इस प्रकार राजदरबारों में भी ध्रुपद के साथ नृत्य की परपंरा रही है। 'सहसरस' इसका प्रमाण है। साथ ही लेखिका ने टी.एल. राणा द्वारा नेपाल दरबार में ध्रुपद–नृत्य की पुश्टि का उल्लेख, ठाकुर जयदेव सिंह का अनुभव व भावभट्ट के ग्रंथ का भी उल्लेख किया है।[7] ध्रुपद रचनाओं में ईश्वरभक्ति गुरू महिमा, नादोपासना के कई उदाहरण है। एक रचना इसप्रकार है–

तुम रब तुम साहेब तुम ही करतार।
घट–घट पूरन जल थल भर भार।।
तुम ही रहीम तुम ही करीम
गावत गुनी गंधर्व सुर नर सुरनार
तुम ही पूरन ब्रम्ह तुम ही सकल
तुम ही जगदगुरु तुम ही सरदार
कहे मियॉं तानसेन तुम ही आप
तुम ही करत सकल जग को भवपार।।[8]

कालान्तर में ख्याल परंपरा का सूत्रपात हुआ, ख्याल गायन के साथ–साथ तबला, कथक, सितार इत्यादि का भी विकास हुआ। ख्याल के ज्यादातर पद श्रृंगारिक होते हुए भी उनमें अध्यात्म व दर्शन के पद पाये जाते है।

राग भटियार की एक रचना है–
"तनिक सुन ही सत्य वचन अब
सुख कल्पना दुख कल्पना, कल्पना है मन की
मन वासना मिटाए, मिटत सब बंध।।9

ख्याल के साथ ठुमरी, भजन, गीत, लोकगीत, फिल्मी गीतों में भी ईश्वरभक्ति के पद पाये जाते है।

निष्कर्ष

इस प्रकार भारतीय संगीत अध्यात्म व दर्शन का प्रतिबिंब है। भारतीय संगीत की आत्मा में उस सृष्टिकर्ता का वास है। जिस प्रकार ईश्वर को किसने देखा? यह प्रश्न विचारणीय है, उसी प्रकार 'स्वर' को किसने देखा? यह प्रश्न भी। अमूर्त से मूर्त व मूर्त से अमूर्त की यह यात्रा आनंददायक तो है साथ ही प्रेरणास्पद भी है। भारतीय संगीत का विकास विश्व बंधुत्व व शांति का विकास है।

संदर्भ सूची

1. नाट्यशास्त्र– भाग प्रथम, डा. पारसनाथ द्विवेदी – पृ. 27–28
2. भारतीय संगीतशास्त्र का दर्शनपरक अनुशीलन– विमला मुसलगॉवकर, पृ. 19
3. ब्रज के देवालयों में संगीत परंपरा– डा. राकेशबाला सक्सेना, पृ. 20
4. प्रेम रसायन एवं संगीत मीमांसा, उर्मिला शर्मा, पृ. 113
5. प्रेम रसायन एवं संगीत मीमांसा, उर्मिला शर्मा, पृ. 129
6. पं0 छोटेलाल मिश्र का साक्षात्कार, छायानट अक्टूबर 2007 मार्च 2008. अंक 120, पृ. 39
7. संगीत संचयन, सुभद्रा चौधरी, पृ. 174–175
8. डागर परंपरा में गाया जाने वाला तानसेन का पद।
9. ख्याल की एक प्रसिद्ध रचना।

6

ब्रज में देवोपासना के विभिन्न सम्प्रदाय एवं उनकी कीर्तन परम्परा

नम्रता मिश्रा

"बन्दहु ब्रजसोभा सहज, सुन्दर सखद सुधाम
जेहि रज रम्य सुपावनी, कोमल ललित ललाम।।"

ब्रज एवं ब्रज संस्कृति भारतीय संस्कृति की प्राण एवं अनमोल धरोहर है जिसका प्रभाव हमारे पूरे देश में ही नहीं बल्कि पूरे विश्व पर परिलक्षित होता है। ब्रज संस्कृति का मूल स्वरूप भगवान कृष्ण में दिखाई देता है अर्थात् श्री कृष्ण की इस संस्कृति के जनक हैं।1

ब्रज के वैष्णव मंदिरों में कीर्तन तथा समाज गायन की परम्परा अत्यधिक प्राचीन एवं समृद्ध रही है। यहाँ पुष्टिमार्गीय मंदिरों की भी अपनी संगीत परम्परा रही है जिसे हवेली संगीत के नाम से प्रसिद्धि मिली। ब्रज के वैष्णवाचार्यो ने श्री राधाकृष्ण की विभिन्न लीलाओं का वर्णन एवं उनका गुणगान करते हुए भक्ति एवं संगीत के सम्बन्ध को स्वीकार किया है।

देवालयों में प्रचलित कीर्तन एवं समाज गायन पद्धति का उदय बहुंत पूर्व हो चुका था। इसके चिन्ह वैदिक काल में सामवैदिक संगीत में यत्र–तत्र मिलते हैं, जहाँ प्रस्तोता, उद्गाता तथा प्रतिहर्ता आदि तीनों गायक मिलकर पंचविध सामगान करते थे। वैदिक युग से ही सामगान, गंधर्वगान, सूक्त स्रोत तथा जयदेव कृत दिव्य प्रबन्ध अष्टपदी आदि सांगीतिक शैलियाँ समय–समय पर देवाराधन का माध्यम थीं।

पूर्व मध्य युग में ब्रज के सगुणोपासक अनेक वैष्णव धर्म सम्प्रदायों का प्रादुर्भाव हुआ, जिनके प्रवर्तकों में वल्लभाचार्य जी, हरिदास जी, हित हरिवंश जी, हरिराम व्यासाचार्य तथा चैतन्य आदि के नाम उल्लेखनीय हैं। ये सभी आचार्य यह सत्य जानते थे कि समाज के

विकास के लिये जितना आवश्यक धर्म है उतना ही जीवन को सुसंस्कृत बनाने के लिये संगीत कला की आवश्यकता है।

कृष्ण भक्तों में यद्यपि साध्य की एकता थी किन्तु उनकी सेवा विधि तथा कृष्ण के विभिन्न रूपों सम्बन्धी मान्यताओं में थोड़ा बहुत अन्तर था जिनके कारण निम्नलिखित प्रमुख धार्मिक सम्प्रदायों की स्थापना हुई –

1. वल्लभ सम्प्रदाय (पुष्टिमार्गीय सम्प्रदाय)
2. राधावल्लभ सम्प्रदाय
3. हरिदासी अथवा सखी सम्प्रदाय
4. गौड़ीय सम्प्रदाय
5. निम्बार्क सम्प्रदाय2

इसके अतिरिक्त ''नन्दगॉव एवं बरसाना की सामूहिक समाज गान परम्परा'' एवं ''रामानुज सम्प्रदाय'' के समाज गान का भी प्रचार–प्रचार खूब हुआ ब्रज की धरती पर।

1. वल्लभ सम्प्रदाय/पुष्ठिटमार्गीय संगीत परम्परा ''हवेली संगीत''

श्री वल्लभाचार्य जी द्वारा प्रवर्तित इस भक्ति सम्प्रदाय (पुष्टिमार्ग) का भारतीय वेदान्त व दर्शन से सीधा सम्बन्ध है। इस सम्प्रदाय की अपनी अलग मान्यताएँ हैं, यथा– गुरू मंत्र, कंठी माला, तिलक, सेव्य स्वरूप, सेवा (श्रृंगार, भोग, राग) सेव्य स्थान, व्रतोपासना आदि। पुष्टिमार्गीय वैष्णव देवालयों अथवा मंदिरों को गुजरात में ''हवेली'' कहते हैं यथा– बाल कृष्ण लाल की हवेली, नवटवर गोपाल की हवेली आदि। इसीलिए यहॉ के संगीत को ''हवेली संगीत'' भी कहते हैं।

पुष्टिमार्गीय वैष्णव देवालय संगीत का उद्भव ब्रज में मथुरा जिले के गोवर्धन कस्बे से 3 मील दक्षिण में जतीपुरा एवं आन्यौर के बीच गोवर्धन पर संवत् 1556 वि. में हुआ। इस सम्प्रदाय के पहले कीर्तनकार श्री कुंभनदास जी हुए। संवत् 1602 वि. में श्री वल्लभाचार्य जी के द्वितीय पुत्र गोस्वामी श्री विट्ठलनाथ जी ने पुष्टिमार्गीय सेवा के तीनों अंगों – श्रृंगार, भोग एवं राग को इतना विस्तृत एवं आकर्षक बनाया कि उनके द्वारा प्रतिष्ठित उस क्रम में वर्तमान तक कोई परिवर्तन एवं परिवर्द्धन करने की आवश्यकता नहीं पड़ी। राग के विस्तार के लिए उन्होंने अष्टयाम[3] की सेवा हेतु अष्ट सखाओं4 की एक मण्डली का निर्माण किया जो अष्टछाप के नाम से प्रसिद्ध हुए।

राजा मान सिंह तोमर के 'मान कौतूहल' ग्रन्थ में ध्रुवपद एवं विष्णुपद दो प्रकार की शैलियों का उल्लेख मिलता है। हवेली संगीत में इन दोनों ही शैलियों का गायन होता है। ध्रुवपद में दो–दो पंक्तियों के चार धातु होते हैं जबकि विष्णुपद में चार–चार पंक्तियों के चार धातु होते हैं।

पुष्टिमार्गीय वैष्णव देवालय संगीत के अन्तर्गत केवल परम्परागत रागों को ही गाया जाता है। इन रागों एवं उनके स्वरूपों में किंचित भी परिवर्तन करना धार्मिक दृष्टि से अपराध माना जाता है। इन परम्परागत रागों के नाम इस प्रकार से हैं – देवगंधार, रामकली, भैरव, विभास, मालकोंस, बिलावल, ललित, सूहा, आसावरी, धनाश्री, सारंग, नट, पूरवी, गौरी, जैतश्री, खमाज, सोरठा, कल्याण, ईमन, कान्हरा, नायकी, हमीर, केदार, अड़ाना, मारू, मालव, वसन्त, मल्हार, काफी, जैजैवन्ती, बिहाग आदि।

पुष्टिमार्गीय संगीत में प्रकारान्तर से मुख्य सात तालें ही प्रयुक्त की जाती हैं – चार ताल (12 मात्रा), धमार (14 मात्रा), आड़ा चार ताल (14 मात्रा) आदि ताल अथवा तीन ताल (16 मात्रा तथा द्रुत गति में 8 मात्रा), झपताल (10 मात्रा), सूलताल (10 मात्रा) तथा झूमरा (14 मात्रा)।

हवेली संगीत में ऋतु–राग सिद्धान्त का भी पालन कियाा जाता है, जैसे – फाल्गुन मास में होरी के पद काफी राग में गाये जाते हैं, चैत्र मास (बसन्त ऋतु) में वसन्त एवं हिण्डोल रागों में गायन किया जाता है तथा वर्षा ऋतु में प्रायः मल्हारें शुरू हो जाती हैं। यहाँ ऋतुओं के अनुसार ठण्डे और गर्म रागों का विधान भी है।

ऐसे ही एक शीतकालीन, पद जिसका प्रयोग शयन कराने के लिये होता है, का उदाहरण इस प्रकार है :–

'राग–बिहागरौ''

''सखियन रूचि–रूचि सेज बनाई।।
रंग महल में परिगए परदा, धरी अंगीठी सुखदाई।
सीत सगै ग्रीष्म ऋतु कीन्हीं, अति सुन्दर वर राई।।
श्री विट्ठल गिरिधारी कृपानिधि पोढे ओढ़ रजाई।।

संगीत की दृष्टि से प्रस्तुत परम्परा के दो प्रमुख केन्द्र हैं – 1, ब्रज 2, नाथद्वारा। यद्यपि पुष्टिमार्ग के मंदिर भारत में सर्वत्र फैले हुए हैं, किन्तु उनमें कीर्तनकार प्रायः इन्हीं दो स्थानों से सम्बद्ध मिलते हैं।

पुष्टिमार्गीय हवेली संगीत के साहित्य में भाव पक्ष एवं कला पक्ष दोनों के साथ भक्ति भावना का पुट इसे सभी दृष्टकोणों से उच्चतम बनाता है।

2. राधावल्लभ सम्प्रदाय का समाज गायन

इस सम्प्रदाय का मुख्य ग्रन्थ श्रीहित हरिवंश जी का 'हित चौरासी' है। यह हित हरिवंश जी के 84 गेय पदों का संग्रह है। इस सम्प्रदाय में प्रेम का स्वरूप अन्य वैष्णव सम्प्रदायों में विलक्षण है। इसमें मुक्ति की कामना के स्थान पर नित्य विहार दर्शन ही सहचरी जीवात्मा का अभीष्ट है।

इस प्रकार श्री हित हरिवंश जी का यह मार्ग आडम्बर रहित निश्छल सहज प्रेम साधना का राज मार्ग है। इस सम्प्रदाय की निजी विशेषता यह है कि यहॉ श्री राधा जी के विग्रह के स्थान पर उनकी गद्दी की सेवा होती है। एक स्वर्ण पत्र पर श्री राधा जी का नाम अंकित करके उसे वस्त्राभूषण से अलंकृत करके आसन पर रखा जाता है जिसे 'गद्दी सेवा' कहते हैं।[5]

संगीत का महत्वपूर्ण स्थान समाज–गान के रूप में देखने को मिलता है। इस सम्प्रदाय में विनय के पद एवं कुछ उपदेशात्मक पदों को छोड़कर अधिकांश पद विभिन्न उत्सवों एवं जयन्तियों से सम्बन्धित हैं। ठाकुर जी के सम्मुख पद गाने वालों को 'समाजी' कहते हैं। यहॉ समाजियों की संख्या कम से कम चार होती है जिसमें एक मुखिया, एक पखावजी तथा दो झेला होते हैं।[6]

इस गायन शैली की रचना इस दृष्टि से की गयी है कि 'वाणी' के शब्द ठीक से उच्चारित हो सकें और श्रोताओं को स्पष्ट सुनाई दे सके। शब्द के स्पष्ट उच्चारण की रक्षा के लिए इस शैली में आलापों का भी निर्धारण कर दिया गया और स्थायी तथा अन्तरा के साथ निर्धारित आलाप ही लिये जाते हैं। इसमें तानों के लिए अधिक अवकाश नहीं होता, केवल छोटी छोटी मुरकियॉ ली जाती हैं।

परम्परागत रसिकों द्वारा रचित पदों का ही इसमें मुख्य रूप से गायन होता है किन्तु अन्य सम्प्रदायों के महापुरूषों के पदो।के गायन की उदात्त भावना इस सम्प्रदाय में सराहनीय है।

श्री राधावल्लभ जी के मंदिर की सेवाचर्या एवं वाणियों के आधार पर इस सम्प्रदाय की सेवा पद्धति चार स्वरूपों में मिलती है :–

1. नाम सेवा
2. समाज (गायन सेवा)
3. नित्य सेवा या अष्टयाम सेवा
4. नैमित्तिक सेवा (उत्सव सेवा)

भोर की प्रथम बेला ऊषा काल से निशान्त तक आठ प्रहर माने गये हैं। इन आठ प्रहरों में चलने वाली श्री प्रिया–प्रियतम की सेवा को नित्य सेवा या अष्टयाम सेवा कहा जाता है। प्रातःकाल में प्रभातियों का गायन करते हुए युगल श्री श्यामाश्याम को शैया पर से उठाया जाता है। उस समय निम्न पद के गायन से समाज होता है –

''जागौ मोहन प्यारी श्री राधा''
ठाड़ी सखीं दरस के कारन
दीजै कुंवरि जु होयन बाधा।।''

इस सम्प्रदाय के प्रमुख संगीतज्ञों में भी ध्रुवदास जी का विशेष स्थान है। इनकी रचना 'बयालीस लीला' के नाम से प्रसिद्ध है।

ध्रुवदास जी के अतिरिक्त श्री हरिराम व्यास जी, चाचा वृन्दावन दास, श्री दामोदर जी, श्री रूपलाल जी आदि आचार्य भी राधावल्लभ सम्प्रदाय के विशिष्ट संगीतज्ञों में गिने जाते हैं।

3. हरिदासी सम्प्रदाय का समाज गान

हरिदासी सम्प्रदाय के महान् प्रवर्तक आचार्य संगीत सम्राट और रससिद्ध कवि स्वामी हरिदास जी ने ऐसी सिद्ध परम्परा को जन्म दिया, जिसने भारतीयों को निगूढ़ प्रेमदर्शन से परिचित कराया। इस सम्प्रदाय की अपनी भावभूमि इतनी गहन, सूक्ष्म और रसपरक है कि उसे किसी भी अन्य सम्प्रदाय के दर्शन, उपासना और लीला क्षेत्र से संयुक्त करके देखना सम्भव ही नहीं है।7

जै जै श्री हरिदास परम गुरू बड़े दयाकर।
प्रगट करी रस रीति मुदित ज्यों उदित दिवाकर।।8

हरिदासी सम्प्रदाय के आठ प्रमुख कवियों को 'अष्टाचार्य' कहा जाता है। श्री स्वामी जी महाराज के द्वारा प्रतिष्ठित और प्रदर्शित नित्य विहार के बॉके पथ के अनुयायी, उनके परम्परावर्ती अधो निर्दिष्ट आठ प्रसिद्ध महानुभाव हुए, जो अष्टाचार्य के नाम से सुप्रसिद्ध है :–

1. स्वामी श्री बीठल विपुल देव जी
2. स्वामी श्री बिहारिन देव जी
3. स्वामी श्री नागरी देव जी
4. स्वामी श्री सरस देव जी
5. स्वामी श्री नरहरि देव जी
6. स्वामी श्री रसिक देव जी
7. स्वामी श्री ललित किशोरी देव जी
8. स्वामी श्री ललित मोहिनी देव जी

'समाज' शब्द का सामान्य अर्थ है 'समूह' और 'समाज गायन' से अभिप्राय है – 'किसी आध्यात्मिक उद्‌देश्य से वृन्दावनीय रसिकाचार्यो के पदों को आदर सहित एक पद्धति विशेष से सामूहिक रूप से गाना।'' अष्टाचार्यो के पदों का संकलन 'श्री केलिमाल' रसिक जगत में बहुत प्रसिद्ध है। इसके सभी पद ध्रुपद शैली में निबद्ध हैं तथा पक्के रागों में गेय हैं।

इस परम्परा के सभी आचार्य उच्चकोटि के गायक थे और स्वामी जी महाराज की गायन शैली का बहुत कुछ प्रभाव परम्परागत रूप में इनमें विद्वमान था। इस सम्प्रदाय में साधकों का यह पद गायन एकाकी भी होता है और सामूहिक भी। इस सम्प्रदाय विशेष के समाज गान में गाये जाने वाले वाणी संग्रहों को 'समाज–श्रृंखला' के नाम से पुकारा जाता है। वाद्य यन्त्रों में हारमोनियम, झॉझ और पखावज अनिवार्य होते हैं। तानपुरा, सारंगी, वंशी

आदि भी सुविधानुसार बजाये जाते हैं। मंगलाचरण के रूप में गुरूदेव 'स्वामी श्री बिहारिन देव जी' की दो साखियों को गाया जाता है।

"प्रथम लड़ाऊँ श्री गुरू, बन्दन करि श्री हरिदास।
विपुल प्रेम निज नेम गहि, कहि सुजस बिहारिनदास।।"

हरिदासी सम्प्रदाय की समाज–परम्परा में प्रायः विलम्बित लय का प्रयोग होता है जबकि अन्य सम्प्रदायों में द्रुत का। श्री धाम वृन्दावन में हरिदासी सम्प्रदाय के समाज–गायन का सर्वाधिक प्राचीन स्थान 'टटिया संस्थान' है।

"बांकौ मारग प्रेम कौ, कहत बनै नहिं बैन।
नैंना होवति हैं श्रवण, श्रवण होत हैं नैन।।'

4. गौड़ीय सम्प्रदाय का समाज गायन

गौड़ीय सम्प्रदाय राधाकृष्णोपासक सम्प्रदाय है। श्री चैतन्य महाप्रभु इस सम्प्रदाय के प्रवर्तक थे। बंगाल में उत्पन्न होने के कारण चैतन्य का सम्प्रदाय गौड़ीय सम्प्रदाय कहलाया। इस सम्प्रदाय में प्रयुक्त होने वाले संगीत के लिये 'समाज' के स्थान पर 'संकीर्तन' शब्द आता है। शास्त्रों में इसके तीन प्रकार बताये गये हैं :– नाम कीर्तन, लीला कीर्तन तथा गुणकीर्तन। इन तीनों प्रकारों में से लीला कीर्तन तथा गुण कीर्तन को वल्लभ सम्प्रदाय के भक्त संगीताचार्यो ने अपनाया तथा नाम कीर्तन के माध्यम से चैतन्य ने भगवद् गुणगान किया।

इस प्रकार 'संकीर्तन' पद्धति के प्रवर्तक श्री चैतन्य महाप्रभु ही माने जाते हैं। उन्होंने संकीर्तन में जाति–पाति, ऊँच–नीच का कोई भेदभाव नहीं रखा। संकीर्तन का एक प्रमुख अंग भक्ति पूर्ण नृत्य था। चैतन्य महाप्रभु ने विद्यापति, चण्डीदास तथा जयदेव कृत 'गीत गोविन्द' आदि का विश्लेषण करके उन्हें शास्त्र की मर्यादा प्रदान की। आज भी खोल और झॉझ की गुरु गम्भीर ताल पर हरिबोल संकीर्तन की टोलियॉ जन मानस को रस–विभोर कर देती हैं।

गौड़ीय सम्प्रदाय के पदावली संकीर्तन में कम से कम तीन गायकों का होना आवश्यक होता है। संकीर्तन के साथएक खोल वादक तथा एक करताल वादक अवश्य होते हैं।

श्री चैतन्य के पश्चात् श्री नरोत्तम ठाकुर, श्री निवास तथा श्री श्यामनन्दन, इन तीनों आचार्यो ने सम्प्रदाय का नेतृत्व किया। इन्हीं के द्वारा बंगाल में कीर्तन की तीन स्वतन्त्र धाराएँ प्रवाहित हुई जो गौड़ानहाटी, श्री मनोहर शाही तथा रानीहाटी के नाम से प्रसिद्ध हुए। इनमें से गौड़ानहाटी "प्रबन्ध तथा ध्रुपद गान शैली" पर आधारित थी। श्री मनोहर शाही कीर्तन शैली "ख्याल शैली" के समान थी तथा रानीहाटी शैली की तुलना उत्तर भारतीय संगीत की "ठुमरी शैली" से की जा सकती है। गौड़ीय सम्प्रदाय में मिश्र रागों में भी कीर्तन किया जाता है जैसे – काफी, पूर्वी, भैरव, बसन्त, गौरी आदि।

गौड़ीय सम्प्रदाय के वरिष्ठ भक्तों में वृन्दावन के छः गोस्वामी सर्वश्री सनातन गोस्वामी, रूप गोस्वामी, गोपाल भट्ट गोस्वामी, रघुनाथ दास, रघुनाथ भट्ट तथा जीव गोस्वामी थे।

5. निम्बार्क सम्प्रदाय में समाज-गान

वैष्णव सम्प्रदायों में प्राचीनतम् माने जाने वाले निम्बार्क सम्प्रदाय में भी समाज गायन की स्वस्थ परम्परा रही है। श्री निम्बार्काचार्य जी ही सबसे प्रथम आचार्य थे जिन्होंने उत्तर भारत में राधा कृष्ण की भक्ति का प्रचार किया था। निम्बार्क वैष्णवों का प्रमुख केन्द्र वृन्दावन धाम है। इस सम्प्रदाय ने ब्रह्म की कल्पना सगुण रूप में करके "द्वैताद्वैतवाद–सिद्धान्त" चलाया तथा युगल भाव से राधाकृष्ण के किशोर रूप को उपास्य तत्व के रूप में स्वीकार किया।

इस सम्प्रदाय का आचार्य पीठ श्री पुष्कर क्षेत्र, निम्बार्क तीर्थ, अजमेर, राजस्थान में है। यहीं पर जगत्‌गुरु श्री निम्बार्काचार्य श्री वृन्दावन देवाचार्यजी ने वि0 सम्वत् 1740 में लगभग चौदह घाटों वाली "गीतामृत गंगा" ग्रन्थ का नव निर्माण किया था। श्री वृन्दावन देवाचार्य जी ने समाज संगीत की परम्परा के विषय में लिखा है :–

"नाद ब्रह्म गान्धर्व है या बिनु सुर नहिं नृत्य।
नहीं गीत या बिनु कुछ तातैं यह है नित्य।।
उठत वायु तैं नाद है जातै सुर संघात।
सुरते उपजत राग सुनि जन विहवल है जात।।
याही तै कलिकाल में सब साधन में मुख्य।
कह्यौ कीर्तन व्यास शुक ज्यों नरवतनि में पुण्य।।9

श्री वृन्दावन देवाचार्य के गुरूदेव श्री नारायण देवाचार्य के गुरुभ्राता और शिष्यों में श्री गोविन्द देवाचार्य बिरजानन्द, आनन्दघन जी, नागरी दास जी आदि सभी समाज गान के विशेषज्ञ थे। इस सम्प्रदाय के हरि व्यास देवाचार्य, श्री वृन्दावन देवाचार्य तथा श्री रूप रसिक देवाचार्य आदि ने अपनी–अपनी वाणियों, 'महावाणी', 'गीतामृत गंगा' तथा 'वृहदुत्सवमणि ।माल' में असंख्य पदों की रचना की। इस सम्प्रदाय के वर्तमान समाज गायकों में श्री महन्त रूपकिशोर दास जी वृन्दावन में मुखिया जी के नाम से विख्यात हैं। इन्हें संगीत शास्त्र एवं गायन का पूर्ण ज्ञान है।10

6. नन्दगाँव-बरसाने की समाज गायन शैली

ब्रज में स्थित बरसाना तथा नन्दगॉव में प्रचलित समाज गान की भी एक विशिष्ट शैली है। नन्दगॉव भगवान श्री कृष्ण की लीला स्थली है तथा बरसाना श्री राधारानी की जन्म स्थली है। इस परम्परा का उदय बरसाने के प्राचीन भवन 'मानगढ़' के निर्माण के समय (लगभग 400 वर्ष पूर्व) से माना जाता है। इसका निर्माण श्री नारायण भट्ट जी ने करवाया था। उन्हीं को इस समाज संगीत परम्परा का सृष्टा माना जाता है।

बरसाना तथा नन्दगॉव में समाज गान मंदिरों में आयोजित सभी सामयिक उत्सवों पर होता है। सॉझी, होली, राधाष्टमी तथा बसन्त के अवसरों पर तो एक मास तक नियमित रूप से समाज गान का क्रम चलता है। राधाष्टमी के दिन राधा जी के मंदिर में जन्म के

विभिन्न बधाऐं गाये जाते हैं। बरसाने में इसके अतिरिक्त हरियाली तीज, गोपाष्टमी, अन्नकूट, जन्माष्टमी, लठामार होली आदि उत्सवों में विशेष समाज गान का आयोजन होता है। यहाँ के समाज गान में लोक धुनों का प्राबल्य रहता है।

यहाँ का समाज गायन पच्चीस–तीस समाजियों के समूह में सम्पन्न होता है। यह समाज का समूह आमने–सामने दो पक्षों या दलों में विभक्त होता है। इसमें 'मृदंग, झाँझ और ढफ' ही पर्याप्त होते हैं। समाज का 'ए हाँ हो' से युक्त सामवेदी घोष अति कर्णप्रिय एवं आनन्दायक होता है।

बरसाने में होली के अवसर पर कुछ दिन पूर्व नन्दगाँव के गोस्वामी सखाओं को होली खेलने का निमंत्रण भेजा जाता है :–

"न्यौतौ नन्दगाँव पठायौ जू।
जन दिन होरी कौ आयौ जू।।"

इस निमंत्रण को स्वीकार कर होली के अवसर पर नन्दगाँव के समाजी अपने दल के साथ बरसाने पधारते हैं। वहाँ का माहौल तब बड़ा ही रंगमय होता है जिसका वर्णन इस पद में देखने को मिलता है :–

"अति रस बरसै बरसाने जू। राजत रमनीक रमानौ जू।
जहाँ मणिमय मंदिर सौहै जू। उपमा को रवि शशि मौहै जू।
जहाँ होत कुलाहल भारी जू। मन मुदित सकल नर नारी जू।।"

7. रामानुज-सम्प्रदाय का समाज गान

वैष्णव धर्म की मर्यादा की रक्षा जिन आचार्यो द्वारा की गयी उनमें से एक नाम है आचार्य नाथमुनि जी का। इनके पौत्र यमुनाचार्य जी के शिष्य रामानुजाचार्य ने अपने गुरू के आदेश पर शंकराचार्य के 'अद्वैतवाद' के सिद्धान्त का खण्डन किया एवं वैष्णव धर्म के प्रथम वेदान्त सम्प्रदाय 'विशिष्टाद्वैत' की स्थापना की। उन्होंने ब्रह्म को सगुण मानकर भक्ति को ही मुक्ति का साधन स्वीकार किया।

इस सम्प्रदाय में ज्ञान की अपेक्षा भक्ति को महत्व देते हुए अपने सिद्धान्तों को उपनिषद् तथा पुराण आदि शास्त्रों पर आधारित माना जाता है। रामानुज सम्प्रदाय में नाम संकीर्तन को ही समाज गायन का उत्कृष्ट रूप माना जाता है। इस सम्प्रदाय के प्रचारक श्री रामानुजाचार्य जी ने तुलसीदास जी कृत 'रामचरित मानस' को ही ग्रन्थ मानकर तुलसीदास जी कृत पदावली तथा रत्नावली के पदों का समाज रूप में गायन किया।

ब्रज में इस सम्प्रदाय का प्रमुख मंदिर मथुरा के विश्राम घाट के समीप 'गताश्रम नारायण' का मंदिर है। सम्प्रति इस समाज सम्प्रदाय में समाज गायन लुप्त प्राय है।

प्राचीन एवं मध्यकालीन भारतीय आध्यात्मिक परम्पराओं की चर्चा जब भी की जाती है, तब ब्रज के मंदिरों की संगीत परम्पराओं का वर्णन भी अत्यन्त प्रासंगिक विषय प्रतीत होता

है। यह परम्परा भारतीय प्राचीन संगीत का वह सशक्त एवं गरिमामय स्वरूप है जिसका संरक्षण एवं संवर्धन आज की नितान्त आवश्यकता है, जिससे यह परम्परा चिरकाल तक जीवित एवं पूर्ण विकसित हो सके, क्योंकि आज भारतीय संगीत के पास जो भी वैभवशाली गायन शैलियाँ हैं उन्हें यदि इस अति प्राचीन देवालय संगीत परम्परा का परिष्कृत रूप कहा जाये तो कोई अतिशयोक्ति नहीं होगी। अतः इस समृद्ध एवं गौरवमय गायन परम्परा से भावी पीढ़ी को अवगत कराना हर संगीतज्ञ एवं संगीत प्रेमी का कर्तव्य है, जिससे भविष्य में यह परम्परा और भी समृद्धशाली हो सके।

संदर्भ सूची

1. ब्रज लोक साहित्य का अध्ययन, डॉ. सत्येन्द्र, पृष्ठ 4
2. ब्रज संस्कृति में संगीत, डॉ. अंजू शर्मा, पृष्ठ 54
3. अष्टयाम सेवा – मंगला, श्रृंगार, ग्वाल, राजभोग, उत्थापन, भोग, संध्या आरती एवं शयन।
4. अष्टछाप– कुम्भन दास, कृष्ण दास, सूरदास, परमानन्द दास, गोविन्द स्वामी, छीत स्वामी, चतुर्भुज दास एवं नन्द दास।
5. ब्रज संस्कृति में संगीत, डॉ. अंजू शर्मा, पृष्ठ 169
6. देवालय उपासना में भक्ति संगीत (प्रपत्र), बालकृष्ण पाण्डेय, कला वसुधा अंक – 5–6 अक्टूबर, 2002–मार्च 2003
7. हरिदासी सम्प्रदाय के अष्टाचार्यो का साहित्य, डॉ. ललित बिहारी गोस्वामी, पृष्ठ 22
8. स्वामी हदिास जी का सम्प्रदायऔर उसका वाणी साहित्य, डॉ. गोपाल दत्त वर्मा, पृष्ठ 124
9. गीता अमृत गंगा, घाट –14, दोहा– 4–5

7

मनुष्य के नैतिक एवं आध्यात्मिक उत्कर्ष में संगीत की भूमिका

शिवानी सोनकर

शिक्षा सदा से मानव को जीवन–यावन करने की विधि और जगत् व्यवहार को जानने का मुख्य माध्यम रही हैं। शिक्षा को मानव जीवन के सही रूप एवं सही नियमों से जोड़ना ही शिक्षा का मूल मात्र उद्देश्य हैं। ज्ञान प्राप्ति का शिक्षा मुख्य आधार रही है, जिससे मानव अज्ञान अधिकार से ग्रसित न होकर ज्ञान प्राप्त कर सके। प्रारम्भ में भारतीय शिक्षा पद्धति मन्दिरों से जुड़ी हुई थी और गुरुओं द्वारा निःशुल्क शिक्षा दी जाती थी। शिक्षा का उद्देश्य चरित्र निर्माण, व्यक्तिगत विकास, प्राचीन भारतीय संस्कृति की रक्षा और धार्मिक कर्तव्यों के परिपालन के लिए दी जाती थी, जिससे व्यक्ति कर्मनिष्ठ बना रहता हैं।[1] अतः शिक्षा का अर्थ वह आयोजित प्रक्रिया है, जो व्यक्ति के व्यक्तित्व के विकास के साथ–साथ उसमें पारलौकिक तत्वों का समावेष करती है।

संगीत शिक्षा की परम्परा प्राचीन काल से चली आ रही है। संगीत मनुष्य की भावनाओं की अभिव्यक्ति का प्रमुख साधन हैं। इसमें शिक्षा का समावेष करने से नैतिकता का अविर्भाव भी हो जाता है। ग्रन्थों एवं पुराणों के अध्ययन से यह प्राप्त होता है कि शिक्षा गुरु–षिष्य परम्परा के रूप में प्राचीन काल से ही प्रचलित हैं।[2] संगीत साधना का अर्थ हैं–''मन को किसी विषेष विषय में एकनिष्ठ भाव से संयुक्त करना।''[3] पुराणों एवं उपनिषदों में शान्ति साधना का आधार इन्द्रिय वशीकरण, मन बुद्धि की निर्मलता और परब्रह्म से तदात्कार होना बताया है। इसकी अनुभूति संगीत द्वारा ही अनुभव की जा सकती है।

संगीत के स्वर कलाकार के मन में सृजित होकर कल्पना के आधार पर नाद सौन्दर्य की सृष्टि करते हैं। संगीत संवेदनाओं की अभिव्यक्ति का सषक्त माध्यम हैं।

भर्त्तहरि के अनुसार

साहित्य संगीत कलाविहिनः
साक्षात पषु पुच्छविषाणहीनः।[4]

अर्थात् जो मनुष्य साहित्य और संगीत को नहीं जानता वो बिना सींग के साक्षात पषु के समान हैं। संगीत कला भारतीय संस्कृति में एक उच्च कोटि की कला मानी गई हैं। सुक्ष्म भावों की अभिव्यक्ति तथा भावनात्मक विकास संगीत कला के द्वारा होता है। संगीत मनुष्य के अन्तस की लोक विलक्षण अनुभूति हैं। जीवन में हर्ष, शोक आदि के सूचक विभिन्न रस भावों को सिद्ध करती है कि संगीत शिक्षा व्यक्ति के हृदय से सबसे निकट हैं। संगीत शिक्षा मनुष्य के जीवन की प्रेरणा, प्रगति एवं प्राण शक्ति है।

मनुष्य जब शारीरिक एवं मानसिक व्यथाओं से ग्रसित होकर थक जाता है तो, मन की उद्विगणता को शान्त कर पुनः सषक्त बनाने की क्षमता एक मात्र संगीत में ही है। जुही कुमारी द्वारा ''भैरवी पत्रिका'' में लिखा गया है कि–'' जब ईश्वर ने सृष्टि रची तब उसने बिखरे हुए महाभूतों की संगीत के द्वारा एकत्र किया इसके पश्चात् ही परमेष्वर ने सृष्टि रचना की।[5]

संगीत में मानव की वृत्तियों को प्रषस्त करने के साथ–साथ आत्मिक शक्ति का अविर्भाव करने की शक्ति भी निहित हैं। मनुष्य के चारित्रिक उत्थान एवं वासनाओं पर विजय प्राप्त करने का सर्वोत्तम साधन संगीत में ही है। संगीत के द्वारा व्यक्ति कठिन से कठिन कार्य को गाते–गाते बड़े आसानी और बिना थके कर लेता है। अतः जन्म से लेकर मृत्यु तक संगीत हमारे साथ है।

संगीत के सूक्ष्म बिन्दु नाद के नियम और संगीत के सातों स्वरों के सिद्धांतों के स्थिरीकरण के पीछे मनुष्य की असीम साधना और कठोर परिश्रम व तपस्या का प्रमाण है।कलाकार पदों के माध्यम से उसे स्वरों में पिरोके अपने अंतर्मन की कल्पना को पंख देकर मनोहारी शब्दों से लोगों के सम्मुख रखता हैं तो सभी उसके साथ–साथ मानव जीवन की गहन अनुभूतियों, भावना, संघर्षो, आशाओं, निराशाओं में डूबने लगते हैं। जब शब्द संगीत के संयोग से लयबद्ध होकर मुखरित होते हैं तो जीवन का सम्पूर्ण अंग–तरंग हृदय के भावों की मधुरता अभिव्यक्ति बन जाती है।

शास्त्रों में संगीत को ईश्वर के प्राप्ति का सरल साधन बताया गया है। कुछ लोगों का मानना है कि जीवन की कठिन से कठिन परिस्थितियों में भी हम ईश्वर की भक्ति कर उस परिस्थिति से उबर जाते हैं। संगीत जीवन की नैतिक अर्थात् बाहरी व्यक्तित्व के साथ–साथ हमारी आत्मिक जीवन पर भी प्रभाव डालता है। जहाँ हम संगीत से अपनी जीवन शैली को एक सकारात्मक दृष्टिकोण प्रदान करते हैं वहीं आत्मिक रूप से हम अपने आत्मबल के साथ मजबूत होते जाते हैं। अतः इसीलिए भक्ति मानव की सहज विभूति हैं। प्रत्येक मनुष्य स्वभावतः अपने से श्रेष्ठ व्यक्तियों के प्रति श्रद्धायुक्त आकर्षण रखता है। इसी श्रद्धा का विस्तार जब असीम, अपरिमित तथा अजेय परमात्मा के प्रति होता है तो वह भक्ति का मार्ग होता है। छंद

और स्वर की दृष्टि से भक्ति संगीत गेय पद पद स्वर, राग एवं ताल से विभूषित होकर जब प्रस्तुत किया जाता है, तो उनसे रस की अजस्त्र धारा प्रवाहित होती हैं।[6] यह रस आत्मा को परम आनंद की ओर ले जाता है तथा हम परमेश्वर में विलिन होने की अनुभूति करते हैं।

संगीत के महत्व को स्वीकार करते हुए श्री उपेन्द्र चन्द्र सिंह ने अपनी कृति "What is Music" में लिखा है–

"To Summaries what is Music, one can safely say it isA kind of Yoga System through the medium of Sonorus sound whichAct upon the human organismAndAwakenAnd develop their proper function to the extent of self realization the ultimate goal of Hindu Philosophy or religion."[7]

इससे इस कथन की पुष्टि होती है कि संगीत एक यौगिक विद्या है जिसकी तीव्र तथा तीव्रतर ध्वनियाँ मनुष्य के सूक्ष्म स्नायुयों को झंकृत कर सुषुप्त कुण्डलियों को जागृत कर देती हैं तथा मानवता को आत्मोन्नति की चरम सीमा, मोक्ष के द्वार तक पहुँचा देती है जो भारतीय जीवन दर्षन का अंतिम लक्ष्य है। स्वयं भगवान कृष्ण ने गीता में कहा है–

नाहं वसामि बैकुण्ठे, गोगिनां, हृदय न च।
मद्भक्ता यत्र गायन्ति, तत्र तिष्ठामि नारद।।[8]

संगीत द्वारा व्यक्ति उच्च प्रेरणायें ग्रहण करता है। मध्यकालीन दरबारी गायकों ने अपने साथ ही अपने आश्रयदाताओं का भी नाम उज्ज्वल और अमर बना दिया। कहते हैं कि अकबर के प्रसिद्ध संगीता तानसेन के गायन से वाद्य–यन्त्र स्वयं ही बज उठते थे, बुझे हुये दीप जल उठते थे और रीते आकाश में श्यामल घटायें घिर आती थी। बैजूबावरा ने अपने सुमधुर आकर्षक गायन द्वारा बावले हाथी को वश में कर लिया और वह खूँखार हाथी उनके पैरों पर लोट गया जो औरों के लिए प्राणघाती सिद्ध हो रहा था। औरंगजेब के अत्याचारों से जब जनता में त्राहि–त्राहि मची थी, क्लांत जन–समूह के लिए सभी द्वार बन्द हो चुके थे तो एक ही मार्ग अवशेष था, संगीत के माध्यम से ईश्वराधना। अगर यह माध्यम इतना शक्तिमान न होता तो शायद सूर, तुलसी, मीरा आदि भक्त कवियों का प्रादुर्भाव न होता।

संगीत साधना को मोक्ष, परब्रह्म अथवा परमानंद का मार्ग कहा गया है। संगीत के द्वारा मुक्ति प्राप्त करते हुए समाधि के आनंद रस का पान भी किया जाता हैं। संगीत के अपरिमेय जीवन का आनन्द, प्रेम भक्ति का स्रोत, आत्मोन्नति, सदाचार, राष्ट्रीयता, जातीयता व जीवन का पवित्र माध्यम माना गया है। संगीत के विद्यार्थी को इन सभी गुणों का अभ्यास शिक्षा के दौरान ही जैसे–प्रेम, दया, क्षमा, सहनशीलता, अहिंसा, धैर्य आदि सद्गुणों का विकास हो सकता है। प्लेटों ने कहा है–संगीत के माध्यम से आत्मा लय सीख जाती है। संगीत चरित्र बनाता है, उनसे धर्म की प्रवृत्ति आ जाती है। ऐसा व्यक्ति अन्याय नहीं करता, क्योंकि वह स्वर लहरों से बन्धा होता है तथा आत्मिक आनंद को प्राप्त करता है।[9]

अतः हम कह सकते हैं कि संगीत शिक्षा सम्पूर्ण मानव जाति को एवं उसके जीवन शैली को एक सकारात्मक दृष्टिकोण प्रदान करता है। वह जीवन की हर अच्छे–बुरे पहलू

में स्थिरता के साथ सामना करने के लिए सशक्त मनोबल प्रदान करता है। साथ ही साथ अध्यात्मिक रूप से भी हमारी आत्मा को बल प्रदान करता है। व्यक्ति को सामाजिक रूप से उन्नत बनाने में संगीत शिक्षा की अहम भूमिका मानी गई है।

सन्दर्भ ग्रन्थ सूची

1. शोध दृष्टि पत्रिका, डॉ. अभिजीत सिंह, (सुषमा कुमारी सिंह) सृजन समिति वाराणसी, 2011, पृ. 428
2. संगीत रत्नावली, अषोक कुमार, अभिषेक पब्लिकेषन चण्डीगढ़, 2008, पृ. 521
3. भैरवी : संगीत शोध पत्रिका, (जुही कुमारी) अंक–62012, डॉ. पुष्पम नारायण, मिथिलांचल, संगीत परिषद्, दरभंगा, पृ. 121
4. भैरवी : संगीत शोध पत्रिका, (जुही कुमारी) अंक–62012, डॉ. पुष्पम नारायण, मिथिलांचल, संगीत परिषद्, दरभंगा, पृ. 121
5. भैरवी : संगीत शोध पत्रिका, (जुही कुमारी) अंक–62012, डॉ. पुष्पम नारायण, मिथिलांचल, संगीत परिषद्, दरभंगा, पृ. 121
6. भैरवी : संगीत शोध पत्रिका, (कुमारी आभा) अंक–62012, डॉ. पुष्पम नारायण, मिथिलांचल, संगीत परिषद्, दरभंगा, पृ. 83
7. संगीत निबन्ध संग्रह, प्रो. हरिष्चन्द्र श्रीवास्तव, संगीत सदन प्रकाशन, इलाहाबाद, पृ. 96
8. संगीत निबन्ध संग्रह, प्रो. हरिष्चन्द्र श्रीवास्तव, संगीत सदन प्रकाशन, इलाहाबाद, पृ. 96
9. शोध दृष्टि पत्रिका, डॉ. अभिजीत सिंह, (महेन्द्र मिश्रा) सृजन समिति वाराणसी, 2011, पृ. 271

8

भारत में सूफीमत का विकास और उसका योगदान

प्रमोद कुमार शर्मा

तसव्वुफ या सूफीमत कई प्रकार के धर्मों, विचारों एवं संस्कृतियों के मेल जोल से निर्मित एक विचार प्रणाली है। जिस पर विविध विचारधाराओं जैसे भभारतीय वेदान्त, बौद्ध धर्म, ईसाई मत, नव–अफलातूनी, यूनानी दर्शन इत्यादि का प्रभाव पड़ा। इसका एक उदाहरण सूफियों के 'अनलहक' को भभारतीय वेदान्त के 'अहं ब्रह्मास्मि' के रूप में देख सकते हैं। बावजूद इसके तसव्वुफ का केन्द्रीय विचार इस्लाम ही रहा। पाश्चात्य विद्वान निकल्सन, ब्राउन जैसे विद्वानों का मानना है कि सूफीमत का मूल स्रोत कुरान है।

सूफीमत नियमों या शास्त्रों से बनी हुई कोई प्रणाली नहीं है, इतना जरूर है कि वह परम्परागत नियमों, शास्त्रों या कतेबों से वैचारिक उर्जा अवय ग्रहण करती रही। सूफी मत एक नैतिक अवस्था है, इसको हम शरीयत, तरीकत, हकीकत एवं मारीफत के रूप में देख सकते हैं। सूफीमत का सम्बंध हृदय की पवित्रता तथा आत्मानुशासन से भभी है।

सूफी साधक वाह्याडम्बरों के स्थान पर भभीतरी तत्वों पर बल देते हैं जिसका प्रतिपादन वे मन, वचन और कर्म से करते हैं। वे व्यक्तिगत रूप से साधनारत होते हुए भभी लोक की अनदेखी नहीं करते। सूफियों के यहाँ एक गहरा मानवीय मूल्यबोध दिखायी पड़ता है जो सम्प्रदाय और साधना की सीमाओं में नहीं अटता। सूफी साधकों की मूल दृष्टि सम्प्रदाय सापेक्ष न होकर मूल्य सापेक्ष रही है। वे ईश्वर या अल्लाह को पाने की प्रक्रिया में 'प्रेम' को मूल तत्व के रूप में स्वीकारते हैं। 'प्रेम' और 'उदारता' सूफियों की केन्द्रीय विशेषता है। इसीलिए उनका रहस्यवाद साधनात्मक न होकर भभावनात्मक है।

''वस्तुतः सूफीमत कई अर्थों की मिलानेवाला एक शब्द है और इसकी प्रमुख रूप रेखाओं का चित्रण करने में व्यक्ति को एक प्रकार का सम्पूर्ण चित्र ही बनाना पड़ता है जो किसी हद तक पद्धति का प्रतिनिधित्व नहीं करता।''[1]

सुफीमत कुरान की पवित्र भावना पर आधारित इस्लाम का स्वाभाविक विकास है। सूफी संत शरीयत को स्वीकार करते थे लेकिन उसमें व्याप्त रुढ़ियों को वे नकारते रहे अर्थात सूफियों का विरोध परम्परा से नहीं बल्कि परम्परा में व्याप्त रुढ़ियों से था।

"नये विचारों के संलेषण की यह प्रवृत्ति तब उभरी जब इस्लाम साम्राज्य के प्रसार के क्रम में नये विचारों और धर्मों का इस्लाम से सम्पक बना। रुढ़िवादी उलेमा ने इन नये विचारों को नकारा और इन्हें इस्लामी उपदेों के प्रतिकूल ठहराया। मगर उदार प्रवृत्ति वाले धर्मोपदेशकों या संतों ने इन नये विचारों को, जहाँ वे इस्लाम के बुनियादी सिद्धान्तों के विपरीत नहीं थे, अपनाया और इसका औचित्य सिद्ध करने के लिए इस्लाम के उपदेशों की रहस्यवादी व्याख्या को प्रधानता दी, क्योंकि इस माध्यम से इस नये विचारों का संलेषण संभव था। इस प्रकार कालातंर में इस्लाम के उपदेों की व्याख्या दो ढंग से होने लगी। एक व्याख्या शरीयत के रुप में हुई जिस पर रुढ़िवादिता या वतजीवकवगल का प्रभाव अधिक था और जिसे उलेमा वर्ग ने प्रधानता दी। दूसरी व्याख्या तरीकत के रुप में हुई जिसमें उदारवादी प्रवृत्ति थी और जिसमें सूफियों का गहरा विश्वास था।"[2]

प्रारंभिक दौर में सूफियों ने कुरान की आयतों की व्याख्या रहस्यात्मक ढंग से की तथा विविध प्रतीकों का सहारा लिया संभवतः अभिव्यक्ति के खतरे रहे होंगे। सूफी आंदोलन के आरंभिक केन्द्रो में मक्का, मदीना, बसरा और कूफा प्रमुख थे। महिला सूफी राबिया (मृत्यु 801ई) के समय में बसरा में सूफी मत अपने चरमोत्कर्ष पर था।

"राबिया बसरा की रहने वाली थी। राबिया में सर्वप्रथम प्रेम–दर्शन का उदात्त और प्रखर रुप सामने आता है। एक स्थान पर वह कहती हैं 'खुदा के प्रेम ने मुझे इतना अभिभूत कर दिया है कि मेरे ह्रदय में अन्य किसी के प्रति न तो प्रेम शेष रहा, न घृणा शेष रही।"[3]

ईरान, खुरासान, मिस्त्र, सीरिया, बगदाद इत्यादि देशेां में प्रारंभिक समय में सूफीमत का विकास हुआ। बगदाद के शुरुआदी सूफियों में 'मंसूर अल हल्लाज' (मृत्यु 923 ई.) का नाम उल्लेखनीय है। उनके कथन 'अनलह्क' अर्थात 'मैं ही सत्य हूँ' या 'मैं ही ईश्वर हूँ', ने सूफी आंदोलन को एक नया आयाम दिया। हल्लाज का यह पद दो, तीन सन्दर्भों की तरफ इंगित करता है। पहला यह कि इस्लाम के परम्परागत विचारों से मुठभेड़ दूसरा कि अहं भाव की अभिव्यक्ति और तीसरा ईश्वर की सत्ता की जगह मनुष्य की सत्ता को स्थापित करना जो कि आधुनिकता का एक लक्षण भी है। ईश्वर और मनुष्य की सत्ता को लेकर रामस्वरूप चतुर्वेदी का कथन है कि "आधुनिक काल में आकर मनुष्य सारे चिंतन का केन्द्र बनता है, और ईश्वर की धारणा व्यक्तिगत आस्था के रुप में स्वीकृत होती है। साहित्य या कि कलाओं में उसका चित्रण प्रासंगिक नहीं रह जाता।"[4]

उलेमाओं ने हल्लाज को 'ईश्वर –निदंक' कहकर आलोचना की। उसे बंदी बनाया गया और अनंतः फाँसी पर चढ़ा दिया गया क्यों कि उलेमाओं की पहुँच बादााहों तक थी। हल्लाज के सिद्धान्तों के आधार पर ही 'इंसान–ए–कामिल' (पूर्व व्यक्ति) की अवधारणा विकसित हुई।

उलेमा सूफीमत को हमेशा संदेह की नजर से देखते थे। उन्हे खासकर 'समा' (भक्ति संगीत) जैसी चीजों से सख्त नफरत थी। कट्टरपंथी इस्लामी शिक्षा प्राप्त कुछ सूफियों ने उलेमा और सूफियों के बीच एक प्रकार का संतुलन स्थापित करने की कोशिश की। अबू हमीद अल–गजाली (1058–1111ई.) इस प्रकार के सूफियों में प्रमुख था। उसने सूफीमत में बाह्य इस्लामी कानूनों का और औपचारिक सिद्धान्तों का पालन करने पर जोर दिया। बावजूद इसके कट्टरपंथी और उदार सूफीमत दोनों मूल्य अलग–अलग रास्ते पर ही विकसित हुए।

भारत में सूफीमत का विकास कब से हुआ इसकी तिथि बताना मुकिल है, लेकिन इतना जरुर है कि इसका प्रारम्भ इस्लाम के आक्रमण से शुरु हुआ। भारत में आकर बसने वाले आरंभिक सूफियों में 'अल–हुजविरि' प्रमुख हैं जो ग्यारहवीं शताब्दी के प्रारंभिक दिनों में लाहौर आकर बसे। सूफीमत से सम्बंधित उनकी पहली प्रसिद्ध रचना 'काफ–उल महजूब' है। यह सूफीमत पर लिखा एक मानक दस्तावेज है।

लगभग बारहवीं शाताब्दी से सूफी मत सम्प्रदाय (सिलसिला) के रुप में अपना स्वरूप ग्रहण करने लगा था। 'खानक़ाह' अब सूफियों के व्यक्तिगत गतिविधि का केन्द्र न रहकर सूफी िक्षा के संस्थागत केन्द्र के रुप में उभर कर सामने आने लगा।

अबूल फजल ने आईन–ए–अकबरी में चौदह सूफी सिलसिलों का जिक्र किया है। इनमें अधिक लोकप्रिय चिश्ती, सुहरावर्दी, कादिरी, शत्तारी और नकबंदी सिलसिले थे। सल्तनकाल के प्रभावाली सम्प्रदायों में चिती और सुहरावर्दी सम्प्रदाय थे।

सुहरावर्दी सिलसिले को भारत में स्थापित करने का श्रेय बहाउद्दीन जकरिया को जाता है। वे खुरासानी थे और शेख शहाबुद्दीन सुहरावर्दी के शिष्य थे, जिन्होंने बगदाद में इस सिलसिला की शुरुआत की थी। सुहरावर्ती परम्परा पर रुढ़िवादी विचारों का अधिक प्रभाव था। इसके संतशासक वर्ग के सम्पक में रहते थे और उनका प्रश्रय भी प्राप्त था। पंजाब, सिंध और बंगाल इसके तीन प्रमुख केन्द्र थे।

भारत में स्थित सूफी सम्प्रदायों में चिती सम्प्रदाय सबसे लोकप्रिय था। इसे ख्वाजा मोईनुद्दीन चिश्ती ने बारहवीं शताब्दी के अंतिम दाक में अजमेर में स्थापित किया। इनके शिश्य कुतुबुद्दीन बख्तियार काकी हुए। बख्तियार काकी के ही शिष्य बाबा फरीद हुए जिन्होंने पंजाब के अजोधन में अपना खानक़ाह बनाया। बाबा फरीद ने लोक और जीवन की सहजता को ज्यादा महत्व दिया। बाबा फरीद के शिष्य निजामुद्दीन औलिया हुए जो दिल्ली में तुगलक शासकों के समकालीन थे इन्होंने शासक वर्ग और अमीरों से दूर रहने की कोशिश की और कभी किसी शासक के दरबार में पैर नहीं रखा। ऐसा माना जाता है कि औलिया के ही शिष्य अमीर खुसरो थे। गुरु की मृत्यु पर लिखी हुई उनकी यह प्रसिद्ध पंक्ति काफी मार्मिक है।

> गोरी सोवे सेज पर मुख पर डारे केस।
> चल खुसरो घर आपने रैन भई चहुं देस।।

भारत में चिश्तियों की लोकप्रियता का कारण यह था कि उन्होंने भारतीय प्रतीकों,

मुहावरों, रीति–रिवाजों और अनुष्ठानों को अपना लिया। उन्होंने गुरु की महत्ता को स्वीकार की। वे समाज के पिछड़े वर्गों के प्रति सहानुभूति रखते थे। भक्ति संगीत (समा) उनके जीवन का एक हिस्सा था जिसका आयोजन वे करते रहते थे।

मध्यकाल में हिन्दू और मुस्लिम दोनों ही संस्कृतियों का प्रभाव एक दूसरे पर पड़ा। उदाहरणस्वरुप देख सकते हैं कि मुस्लिमों के एकेवरवाद का प्रभाव जो कि हिन्दू संस्कृति में पहले से ही बीज रुप में निहित था, बहुदेववाद की जगह जाग उठा। मुस्लिम समाज भी जाति–प्रथा से प्रभावित हुआ। उनमें 'आराफ' और 'अजलाफ' की कोटियाँ बनीं। सैयद, शेख, पठान, जुलाहा विविध जातियाँ अपना रुप धारण कीं।

सूफी संतों और नाथपंथी जोगियों के बीच एक अच्छे वैचारिक तालमेल देखने को मिलते हैं। सूफी कवि मलिक मुहम्मद जायसी अपनी रचनाओं में गोरखनाथ, मछिदंरनाथ का जिक्र करते हैं।

लीन्हेसि धँसि सुवाँस मन मारे। गुरु मछिदंरनाथ सँभारे।।[5]

सूफी सन्तों की सांस्कृतिक दृष्टि इसलिए भी महत्वपूर्ण है कि वे एक ही रचना में मसनवी शैली और भारतीय लोक कथाओं का निर्वाह बहुत ही सहजता से करते हैं, जहाँ स्थानीयता की गंध बराबर मौजूद रहती है। मध्यकाल में हिन्दू–मुस्लिम संस्कृति के साथ धर्म, भाषा इत्यादि में भी एकता की तलाा या उसके समन्वय का कार्य सबसे अधिक सूफी एवं सन्त कवियों ने किया जिसमें महामति प्राणनाथ का योगदान सबसे अधिक है। महामति प्राणनाथ औरगंजेब के समकालीन थे। इनकी नोटिस साहित्यकारों एवं इतिहासकारों द्वारा बहुत कम ली गयी। ''वास्तव में भारत के मध्यकालीन इतिहास में स्वामी प्राणनाथ ही ऐसे महान समन्वयात्मक दृष्टि वाले संत थे जिनकी धर्म सभाओं में कुरान, भागवत, उपनिषद का नित्य पाठ होता था। उन्होंने एक ऐसे सम्प्रदाय की स्थापना की जिसमें स्पष्ट रूप से हिन्दू, मुसलमानों और ईसाइयों को एक घोषित किया गया।''[6]

महामति एक ऐसे संत थे जिन्होने अरब के कई देशों की यात्राएँ की तथा कुरान का विधिवत अध्ययन किया। वे अजान सुनते हुए ला, इल्लाह, अल्लाह को हिन्दुओं के क्षर, अक्षर, अक्षरातीत के समान पाए। महामति कहते हैं कि–

भेष भाषा जिन रचो, रचियो माएने असल।
भई रोसन जोत रसूल की, अब खुले माएने सकल।
करना सारा एक रस, हिन्दू मुसलमान।
धोखा सबका भांन के, सब का कहूंगी ग्यान।।[7]

प्राणनाथ जी कहते हैं कि वेद और कतेब का विवाद भाषा का है जो निरर्थक है क्योंकि दोनों दो विरोधी बात नहीं बल्कि एक ही बात कर रहे हैं। इसीलिए महामति हिन्दुस्तानी भाषा की पैरवी करते रहे जो दोनों वर्गों की मिली–जुली भाषा थी।

जो कछू कह्या कतेब ने, सोई कह्या वेद।

दोऊ बंदे एक साहेब के, पर लड़त बिना पाए भेद।[8]

कबीर इस वेद, कतेब के झगड़े को पहले ही नकार चुके थे उनका विवास 'कागद लेखी' की जगह 'आँखन देखी' पर अधिक था।

सूफी एवं संत कवि दोनों समुदायों में एक सौहार्दपूर्ण वातावरण चाहते थे रैदास कहते हैं कि–

मुसलमान सों दोस्ती, हिन्दुअन सों कर प्रीत।
रैदास जोति सभ राम की, सभ हैं अपने मीत।।[9]

सूफियों एवं संतों में संगीत – गायन की परम्परा अभूत थी जिसका दोनों ही संस्कृतियों पर भावनात्मक प्रभाव पड़ा। हिन्दू–मुस्लिम दोनों समुदायों पर जितना अधिक प्रभाव संगीत और उसकी राग–रागिनियों का पड़ा उतना अधिक चित्रकला या स्थापत्य कला का नहीं पड़ा।

''जौनपुर के सुल्तान हुसैन फारकी ने, ऐसा कहा जाता है कि, एक नयी संगीत शैली 'ख्याल' को प्रवर्तित किया जो हिन्दुओं और मुसलमानों दोनों में समान रुप से लोकप्रिय हुई। 'ध्रुपद' शास्त्रीय हिन्दू शैली परिमार्जित रुचि के मुसलमानों द्वारा बहुत अधिक पसन्द की जाता थी।''[10]

सूफियों के प्रेम में एक अनुभूति की पीड़ा दिखायी पड़ती है।
प्रीति बेलि संग बिरह अपारा। सरग पतार जरै तेहि झारा।।[11]

यह वियोगजनित पीड़ा ही मनुष्य को दिव्यता से बचाता है और मनुष्य अपने सारे मानवीय सारोकारों के साथ उपस्थित होता है। जायसी कृत पदमावत में नागमती वियोग की स्थिति में अपना सारा रानीपन भूल जाती है और एक विरहिणी या साधारण स्त्री के रुप में दिखायी पड़ती है। सूफियों का विरह और प्रेम हमें बैकुंठी भी बनाता है और जीवन से जुड़कर उसकी सच्चाईयों से रुबरु भी कराता है।

सूफी, उलेमाओं की तरह विलासिता और दरबार का मार्ग नहीं अपनाते बल्कि उसकी जगह त्याग, संतोश और प्रेम का मार्ग अपनाते हैं। बाबा फरीद कहते हैं कि–

फरीदा चिंत खटोला वाणु दुखु बिरह बिछावन लेफु।
एह हमारा जीवणा तू साहिब सचे वेखु।।[12]

सूफी काव्य में केवल पात्रों का विकास दिखायी नहीं पड़ता बल्कि उनमें उलटफेर या उतार–चढ़ाव आता रहता है। पात्रों का यह उलट–फेर तत्कालीन जीवन, समय एवं मनुष्य की प्रवृत्तियों से जुड़ा हुआ है। इसलिए सूफी कवियों की रचनाओं में केवल प्रेम का अलौकिक पुट देखना ठीक नहीं बल्कि मानवीय जीवन की त्रासदी को देखना ज्यादा उचित है। मध्यकाल में वीरता, युद्ध और भोग सामंती मूल्य थे, इसके समानान्तर प्रेम, त्याग और भक्ति प्रतिरोधी मूल्य थे जो सामंती व्यवस्था को चुनौती दे रहे थे।

उपर्युक्त इन दोनों मूल्यों को लेकर सूफी कवि अपनी रचनाओं में एक त्रासद तस्वीर

गढ़ते हैं जिसकी अन्तिम परिणति प्रेम और त्याग में होती है। 'पदमावद' के सन्दर्भ में विजयदेव नारायण साही का कथन है–

"पदमावत केवल प्रेम की कहानी नहीं है प्रेम और युद्ध की मिली जुली कहानी है।"[13]

सूफी संत जीवन को केवल देखते नहीं है बल्कि उसे गहन अनुभूतियों से महसूस करते हैं, इसलिए उनकी रचनाएँ मध्यकाल की एक त्रासद छवि दिखा पाती है। पाश्चात्य चिन्तक 'होरेस वालपोल' का कथन है कि–

"Life is comedy for those who think and a tragedy for those who feel."[14]

मध्यकालीन सूफी कवियों की विशिष्टता इस बात में दिखायी पड़ती है कि सामंती दौर में भी उनके लगभग सारे प्रेमाख्यानक स्त्री पात्रों के नाम पर हैं, जैसे– चन्दायन, मृगावती, मधुमालती, पदमावत इत्यादि।

इन प्रेमाख्यानकों की बुनावट में हिन्दू घरों की लोककथाएँ भी हैं, फारसी का प्रभाव भी झलकता है तथा अंधविवास, बहु विवाह, बाल विवाह, नारी की विवाता, सती प्रथा, दास प्रथा, युद्ध की समस्या, स्थानीयता का प्रभाव, पौराणिकता सब कुछ दिखायी पड़ता है। जिनमें प्रतिरोध के साथ त्रासदी और विडम्बना भी उजागर होती है और कुछ परम्परागत, रुढ़िगत मूल्यों का समर्थन भी दिखायी पड़ता है। इसको हम स्त्री जीवन से जुड़े कुछ उदाहरण से देख सकते हैं। सूफी कवि जायसी अपनी रचना पदमावत में स्त्री जीवन की दारुण कथा को व्यक्त करते हैं कि किस प्रकार सामंती समाज में स्त्री ससुराल में विविध बन्धनों में बँधी दिखायी पड़ती है।

ऐ रानी मन देखु विचारी। एहि नैहर रहना दिन चारी।।
जौ लहि अहै पिता कर राजू। खेलि लेहु जौं खेलन आजू।।
सासु नंनद बोलिन्ह जिउ लेहीं। दारून ससुर न आवै देहीं।।
पिउ पिआर सब ऊपर सो पुनि करै दहुँ काह।
कहुँ सुख राखै की दुख दहुँ कस जरम निबाह।।[15]

सूफी संतो ने सामंती मूल्य एवं पितृसत्तात्मक मानसिकता के विकल्प स्वरूप प्रेम को रखा जो तथाकथित शुद्धतावादी भाव, आडम्बरी नैतिकता को तोड़ता है। प्रेम निर्बन्ध होता है इसका उदाहरण हिन्दी का प्रथम सूफी काव्य 'चन्दायन' में 'चन्दा' और 'लोरिक' की प्रेम कहानी में भी देख सकते हैं।

हम देखेंगे कि बहुत पहले से ही धर्मतंत्र और राजतंत्र का आपसी गठजोड़ रहा है। वे यूरोप के देश रहे हों या अरब, एशिया के देश। इन दोनों में से कभी राज्य की शक्ति मजबूत होती रही है तो कभी धर्म की। पोप, चर्च, खलीफा तथा सुल्तान इत्यादि इसी दायरे में आते हैं।

मध्यकाल में धर्मतंत्र पर उलेमाओं और मौलवियों का एकाधिकार था तो राजतंत्र पर अमीरो और सामंतों का। इसी धर्म (मठ) और राज्य (गढ़) की 'हेजेमॅनी' (Hegemony) को

सूफी, संत एवं भक्त कवि तोड़ते हैं। बाबा फरीद कहते हैं–

फरीदा मनु मैदानु करि, टोए टिबे लाहि।[16]

अर्थात तुम अपने मन रुपी मैदान से गढ़ों एवं टीलों को साफ करके इसे समतल कर लो। जायसी पदमावत में इस 'मठ' और 'गढ़' को टूटते हुए दिखाते हैं–

गढ़ कै गरब खेह मिलि गए। मंदिर उठहिं ढहहिं भै नए।।
अंत जो चलना कोऊ न चीन्हा। जो आवै सो आपुन्ह कीन्हा।।[17]

अर्थात हमारे अहंकार के जो प्रतीक मठ और गढ़ हैं वे जीवन के अन्तिम दिनों में हमारे साथ नहीं जायेंगे। इन्हीं सामंती मूल्यों को तोड़ने की बात आधुनिक काल में मुक्तिबोध अपनी लम्बी कविता 'अँधेरे में' में करते हैं–

''अब अभिव्यक्ति के सारे खतरे उठाने ही होंगे,
तोड़ने ही होंगे मठ और गढ़ सब।''

यहाँ 'मठ' पुरोहितवाद का प्रतीक है और 'गढ़' सामंतवाद का। सूफी संत और खासकर चिती सम्प्रदाय के सूफी जिनका सम्बंध राजदरबार रो नहीं रहा, बार–बार राजाओं की विलासिता एवं उनके कुकृत्यों के प्रति सचेत करते हुए समानता की बात करते रहे।

बाबा फरीद कहते हैं–

पासि दमामे छत सिरि मेरी सडो रड।
जाइ सुते जीराण महि थीए अतीमा गड।।[18]

अर्थात् जिनके द्वार पर नगाड़े बजते हैं, सिर पर छत्र झुलते हैं, वे भी कब्रिस्तान में सो गए और अनाथों की तरह दब गए।

हम देखेंगे कि भक्ति आंदोलन के सारे रचनाकारों का मूल स्वर लोकजागरण है। वे रचनाकार केवल सामाजिक मूल्यों के प्रति सचेत नहीं कर रहे थे बल्कि जीव, जीवन की एक मुकम्मल व्याख्या प्रस्तुत कर रहे थे। वे सूफी जीवन के हर्श और उल्लास के समानान्तर आत्मजागरण और मृत्युबोध को भी रच रहे थे। 'आत्मजागरण' और 'मृत्युबोध' की उतनी अधिक कविताएँ न मध्यकाल के पहले लिखी गयी और न ही बाद में। जायसी लिखते हैं कि–

मैं घर बार कहाँ कर पावा। घर काया पुनि अंत परावा।।19
अर्थात यह शरीर रुपी जो घर है वह दूसरे का हो जायेगा।

उत्तर भारत या हिन्दी सूफी कवियों के यहाँ लोक की भीनी गंध तथा स्थानीयता की अभूत छाप दिखायी पड़ती है। उनका सारा काव्य ठेठ अवधी में है। संस्सृत और अरबी जो कि धर्म की और फारसी जो कि राज्य के काम काज की भाषा थी, इन दोनों की जगह उन्होंने क्षेत्रीय भाषा या स्थानीय बोली अवधी का चुनाव किया। वे रचनाकर भाषा के माध्यम से भी तत्कालीन सामंती समाज को चुनौती देते रहे। अर्थात सूफियों का सारा चिन्तन मानवीयता पर आधारित है जहाँ आलोचनात्मक विवेक भी है। उनके केन्द्र में मनुष्य अपनी सांस्कृतिक,

सामाजिक, स्थानीय गुण–दुर्गुणों के साथ उपस्थित है जहाँ ईश्वर या अल्लाह से मिलने की व्याकुलता भी दिखायी पड़ती है।

सन्दर्भ सूची

1. हिन्दी सूफी काव्य का समग्र अनुशीलन – शिवसहाय पाठक, पृ. 25
2. मध्यकालीन भारत : एक सर्वेक्षण – इमत्याज अहमद, पृ. 148
3. मध्ययुगीय प्रेमाख्यानक – याममनोहर पाण्डेय, पृ. 27
4. हिन्दी साहित्य और संवेदना का विकास – पृ. 79
5. पदमावत – सं. वासुदेवारण अग्रवाल, पृ. 228
6. मध्यकालीन हिन्दी काव्य में सांस्कृतिक समन्वय – डा. अब्दुल बिस्मिल्लाह, पृ.30
7. श्रीतारतमवाणी – सनंध, प्रकरण 3, चौपाई 1,3
8. वही, खुलासा, प्र. 12, चौ. 42
9. रैदास ग्रंथावली – डॉ. जगदी‌ा शरण, पृ. 107
10. भारत की राष्ट्रीय संस्कृति – प्रो. एस. आबिद हुसैन, पृ. 76
11. पदमावत – वासुदेवारण अग्रवाल, पृ.242
12. शेख बाबा फरीद और उनका काव्य – डा. जयभगवान गोयल, पृ.50
13. जायसी – पृ.82
14. Emotional Intelligence-Daniel Goleman, Page.13
15. पदमावत– वासुदेवारण अग्रवाल पृ.61
16. शेख बाबा फरीद और उनका काव्य – डॉ. जयभगवान गोयल, पृ.58
17. पदमावत – वासुदेवारण अग्रवाल, पृ.212
18. शेख बाबा फरीद और उनका काव्य – डॉ. जयभगवान गोयल, पृ.52
19. पदमावत – वासुदेवारण अग्रवाल, पृ. 123